PEACE, DEFENSE AND ECONOMIC ANALYSIS

Peace, Defense and Economic Analysis

Proceedings of a Conference held in Stockholm jointly by the International Economic Association and the Stockholm International Peace Research Institute

Edited by
Christian Schmidt

and

Frank Blackaby

St. Martin's Press   New York

First published in the United States of America in 1987

Printed in Great Britain

ISBN 0–312–01321–3

Library of Congress Cataloging-in-Publication Data
Peace, defense, and economic analysis: proceedings of a conference
held in Stockholm jointly by the International Economic Association
and the Stockholm International Peace Research Institute / edited by
Christian Schmidt and Frank Blackaby.
p. cm.
Bibliography: p.
Includes index.
ISBN 0–312–01321–3 : $35.00 (est.)
1. Munitions—Economic aspects—Congresses. 2. Armaments–
–Economic aspects—Congresses. I. Schmidt, Christian.
II. Blackaby, Frank. III. International Economic Association.
IV. Stockholm International Peace Research Institute.
HC79.D4P43 1987
338.4'7355—dc19   87–19708
                                                                       CIP

Contents

v

PART IV ECONOMETRICS AND APPLIED
MICROECONOMICS

Acknowledgements

The conference reported in this volume was made possible only by the joint efforts of a number of persons and organisations.

We should like first to thank SIPRI for providing the venue for the conference, for their hospitality and for the administrative arrangements, including much editorial work.

The hospitality offered by the Swedish Minister of Defence in the impressive setting of the Swedish Foreign Office and the evening reception given by the Swedish Economic Association greatly added to the enjoyment of the participants and created a relaxed atmosphere for informal discussion. The IEA is indebted to the Rockefeller Foundation and to the Ford Foundation for financial support without which the conference would not have been possible.

Lastly we are grateful for the continuing financial assistance given by UNESCO* to the IEA which enables the work of the organisation to proceed and to arrange conferences of this kind.

PROGRAMME COMMITTEE

Christian Schmidt ⎫ Co-Chairmen
Frank Blackaby ⎭
K. Boulding
M. D. Intriligator
A. Sen
K. W. Rothschild
V. L. Urquidi

* Under the auspices of the International Social Sciences Council and with a grant from UNESCO (1986–1987/DG/7.6.2/SUB.16(SHS)).

List of Participants and Contributors

Dr Jacques Aben, Université de Montpellier UER de Sciences Economiques, France.

Dr Gordon Adams, Center on Budget and Policy Priorities, Washington DC, USA.

Professor Ulrich Albrecht, Institut für Internationale Politik und Regionalstudien (WE4), Freie Universität, Berlin.

Dr Thomas O. Bayard, Ford Foundation, New York, USA.

Professor Dr Nansen Behar, Institute for Contemporary Social Studies, Bulgarian Academy of Sciences, Bulgaria.

Mr Frank Blackaby, SIPRI (1981–6), Sweden.

Dr Evgheny Bougrov, Institute of World Economy & International Relations, Academy of Sciences of the USSR, Moscow, USSR.

Professor Kenneth E. Boulding, Institute of Behavioral Science, Colorado University, USA.

Professor Dagobert L. Brito, Economics Dept., Rice University, Texas, USA.

Professor Andrew Brody, Institute of Economics, Hungarian Academy of Sciences, Budapest, Hungary.

Dr Hans Christian Cars, Försvarsdepartementet, Stockholm, Sweden.

Dr Saadet Deger, Economics Department, Birkbeck College, London, UK.

Professor Pierre Dussauge, Centre d'Enseignement Supérieur des Affaires, France.

Professor R. Faramazyan, Institute of World Economy & International Relations, Academy of Sciences of the USSR, Moscow, USSR.

Professor John P. Farrell, Economics Department, Oregon State University, USA.

Dr Jacques Fontanel, CEDSI, University of Grenoble, France.

Dr Daniel Gallick, ACDA, Washington DC, USA.

Professor Gilbert Ghez, Roosevelt University, Chicago, USA.

Mr A. R. Gigengack, Faculteit der Economische Wetenschappen, Rijksuniversiteit, Netherlands.

Mr D. A. Gold, Center on Budget and Policy Priorities, Washington DC, USA.

Professor Dr H. de Haan, Faculteit der Economische, Wetenschappen, Rijksuniversiteit, Netherlands.

Dr Keith Hartley, Institute for Research in the Social Sciences, York University, UK.

Dr Patricia M. Hillebrandt, IEA Conference Editor and Reading University, UK.

Ms Marie Hosinsky, National Defence Research Institute (FOA), Stockholm, Sweden.

Professor Michael D. Intriligator, Center for International and Strategic Affairs, University of California, Los Angeles, USA.

Professor Walter Isard, School of Arts and Sciences, Pennsylvania University, USA.

Ms Catherine J. Jepma, Faculteit der Economische Wetenschappen, Rijksuniversiteit, Netherlands.

Professor Edward A. Kolodziej, Program in Arms Control, Disarmament and International Security, University of Illinois, USA.

Professor Jean-Christian Lambelet, DEEP, Université de Lausanne, Switzerland.

Professor Urs Luterbacher, Graduate Institute of International Studies, Geneva, and Universities of Lausanne and Geneva, Switzerland.

Dr Stephen Martin, Birkbeck College, University of London, UK.

Professor Martin C. McGuire, Economics Department, University of Maryland, USA.

Ms Rita McWilliams Tullberg, SIPRI, Sweden.

Dr Christos Passadeos, Paris, France.

Professor Mark Perlman, Department of Economics, University of Pittsburgh, USA.

Professor Louis Pilandon, Mission d'Enseignement et d'Etude de la Défense, Secrétariat Général de la Défense Nationale, Paris, France.

Professor Kurt W. Rothschild, Vienna, Austria.

Professor Bruce Russett, Department of Political Science, Yale University, USA.

Professor Todd Sandler, Economics Department, Iowa State University, USA.

Professor Christian Schmidt, Université de Paris IX Dauphine and LESOD, France.

Professor Amartya Sen, All Souls College, Oxford, UK.

Professor Martin Shubik, Economics Department, Yale University, USA.

Professor Ron P. Smith, Birkbeck College, University of London, UK.

Professor Wally Struys, Ecole Royale Militaire, Brussels, Belgium.

Professor Jan Tinbergen, The Hague, Netherlands.

Professor Bernard Udis, Economics Department, Colorado University, USA.

Professor Victor L. Urquidi, El Colegio de Mexico, Mexico.

Professor Raimo Väyrynen, Department of Political Science, Helsinki University, Finland.

Professor Miguel S. Wionczek, El Colegio de Mexico, Mexico.

Professor Murray Wolfson, Economics Department, Oregon State University, USA.

Abbreviations and Acronyms

ABM	Anti-ballistic missile
ACDA	Arms Control and Disarmament Agency (US)
AVATAR	Modèle d'analyse variantielle de l'INSEE
BIS	Bank of International Settlements
BMD	Ballistic missile defence
CANDU	Canada's natural-uranium-fuelled, heavy-water-moderated reactor
CBO	Congressional Budget Office
CEA	Commissariat à l'Energie Atomique
CEDSI	Centre d'Etudes de Défense et de Securité Internationales
CGE	Central Government Expenditure
CIT–ALCATEL	French firm
Cmnd	A Command Paper
CND	Campaign for Nuclear Disarmament
CNRS	Centre Nationale de la Recherche Scientifique
CRERI	Centre de recherches empiriques en relations internationales (Geneva)
CSGG	Cahiers du Séminaire Charles Gide, Montpellier tome XV, 1981
CSO	Central Statistics Office
DEEP	Départment d'économétrie et d'économie politique (University of Lausanne)
DGA	Délégation Générale pour l'Armement (Ministère de la défense)
DSAA	Department of Defense Security Assistance Agency
EEC	European Economic Community
ESD	Electronique Serge Dassault
ESRC	Economic and Social Research Council
FAO	Food and Agriculture Organisation
FRG	Federal Republic of Germany
FY	Fiscal year
GATT	General Agreement on Trade and Tariffs
GDP	Gross Domestic Product
G–MAPP	Global Models and the Policy Process
GNP	Gross National Product

HCP	House of Commons paper
IBD	Independent Bids for Development
IBRD	International Bank for Reconstruction and Development
ICBM	Intercontinental ballistic missile
IDA	International Development Association
IDEA	International Defence Economics Association
IISS	International Institute for Strategic Studies
IMF	International Monetary Fund
INSEE	Institut national de la statistique et des études économiques
LDC	Less-developed country
LESOD	Laboratoire d'Economie et de Sociologie des Organisations de Défense
LIBOR	London Inter-Bank Offered Rate
MAD	Mutual assured destruction
MAP	Military Assistance Program
ME	Military expenditure
MIC	Military–industrial complex
MILCOM	Military commodity (sector of SARUM)
MIRV	Multiple independently targetable re-entry vehicle
MIST(S)	Military industrial–scientific technological complex(es)
MoD	Ministry of Defence
MRS	Marginal rate of substitution
NASA	National Aeronautics and Space Administration
NATO	North Atlantic Treaty Organisation
NIC	Newly industrialising country
NIESR	National Institute of Economic and Social Research
NOC	Not otherwise classified
OECD	Organisation for Economic Cooperation and Development
OLS	Ordinary least squares
OPEC	Organisation of Petroleum Exporting Countries
PME	Politico-military exercise
PPP	Purchasing-power parity
PROPAGE	Modèle de projections multisectorielles glissantes de l'INSEE
RAF	Royal Air Force

R&D	Research and Development
RPE	Retrogressive path equations
SAGEM	Société d'Applications Générales d' Electricité et de Méchanique
SALT	Strategic Arms Limitation Talks
SANA	Scientists Against Nuclear Arms
SARU	Systems Analysis Research Unit
SARUM	SARU model
SBU	Strategic business unit
SDI	Strategic Defense Initiative (US)
SER	Standard Error of Regression
SIAR	Surveillance Industrielle de l'Armement (Ministère de la défense)
SIPRI	Stockholm International Peace Research Institute
SIRPA	Service d'information et de relations publiques des armées (Ministère de la défense)
SLBM	Submarine-launched ballistic missile
3SLS	Three-stage least squares
SNA	System of National Accounts
SNECMA	Société Nationale d'Etude et de Construction de Moteurs d'Avions
SNPE	Société Nationale des Poudres et Explosifs
START	Strategic Arms Reduction Talks
STEALTH	A technology to reduce radar visibility of aircraft or missiles
TRW	A US firm
UNCTAD	UN Conference on Trade and Development
UNDO	Unilateral National Defence Organisation
UNIDO	UN Industrial Development Organisation
USACDA	US Arms Control and Disarmament Agency (see also ACDA)
WDR	World Development Report (published by the World Bank)
WDT	World Debt Tables (published by the World Bank)
WEO	World Economic Outlook (published by IMF)
WMP	World Model Project, University of Groningen

Preface

Frank Blackaby
STOCKHOLM INTERNATIONAL PEACE RESEARCH
INSTITUTE (1981–6)

Science is organised and tested knowledge; and in that knowledge lies the potential control of phenomena. In regard to war, science can have two functions, the one promoting and the other impeding war. It can amass knowledge about the methods of prosecuting war so as to make war more efficient: or it can amass knowledge about the nature, causes and activities of war with a view to checking or preventing it. Julian Huxley, Peace through Science in *Challenge to Death* (London, Constable, 1934).

When Julian Huxley wrote this he had, of course, physical scientists in mind. In the post-war period, it does seem that physical scientists have shown more concern about the problem of war than social scientists: the Pugwash movement is a case in point. This may be because physical scientists are largely engaged in studies where national boundaries are irrelevant. Theoretical physics is the same in the Soviet Union as it is in the United States of America. Further, many of the applied physical scientists deal with problems which are obviously planetary problems, and which have no respect for national boundaries – the spread of disease, the possibility of long-term meteorological changes, and so on. To the physical scientist concerned with problems of this kind, wars across national boundaries appear somewhat absurd.

Social scientists have come to the problems of war somewhat later, and perhaps in a rather more tentative way. This may be because the study of economics and politics is not supranational in the same way as the study of physics and astronomy; the teaching of economics and politics in the USA is very different from that in the USSR. In particular, economists' academic interest in the economic issues raised by the phenomenon of war, and by the size of the world military sector, is rather recent and somewhat tentative.

There are reasons for this tentativeness, and they can be illustrated by observing how the approach to the study of government military expenditure differs from the approach to the study of other major items of government expenditure – for example, expenditure on health. The economic study of government expenditure, of course, falls into the category of economic policy studies: economists working in these fields are essentially concerned with the most efficient way of meeting certain policy objectives.

In the matter of government expenditure on health, it is not fanciful to consider the possibility of quantification of the objective. A variety of indicators exists on the state of health of a particular community – expectation of life, infant death rates, and so on. It is therefore quite possible to examine alternative policies of health expenditure for improving the state of health in a country: what are the relative returns, for example, on an intensive campaign to reduce cigarette smoking, as against the expenditure of a similar sum of money on heart operations? The studies can be broadened to consider a wide variety of ways of reducing the risk of death, and these can serve as policy guidance in the choice which governments have to make with their limited resources. The contribution which an economist can make to a more efficient allocation of resources for improving national health is, conceptually, reasonably clear.

With military expenditure, there is a very different situation. It is, of course, possible to produce narrow studies addressed to the efficacy of particular weapon systems – 'efficacy' necessarily being defined by the number of casualties (divided into dead and wounded) which can be caused for a given quantum of expenditure. (By this measure, of course, nuclear weapons are remarkably efficient.) This is an extremely limited definition of the objective of this category of government expenditure – though it may indeed be more realistic than some of the more euphemistic formulations which policy-makers tend to present. No doubt there are many studies of the relative killing efficacy both of alternative weapons and also of alternative weapon deployments; however, not many of them are to be found in mainstream economic literature. No doubt there are economists who are engaged in the study of ways of 'making war more efficient' in the words of Julian Huxley; however, in general they are not particularly concerned to draw attention to the fact that they are so engaged.

The objective of health expenditure is to improve health and to reduce disease. What is the objective of military expenditure? In the latter half of this century, there has been a radical change in thinking about the answer to this question. It is best encapsulated in the classic statement of the American strategic thinker Bernard Brodie, who wrote in 1946: 'Thus far the chief purpose of our military establishment has been to win wars. From now on its chief purpose must be to avert them. It can have almost no other purpose.'[1] That amended statement of the objective radically changes the appropriate nature of the analysis. First, the question to be put to the military sector in any country is no longer a question about its efficacy as a military machine: it is a question about its efficacy as an instrument for preventing war. Second, if the objective is the prevention of war, then clearly the study of this question should not be limited to the study of the military sector alone.

Economists have moved somewhat tentatively into this field. This is perhaps somewhat surprising because, of all the social sciences, economics has probably developed the best methodology for thinking about the problems of policy addressed to particular objectives; it is an apparatus of thought initially developed by Professor Tinbergen whose essay follows this introduction. The apparatus of thought essentially requires two things: a precise definition of the objective, and a knowledge of the system in which policy operates. The policy-maker needs to know what instruments of policy he or she has available, and what the consequences of their use would be – and for that the knowledge of the interrelationships embodied in the system is needed. It is true that in economics there are many competing models, from which different policy prescriptions can be derived. However, in the very long run it can be assumed that 'organised and tested knowledge', in the words of Julian Huxley, well serve to distinguish which model fits the facts of the situation better. At least there is now in economics the way of thinking about policy which has some degree of intellectual vigour. It should be possible to adapt this way of thinking – the apparatus of objectives, instruments, and knowledge of the system – to the problem of reducing the risk of war.

Economists do have both a theoretical and practical contribution to the problem of the prevention of war. There is also a great deal they can usefully do in the study of the world military sector itself. As many of the contributions in this volume show, there are indigenous processes in the world military sector which must be understood. There is the nature of arms competition, which differs from other economic competitive processes. The weapons industries themselves – partly market, partly non-market – have their own patterns of behaviour. The spread of weapons round the world, and the rise of military industries where they did not previously exist, needs a form of analysis which is not precisely identical with the analysis of changes in the world structure of other industries. As the variety of approaches set out in this volume shows, there are a great many questions to be examined to improve our knowledge of the world military sector, and make some contribution to reducing the risks of war.

Note

1. Brodie, Bernard, *Strategy in the Nuclear Age* (Princeton University Press, 1959) p. 153.

Introduction

Christian Schmidt
UNIVERSITÉ DE PARIS IX DAUPHINE AND LESOD

The International Economic Association organised a meeting in Paris in June 1982 in order to assess our knowledge about the effects of military expenditures in the light of the recent trends in economic thought.[1]

The Stockholm meeting held in October 1985 represents a second step forward. Indeed, the chosen topic is without doubt more ambitious and also, perhaps, more questionable. Translated into crude provocative terms, it means: Does economic analysis have something to say about defence and peace? In spite of its intuitive appearance, neither the answers nor the question itself are trivial, or even perfectly clear.

I THREE PREREQUISITE QUESTIONS

Indeed, if war and peace activities obviously produce economic consequences, via military budgets, this does not imply anything about the relevance of economics to understanding defence and to promoting peace. Therefore its complete investigation requires answers to the following questions:

(1) Are defence and peace functionally related in economic terms such as input/output or substitutes/complements?
(2) Is defence an economic activity?
(3) Is peace an economic good?

The first question leads far beyond the economist's concern. It cannot be debated without the introduction of two other concepts, namely military expenditure and war. Indeed, military expenditures are, through strategic doctrines including those of nuclear deterrence, potentially related to war and peace according to the use (or non-use) of arms. Therefore a correct answer to this question is highly dependent on the relevance of economic concepts for a study of military strategy. The profession seems to be divided into two groups which may be labelled, following a suggestion of Intriligator,[2] the 'defence' economists and the 'peace' economists. Roughly speaking, for the first group, defence expenditures are assumed to be a necessary condition to lead towards a state of peace; for the second group, the negative aspect of a military arsenal in the peace-making process is regarded as dominant.

But if the two groups start from different presuppositions, both focus their researches on phenomena such as the arms race, war preparations, and the outbreak of war, perhaps in order to avoid such a situation. Only a few studies are prepared by economists on peace itself. Obviously, observations of the real world provide arguments in favour of such an orientation, but some theoretical considerations are also relevant. Individual rationality and traditional competitive assumptions of economic theory appear, at first glance, to be more easily related to situations of conflict than of peace. Furthermore, if the price of war is difficult to compute, the definition of a price of peace opens a still more fundamental debate in economic theory.

The answer to the second question is cumbersome. Some facets of defence activity belong to the world of markets, including the arms industry and international transfers; others remain outside this realm, for instance, the defence spirit of a population. In other respects, defence pictured as a whole seems to provide an excellent example of a so-called pure public good, as opposed to a pure private good.[3] Thus Public Economics is relevant to defence studies.

From an institutional point of view, defence organisation can hardly be described as an economic system because of the very specific content of its 'satisficing principle'.[4] But this does not mean that the non-economic defence organisation has no economic effect. On the contrary, Boulding's claim for a need for economic analysis of such non-economic organisation sounds right.

The third question is related to the other two. National security enters into the utility function of every citizen of a given country. But the answer for national security does not solve the dispute about the meaning of peace. For a defence economist, peace cannot be directly appraised, but can only be taken into account indirectly by means of a treatment of war risk. Shadow prices, indirect utility function and expected utility theory have already provided useful tools for the evaluation of strategic states of the world under the restrictive optimal assumptions. Peace is then a limit situation, where the probability for war would be zero. For a peace economist, peace must be conceptualised as a principle for economic calculation without using defence outlays, like justice in the utilitarian tradition. Concepts such as fair division can be applied to processes such as peace negotiations.[5] But this normative extension of economics seems at the moment merely like an agenda for tentative research programmes. Yet let us observe that if peace can be understood as a limiting case in a war's prospect, war also can be interpreted as a stop point in an implicit negotiation process.

Such fundamental questions were obviously not solved during the Stockholm meeting. However, the participation of economists from various backgrounds enabled the subject to be considered from many different angles. From an analytical point of view, the contributions may be classified into two distinct groups namely war and peace economic analysis and the economy of defence systems.

II GUIDELINES FOR THEORETICAL INVESTIGATIONS

According to a prevalent view, defence studies require research on warfare and on modelling of strategy. Three major parts of economic analysis were used to explore this unfamiliar field.

The first is game theory, which provides a common matrix to set and solve many problems in economics as well as in military strategy. Shubik has contributed a critical survey of the possibilities and the actual limits of the game theory approach in defence matters. Another example of its use is found in the chapter by Sandler through the economic theory of alliances as a by-product of the games approach.

The economic theory of utility, with its extension to risk treatment and individual expectations was, in various modes, also used extensively for different purposes by Brito and Intriligator on the one hand and by McGuire on the other.

Finally, the theory of public choice also supplies an interesting schema, mainly used to discuss the performance of the resources allocative process for defence. Keith Hartley, who began such an investigation ten years ago, used its features to introduce the debate on a case study of reducing defence studies in the UK.

It would be wrong to deduce from this list that only microeconomic tools, belonging to the neoclassical arsenal, are relevant to the study of defence matters, although researches along these lines are probably more numerous because of the need for the decision-making process to explain rational military or political behaviour in defence fields. But other approaches, traditionally labelled as macroeconomic, can also legitimately be explored. Thus Brody has presented a paper dealing with a von Neumann growth model where defence is considered as a 'priority good'. The relevance of this framework is discussed by Sen.

One is surprised at the relatively few studies referring to the features of economic welfare theory. An evaluation of defence from a welfarist point of view is supported with different arguments in this volume by two political scientists, Albrecht and Kolodziej, who have both worked at the borderline of Political Economy. A little reflection about semantics shows that welfare refers, at least implicitly, to some social 'well' or 'good' order. Translating into an appropriate language, war should be designated as a kind of 'illfare'. Unfortunately, several of the conditions traditionally assumed for welfare do not operate for illfare, for instance, the positive association of social individual values.[6] Indeed, welfare and illfare are no more symmetrical than peace and war in the international world. But the measurement of military burden in terms of social entitlements suggested some relevance of the welfare approach to the topic through public expenditure analyses.

III FRAMEWORKS FOR EMPIRICAL TREATMENTS

The relationship between economics and war (or peace) situations cannot be reduced to pure theoretical constructions, built on the unique basis of economic logic and referring only to hypothetical and stylised warfare. There are interesting contributions on the relationship between economic depression and international conflict.

Econometric cross-section techniques have been used, as well as input–output models, in order to support empirical estimates for the traditional economic analysis of military expenditure at various levels – national, regional and international.[7] One of the main limitations of such techniques concerns the timing schedule treatment. So Martin, Smith and Fontanel together propose a time-series model for a comparative study of the macroeconomics impact of the military budget in France and the UK.

In order to investigate the military dynamics inside an econometric network, two routes are available. The first, following a line of reasoning suggested by Isard, consists of introducing an interactive international process to arms races into a world econometric model.

In that spirit, the world SARU model described by Gigengack, de Haan and Jepma incorporates an arms dynamics submodel mainly deduced from a simple econometric translation of the Richardson equations.

The other route seeks to find a correct linkage between separate models containing various types of variables and parameters. This direction is investigated by Lambelet and Luterbacher relating allocative resources, diplomatic relationships and war.

IV AN OPEN FIELD

A brief survey of ordered, but very eclectic, contributions discussed at Stockhom and collected in this volume, gives the picture of a patchwork. No dominant features emerge from it as a premise for a unified corpus of knowledge corresponding to an economic theory of defence. Yet the observed diversity of the economists now involved in one or another defence topic can be seen as a signal both of vivid scientific expectation and of increasing political demands. The creation of the first International Defence Economics Association (IDEA) as one of the concrete results of the Stockholm IEA meeting is a supplementary indication that today several professional economists are convinced that defence opens new horizons for stimulating economic investigation in close relation with scientists from other disciplines.

Notes and References

1. Schmidt, Christian (ed.), *The Economics of Military Expenditures* (London: Macmillan, 1986).
2. Intriligator, M. D., 'Strategy in a Missile War: Targets and Rates of Fire', Security Studies project, UCLA, Los Angeles, 1967; and various contributions in MacKeanes, R., *Issues in Defence Economics* (New York, 1982). For a discussion of their relevance cf. C. Schmidt, 'Logique de la décision économique, Logique de la dissuasion nucléaire', *Revue d'Economie Politique* no. 4, June–July 1982.
3. Samuelson, P. A., 'The Pure Theory of Public Expenditure', *Review of Economics and Statistics*, vol. XXXVI, 1954, and 'Pure Theory of Public Expenditure and Taxation' in J. Margolis and H. Guitton (eds) *Public Economics* (London: Macmillan, 1969) pp. 107–10. For a discussion of defence application see C. Schmidt, 'An Economic Contribution to War and Peace Analysis' in R. Väyrynen, D. Senghas and C. Schmidt (eds) *Quest for Peace* (New York: Sage Press, forthcoming).

4.   In the sense of H. Simon, *Model of Man* (New York: John Wiley 1957).
5.   Raiffa, H., *The Science and the Art of Negotiation* (Cambridge, Massachusetts: Harvard University Press 1982).
6.   This open question of an 'illfare' was briefly mentioned in Kenneth J. Arrow, *Social Choice and Justice*, collected papers, vol. 1 (Cambridge, Massachusetts: Harvard University Press, 1983) p. 15.
7.   For an input exercise at world level, cf. W. Leontief and F. Duchin, *Military Spending, Facts, Figures, Worldwide Implications and Future Outlook* (Oxford: Oxford University Press, 1983).

Note by the Editors

In view of the number and length of the papers presented at the Conference the editors of this volume have had to be very selective in what they could include. In particular they have been able to publish only a selection of the points made in the discussion, often in a very condensed form.

C. S.
F. B.

Opening Presentation: World Peace Policy

Jan Tinbergen*
THE HAGUE

I NECESSITY OF PEACE POLICY

After the First World War the Allied governments imposed heavy reparation payments on Germany and even occupied the Ruhr region as a punishment for delayed payments. The war's aftermath could not be held under control by the early post-war governments and the economy's disorganisation demonstrated itself in a run-away inflation which reduced the mark's buying power to one billionth (in the European sense of 10^{-12}) of its pre-war value. The young economist John Maynard Keynes had warned against such a policy,[1] but at the time of the negotiations was unable to persuade the politicians involved.

After the 1929 economic crisis, which finished in the Great Depression, the joint impact of the 1922/3 inflation and of cyclical unemployment brought Hitler to power, who wanted war and dreamt of a powerful Germany. It took unbelievable efforts to defeat Germany, especially by communist Russia. Only at that time were Keynes' views understood: instead of reparation payments considerable assistance to rebuild the German economy (as far as occupied by the USA, the UK and France) was offered by the USA. After some time, in which reparation payments in kind had been imposed by the Soviet Union, the part occupied by Soviet forces was also treated more positively.

Keynes as an economist had dealt with the consequences of the First World War in an incidental way, taking as given the choices that the politicians had made and analysing the consequences. Similarly, during the Second World War, he took the political decisions as given and indicated how best to finance that war. Until quite recently, the choice between a policy of war and one of peace was not considered a subject for economists to deal with. Yet, good arguments can be offered to do so. Wars have increasingly affected various aspects of human welfare: enormous losses of goods and human lives as well as enormous efforts – productive and destructive – are involved, considerably larger than the consequences of economic policy in the traditional sense, such as an anti-cyclical policy or a policy of structural change, such as development policies. In a recent article I therefore suggested that economic science 'internalise' peace policy as an important chapter in 'total economic policy', the possible new name to give to that integration process.[2]

If this proposal is accepted, a first step may consist of what is normal in the preparation of an economic policy for a given country (or other area) during a given time period: a correction of the population's preferences. Some corrections are corrections for short-sightedness, for instance compulsory schooling for youngsters up to the age of 18. Other corrections consist of the encouragement to consume merit goods and the discouragement of unhealthy goods by making the former available at prices below cost and by taxing the latter. A third correction of preferences may be quality control or information on quality (for instance by consumer unions) as a correction on quality suggestions by advertising. Similarly a peace policy may require a correction on exaggerated nationalism or patriotism, which are often based on the idea that one's own compatriots are better, abler or nobler than citizens of other countries. This cannot be true simultaneously for two or more nations and so a correction is necessary. Similarly also a correction may be needed for the underestimation of the sufferings that accompany war, if only because war victims of previous wars do not vote. Another reason for a systematic underestimation of war suffering is the technological development in weapons. Nuclear weapons of today's generation are able to annihilate human and other life.

The preparation of an optimal 'total economic policy' may be set up as recommended by economists in texts on economic policy.[3] The first step consists of the construction of a model of the operation of the economy considered; the next steps are choosing targets and instruments – or more generally aims and means – and the final step consists of the solution for the optimal numerical values to be given to the instruments or the structure of the economies involved. By 'structure' we mean the set of institutions and their instruments. These constitute the qualitative aspects of an optimal policy, whereas the numerical values to be given to the instruments constitute the quantitative aspects. Examples of the latter may be the levels of import duties or the size of the defence budget. In this essay we will discuss some of the additions to be made to this procedure as a consequence of the inclusion of peace among the aims.

II   LEVELS OF DECISION MAKING

One consequence is the necessity to consider at least two economies or nations, since an integrated nation does not know war as a means of policy. We will restrict ourselves to only two nations, because in today's world the coexistence of the United States of America (USA) and the Union of Socialist Soviet Republics (USSR) constitutes the most important problem of peace policy. A policy of sovereign decisions by each of these two nations (or their creations of NATO and the Warsaw Pact) will be called a policy 'at the lower level' or 'at level 2'. An alternative policy in which common decisions of the two nations (or the two alliances) – to be indicated as United Nations (UN) decisions – are made will be called a policy 'at the higher level' or 'at level 1'.

In this section will be discussed the problem of which level of decision-making is optimal, that is, produces a higher total welfare. This may be called a problem of management and so another contribution of economic science can be made: management science finds its main (though not its only) application in business economics. Our model is the simplest form of a hierarchy, where larger numbers of levels of decision-making are more often involved. It depends on the nature of the problem to be solved which of a number of possible levels of decision-making is optimal. Any decision at a given level will have an impact on the population controlled by that level and an impact on the population not controlled. The latter will be called external effects. It will be assumed that external effects will be underestimated. As a consequence the interests of the total population will be taken care of in the best way if external effects are negligible.

This proposition may be illustrated by a topical example, the one of environmental quality, such as acid rain or the quality of Rhine water. In both cases the optimal level of decision-making is supranational. British policy does not guarantee that the interests of the European Continent are taken care of sufficiently and French decisions are no guarantee that the interests of other nations in the Rhine valley are taken care of sufficiently. Both examples illustrate that sticking to national sovereignty is not an optimal policy to solve these environmental quality problems.

Some politicians are victims of a misunderstanding concerning the consequences of national sovereignty. They seem to think that sovereignty warrants keeping the nation's welfare under control. This is not correct, however: a nation's welfare may very well be co-determined by the decisions of other nations.

Of course a large number of decisions can be taken at or even below the national level, since their effects depend on such decisions only and not on decisions taken elsewhere. The choice of food consumed can be left to families. The question where to place traffic lights cannot be influenced by authorites of towns other than the two under consideration. (The colours of traffic lights, however, should not be chosen locally.)

A sovereign decision may also be taken on the country's social system, at least within certain limits. Thus, the Warsaw Pact countries are technically free to choose their own way to socialism (Berlin 1976 meeting of the Council for Mutual Economic Assistance or Comecon). The choice made by Hungary in 1956 or that made by Czechoslovakia in 1968, was not accepted by the USSR, however. NATO countries are somwhat freer; yet, a seizure of power by the communist party without a regular vote would not be accepted in the West, and correctly so. Even so the 1948 coup in Czechoslovakia was accepted grudgingly.

The most important conclusion with regard to our subject is, of course, that for peace policy, the optimal level of decision-making is level 1, the United Nations level. For this problem – the maintenance of peace – national sovereignty is not appropriate. In other language, coexistence requires common decision-making of all nations involved. In still other language, the one of the Palme Commission, security must be common security.[4] The new institution needed for peace policy is a Security Council with the competence to take decisions (without veto power of some members) and the power to implement these decisions (United Nations Peace Force).

Before pursuing our main subject it seems useful to add a few other problems whose optimal solution requires decisions at world level. In a way these are the problems dealt with in the report to the Club of Rome on the New International (Economic) Order, Reshaping the International Order. The problems covered may be indicated briefly as financing world development (the World Bank's activities), financing short-term fluctuations in international payments (the activities of the International Monetary Fund), food production and distribution (the activities of the Food and Agricultural Organisation), international trade and industrialisation (the activities of the General Agreement on Tariffs and Trade, of the United Nations Conference on Trade and Development and the United Nations Industrial Development Organisation), energy and minerals production and distribution, research and development, transnational enterprises and the management of the oceans (the activities dealt with in the new Law of the Sea, in preparation), It is to be hoped that the forty-year jubilee of the United Nations will be a stimulus to reconsider the ways and means needed to perform these tasks in a more satisfactory way than so far.

III   MUTUAL DETERRENCE NOT AN OPTIMAL SOVEREIGN POLICY

Pursuing our main theme let us now consider the methods presently used by the USA and the USSR in order to maintain peace. At present national sovereignty is adhered to, and not even in the best way. Although a beginning of understanding for common security shows up with some administrators in the USA,[6] so far a system of mutual deterrence is practised, which has resulted in an arms race and even a nuclear arms race, at astronomical cost and great risks.

This development is the result of a high degree of mutual distrust and ignorance about the other superpower's aims, a dangerous and insufficiently understood preference for offensive weapons and an insufficiently founded strategy. Recently some economists, and in particular Professor Dietrich Fischer, have contributed valuable analyses of the mechanisms involved and formulated proposals for better policies,[7] even if national sovereignty were maintained. In the remainder of this essay more details of these analyses and proposals will be discussed.

A very important tool of analysis used by Fischer is the distinction between *offensive* and *defensive* arms. A generalisation of this distinction consists of a similar distinction between the means to produce security. These means need not consist of military means only. The use of some non-military means of economic policy as long as peace is maintained may contribute to the security of both nations. Even non-economic but general political means may be used to raise the level of security. Finally, even the possibility of raising the security level of both countries without negotiations and without a treaty exists. The tools of analysis mentioned may now be applied by listing a number of alternative strategies to safeguard peace.

The distinction between offensive and defensive arms may be applied by listing a number of both types. Whereas battleships, aircraft and tanks are offensive, minefields, anti-aircraft guns and anti-tank artillery are defensive. While missiles are offensive, anti-ballistic missiles weapons (ABM) are defensive.

The distinction between offensive and defensive non-military means may be illustrated by economic wars and economic cooperation. Trade restrictions, whether on imports or exports, are the main instruments of economic wars. Economic cooperation may consist of the furthering of trade, of financial transfers or of transfer of technological information. Examples of general political means are public addresses and scientific and cultural cooperation. Qualifications in public addresses may be destructive or constructive, as recent examples show. Examples of one-sided measures which may contribute to a better climate for negotiations have been given by former Secretary of Defence of the USA – Robert S. McNamara.[8]

Alongside the tools of analysis mentioned other concepts also are useful to understand the strategic choices available. One of these is the concept of vulnerability. Missiles in silos are much more vulnerable than mobile missiles. Missiles not visible to reconnaissance satellites are also, of course, less vulnerable. The level of security at present depends very much on the existence of missiles of unknown location.

IV PROPOSALS OF SOVEREIGN PEACE POLICIES

Let us now mention some proposals of sovereign policies made by Fischer and others which may both raise nations' security and reduce the cost of security in comparison with the policy of mutual deterrence with the aid of threatening weapons.

One set of measures is offered under the heading of *transarmament*, meaning a shift from offensive to defensive weapons. Thus a shift from tanks to anti-tank artillery, or to minefields may indeed show a nation's aversion to war. The transarmament process is more complicated if missiles are to be replaced by anti-missile weapons. The latter are in the process of being tried out only. One system only – meant to defend the Moscow area – has been accepted in the

1972 ABM Treaty. The American Strategic Defense Initiative (SDI) aims at finding alternatives and the USSR is reported by the USA to be trying out other systems. Sovereign policies may lead to a situation in which one nation would attain first-strike capacity and the other would not. This would mean a less stable equilibrium of deterrence and lead to an additional arms race. This possibility again illustrates the limitations of a sovereign policy.

Reducing the chance that the opponent attains first-strike capability is also possible by spreading warheads over a larger number of locations. This implies the reduction of the number of warheads per missile. However, there are possibilities such as those mentioned by Fischer and McNamara,[9] some of which have been mentioned above. To the extent that a reduction in arms production would be attained by negotiations an economic problem will turn up; how can society profit, in terms of employment and consumption or growth, from such a reduction? This is known as the problem of conversion, switching from military to civil production. The member nations of the United Nations have been requested by the Secretary General to report on conversion possibilities and, as usual, Sweden was the first nation to report.[10]

V   SUMMARY

In the preceding sections we submitted the following propositions:

1.   Economists are able to contribute to finding a better peace policy.
2.   War is even worse than expressed by public opinion.
3.   Optimal policy has to use qualitative and quantitative means, that is, the creation of new institutions and a better use of existing institutions and their instruments.
4.   The most important new institution needed is world-level decision making or a reorganised Security Council with the competence to decide (without veto power of some nations) and the power to implement decisions (a United Nations Peace Force).
5.   A beginning of understanding in the USA for the necessity of cooperation of the USA and the USSR on defensive weapons was reported in the Dutch press.
6.   Sovereign policies so far have led to mutual deterrence which is very expensive and does not warrant a lasting peace.

7. Some better forms of sovereign policies exist. A shift from offensive to defensive weapons (transarmament) may raise security.
8. Non-military means (trade policy, technical cooperation, public pronouncements) may also raise security.

Notes and References

*Unfortunately Professor Tinbergen was unable to present this address in person.

1. Keynes, J. M., *The Economic Consequences of the Peace* (London: Macmillan, 1920).
2. Tinbergen, J., 'De economie van de oorlog' ('The Economics of Warfare') *Economisch Statistische Berichten*, 20 February 1985, pp. 172–5.
3. cf. Tinbergen, J., *Economic Policy: Principles and Design* (Amsterdam: North Holland, 1956); Preston, A. J. and Pagan, A. R., *The Theory of Economic Policy* (Cambridge, New York, etc.: Cambridge University Press, 1982); Hughes Hallet, A. and Rees, H., *Quantitative Economic Policies and Interactive Planning* (Cambridge, London, New York, etc.: Cambridge University Press, 1983).
4. Palme, O. *et al.* (Independent Commission on Disarmament and Security Issues), *Common Security* (New York: Simon & Schuster, 1982).
5. Tinbergen, J. *et al.*, *Reshaping the International Order* (New York: Dutton, 1976).
6. Spoor, A., 'Defensieschild alleen samen met Russen acceptabel' ('Defence shield acceptable only together with Russians'), *NRC–Handelsblad*, 11 February 1985, p.8.
7. Fischer, D., *Preventing War in the Nuclear Age* (London: Croom Helm, 1984); Fischer, D., 'Peace as a Road to Disarmament', *Disarmament* VII, 3, 1984, pp. 81–7; Fischer, D., 'Weapons Technology and the Intensity of Arms Races', *Conflict Management and Peace Science*, no. 1., Fall, 1985.
8. McNamara, R. S., 'What the US can do', *Newsweek*, 5 December 1983, pp. 114–18.
9. Fischer, D., 'Peace as a Road to Disarmament', *Disarmament* VII, 3, 1984, and McNamara, R. S., 'What the US can do', *Newsweek*, 5 December 1983.
10. Cf. Thorsson, Inga, *In Pursuit of Disarmament, Conversion from Military to Civil Production in Sweden*, vols. 1A, 1B (Stockholm: liber Allmänna Förlaget, 1984).

Part I
General Perspectives

1 Unilateral National Defence Organisations: An Economic Analysis of Non-economic Structures

Kenneth E. Boulding*
INSTITUTE OF BEHAVIORAL SCIENCE,
COLORADO UNIVERSITY

The 'war industry' is that segment of economic structures and activities which produces what is purchased with military expenditures, mainly out of nation-states' military budgets. Unilateral National Defence Organisations (UNDOs) are those departments within governments that organise the war industry. We may add terrorist organisations (soldiers without governments) to this list.

UNDOs are essentially non-economic organisations, in that while they have a capital stock and a cash flow, they are not governed by measures of the value of product relative to cost (profit) and do not have a balance sheet or 'bottom line' (net worth). If they did, it would probably be a very large negative number. Their product is supposed to be national security, but as each UNDO has large external diseconomies, producing insecurity in other nations, especially though not exclusively in those regarded as enemies, UNDOs as a world system have a large negative product, and represent a kind of cancer in the world economy.

Technical change, especially long-range missiles with nuclear warheads, have moved us into a new 'region of time' where the parameters of the world war industry have changed, so that the immediate past is a poor guide to the future. National defence indeed has become incapable of producing national security, and other means must be found.

I HOW THE WAR INDUSTRY OPERATES

The war industry in any country can be indentified fairly easily as that
part of the national product which is purchased with the military or
'defence' budget. This identifies a substantial area of organisational,
economic and political activity which would not exist if there were not
a defence budget. It could be argued that perhaps local militia and
even private guerrilla organisations might be added to this, but these
are usually very small. Fundamentally, the war industry is a creation
of the national state and the budget of the national state. It could be
regarded either as a proportion of the national product or the net
national product, or even some other aggregate. All aggregates are a
little misleading because of the virtual absence of capital accounting
in government, especially in the war industry. With the possible
exception of private firms within it, the war industry does not
contribute as much as it should to the official statistics for capital
consumption and hence tends to exaggerate the value of the net
national product. But these are relatively minor points.

The war industry is subject to enormous fluctuations, more than
any other segment of the economy. In the USA, for instance, it was
less than 1.0 per cent of the economy in the early 1930s. It rose
to about 42 per cent by 1943 or 1944, fell to about 6 per cent in the
'great disarmament' which followed the Second World War, when
the USA transferred well over 30 per cent of the economy from the
war industry into civilian industry without unemployment ever rising
above 3 per cent, a remarkable achievement, which, strangely
enough, is not in the popular imagination. In the USA, again, the war
industry increased to about 14 per cent of the economy in the Korean
War. Except for the relatively small rise in the Vietnam War, it has
been falling ever since, until the Reagan Administration. Even now it
is only about 7 per cent of the economy.

Organisationally, the war industry consists, first, of departments of
defence, which spend the defence budget. There seems to be no
general name for these organisations. I suggest 'unilateral national
defence organisation' which has the agreeable acronym of UNDO.
The war industry also consists of those organisations which provide
what is purchased by the UNDOs. In the capitalist countries, these
are frequently at least quasi-private organisations, which have to
show profits in order to survive, but they are still an essential part of
the war industry. In the communist countries, of course, the private

sector is very small indeed, and virtually the entire war industry is publicly owned and operated. This difference, however, may not really be very large in actual behavioural terms. There must be some equivalent of the Lockheed Corporation in the USSR. Its managers have to please a slightly different set of people from those of the Lockheed Corporation in the USA, but both are governed by some sort of accounting system and the decision-making process is probably not radically different.

Like all other segments of an economy or, for that matter, of a whole society, the war industry can be described in both what might be called a 'capital mode' and an 'income mode', both of these being necessary for a full description. In the capital mode, the war industry can be described in terms of a position statement or structure, a 'flashlight photograph' describing the land, buildings, weapons, vehicles, machines, cash-in-hand, debt and other financial obligations, and so on, and also its personnel ranging from the commander-in-chief or war minister, down all the ranks of the military hierarchy to business executives, civilian employees, veteran-hospitals' staffs, and so on. The 'income mode' has to be described in terms of the changes in the flashlight photograph from day to day or, more strictly, from second to second. The income description then is a 'movie' of which the position statements, which may be thought of as extended balance sheets, are frames.

Income statements describe such events as the depreciation and destruction of stocks of all kinds, including obsolescence. Such statements also describe the creation of new stocks by production or purchase, such items as weapons, fuel supplies, food, and so on. These statements should also include additions to and subtractions from personnel – those people who are hired, fired or conscripted, or who retire, quit, or die. These subtractions occasionally become dramatic, when personnel are killed in war or in accidents. They describe also financial changes – increases in money stocks from government budgets, the exchange of money stocks for purchases of all kinds, the creation and redemption of debt, and so on. In that part of the war industry which is privately owned there are balance sheets which evaluate at least a significant part of the total flashlight photograph and have some kind of 'bottom line' that is, a net worth, which is the sum of all positive assets minus the sum of all negative assets or liabilities. As a result of the continual changes and transformations in the balance sheet, the revaluation of assets and so on, the net worth may increase or decrease. An increase in the net worth, gross of disbursements to stockholders or owners, is net profit. If this is a decrease, it is called a net loss.

In the publicly owned sector of the war industry, as in the whole government sector, balance sheets are rarely, if ever, constructed. In national income accounting the product of the industry is presumed to be identical with the cost, that is, the budget, which is fundamentally a cost but is entered in national income accounts as a product. There is no necessity to calculate a rate of return or rate of profit, nor indeed even to calculate a net worth. Sometimes this is tried roughly, as when cost–benefit analysis is done, mostly for civilian investment projects, such as dams. A very half-hearted attempt was made in the USA at war-industry accounting during the time that Robert McNamara was Secretary of Defense in the early 1960s, but there is not much evidence that it had any significant effect on decision-making and the process had considerable elements of ritual. It is this fact that UNDOs never have to show a 'bottom line' or a rate of return on their investment that demonstrates the fundamentally 'non-economic' aspect of the war industry and of the whole concept of national defence. The product of the war industry is never simply calculated, as is demonstrated by the fact that we assume in national income accounting that its product is measured by its cost. If product is defined by cost, it is not surprising that we have the phenomena of cost overruns, waste, and corruption, which have been documented so successfully, for instance, by Seymour Melman and Lloyd Dumas. [1, 2]

II   IMPACTS OF WAR INDUSTRY ON CIVILIAN ECONOMY

The more immediate impacts of the war industry on the civilian economy can be analysed and identified fairly easily. The overall impact will depend a good deal on how the war industry is financed, whether by taxes, by expanding the national debt, or by increasing the money supply. The impact depends also to some extent on certain psychological reactions on decision-making in the civilian sector itself in terms of such things as general optimism and pessimism about the future, expectations of inflation or deflation, general willingness to adapt and adjust, mobility of capital and labour, and so on. As the war industry does not produce very much in the way of physical product which is purchased by the civilian sector, except by way of occasional 'garage sales' of surplus equipment and materials, the war industry has a certain inflationary bias unless it is financed by an excess of taxes over the expenditure on it. This inflationary bias may be offset to some extent if the war industry absorbs labour and other resources which had previously been unemployed. This was very noticeable in the early years of the expansion of the war industry in the USA during the Second World War, when the expansion began about 1939 with unemployment running at almost 20 per cent.

The success of the previously noted 'great disarmament' of 1945–7 certainly had something to do with the fact that the production of consumer capital, especially automobiles, had been very sharply curtailed during the war and also that net investment in the civilian sector had been extremely small, practically zero, for some years, so that there were large deficiencies to be made up in both the business and the household capital structures. Local community planning for the transition from war to peace, largely sponsored by the Committee for Economic Development, also played a very important role. And, of course, there was a considerable inflation, especially after price controls were removed, which reduced real interest rates and also helped to reduce unemployment. There is one other example in the experience of the USA, in which a noticeable reduction in the war industry in the early 1960s was also accompanied by a decline in unemployment, largely because of an expansion of state and local government, especially in education. It is only a partial oversimplification to say that the great expansion, especially in US university education in the early 1960s, came about as a result of resources released from the war industry.

III   LOCAL AND REGIONAL IMPACT ON THE WAR INDUSTRY

The local and regional impact of the war industry, and especially of changes in the war industry, can be very significant. Estimates have been made for the USA for net regional impact – that is, income brought in by the war industry minus income taken out in taxes and other things – which do show a considerable regional redistribution. There is not much evidence, however, that this very much affects the votes in Congress, with a few exceptions. Over longer periods, the very instability of the war industry tends to make it a liability rather than an asset to a region or a community, as it is far and away the most volatile segment of the total economy, as we have seen. Studies by the US Arms Control and Disarmament Agency have indicated that the adaptability of local communities in the USA is quite high. When, for instance, a war plant or an army base is shut down, the first reaction is great gloom and anxiety in the local community. Then not infrequently there is a realisation that the community has an asset in the closed base and it is then turned into an industrial park or something of that sort and frequently the community emerges better off, with a more stable economy than it had before. Over the long run, regional differences depend much more on the longer-run aspects of regional culture (and especially political culture) than they do on the ups and downs of federal spending. The war industry is so isolated from the rest of society – it is indeed something of a ghetto – that is makes much less impact upon local civilian culture than does, say, a technical college or a state university. In 1862 the US Government passed the Morrill Act, which set up the land grant colleges of agriculture and mechanic arts in each state. This act probably did far more for the US economy than all expenditure on the war industry over 200 years.

IV   EFFECT OF WAR INDUSTRY ON SCIENTIFIC TECHNOLOGY AND RESULTANT IMPACT ON CIVILIAN ECONOMY

Probably the largest and most significant impact of the war industry on the civilian economy in the long run arises out of the fact that, especially in the twentieth century, the war industry has become intimately associated with high scientific technology and hence constitutes an internal 'brain drain' on a national economy. This element was probably much less important in earlier times, when the war industry attracted 'macho heroes' – aristocrats at the one end and ne'er-do-wells at the other end of the hierarchy, who probably would not have made much contribution to the civilian economy anyway. The traditional armed forces could almost be regarded as an economic substitute for jails; a picturesque and romantic way of dealing with profligacy, libertinism, and sadism. What contribution indeed would Achilles have made to a civilian economy? The answer is almost certainly a negative one. This is not to deny, of course, that some very find human beings have been in the military, but an industry whose principal product is death and destruction is hardly likely to attract the most productive and creative types.

In the twentieth century this situation has profoundly changed with the applications of science to weaponry, and even to persuasion, marketing, and propaganda. Even from earliest times, of course, weapons have been made by civilians. So have medals and epaulettes and fancy dress, means of transportation and commissariats. These civilians in the war industry very rarely participated in actual combat. They were certainly closer to civilian life than the military in their ghettos, and some of their skills in metal working and so on in earlier times undoubtedly spilled over into civilian industry. With the application of science to technology, however, which really only begins in the middle of the nineteenth century, the whole situation was changed radically. The technology of weaponry and military equipment has become increasingly divorced from that of the civilian economy. The nuclear weapon has no civilian uses, apart from that of destruction. It is far too dangerous and messy to be used as a civilian explosive.

The principal 'spillover' from the nuclear weapon into the civilian economy was the light-water reactor, which has turned out to be an economic disaster. It is certainly no solution whatever to the long-run energy problem. It seems now that if we had developed nuclear power without the intervention of the military, we would have done it very differently, and almost certainly more usefully, perhaps more along the lines of the CANDU (Canadian-designed natural-uranium-fuelled, heavy-water-moderated reactor), the heavy-water reactor, or perhaps the gas-cooled reactor. We might even have gone more directly to the breeder, which is certainly more attractive from the point of view of the long-run energy problem, as it can use something like 70 per cent of the energy available in uranium, whereas the light-water reactor uses much less than 1.0 per cent of this pretty scarce resource. Other 'spillovers' from the military, such as heavily computerised machine tools, have also turned out to be of somewhat dubious civilian value.[3] The awful truth seems to be that swords make pretty miserable ploughshares; they are the wrong kind of material and very expensive. If we want ploughshares, it is much better to make them directly and to put research into them directly. All good rules have exceptions, of course, and perhaps the jet plane is a net civilian asset which certainly owes something to the military. But it would be a foolish housewife who proposed to feed the family on spillovers.

   The evidence for the adverse effects on the civilian economy in the long run in terms of technology and productivity is very strong as we compare the USA with Japan and West Germany. Economically it was the defeated countries who won the Second World War. They became psychologically demilitarised societies and so were able to devote virtually all their intellectual and technological resources to getting richer. Japan, especially, achieved a rate of economic development unprecedented in human history over two or three decades. One might oversimplify the situation by saying that the man who should have been designing Hondas in Detroit was probably building missiles for Lockheed. Especially since the 1970s, US productivity and per capita incomes have virtually stagnated after the great 'golden age' of the 1950s, 1960s, and early 1970s, when per capita income more than doubled and poverty by any standard was more than halved. Now in the USA poverty is increasing, slowly but noticeably, and for this the militarisation of the economy and of the whole society which followed the victory in the Second World War must bear a great deal of the responsibility, though exactly how much is hard to assess.

V   SECURITY AS A PRODUCT OF THE WAR INDUSTRY AND UNDOs

This brings us up against a most fundamental and difficult question: What is the product of the war industry and of the unilateral national defence organisations, and how is this product distributed, both internally and among the nations themselves? The conventional answer to this question, of course, is that the product is national security, and there is usually no further inquiry as to how this is defined, what it means, or how it is measured or evaluated. Security is by no means a meaningless concept. Up to a point it is something we all want, although like any other partial good, it is subject to the universal principle of diminishing marginal utility – perhaps the greatest principle that emerges out of an economic way of thinking. In economics there are no absolute values, except the ultimate good. Intermediate goods, of which security is one, all follow what I have sometimes called the 'parabola principle' – that the function which relates absolute goods to intermediate goods is always shaped something like a parabola and has a maximum. Thus, all virtues become vices if we have too much of them; all goods become bads if there is too much of them.

There are some troubling discontinuties in these 'goodness functions' which may create illusions of absolute value, or which involve what are essentially negative values. Good health is a good example. One can certainly range states of the human organism in regard to health from being on the point of death, through various stages of disease or imperfect health, up to perfect health, which is simply the absence of anything that can be identified as disease or deficiency. On the other hand, when it comes to athletic prowess, the perfect health boundary becomes a little vague. A person could have no disease and yet be a very poor athlete, or in another dimension may have no disease and yet be unable to pass examinations. In this respect, the concept of security is a little bit like health, and insecurity like disease, or perhaps the prospects of probability of disease. Security relates to the structure of our images of the future. It relates particularly to the probability of our condition worsening. This raises the question: Can we buy security? This would mean some 'price' or sacrifice of our present condition in order to give us a smaller probability of a worsening of condition in the future.

The clearest case of the purchase of security is, of course, insurance. Buying insurance is a present sacrifice which we believe will change the probability structure, especially of losses and severe losses, in the future. Without insurance, we feel less secure as we contemplate the fact that there is a positive probability that our house will burn down, that we will be involved in an automobile accident, that we will be sued for something, that we will have large doctor bills, or even that we will die within a certain period of time. These insecurities are perceived as a positive disutility, the diminution of which is worth some sacrifice of an insurance premium in the present. Insurance, that is to say, is a form of deterrence. It involves current sacrifice in order to diminish the probability that unacceptable change will happen to us in the future.

VI   THE WAR INDUSTRY AS A THREAT SYSTEM

Historically, the war industry produces two very different kinds of products. One is conquest, or the prevention of conquest, and the other is deterrence. The war industry is part of the threat system. It is concerned with the capability of carrying out threats. In the broadest sense, a threat system originates with a statement on the part of the threatener to the threatened, 'You do something that I want or I will do something that you don't want'. In this it differs sharply from exchange, which originates with a statement such as 'You do some-thing I want and I will do something you want'. A threat is an offer of a negative commodity. What system is produced by a threat depends, of course, on the reaction of the threatened. I distinguish at least five classes of reaction: submission ('It's O.K., I will do what you ask.'); defiance ('I won't do what you ask; carry out the threat if you can.'); counterthreat ('You do something nasty to me and I will do some-thing nasty to you.'); threat reduction ('I will do something that will diminish your threat.') One form of threat reduction is flight, simply running away, a very common reaction, which rests on the principle that the capability of carrying out threat diminishes with increase in distance between the threatener and the threatened. A second form of threat reduction is defensive structures – armour, city walls, and so on . . . the list could certainly be extended.

All these different systems have economic aspects. An initial threat raises the question as to whether the gain to the threatener from the ensuing system is going to be worth the cost, for both making and carrying out a threat always involves cost to the threatener as well as to the threatened. On the whole, the evidence of history suggests that initial threats do not pay off very well to the threatener, simply because of the great variety of reactions open to the threatened, and also because alternative initiatives, such as an offer to exchange, usually pay off much better than threat. Combinations of exchange and integrative relationships are particularly profitable. Rape is a poor method of sexual satisfaction. 'Marry me or I will kill you' rarely results in a very happy marriage for either party. 'Marry me and I will love you' usually works out much better. Even 'Marry me and with all my worldly goods I will thee endow' often works out quite well.

An overwhelming argument against threat initiation, even for conquest, is the accumulating evidence of the unprofitability of empire for the imperial power (frequently, even in the short run; almost 100 per cent in the long run). The Roman Empire bled Rome white, the Spanish Empire impoverished Spain for 400 years, as did the Portuguese Empire impoverish Portugal. It took France more than 100 years to recover from Napoleon and from its later empire. In both France and Britain the abandonment of empire after 1950 promoted a substantial increase in the rate of economic growth. There is overwhelming evidence for the proposition that the way to get rich is to stay home and mind your own business well. The Swedes are a very good example. One of the poorest countries in Europe in

1860, Sweden had a much more rapid rate of economic growth in the ensuing 100 years than did either France or Britain. The German overseas empire in the late nineteenth and early twentieth centuries was a dead loss from the very beginning in economic terms. The Japanese conquest of Korea cost it some ten years of economic growth.[4] The evidence is that exploitation has a very low pay-off for the exploiter, simply because threats produce hostility and divert resources into the threat system and away from the system of production and exchange. Slavery, for instance, always seems to have led to economic stagnation by comparison with free labour markets.

If we broaden our gauge beyond the economic to the cultural, again there are a very large number of examples in which military defeat has set off an outburst of culture in the defeated country and has led the victor to stagnate. After the defeat of France by Germany in 1870–1, Paris became the cultural capital of the world in art, literature, music – one thinks of Cézanne, Victor Hugo, Debussy – whereas Berlin became a provincial capital full of strutting soldiers – the great days of Goethe, Beethoven, and Schubert were over. Indeed, after the defeat of Austria by Germany in 1866, Vienna became the cultural capital of the German world, as symbolised by the Strausses, Freud, and Logical Positivism. Berlin after the defeat of 1919, until Hitler stopped it all, produced modern architecture and the Bauhaus, Brecht, the 'Blue Riders' in art, and so on. Even in the USA after the Civil War, American literature tended to move to the defeated South. No rule, of course, is universal. Carthage certainly did not do very well after its defeat by Rome, but perhaps it deserved that for nurturing the cult of Moloch.

The wars of the twentieth century, on the whole, have been wars of the breakdown of deterrence rather than wars of conquest as such. The First World War was certainly a breakdown of a previous system of deterrence as a result of an arms race. To some extent it was also a war of nationalisms, in that it resulted in the creation of some new nation-states in Poland, Czechoslovakia, and the break-up of Austria–Hungary. The Second World War is a very exceptional case, something like a 1000-year flood. In part it was a result of an arms race; in part the 'Drang Nach Osten' for Germany was an attempted war of territorial conquest of the Ukraine. The war was also complicated by ideologies of genocide and also by a profound change in aerial warfare technology, even before the atom bomb. Dresden was just as bad as Hiroshima.

VII CHANGES IN WAR PARAMETERS BROUGHT ABOUT BY NUCLEAR MISSILES

The development of long-range missiles with nuclear warheads has profoundly changed the parameters of war and has moved us from 'fighting' like the wars of the eighteenth century in which there were battles (which still survived somewhat in the Second World War) into wars of mutual genocide of civilian populations. To find equivalents for Auschwitz, Hiroshima, Nagasaki, and Dresden, one would almost have to go back to the Mongols, who also destroyed cities with all their inhabitants rather than merely conquering them. All complex systems – and the human race is the most complex – are capable of moving into unfamiliar and improbable regions. Over the course of human history, what I have called 'inclusive peace' – everything that is not war – has been at least 95 per cent of human activity. This is ploughing, sowing, reaping, manufacturing, dancing, singing, raising children, art, literature, religion, and so on.

War is a relatively rare pathology of the system and extreme war in the form of genocide is still more rare. Nevertheless, no matter how low the probability of anything, it is a fundamental principle that if we wait long enough it will happen. This is why a system of deterrence cannot be stable in the long run, though it can be stable in the short run, as indeed nuclear deterrence has been for forty years. If deterrence were 100 per cent stable, however, it would cease to deter. If the probability of nuclear weapons exploding were zero, they would not deter anybody. That would be the same thing as not having them. The present situation, therefore, has within it a positive probability of nuclear war which could very well lead to the end of the human race or even of the evolutionary process on this planet. It could be argued, of course, that economics and accounting simply break down in a situation of this kind. Nevertheless, the pretence that defence gives security should be exposed. The product of the US Department of Defense (and its counterparts elsewhere) is not national security but a certainty that within X years the USA and the USSR will destroy each other and possibly all the rest of the world as well. One is tempted to put negative infinity as the bottom line of the balance sheet of the US Department of Defense. Infinite loss discounted at any rate of discount is still infinite loss.

It is worth raising the question, therefore, as to whether any other structure of threat systems would have a positive net worth. At certain times and places in human history threat-reducing structures have at least been thought to have positive net worth, to judge by the castles and the city walls which are now tourist attractions and by the suits of armour which are mostly found in museums, but which survive perhaps in the shape of bullet-proof vests, soon I understand to be made obsolete. The 'Star Wars' proposals of the Reagan Administration are at least intended to be threat-reducing structures. The probability of their being successful, however, seems very small. They are equivalent to shooting the bullet that comes towards you rather than the cowboy who has just shot it. The cowboy certainly seems to be an easier target. Indeed, the preparation to cock the laser gun to shoot the bullet would seem to be a pure invitation to the aggressor to a first strike before the laser gun is cocked, and one would expect it to increase the probability of nuclear war very substantially.

Human history suggests that the improvement in offensive weaponry usually seems to have outdistanced any improvement in defensive structures. The collapse both of the feudal system, the feudal castle, and the walled city after the invention of gunpowder and the effective cannon is a good case in point. The virtual abandonment of civil defence except as ritual in an age of nuclear and long-range missiles certainly suggests that the same thing is happening again – that is, the nuclear weapon has made traditional national defence as obsolete as the effective cannon made the feudal baron.

VIII THE MEANING OF NATIONAL SECURITY IN THE NUCLEAR AGE

The insistent question remains, therefore: What is the meaning of national security in the nuclear age and against what are we trying to defend ourselves? One way of approaching this question is to ask ourselves: What would the system be like if either one of the superpowers disarmed unilaterally, as Costa Rica has done up to a point? Would this be followed by invasion and conquest? The answer would seem to be that this scenario would be so highly improbable that it could virtually be neglected. Only relatively simple societies can be conquered, in the sense of being annexed, and political heterogeneity has very low pay-offs. We can argue that Japan was conquered by the USA in the Second World War. Indeed, we still have military bases there. These military bases, however, are

remarkably ineffective in prevening the Japanese having a spectacular economic development, and indeed in creating (in some minds at
least) something of an economic threat to the USA, which is probably
more imaginary than real. If one side does not follow the conventions
of war, it is extremely difficult for the other side to follow them. This
is indeed the philosophy behind Ghandian non-violence or even
karate, which involve non-imitation of the opponent. If the USSR
disarmed unilaterally, what would the USA do? The answer is,
probably nothing. The USSR might dissolve into fourteen independent states. The principal beneficiary of this would undoubtedly be
the Russians, who now have to impoverish themselves in order to
keep the other nationalities within the Soviet Union, just as China
has impoverished itself to subsidise Tibet. Would the situation be
parallel if the USA disarmed unilaterally? Would the USSR send
armed forces to take Washington and instal Mr Guy Hall as president? Even in 1814 when the British burnt Washington they did not
attempt to conquer the USA. Adam Smith saw very clearly that if
there had not been an American Revolution, the centre of the British
Empire would have been removed to the American colonies in a few
decades as they came to exceed the mother country in population and
revenue, and Britain would have become a minor province in a great
American empire. One suspects that the American Revolution was
provoked by the British to preserve British independence.

IX   A CRITIQUE OF THE US AND SOVIET ECONOMIC SYSTEMS

It is true that there is some asymmetry between the USSR and the
USA. The USSR may be a little more ideologically aggressive,
although the asymmetry is not so striking under the Reagan Administration. A common defence of the US Department of Defense is that
if it did not exist the USSR would 'take over the world' with Cuba as
the example. The fact that devoting some 7 per cent of the economy
to the war industry enabled the USA to take over Grenada but did not
enable it to take over Cuba is some indication of its productivity. If
we do a cost–benefit analysis of the Cuban Revolution, however, it is
pretty clear that the USA is the principal benefactor. It gained over
200 000 able people who did not have to be educated and who are a
great economic asset to the USA, although there were a few liabilities
flown in at the end. The USA does not have to buy Cuba's sugar, it

does not have to subsidise Cuba and the Russians do. One is tempted to ask: What more could the USA want?

The USSR, like the Peoples' Republic of China, is an anomalous nineteenth-century empire, a cost–benefit analysis of which would certainly reveal that both the Russians and the Chinese would be well advised economically to abandon their empires, which they would then not have to subsidise. Furthermore, communist ideology is in a state of considerable disrepair simply because a great deal of it simply is not true. What is not true will eventually be found out, threat system or no threat system. China is learning this very rapidly. If the USSR learns it, it may become an economic competitor in the world market, which it certainly is not now, but even that would be no real threat to the USA. When the poor get richer, it is almost universally the case that the rich get richer too. It would certainly be to the advantage of the USSR to abandon its rigid planned economy, which is an economic dinosaur, and to follow the Chinese example, or even Lenin's example of the new economic policy when he found that communism simply did not work.

On the other hand, the capitalist world has it troubles too. Something can go wrong with anything – the international debt situation, the gobbling up of profit by interest, the enormous redistributions which are going on as a result of the debt structure in the face of declining land- and real-estate values, the precarious and casino-like quality of stock-markets and commodity markets, and so on, suggests that something might be a little rotten even in the state of Denmark and its fellow capitalist societies. The Great Depression was a much more severe crisis than any which seems to be coming up now, however, and the world survived it, and even learned something from it. There is a good case for cautious optimism regarding the economic future of the capitalist world. A similar cautious optimism is not unreasonable in regard to the communist world, simply because ideological illusions have failed to be realised in practice. What is happening in China could easily happen in the USSR under new leadership.

The economics of tribute versus defence is another aspect of this subject which requires careful study. We might be well advised to reverse the famous dictum of John Paul Jones, and say 'Billions for tribute, but not a penny for defence', simply on the grounds that tribute is much cheaper. In effect this is what was done with OPEC, to whom the USA and the rest of the world paid very substantial tribute over the past twelve years, now somewhat diminishing, as

economists should have predicted. Somebody must have reckoned
that the cost of conquest of the OPEC countries was greater than the
tribute paid to them. This principle applies, incidentally, in the
relations of civilian populations to their own countries. US citizens
pay tribute to their own country in the shape of taxes, for much of
which they get little in return except insecurity and the certainty of
eventual annihilation. The costs of revolt and tax refusal are usually
estimated to be greater than the costs of the tribute that they pay.

X   CONCLUSION

The conclusion seems inescapable that war and the war industry are a
non-economic section of society, guided by considerations of values
which are quite alien to the economic way of thinking. The question
which this conclusion raises is: Is there any possibility of transforming
the military culture into one that has a more economic direction? If
only one could persuade the military that it is much better to draw
wars than to win them, that winning wars nearly always means losing
the peace, and that in the present situation they are indeed a threat to
the continued existence of the human race, then a transformation
within the military culture should not be inconceivable. After the
transformation that I have seen in my lifetime in the Catholic Church,
I sometimes have hope even for the military, who are also human
beings, even if they do belong to a culture that is almost inevitably
rather pathological. The great problem with the military is that,
particularly if the theory of national security is deterrence, they are
useful only as long as they are not being used. They are rather like a
football team that practises and practises for long periods of time
without ever being allowed to play an official game. Perhaps indeed
the Falkland (Malvinas) War and the Grenada invasion do represent
ritual war, designed mainly to give the military some activity. We
manage to ritualise human sacrifice in religion. We may be able to do
the same thing with war.
    One note of hope is that national security through stable peace,
which in the present day is the only national security really available,
has actually spread to a large number of countries that have no plans
whatever to go to war with each other, and who are determined to
put national boundaries off their agendas, which is almost a sufficient
condition for stable peace. Economic conflicts have very little to do
with war. The USA, for instance, has virtually no economic conflicts

with the USSR and has much more intense economic conflicts with its allies and friends. There is some hope in the feeling that is found among some members of the military, that the nuclear weapon and the guided missile have destroyed what might be called the traditional 'ethos' of the military, involving courage, fighting, self-sacrifice, and so on, and have turned war into pure genocide. If this feeling could be encouraged, if more members of the military could come out of their ghettos and actively interact with the civilians who are concerned about their true welfare, then there can be some hope for the future.

Notes and References

* In the preparation of this paper, I was greatly assisted by the ideas and data contained in the recent unpublished manuscript entitled, 'The Nation Is Secure: Lessons From Stable Competition and Inherent National Security' by G. Shepherd and B. Shepherd of the University of Michigan, Ann Arbor, Michigan.

1. Melman, S., *The Permanent War Economy: American Capitalism in Decline* (New York: Simon & Schuster, 1974).
2. Dumas, L. J., (ed.) *The Political Economy of Arms Reduction: Reversing Economic Decay* (AAAS Selected Symposium 80) (Boulder, Colorado: Westview Press, 1982).
3. Noble, D. F., 'The Social and Economic Consequences of the Military Influence on the Development of Industrial Technologies', in Dumas, L. J. (1982) p. 91.
4. Boulding, K. E., and Gleason, A. H., 'War as an Investment: The Strange Case of Japan', *Peace Research Society (International) Papers* (Chicago Conference, 1964) vol. III (1965) pp. 1–17.

2 Peace and War Economics in Retrospect: Some Reflections on the Historical Background of Defence Economics

Christian Schmidt
UNIVERSITE DE PARIS IX DAUPHINE AND LESOD

The chapter first reviews the different approaches of economists to peace, to defence, to war and the semantics of the subject. Then the present state of the art and its development is considered, using historical material. The inheritance from Adam Smith is examined, followed by that from F. Y. Edgeworth, and it is found that both have substantial contributions to make to our understanding from their different approaches to questions of war, peace and defence.

I INTRODUCTION

1 Peace, Economic Theory and Defence Economics: Semantic Preconsiderations

When G. Kennedy prepared a new edition of his book, he decided to change its title from *Economics of Defence* (1975) to *Defence Economics*, arguing the extent of new material and different concern.[1] The reasons used by Kennedy were unclear and a touch of ambiguity still surrounds the topic. Does it mean that defence matters allow more room for the application of economic analytical tools, or that defence activities create economic problems with new concepts?

Behind the conventions of terminology a more serious debate about the concern of economics in these fields has emerged.

The literature published since 1975 provides examples of both interpretations. On the one hand, utility and cost functions, expected utility theory, economic equilibria definitions, optimality theory, cooperative and non-cooperative game solutions are extensively used by some economists to describe and explain such phenomena as battles, wars (especially nuclear wars), warfare, deterrence, alliance, the arms race and arms negotiations.[2] One could not help but notice the more frequent appeal to economic concepts for war than for peace. On the other hand, numerous economic studies exist concerning national accounting systems for national defence budgets, the costs and burden of the military sector, dynamics of defence programmes, and mechanisms of international arms transfer.[3] A quick comparison of these two groups of subjects leads to a strange and paradoxical observation: the traditional economic concepts look more satisfactory when they are applied to strategic or diplomatic topics (that is to say non-economic fields) rather than to the economic consequences of defence activities. Indeed, recent history reveals a contrasting picture: the process of accumulating knowledge produces self-satisfaction for the first group, while difficulties and controversial results generate a certain scepticism for the second.

Part of this difference can be attributed to the economic tools themselves and their different uses in the two cases. On the one hand there are concepts mainly provided by microeconomic theory, with the help of mathematics, to clarify the logical structure of war or its strategic doctrines; and on the other hand, using econometric techniques, there are macroeconomic concepts – mostly Keynesian-oriented – to scrutinise the data. But the topics themselves are not exactly the same. The general framework of microeconomic theory represents a starting point for elaborating theories, or, more precisely, for interpretative theoretical models of a strategic object. One of the most accurate examples is provided by models viewing nuclear war as a problem of optimal allocation of targets and rates of fire between two countries possessing a given number of nuclear missiles.[4] The general framework of macroeconomics is used to provide an explanation of the economic impact of a defence object. This approach is well exemplified by the tentative treatment of disarmament figures in an input linear system.[5] According to this divergence, the label *Economic Theory of War (or Peace)* can be given to the first topic and *Defence Economics* can be reserved for the second.[6]

In investigating the relationship between defence economics and the economic theory of war, this chapter will aim at referring to the previous distinction. Some researchers have certainly worked simultaneously in the two fields; for instance, Boulding and Isard, who have pictured a peace economic theory, while studying some aspects of defence economics, or Schelling, who particularly contributed to elaborating strategic models based on economic concepts but who was also interested in several facets of defence economics. But their synthesis, if it exists, is built more or less on the basis of their individual moral preferences. Oddly enough, one of the unique tentative attempts to bridge the gap between the two approaches did not emerge from a professional economist but from a mathematician–meteorologist, L. W. Richardson, who tried to propose, within the same model, a theoretical explanation of dynamics leading to war and a network to treat empirical economic data on military expenditures.[7]

The very broad question raised by this investigation is related to the place occupied by peace and war in economics as a specific area of knowledge. In order to formulate some prime elements, the point of view adopted here is the retrospective use of historical material providing information from the historical background of the present state of the art, and additional suggestions about its development. But one should note that this contribution is not a purely historical one. Therefore I have deliberately chosen to concentrate on, and restrict my analysis to, only two past economists: A. Smith and F. Y. Edgeworth. First, each of them has written at a crucial time in the history of political economy – the early years of classical economics (*An inquiry into the Nature and Cause of the Wealth of Nations, 1774*), and the beginning of marginalism school (*Mathematical Psychics* 1881). Second, Smith's and Edgeworth's writings on war, peace and defence have pictured two alternative ways to pose the question, from which two kinds of construction could be developed in order to clarify the background of the present situation. The Smithian view will be examined in the next section and the Edgeworthian analysis in the subsequent one. Finally, additional analytical suggestions will be drawn from this return to the past.

II DEFENCE AS A BRANCH OF PUBLIC ECONOMICS: THE INHERITANCE FROM ADAM SMITH

It is a common fallacy to speak of Adam Smith as an early father of the individualistic ultra-liberal economic school.[8] Such views on Smith's economic contributions do not take into account Books IV and V of *An Inquiry into the Nature and Causes of the Wealth of Nations*, and misunderstand key concepts, such as the 'division of labour', the 'invisible hand' and the particular meaning of 'market'. The summary of Book V given by Smith in his introduction and repeated at the end of Book IV, however, appears, quite clearly, to be a complete research programme on public economy:

> In this book, I have endeavoured to show: first what are the necessary expenses of the sovereign, or commonwealth; which of those expenses ought to be defrayed by the general contribution of the noble society; and which of them by that of some particular part only, or some particular members of it; secondly, what are the different methods in which the whole society may be made to contribute towards defraying the expenses incumbent on the whole society, and what are the principal advantages and inconsistencies of those methods; and, thirdly and lastly, what are the reasons and causes which have induced almost all modern governments to mortgage some parts of this revenue, or to contract debts, and what have been the effects of those debts upon the real wealth, the annual produce of the land and labour of society.[9]

For Smith, the expenses of the sovereign or commonwealth are directly induced from three major duties: (i) protecting society from violence and invasion of other independent countries (defence); (ii) protecting every member of society from injustice and oppression of every other member of it (justice); and (iii) erecting and maintaining certain public works and public institutions (public work and education).[10]

A more detailed examination of Smith's pages reveal two more precisions. First, he puts together as elements of the same set the first four books of the *Wealth of Nations* and considers Book V separately. Indeed for Smith the contents of these first four books relate to one scientific object (explanation of wealth production and income distribution in trade market economies), while the contents of the fifth book apply to another one (control and management of public goods in non-trade market economies). Second, among the different duties identified by Smith to support public expenses, the first place is reserved for defence.[11] Bringing together these observations, we can assume from the general framework of the *Wealth of Nations* that:

1. Public economy is a full part of political economy.
2. Defence is a predominant branch of public economy.

It is possible to go further in that direction and to propose an unfamiliar interpretation of *Wealth of Nations*, starting from Book V in order to shed some light on the shaded areas of the other four. Let us consider, for example, the division of labour introduced by Smith in the first two chapters of Book I. Smith did not consider division of labour as a primitive principle, but rather as a consequence of another hypothesis relative to 'a general propensity to truck, barter, and exchange one thing for another'.[12] But in order to transform the opportunities opened by such disposition to an allocative process corresponding to the division of labour, some social conditions would be required to organise the market mechanisms.

The three fields mentioned by Smith in Book V correspond exactly to these prerequisites. The existence of a 'marketable space' needs defence, justice, public works and education. Therefore, referring to the Smithian conception of wealth, it becomes arguable that the public economy described in Book V determines, in the end, the private one analysed in the four previous books, because only the proper management of public expenses offers the necessary conditions for the development of trade market economies. As a priority among the other fields of public economy, defence is not treated by Smith as a by-product, but as an economic matter in itself.

1   Public versus Private Economics: The Ideal Defence Case

The Smithian definition of public economy could be deduced from two types of criteria: positive ones that have only an indirect economic meaning, as it appears in the economic foundations of the three governmental duties previously discussed; and negative ones that possess a direct economic meaning. Two main criteria of the latter group must be mentioned: (i) the lack of correspondence between the results of an individual economic evaluation and those of a collective evaluation; and (ii) the disconnection between the division of labour principle and the hypothesis of a general propensity to trade. These are related but distinct statements. To understand better the nature of their relationship, let us quote Smith himself with regard to (i):

> The profit could never repay the expense to any individual or small number of individuals, though it may frequently do much more than repay it to a great society.[13]

and with regard to (ii) specifically regarding expenses:

> Into the other arts, the division of labour is naturally introduced by the prudence of individuals, who find that they promote their private interest better by confining themselves to a particular trade, than by exercising a great number. But it is the wisdom of the State only which can render the trade of soldier a particular trade separate and distinct from all others.[14]

With (i) and (ii) a breakdown in invisible hand becomes possible. The latter indeed schemes that division of labour can be derived from other sources than self-interest calculations. The fact that the defence case with standing army versus militia is chosen by Smith to exemplify this statement is meaningful. It shows the existence of cases where private self-interest coming from individual persons, or even small groups, becomes contradictory with public interest considered as a whole. It should be noted that the breakdown in the invisible hand does not have the same theoretical meaning in (i) and (ii). In the case of defence there is no contradiction between individual and collective protection; on the contrary both are entirely the same – individual protection from an enemy's attack could be considered as meaning-less. The question pointed out by Smith regarding division of labour is the absence of an economic individual incentive to become a military 'trader' unless a governmental (that is, collective) interven-tion occurs.

A retrospective mistake would be to reduce the Smithian analysis to the modern well-known notion of 'market-failure', which was, until now, one of the public economic foundations. If the invisible hand operates through the market process, it also operates through other social processes, for example voting systems. (Is the voting system a political market? I do not think so.) However, the invisible hand is only one of the components of certain markets (large-scale). A person-to-person direct-trade process with 'recontract' is really a market without an 'invisible hand' operation. Therefore, the break-down of an invisible hand must be considered as different from the failure of a market.

Furthermore, the Smith quotations suggest a positive content for (i) and (ii). The former not only ascertains the irrelevance of individual evaluation, but also asks for an alternative calculation, which could be related to the 'social utility', a notion frequently invoked by Smith, which does not correspond to the modern meaning of that term because it is not derived in any way from the individual utility concept.[15] Unfortunately, social utility remains vague in Smith's writing, and must be made more elaborate to sustain an operational mode of evaluation. As regards (ii), the division of labour principle can also operate in a centrally controlled part of an economy, which means that it is then the result of the 'State's wisdom', referring also to a public type of economic caculation. Now let us remember that for Smith, in general, the division of labour is not originally 'the effect of any human wisdom, which foresees and intends that general opulence'.[16]

We can conclude from a careful examination of Smith's thought that:

1. Public economy (defence, justice, public works, education) must be studied using public economics.
2. Public economics is economic knowledge based on assumptions different from those made by private economics.
3. Defence economics is one of the main branches of public economics.

2 Defence Economics in the 'Pre-welfarist' Perspective

Among the different components of public economics, defence occupies a preferential place. It is set forth as the first public expense, it serves as a favourite example, and is summarised by Smith in these words:

> The expense of defending the Society, and that of supporting the dignity of the chief magistrate are both laid out for the general benefit of the whole society. It is reasonable, therefore, that they should be defrayed by the general contribution of the whole society, all the different members contributing, as nearly as possible, in proportion to their respective abilities.[17]

This question highlights that for Smith defence is a 'pure' public good in the analytical meaning of this term using modern terminology because, for him, every individual member or group belongs to a national community and is directly affected by 'defence duty'.[18] It must be added immediately that such a definition of defence as a public good does not obviously preclude the question of the positive, negative or even zero value assigned to military expenditures by each component of the community, which could hardly result from a hypothetical comparison between defence benefit and, on the expenses side, military cost. Smith remained sceptical because the outcome's evaluation (defence benefit) depends on the art of war which, according to Smith 'becomes one of the most complicated among them [the arts]'.[19] Anyway, defence is a very appropriate example of a pure public good where, according to Baumol, every person has a non-arguable interest in obtaining the collective advantage of protection against risk of attack from abroad while at the same time avoiding contribution to the expense as long as he can.[20] Furthermore, an analysis in terms of externalities in the case of military expenditures seems quite irrelevant because no reference to something like a market process is consistent with such an hypothesis.

Therefore, Smith's own conclusions on this matter are perfectly logical:

1. The defence expenses must be entirely 'defrayed by the general contribution of the whole society', which was not at all obvious in Smith's time.[21]
2. The allocation of this contribution between the different members must be 'in proportion to their abilities', which implicitly refers to the criterion of equity. And so, defence economics, viewed by Smith, has a very 'welfarist' look and puts it, without discussion, in the normative basket of economic theory.

Another interesting aspect of Smith's view is pointed out by the difference between defence and all other public goods identified in *The Wealth of Nations*; justice, education and public works, on the contrary, are not pure public goods. Justice, for example, is jointly consumed by members of a community but one must pay attention in order to avoid confusion between a potential (or national) use of justice and an effective legal dispute. The gap becomes larger and larger with education and public works. But coming back to the case of justice, even if everyone has a potential benefit from a judiciary service, only some of the citizens will use it during the course of their lives. Therefore the allocative systems imagined by Smith for defence and justice are quite different.[22]

More precisely, Smith brings to light some difficulties with Samuelson's initial definition of a 'pure' public good as one which enters into everybody's utility.[23] Such a definition is too broad and remains ambiguous until the relevant domain of utility is carefully specified. If it means only that no member of a community is immune from the risk of foreign attack or national injustice, then defence and justice are both trivially 'pure' public goods. But if it requires a little more and, for instance, a similar or at least approximate risk-distribution of probability for each member of the community, then defence would perhaps still be a pure public good but justice certainly would not. Indeed it remains debatable that there exists a kind of equiprobability of the casualties of war in every part of any national territory. However, if the outcome of defence is a peace guarantee, often provided nowadays by a deterrence doctrine, then this equiprobability assumption becomes not completely unrealistic.[24] Anyway, the foundations of probability calculations when the states of the world are at peace (or at war), as in defence models, are not the same as for legal proceedings, as in justice models.

Finally, Smith's outline classification of various public goods can be brought together with his reluctance to put the economic problem of public expenses in terms of alternative allocations – defence, justice, education and public works. Each of them belongs to different categories of the public good which could not be represented as a continuum. Therefore no common scale can be fitted to them in order to authorise such comparative processes. The only way to solve the problem formally is to represent the set of governmental duties in lexicographic order. Following this interpretation, the Smithian view of defence as a priority means only that it has first place in such a social lexicographic order. In any case such interpretation is consistent with Smith's conception developed in Book V of social utility requiring treatment different from the rest of *The Wealth of Nations*. Then, the question opened by Smith's statement, supposedly still unsolved, concerns the possibility (or the impossibility) of constructing a social lexicographic order among public goods, satisfying some reasonable or at least 'acceptable' conditions.[25]

Incidentally and curiously enough, there are some similarities between this Smithian view and Jevons' position on the same matter. Referring to Bentham's tradition, Jevons tries to link economic theory to the 'calculus of pleasures and pains', but proposes different levels where Bentham's general principle can be applied. The utility calculus in the marginalist sense, occupies for him the lowest rank in the hierarchy of the types of calculus to be derived from Bentham's framework.[26] Jevons suggests the possibility of a public calculus below the private one and different by nature. As he wrote in the introduction to the *Theory of Political Economy*:

> The safety of a Nation, the welfare of great populations may happen to depend upon his extortions, if he be a solider or a statesman; claims of a very strong kind may now be overbalanced by claims of a still stronger kind . . . The statesman may discover a conflict between motives; a measure may promise, as it would seem, the greatest good to great numbers, and yet these may be motives of uprightness and honour that may hinder his promoting the measure. How this may be rightly determined it is not my purpose to inquire here.[27]

Consequently, it is proposed as a conjecture that for Jevons:

1. Public dominates private calculus.
2. Public calculus cannot be solved with the marginal utility theory.

Under these conditions, the principal difference between Smith and Jevons is that the public sphere belongs to economics for the former but stays outside the economic theory for the latter. Therefore there is no room for defence economics in Jevons' political economy and more generally in the majority of the first generation of marginalist economists.

In conclusion, Smith's analysis puts defence economics at the top as a specific branch of public economics. The author of *The Wealth of Nations* draws the main lines of an original research programme which has not yet even been fulfilled. Indeed, he mentions in different passages that defence economics does not operate in the same way in peace-time and wartime.[28] Following the line of the argument developed here, defence as a public good does not have the same characteristics with regard to peace and to war states of the world. Therefore, in Smith's sense the strategic concepts such as deterrence doctrines, defence postures, or more recently, strategic defence, pose new theoretical problems to defence economists. And no precise material can be found in Smith's writing that elaborates on any economic theory of war (or peace).

III ECONOMICS AS A PECULIAR FRAMEWORK FOR PEACE AND WAR MODELS: THE INHERITANCE FROM EDGEWORTH

Moving to Edgeworth, the landscape becomes different. In *Mathematical Psychics*, F. Y. Edgeworth investigates the logical possibility of applying a mathematical calculation to human affairs.[29] He starts with a refinement of Sidgwick distinction between two extreme types of calculus of pleasure and pain – 'economical' and 'utilitarian'. Let us quote Edgeworth:

> The economical calculus investigates the equilibrium of a system of hedonic forces each tending to maximum individual utility; the utilitarian calculus, the equilibrium of a system in which each and all tend to maximum universal utility.[30]

Such a definition of an economic system by means of this concept of economic calculus leads to an economic theory which is, simultaneously, too narrow and too broad: too narrow because economic calculus according to Edgeworth is based on the principle of an assumption of self-interest;[31] too broad, because many other systems in social life can also be described in the framework considered as economic. Edgeworth himself points out this last feature and observes, incidentally:

> Let us glance at the elements of economic calculus, observing that the connotation (and some of reasoning) extends beyond the usual denotation, to the political struggle for power, as well as to the commercial struggle for wealth.[32]

Some observations emerge from the scope of the definition:

1. Many concepts, such as preference relation, marginal utility, marginal cost, maximisation criteria and equilibria types, though not all the traditional economic concepts, are relevant for the understanding of both commercial and political activities.
2. An opportune choice of the relevant concept from among this general set requires an elaboration in a more analytical way of what is power and what is wealth (until these precisions are given, an economic theory of political power remains questionable).

Beyond Edgeworth's own exposition, two other implicit hypotheses must be clarified in order to judge the relevance of a bridge, as suggested by the author, between commercial struggle on one side and military battles on the other.

One hypothesis is to refer to the determination of the necessary and sufficient conditions for a well-founded link between the theories of decision-making of a politican and those of a private contractor. Let us observe that it implies the exploration of two types of question: the well-known aggregation problem of passing from a private to a public decision and the nature of the relation between a decision process with *prima facie*, purely internal, consequences (private choice) from that which has purely external consequences from the decision-maker's point of view (political choice). Once may observe that the treatment of countries as economic private individual persons is common to classical and neoclassical international trade theory, and Edgeworth himself has used this convention extensively in works relative to these matters.[33] Incidentally, it is not uninteresting to note that the starting-point of Arrow's work on welfare and social utility function is a question asked by Helmer about the opportunity to apply game theory developed for individual players to international relations where the players are countries.[34]

Another hypothesis concerns the analogue between the field of competition where commercial struggle takes place and the battlefield where war takes place. It requires a more detailed examination of the theoretical features of these two domains which probably exceeds the analytical power of purely economic tools, as will be demonstrated later.

A last point relates to the ability to integrate the logical background of all military strategic actions into the logical framework of economic decision. Such a possibility may be especially arguable with reference to deterrence concepts and doctrines more recently developed by the military thinkers.

IV   COULD WAR BE AN ECONOMIC CONCEPT?

Edgeworth has found a close link between war and commercial action inside the economic process itself. He proposes, for that reason, to call 'war' all the situations 'where every agent actuated only by self-interest, act without consents of others affected by their actions'.[35] Translated in modern games-theory terminology, the general expression of war then covers the large class of non-cooperative games.[36]

A more detailed examination shows that war in Edgeworth's economic sense is characterised by only two criteria: (i) the pure self-interest motivation, and (ii) the unilaterality of the decision process; however, these seemed to be not sufficient and the definition of 'war' as a rational act requires a third criterion – (iii) the incentive to start.

This adjunction underlines a weakness in Edgeworth's economic approach to war. For Edgeworth indeed, the final purpose of economic activity is to 'contract', which means to find a negotiated solution. But such negotiated solutions imply a consent between the parties corresponding to a kind of peace. Therefore, the very goal of the economic process is not to win (a war) but to conclude a self-interest agreement which could be characterised by a type of peaceful content. However, Edgeworth, as was previously mentioned, was viewing the competitive field as a battlefield. More precisely the field of economic competition is both a battlefield and a space for negotiations. Its main consequence is that war, as a topic of decision-making study, remained logically outside the domain of interpretation of economic theory in spite of the fact that Edgeworth took war into account at the core of his economic analysis. Even if the definition of a competitive field presupposes the existence of a tentative battlefield, it does not, however, provide sufficient elements for modelling the decision of an attack in a military sense, which is required for any war theory. This observation, however, does not mean that the economic concepts are useless for modelling a military war case, but rather that those erected by Edgeworth from the marginalist 'tool-chest box' are not sufficient for that purpose.

As is well understandable, the key of the analogy between economics on the one hand and war and peace on the other is located in the existence of a competitive field. Edgeworth himself elaborates his intuition on that topic when he writes, in his very personal tricky style:

> 'Is it peace or war?' asks the 'lover of Maud', of economic *competition*, and answers hastily: it is both, *pax* or *pact* between contractors during contract, *war*, when some of the contractors without the consent of other recontract.[37]

Let us observe that Edgeworth refers to the features of competition and not at all to the market in the Smithian conception previously evoked.

Furthermore, Edgeworth's definitions of war and peace are obviously connected with his own conception of a field of competition viewing as the set all the individuals who are willing and able to recontract about goods. It provides a precise foundation for the analogy between the economic field of competition and a military battlefield which underlines the specific role of war in the whole construction.

A more detailed analysis demonstrates the dependence of the definition of war and peace on the competitive structures in such a general sketch. It leads sometimes to paradoxical results. Examine, for instance, the well-known bilateral monopoly case, wrongly labelled Edgeworth's box-diagram, where there are only two persons. No war would be theoretically possible, because, by definition, no one is able to recontract without the consent of the other. But, curiously enough, there is also no way in such a situation to determine a peaceful conclusion, because the result of economic calculus applied to contract and recontract leads to an indeterminate result. Therefore we know now that a Nash non-cooperative game could provide a solution under supplementary assumptions. But the interpretation of threat traditionally linked to Nash non-cooperative game is indeed unfortunately war-oriented, and then becomes inconsistent with Edgeworth's war starting-point.

Therefore, Edgeworth's solution is sought in a quite different direction, by the utilisation of the other type of calculus (universalist) derived from the utilitarian system and completely outside the competitive economic field and its war connotation.[38]

In the other extreme case, the number of persons tends towards infinity and each of them views himself as an insignificant part of the negotiation set, as was idealised for instance by Walras. In such a case, often labelled as perfectly competitive, the war would theoretically operate between the contractors. On the contrary, however, it could demonstrate that under additional assumptions, a Pareto cooperative solution could provide an answer. Unfortunately again for Edgeworth's semantics, the Paretian cooperative equilibrium excludes by definition recontracts without consent and eliminates any war content. However it is doubtful whether pure competitive equilibrium can be used as an economic peace model.[39]

These kinds of retrospective interpretations,[40] in spite of a certain unfairness to Edgeworth's spirit, have the advantage of underlining some of the main difficulties in transposing economic concepts from a set of recontracting processes to a set of military conflicts and diplomatic negotiations.

1 Peace or Simple Consent: Weak and Strong Economic Meanings

The use of the term 'peace' in Edgeworth's analytical framework must also be studied cautiously. In the context of his 'Economical Calculus System', it only means a possible consent between all contractors. Therefore, first, a peace (or even a war) economic model can be built only on the foundation of an interactive decision-making representation, which explains the success of game theory as a preferential general matrix;[41] second, there is no semantic connection between economic equilibrium and peace, as, in Edgeworth's formulation, all the points of the contract curve correspond to peace; third, peace implies no reference at all to any concept of stability whatever because Edgeworth's framework remains static.

It could be argued that such an acceptance of peace continues as rather poor. But it must be noticed that when he introduces the distinction between *economic calculus* and *utilitarian calculus*, Edgeworth, who referred to struggle and war, did not even mention the word 'peace'. In order to explain this strange asymmetry between peace and war in his economic model, one can suggest the existence of two concepts of peace in Edgeworth's thoughts, corresponding respectively to a *weak* form and a *strong* one. The former which has been previously studied takes place in his war-interpretative economic model, with its own limitations; on the contrary the latter has a meaning only in the utilitarian alternative system developed by Edgeworth on the basis of the utilitarian calculus formula, briefly mentioned in the introduction. The examination of *strong* peace would be outside this investigation,[42] but such a category demonstrates that peace economic models, as well as defence economics, studied in the first part, refer also – for other reasons – to a normative welfare prospect.

In conclusion, Edgeworth's exposition highlights some crucial difficulties for using the same microeconomic framework to understand competitive and non-competitive processes on the one hand, and war and peace mechanisms on the other.

Furthermore, an indirect link between defence economics and economic models of war and peace is provided by the research programme initiated by Edgeworth via the two meanings of peace. Peace in the weak sense is a necessary concept to provide a logical foundation for the war economic model, while peace in the strong sense is obviously a pure public good, which could be defined only inside an alternative system derived from utilitarian calculus but which could also be consistent with the Smithian defence economics prospect.

V CONCLUSION: DIFFERENT TOPICS AND TENTATIVE LINKAGES

Three main features emerge from this very selective, but hardly arbitrary historical sketch. First, defence economics as well as the economic modelling of war and peace are by no means new exercises. Even excepting the mercantilist economists and retrospectively starting with the classics, the two examples exhibited here largely demonstrate their deep roots in the history of economic thought. Therefore, it would probably be wrong to consider such domains as new economic fields.

Second, the hypothesis of two rather different topics seems corroborated by the historical evidence. Defence economics is related to classical political economy tradition (Smith), and economic models of war and peace to that of marginal economic theory (Edgeworth). Then, indeed, despite the broad Smithian conception of political economy, no mention can be found throughout the five books of the *Wealth of Nations* of a possible economic theory of war. Smith treats the art of war as 'the noblest of all arts . . . and one of the most complicated among them'.[43] In other words, strategy has its own specificity and used an original conceptual framework.[44] After Smith, Ricardo's interest for defence economics, and, moreover, J. S. Mill's contributions, remained restricted to the economic impact of war expenditures on their financing methods.[45] On the contrary, and symmetrically, nothing is said about defence economics in Edgeworth's writings, despite his largely theoretical economic pattern. The same is observed among the major British marginalists of the first generation. Referring to the works of Jevons, Marshall and even to Wicksteed, defence economics appears outside their theoretical outline. Such a disconnected situation must be related to the general changes from political economy to economic theory, with the additional observation of a persistent current of the first approach through Keynes and some of the modern neo-Cambridge School of Economists.

Third, there does exist from a purely analytical point of view, a bridge between these two isolated pieces of economic knowledge provided by the welfare approach. Identified as a public good by Smith, defence requires the solution of welfare questions. Peace and negotiations suggestively linked to economic analysis by Edgeworth lead to the utilitarian calculation in a large sense. Finally, utilitarianism and welfarism have some common basis,[46] which must be used to elaborate the understanding of their relationship.

If such reconsideration of several welfare statements is able to provide a fruitful linkage between defence economics and peace economics theoretical models, its relation to war models remains unsolved. Anyway, there are other ways to present this question. Some phenomena, such as an arms race, can be viewed in the framework of economic models, strategic models or even mixed models. A model is now labelled economic or strategic, according to the meaning of its variables and parameters independently from its formal structures, which might indeed include mathematical tools successfully used in economic theory (as continuous functions with a maximum value). Two different cases can then occur: either the economic and the strategic models are both two alternative interpretations of the same mathematical system, as for instance in the Richardson case,[47] or economic and strategic models are also mathematically distinct, as for example when we ask if economic downturn leads to war.[48] The former case leads to a transformation problem, which consists in finding a set of general conditions to transform one model into another (in the Richardson example, the economic interpretation is a strategic one, and vice versa);[49] the latter requires finding original processes to connect the two types of model. But such operations belong to the borderlines of economics; Therefore their studies would be outside the topic of this paper. But defence economics, as well as peace- and war- economic models, need such interdisciplinary raids to reinforce their own foundations.

Notes and References

1. Kennedy, G., *Defence Economics* (London: Duckworth, 1983) p. viii.
2. For a complete survey cf. Intriligator, M., 'Research on Conflict Theory: Analytic Approaches and Areas of Application', *Journal of Conflict Resolution* (26) 1982.
3. Recent studies in that field are reviewed in Schmidt, C., 'Dépenses militaires et analyse économique', in *Conséquences Économiques et Sociales de la Course aux Armaments*, (Paris: UN Economica, 1983).
4. Intriligator, M., *Strategy in a Missile War: Targets and Rates of Fire*, Security Studies Paper no. 10 (Los Angeles: 1967).
5. Leontief, W. and Duchin, F., *Military Spending Facts and Figures, Worldwide Implications and Future Outlook* (Oxford: Oxford University Press, 1983).
6. Assumes that the existence of a defence economics corresponding to the domain of defence economy would be stated.
7. For a discussion of the status of Richardson's model, cf. Schmidt, C., 'Semantic Variations on Richardson's Model', in *Economics of Military Expenditures* (London: Macmillan, 1987).
8. Smith, A., *An Inquiry into the Nature and Causes of the Wealth of Nations*, Campbell and Skinner (eds.) (Oxford: Clarendon, 1976) vol. I, p. 12.
9. Ibid, vol. II, pp. 687–8.
10. Ibid, vol. I, pp. 11–12.
11. Ibid, vol. II, p. 689.
12. Ibid, vol. I, p. 25.
13. Ibid, vol. II, p. 688.
14. Ibid, vol. II, p. 697.
15. It can be argued that, when Smith uses the term 'use', he refers to a social acceptance rather than to an individual meaning familiar to the marginalist economists. A careful study of various manuscripts in the *Lectures* sheds some light on this peculiar Smithian intepretation. Cf. the discussion in vol. V, pp. 44 and 46 (footnotes).
16. Smith, *Wealth of Nations* (Clarendon edn, 1976) vol. I, p. 25. But Smith adds that 'the general propensity to trade' is probably a consequence of reasoning and the use of the language. It must be noticed that Smith has previously written an essay on the origin of language. Cf. *Essays on Philosophical Subjects*.
17. Smith *Wealth of Nations* (Clarendon edn, 1976) vol. II, p. 814.
18. It is the reason Smith considers, for example, that the expense of 'Defending the Society' and those 'supporting the Dignity of the Sovereign' as belonging to the same category. Cf. Smith, *Wealth of Nations* (Clarendon ed. 1976) vol. II, p. 814.
19. Ibid, vol. II, p. 697.
20. Baumol, W. J., *Welfare Economics and the Theory of the State* (Cambridge: Cambridge University Press, 1952).
21. This position must be connected to the Smith support for a standing army versus a militia; Smith, *Wealth of Nations* (Clarendon edn, 1976) vol. II, p. 698 and footnote.

22. Ibid, vol. II, p. 815.
23. Cf. Samuelson, P. A., 'Pure Theory of Public Expenditure', *Review of Economics and Statistics*, XXXVI, 1954. For a semantic discussion, cf. Samuelson, P. A., 'Pure Theory of Public Expenditure and Taxation' in Margolis, J. and Guitton, H. (eds) *Public Economics* (London: Macmillan, 1969) pp. 107–10.
24. The logical background of such an equi-probability assumption can be found in Harsanyi's interpretation of utilitarian normative tradition; cf. Harsanyi, J. C., *Essay in Ethics, Social Behaviour and Scientific Explanation* (Amsterdam: Dortretch-Reidel, 1976) and 'Morality and the Theory of Rational Behaviour' in Sen, A. and Williams, B. (eds) *Utilitarianism and Beyond* (Cambridge: Cambridge University Press, 1982) pp. 44–6. Some suggestions to apply the public good theory to deterrence can be found in Kennedy, *Defence Economics* (Duckworth, 1983), pp. 27–28.
25. In the same meaning as the 'reasonable' conditions imposed by Arrow to any constitution; cf. Arrow, K., 'Values and Collective Decision-making' reprinted in *Social Choice and Justice* (Cambridge, Massachussetts: The Belknap Press of Harvard University Press) pp. 70–1. But such a notion of acceptability remains slightly debatable.
26. Jevons, S. (1871) *The Theory of Political Economy*, edited by R. D. Collinson Black and reprinted (Harmondsworth: Penguin, 1970).
27. Ibid, p. 92.
28. For instance, Smith, *Wealth of Nations* (Clarendon edn, 1976) vol. II, p. 689. Many observations on that topic can be found in Cannan, E. (ed.) (1763) *Lectures on Police, Justice, Revenue and Arms* (New York: 1964).
29. According to its subtitle 'On the Application of Mathematics to the Moral Science'. For a detailed analysis on F. Y. Edgeworth's views on this matter, cf. Schmidt, C., *La Sémantique Économique en Question: Recherche sur les Fondements de l'Economie Théorique* (Paris: Calman-Lévy, 1985) pp. 91–4.
30. Edgeworth, F. Y., *Mathematical Psychics* (1881), reprinted (New York: A. M. Kelley, 1967) pp. 15 and 16. It should be noticed that Edgeworth just started by working on moral philosophical topics in the line of Sidgwick's works, cf. 'Hedonical calculus', *MIND* (July 1878).
31. Edgeworth, *Mathematical Psychics* (Kelley edn, 1967) p. 16. Edgeworth accurately expresses in a footnote that status of the self-interest assumption which is not a principle but corresponds to *observati*. Therefore, Edgeworth's economic calculus must be considered more from a 'descriptive' than from an 'axiomatic' point of view.
32. Edgeworth, *Mathematical Psychics* (Kelley edn, 1967) p. 16.
33. Edgeworth, F. Y., Review of Bastable, 'The Theory of International Trade', *Economic Journal*, VII, (1897) pp. 397–403; see also *Papers Relating to Political Economy*, 1916, T II.
34. Sen, A., 'Review of Arrow's Social Choice and Justice' *Journal of Economic Literature*, XXIII (4) (December 1985).
35. Edgeworth, *Mathematical Psychics* (Kelley edn, 1967) p. 17.

36.   An extensive investigation of Edgeworth's contribution to the concep-
      tual foundations of game theory is provided by Shubik, M. (1983,
      1984) *Game Theory in the Social Science*, vol. I; *Concepts and
      Solutions*, vol. II; *Game Theory Approach to Political Economy*
      (Cambridge, Massachusetts: MIT Press, 1983 and 1984). For Political
      Economy applications cf. vol. II, pp. 251–85.
37.   Edgeworth, *Mathematical Psychics* (Kelley edn, 1967) p. 17.
38.   Edgeworth, *Mathematical Psychics* (Kelley edn, 1967) p. 66.
39.   In the sense of a general equilibrium solution explored in modern
      literature in particular Arrow and Debreu and their followers.
40.   This could be developed as an interesting logical consequence of
      Edgeworth's and Walras's alternative approaches to a trade equili-
      brium system well pictured, for example, by Hildenbrand, W., and
      Kirman, A. P., *Introduction to Equilibrium Analysis: Variation on
      Themes by Edgeworth and Walras* (Amsterdam: North Holland, 1976)
      especially pp. 1–33. Following that line of thought, one could mention
      Walras's constant interest in peace questions which could be compared
      with his economic understanding of a *competitive solution*. Cf. Jaffe,
      W. (ed.) *Correspondence of Leon Walras and Related Papers*, vols. II
      and III (Amsterdam: North Holland, 1965).
41.   That was particularly Schelling's own conviction; cf. Schelling, T.,
      Preface to the 1980 edition of *The Strategy of Conflict* (Cambridge,
      Massachusetts: Harvard University Press, 1980) p. VI.
42.   To be erected from Edgeworth's guidelines, cf. *Mathematical Psychics*
      (Kelley edn, 1967) Appendix VII, pp. 126–48. A suggested compari-
      son with Kant's writings on Peace (namely *Werke in sechs Bänden*)
      would be fruitful.
43.   Smith, *Wealth of Nations* (Clarendon edn, 1976) vol. II, p. 697).
44.   Note that 'strategic', as an original system of concepts was erected at
      the end of the eighteenth and the beginning of the nineteenth centuries
      with thinkers such as Guibert in France and Clausewitz in Prussia. For
      a modern reappraisal of the difference between economic and strategic
      logic, see Schmidt, C. 'Logique de la décision économique, Logique de
      la dissuasion nucléaire, *Revue d'Economic Politique* (Août–Septembre
      1982).
45.   One of the most complete expositions can be found in Mill, J. S.
      (1824) 'War expenditure', in *Collected Works* (Toronto University
      Press, 1967) vol. IV, pp. 1–22.
46.   About some logical inconsistencies of Christian Schmidt, 'Logique de
      la decision économique, Logique de la dissuasion nucléairé, *Revue
      d'Economie Politique* (Juillet–Août 1985) (4).
47.   For a more detailed analysis, see Note 7.
48.   See Russett, B., 'Economic Change as a Cause of International
      Conflict', p. 185 of this volume.
49.   Cf. Rudnianski, M. and Schmidt, C., 'Economic and Military Arms
      Race Models: the Transformation Problem.' Communication pre-
      pared for the *Twentieth European Peace Science Society Meeting*
      (September 1985).

3 Defence Spending as a Priority

Andrew Brody
INSTITUTE OF ECONOMICS, HUNGARIAN
ACADEMY OF SCIENCES

Defence spending diminishes consumption and also hampers development by draining investible funds. But its most harmful effect consists in the disarray of economic proportions. The present slowdown and high level of pollution may be attributed to the forced industrialisation and militarisation of the 1950s and 1960s. This kind of defence and industrial priority is counter-productive: though it may boost the economy for a shorter or longer stretch of time, it necessarily leads to crippled relationships, mismatches and growing economic, social and political tensions.

———————

Leontief repeatedly computed the more attractive economic scenarios to be gained by an arms cut. [1,2,3,4] I would like to point out the fact that the real loss caused by defence spending lies not only in these foregone advantages. The present trend of militarisation is responsible for deeper economic maladies. Both the economic slowdown and the increase in environmental deterioration are natural consequences of defence priorities, resulting in crippled and distorted economic proportions.

I THE THEORETICAL PROBLEM

It is generally possible to identify at least one 'Equilibrium Growth Path' for every economy determined by its structure, expressed by all the requirements of production. In an approximate manner this path can be computed 'linearising' these requirements, according to models proposed by von Neumann's activity analysis, Leontief's dynamic input output analysis, or Pasinetti's growth models.[5,6] Yet there are no *a priori* reasons, except theoretical considerations of efficiency, for any economy to remain on this path. Indeed an actual economy will almost never be found to be in equilibrium. Mankind's present means of control – be they market forces or plan directives – can at most achieve a path moving towards the neighbourhood of equilibrium. At the same time very strong influences work in all known economic systems causing deviations from equilibrium steady-state.

We may call such an enforced deviation from a theoretical equilibrium a priority, pointing towards some preferred direction. This concept of priority can be elaborated but basically a government governs by assigning priorities and enforcing them by various means; taxes, subsidies, quotas and outright directives. It must be pointed out that with the increasing emphasis on priorities there seems to be a general tendency to shift from monetary stimulus to coercive action. As explained in the sequel, a priority, if adhered to, creates increasing stress in every economic system. The mounting stress can be resisted only by reverting to increasingly direct methods; outright orders tend to replace incentives. This is the case for military purposes. A government priority may also be directed towards other aims too, for instance, 'import substitution', 'export drive', 'mass employment' or 'abolition of illiteracy' and so forth. The objectives will sooner or later be spelled out in kind and the political language will be inundated by expressions such as 'fight', 'battle', 'victory', all of military origin.

Now every priority whatsoever can and will be rationalised by economic arguments supporting that the priority policy in question leads to faster development, that is, greater growth than usual. And this is indeed the case in the short run because equilibrium growth being the slowest among all the possible growth paths, any modification or deviation can be proved to lead first to an upswing.

In order to demonstrate this perplexing character of economic systems, let us briefly inspect a closed dynamic Leontief system, with flow coefficient matrix A and stock coefficient matrix B. At any point x of total production, the surplus available for investment will be $(1 - A)x$. An addition to existing capacities, x, can be achieved as long as its requirements do not exceed the available surplus

$$Bx \le (1 - A)x$$

The Leontief inverse $Q = (1 - A)^{-1}$ is strictly positive and may be used to pre-multiply both sides of the inequality

$$QBx \leq x$$

If growth rates differ, then $x = Rx$, with $R = (r_i, \ldots, r_n)$, the diagonal matrix of growth rates, save one in sector i,

$$r_i QB._i i \leq x$$

That is growth in sector i will be maximised in this sense if

$$(1 - r_i QB._i) x = 0$$

The determinant on the left side vanishes if, and only if

$$r_i = \frac{1}{QB_{ii}}$$

Priority growth rates will thus be constrained only by the reciprocal of the diagonal elements of the matrix QB.

Without exception, these growth rates will be much greater than the equilibrium rate, given by the *reciprocal* of the greatest and positive eigenvalue of the Frobenius-matrix QB. This eigenvalue will be approximately equal to the average column sum of the matrix QB thus necessarily much greater than its diagonal elements.[7]

By concentrating resources on boosting one or more preferred sectors, the expansion of the economy can be accelerated. By manipulating the price system (pushing non-preferred sectors into the background) the above maximal values may be approximated.

II   SOME ECONOMIC CONSEQUENCES

Two main economic results may be deduced from the previous analysis:

1. Maximal growth can be achieved only with a peculiar economic configuration.
2. The growth thus achieved will modify the initial proportions. In a dynamic situation such a continuous modification cannot be

maintained in the long run because it generates increasing disequilibrium. By definition the 'Equilibrium Path' is the only direction which can be maintained indefinitely – all other directions lead sooner or later to a deadlock where surplus in some sectors becomes zero.

The lift given to any economy by any kind of priority is therefore transitory and carries its own antidote.

Given a certain amount of surplus, we may invest it in various ways. If our purpose is not equilibrium but short-run maximal growth, then it will be the capital/output ratios which govern the allocation. Among all the branches of an economy it is usually the engineering industries which exhibit the lowest capital requirements per unit of output. Thus if we neglect education, health care, housing, and so on, because of their high requirements per unit, we may trigger a seemingly felicitous 'great leap'. And the next period will look even better; the fast-growing engineering industries bring forward a profusion of machines ready to be invested again.

It is only with a delay of decades that such an 'industrialisation drive' – hardly discernible from defence priorities – meets its intrinsic barriers. Sooner or later the neglected sectors corresponding to all the previously ignored capital-intensive social problems will claim their share, and this will slow down the general thrust. The ever-more-widely-spreading symptoms of economic and social maladjustment then come to the surface. And in the meantime, the 'industrial' and 'defence' sectors (engineering, metallurgy, chemicals and energy) will have produced their over-average share of pollutants, so that intractable environmental problems will have emerged at the same time.

III CONCLUDING REMARKS

The equilibrium rate of growth is by no means the maximal rate of growth in the short run. It is only in the long run or more precisely in the trend that it cannot be surpassed, as demonstrated in full generality by all the various turnpike theorems.

How the long and short run may be separated in any given instance depends on the priority policy, the strictness with which it is enforced, and, possibly, also on the vagaries of economic life.

Looking to past experiments, Hindenberg's plan to boost German military production in 1916 ruined the economy within two years.[8] Meanwhile the more circumspect policy in the Second World War brought a production peak in 1943.[9] The favourable effects of a priority policy may have a shorter or longer duration. But in any case after a transient period, the advantages vanish and the economy is left in disarray, farther from equilibrium than it was when the exercise was begun.

How deep is the disarray in the 1980s? The remaining growth potential is again at least halved because of the maladjustment discernible in all economies. The remaining growth tends towards zero with killing-potential doubling and the potential for survival halved every five years. It is only discomfort and not happiness that grows.

If mankind decides to halt its own development, it does not have to detonate those bombs. By continuing the present trend in producing them, they will have an impact just as terrific.

Notes and References

1. Leontief, W., 'Alternatives to Armament Expenditures', *Bulletin of the Atomic Scientists* (June) 1964, pp. 19–21.
2. Leontief, W., 'The Economic Impact – Industrial and Regional – of an Arms Cut', *Review of Economics and Statistics* (August) 1965 pp. 217–41.
3. Leontief, W., statement in 'Economic Effect of Vietnam Spending', *Hearings before the Joint Economic Committee* (Washington, DC: US Government Printing Office) 1967 pp. 237–63 and 291–2.
4. Leontief, W. and Duchin, F., *Military Spending: Facts, Figures, Worldwide Implications and Future Outlook* (New York: Oxford University Press 1983).
5. Pasinetti, L. L., *Lectures on the Theory of Production* (London: Macmillan, 1977).
6. Pasinetti, L. L., *Structural Changes and Economic Growth* (Cambridge: Cambridge University Press, 1981).
7. Professor Sen in his comment at the Conference during my presentation of this paper pointed out the simplistic character of the von Neumann–Leontief representations because of their 'fixed coefficients'. I believe the proof given above generally stands in any case. However complicated the functions of the matrix-coefficients may be (depending on prices, quantities, technological choice, and so on) the diagonal elements remain necessarily and always smaller than the maximal and positiven eigenvalue.
8. Hardach, G., *The First World War, 1914–1918* (Berkeley and Los Angeles: University of California Press 1977).
9. Milward, A. S., *War, Economy and Society, 1939–1945* (Berkeley and Los Angeles: University of California Press 1977).

COMMENT

Amartya Sen

'*Qui desidarat pacem, praeparet bellum.*' So said the fourth-century military writer Flavius Vegetius Renatus. Translated into English this aphorism advised: 'He who desires peace, let him prepare for war!' It is not obvious what precise good preparation for war does for peace, no matter what Vegetius thought (in line with what militarists of our times also solemnly affirm). But it is absolutely certain that preparation for war ruins the working of many economies and impoverishes the material lives of countless millions. Professor Andrew Brody, in his crisp and sharp paper, discusses how defence spending can blight economic prosperity and progress, and how the present level of military expenditure makes sure that 'it is only discomfort and not happiness that grows'.

The wastefulness – from an economic point of view – of military expenditure is obvious enough. (So is the wastefulness of that expenditure from the *political* point of view, for *the world as a whole*.) Defence spending diverts resources from more useful activities; reduces the productive potential of commodities vital for human well-being; limits the expenditure that could be devoted to eliminating poverty, hunger, disease and mortality; and so on. Even when aggregate production is demand-constrained (with the resource constraints being 'slack') for example, in situations of Keynesian unemployment, the demand-expanding role of defence expenditure can be taken over by other more fruitful forms of public spending. All this we know well enough. So what is new?

Advances

There is, in fact, much that is new in Andrew Brody's paper. He develops a line of reasoning that is interestingly different from the usual arguments. He draws on the works of von Neumann and Leontief,[1] and bases his analysis on the diagnoses that 'every economy has an equilibrium growth path' determined by its structure, expressed by all the requirements of production'. He notes that 'the "equilibrium path" is the only direction which can be maintained indefinitely'. However, it is possible in the short run to have faster rates of growth than that of the equilibrium. Indeed, by concentrating attention on some specific sector, greater growth rates for it can be easily achieved, and this can even lead – in the short run – to a higher over-all growth rate. Brody notes, 'by concentrating resources on boosting one or more preferred sectors the expansion of the economy can be accelerated'. Thus giving 'priority' to the defence sector may make the economy grow faster in the short run compared with the 'equilibrium' growth path. This will be achieved by continuing to modify the balance of sectors, but this continuous modification cannot be maintained in the long run because it causes ever increasing disequilibrium. Since engineering industries, Brody argues, 'exhibit the lowest capital requirements per unit of output', concentrating on these industries will also enhance growth in the short run. 'It is only with a delay of decades that such an "industrialisation drive" – hardly discernible from defence priorities – meets its intrinsic barriers'. But 'sooner or later' the neglected sectors 'will slow down the general thrust'.

It is in this light of inevitable 'disarray' that Brody views the economic predicament of the modern world. His diagnosis of the deep disarray of the 1980s is coupled with a prediction of worse to come if the 'maladjustment' caused by defence priority and overemphasis on engineering industries are continued. 'If Mankind decides to halt its own development it does not have to detonate those bombs.' It is sufficient 'to continue the present trend in producing them'.

This is a well-knit analysis with considerable power and reach. Defence priority comes under fire from an unusual angle, to wit, the self-defeating nature of raising growth rates in the short run through creating more and more 'disequilibrium' and through the harm that this escalating disequilibrium does. There is certainly something quite novel in the argument. But is the argument convincing?

Disputation

The equilibrium properties of the dynamic systems developed by Leontief and von Neumann are extremely contingent on the nature of the technological assumptions made respectively by them. The classic formulation of the dynamic Leontief system involves fixed coefficients and avoids the problem of choice of techniques. This is surely a limitation, since alternative techniques do undoubtedly exist. The possibility of effectively eliminating choice of techniques through some additional assumption (for example, through the use of the so-called 'non-substitution theorem' in a model of one primary factor and no joint production),[2] does undoubtedly exist. But even these possibilities are scarcely realistic (for example, there are various complex forms of joint production in actual production structures, and also primary resources other than labour).[3]

The von Neumann model is also severely limited, even though it explicitly builds in the choice of techniques. Given its assumptions, a particular set of technical-choice-combination emerges and a corresponding set of relative prices rules for equilibrium growth, which is both maximal and uniform for all sectors. In this model all *inputs* are also *outputs*, which are producible (including labour which expands with the expansion of wage-earners' consumer goods). And there is no technical change over time.[4] The results are thoroughly dependent on the restrictive set of assumptions and can be varied with changes in production conditions (for example, having non-produced means of production, incorporating non-trivial technical progress).[5]

Luigi Pasinetti has cogently argued that despite the 'elegant and exciting' nature of the Leontief-von Neumann models from 'an analytical point of view'[6] the severely limiting nature of the underlying assumptions makes this set of models have 'sense only if considered *as an intermediate analytical step* to a more relevant type of dynamic analysis'. 'Taken as such, it can have, on strictly empirical grounds, very little practical relevance' (p. 119). The criticism would, I am afraid, apply to Brody's use – interesting and thought-provoking as it is – of the von Neumann–Leontief models to interpret the contemporary economic 'disarray' and to assess the destructive role of the priority on defence spending.[7] The models employed to develop the argument and the results invoked (in particular, the existence of a unique equilibrium growth rate which cannot be influenced and is uniform for all sectors, specifying the maximal sustainable possibility of expansion) are much too special to serve as the basis for the kind of general lessons that Brody derives from them. There is too big a leap from special theory to general wisdom.

Acclamation

Despite these limitations, the contribution made by Brody's paper is, I believe, valuable and worth following up. The contribution lies partly in the interesting and important observations that Brody makes in passing in the process of presenting his main argument. Brody suggests that defence production and the related activities in 'engineering, metallurgy, chemicals and energy' produce an 'over-average share of pollutants', and that consequently militarisation contributes to 'the increase in environmental deterioration'. Brody also points illuminatingly to the important possibility that defence priority contributes to 'the militarisation of the society'. He also refers to the reduction in 'the possible speed of development' because 'about half the surplus is being spent on defence' (coming close to a traditional argument, but none the worse for that). But the main contribution of Brody's paper does not lie in these diverse bits of cogent arguments, but in his general pointer to the possibility that the harmful effects of defence spending may be very much more powerful in the long run than in the short period. This line of argument does, of course, relate closely to Brody's use of von Neumann–Leontief models, but the relevance of the intertemporal contrast extends well beyond the narrow limits of these particular models.

One could well dispute whether there is a unique equilibrium growth rate, the same for all sectors, maximal in the long run for all sustainable possibilities and without being subject to influence. But the idea that if enhanced defence spending speeds things up in the short run then the long run is secure too, is deeply defective. By forcing this question into the open, Brody does make a valuable contribution to the assessment of the debates surrounding the impact of defence spending. Stylistically, I believe the point is not best made by concentrating on a very narrow set of models, the limitations of which would seem to limit the cogency of the principal argument. But in the context of styles now dominant in economic theory (in my judgement this is no matter of glory for economic theory) arguments based on *formal* models seem to command more attention than do the more general arguments, presented on their own. In fairness to the formal argument, it could also be said that the applicability of the general argument to the particular models can serve an important illustrative purpose (even if the illustration is somewhat misleadingly presented as if it were the only possibility, covering all the relevant cases).

The post-Second-World-War booms and the balmy nature of the 1950s, the 1960s and even some of the 1970s have received a good deal of attention and praise. These have been seen as 'successes', followed later by problems of external origin (for example, oil crisis), or policy change (for example, monetary conservatism). But it is quite possible that the same forces that made sure that 'we have never had it so good' also made it inevitable that we could not have it so good for long. The post-war economic experiences of the world have been studied perhaps in too-temporally-fragmented terms. There is a good case for paying attention to the contrast between short run success *vis-à-vis* long-run problems, which may arise precisely from the same process that led to the short-run success. This is really the central point of Brody's paper. Leontief and von Neumann can come and go as illustrations in outlining the seriousness of this possibility, but the central point goes beyond the special features of these models. For this important pointer in a valuable direction of economic investigation, we are indebted to Brody.

Notes and References

1. von Neumann, J., 'Über ein ökonomisches Gleichungssystem und eine Verallgemeinergung des Brouwerschen Fixpunktsatzes' (A Model of General Equilibrium), *Review of Economic Studies*, 13, (1937) 1945–6; Leontief, W. W. *The Structure of American Economy 1919–1939* (New York: Oxford University Press, 1941). Leontief, W. W., (ed.) *Studies in the Structure of the American Economy* (New York: Oxford University Press, 1953).
2. See for example Dorfman, R., Samuelson, P. A. and Solow, R. M. *Linear Programming and Economic Analysis* (New York: McGraw-Hill, 1958).
3. Cf. 'Labour is *not* the source of all weath. *Nature* is just as much the source of use values (and it is surely as such that material wealth consists!) as is labour which itself is only the manifestation of a natural force, human labour power', Marx, K. (1875) *Critique of the Gotha Programme*, English translation, edited by C. P. Dutt (New York: International Publishers).
4. There is also the assumption of constant returns to scale, shared with the Leontief model.
5. For an illuminating analysis of the contingent nature of these results depending on the precise set of assumptions involved, see Chakravarty S. *Capital and Development Planning* (Cambridge, Massachusetts: MIT Press, 1969); See also Brody, A. *Proportions, Prices and Planning* (Amsterdam: North Holland, 1970), and Marglin, S. A. *Growth, Distribution and Prices* (Cambridge, Massachusetts: Harvard University Press, 1984).
6. Pasinetti, L. L. *Structural Change and Economic Growth* (Cambridge; Cambridge University Press, 1981).
7. For example, the presence of primary (non-produced) resources and of technical progress can alter the unique and maximal properties of a specific equilibrium growth rate. Furthermore, *induced* technical progress introduces complexities in the determination of the long-run effects of enhanced defence spending on equilibrium growth.

Part II

Defence and War Modelling

4 The Uses, Value and Limitations of Game Theoretic Methods in Defence Analysis[1]

M. Shubik

An overview of the applications of the theory of games to defence analysis is given. The important distinction is made between those models of conflict which can be adequately modelled as two-person constant-sum games and those which model as non-constant-sum games with two or more players.

The zero-sum game models are in general relevant to the study of tactical processes and even for dynamics a reasonably good theory exists. Thus weapon evaluation involving duelling, search and pursuit is of direct interest.

When we move to non-constant-sum games with more than one player the applications are primarily to strategic and diplomatic problems. Game theory has provided a host of 2×2 examples to illustrate the dangers of extrapolating from individual rational behaviour to jointly rational behaviour. The paradoxes of myopic and local rationality are considerable.

A key difficulty which appears even with 2×2 games is in the evaluation of pay-offs. From Ghengiz Khan to Herman Kahn, how do we evaluate 'megadeaths'?

Game theorists have concentrated upon exploring the limitations of rational behaviour of the individual. But it is easy to observe that individuals at best have limited cognitive and computation abilities. Thus rational behaviour must be in reference to the individual's reduced picture of his actual environment which may be determined by cultural and societal phenomena.

Much of strategic analysis is based upon the concepts of subjective probability but empirical evidence casts doubt upon expected utility behaviour especially for low- and high-probability events. A suggestion is made for an experimental programme to study risk behaviour.

I INTRODUCTION

It has been approximately forty years since the publication of the seminal work on the theory of games,[2] and about twenty-five years since the stimulating series of essays by Schelling raised a series of questions concerning the application of an intermixture of game theory and gamesmanship to strategic analysis.[3]

The recognition of the need to study and formulate the principles of war, taking into account the intermixture of behavioural and technological factors, dates back some 2500 years to the writings of Sun Tzu (*circa* 500 BC).[4]

Wisdom often begins with the recognition of a problem and an evaluation of the importance of its solution. Unfortunately the recognition of the importance of a problem and our ability to find a solution may be separated by centuries if not millenia. Thus there has been a steady stream of invention and increase in the killing-power of weaponry over the centuries together with an explosion in the means of communication in the last century. Yet it would be difficult to attribute the same level of progress to society's ability to control war.

Although the seeds for the mathematical formalisation of tactical, strategical and diplomatic procedures are already present in Sun Tzu, the specific development of a mathematical language for the study of conflict, cooperation and negotiation did not occur until the advent of the theory of games. Paradoxically the precision of the mathematical methods of game theory have helped to illustrate the imprecision and the elusiveness of many of the concepts at the basis of the science, art and social process of war.

The prodigious growth in the destructiveness of weapons has made it imperative that in order to survive we develop a capability to control the use of war. But this capability must be manifested in many ways such as the political and bureaucratic control of crisis instability; the ability to interpret ambiguous information and to prevent the propagation of error in command and control systems as well as the overall psychological and political ability to prevent passion or panic from dominating decisions. The dangers of going to 'red alert' have been appreciated at least since the time of Xenophon.[5] Yet our ability to cope with tension and mutual suspicion is probably no greater today than it was over 2000 years ago.

The perception of and concern with the current dangers is manifested in the activities of physicists, senior defence officials, both active and retired, diplomats and political scientists, economists, game theorists, military operations researchers, lawyers, social-psychologists and others. Conferences involving interdisciplinary approaches serve to indicate that there is an understanding that the control of conflict will not come from a single technological, legal, economic or socio-psychological fix. Reality is too complex to have our problems fully solved by a new piece of hardware, a change in costs, a new treaty or a modification to international law.

In spite of the recognition of basic problems requiring study and collaboration among individuals with highly diverse backgrounds and views, our success in developing an adequate understanding of threat or crisis control has been minimal.

Even some of the most elemental questions are not clear. Virtually all professionals concerned with defence foresee the horrors of nuclear war and subscribe to the desire to avoid it. Yet the goal of making the world free from nuclear war is not inconsistent with making the world safe for conventional limited war. Empires grow and decay. Nation-states emerge and evolve. National and tribal boundaries change. 'No war' should not be a synonym for no international change. The traditional way in which the map of the world has been remade has been by armies, navies, cavalry sweeps, sieges, bombardments and other acts of force. Possibly there are better ways but they have yet to be institutionalised.

The growth of civilisation requires self-understanding and self-control. The necessities of this current stage in world history require a deep examination of our ability to build and control national and international systems for the command, control and communication over weaponry of a destructive power sufficient to endanger the survival of our societies.

Much of the analysis done by physical or social scientists is based upon an implicit or explicit assumption of rational behaviour. The central actor in much of economic theory is *homo oeconomicus* (economic man), a direct descendant of Benthamite man. The actor in game theory is a direct descendant of economic man. He knows what he wants, knows what actions are available to him, is able to calculate without passion or other distractions. He understands the logic of cross-purposes optimisation in situations involving two or more strategic actors. In particular he knows that in general the concept of individual rationality does not generalise to situations with more than one actor.

The central contribution of game theory to defence analysis has been a language for the understanding of how to formulate and study strategic or cross-purpose optimisation in situations involving two or more actors. It is suggested here in the remainder of this discussion that two fundamentally different classes of application of game theory to problems in defence have emerged. The first is the application of two-person zero-sum game theory to military, primarily tactical, situations which for the purposes at hand can be reasonably well modelled in this manner. The second is the application of two-or-more-person non-constant-sum-game theory to strategic problems involving threat analysis, crisis control and the interface between international diplomatic relations and war.

When our interests are confined to applications of the two-person zero-sum theory, a reasonably strong case can be made for *homo ludens* (game-playing man) as an intelligent, calculating entity with no personality or psychological foibles playing against an equally bloodless opponent. It can even be argued that there is a natural way to extend the concept of individual rational behaviour to the two-person zero-sum game.

When our concerns are strategic and the game is naturally a non-zero-sum cross-purposes or mixed-motive optimisation, where there is neither total coincidence nor total opposition of interests, the model of the individual actor raises many basic problems. The USSR and the USA may not be adequately described as two abstract players. Yet for some purposes such as the study of mass market behaviour, the model of many agents as intelligent economic men devoid of personality and concerned in a single-minded manner with the pursuit of profit may be adequate.[6,7]

Implicit in setting up a model of some aspect of reality for analysis is a host of basic assumptions concerning the players and their environment. Once the implicit and explicit assumptions have been accepted, analysis, calculation, logic and mathematics take over. The two critical sets of assumptions which must be made concern the players and their environment. Social psychologists, biologists and field commanders are concerned with individual differences. Yet underlying most analytical models more or less as a simplifying necessity for analytical purposes is the condition of external symmetry. Any difference in abilities of individuals must be specified within the model, otherwise all non-specified attributes are regarded as the same.

Unlike formal games such as chess, bridge or poker which have well-defined beginnings and endings, most models of strategic situations cannot be easily cut away from history or assigned a clear termination. In essence, it is the responsibility of the modeller to establish the context in which the game is played. This is most clearly seen when a scenario is prepared for a war game or a politico-military exercise (PME).

The importance of context is such that rather than use the phrase 'rational behaviour' I suggest that the phrase 'context rational behaviour' provides the analyst with a reminder that behaviour must be assessed in the context of the situation at hand and it warns against spurious generality.

The value of the assumption of external symmetry is enormous as a device for simplification. But it must be justified in an *ad hoc* manner. Thus, for example, if we wish to apply the two-person zero-sum game theory to a weapon-evaluation problem involving a task on tank duel, the assumption that the opposing crews are equal in all respects appears to be reasonable.

In much of economic theory the assumption of *ceteris paribus* (all other things being equal) plays the same role as external symmetry. In both instances underlying the assumption is that unless otherwise specified, individuals are fully-rational perceptive optimisers. But the assumption of the existence of *homo oeconomicus* or his strategic cousin *homo ludens* should not be regarded as a step towards some ultimate abstraction of a Platonic rational man, but as a simplification for an individual who, no matter how intelligent or perceptive, is limited in his capacity to see, comprehend, process and act upon all the information available.

Especially in the study of threats, bargaining and negotiation, there has been a realisation that it may be worth considering richer models of man. Yet, when behavioural models are proposed, phrases such as 'limited rationality' are used to describe the actors. Unfortunately, the world 'limited' frequently carries with it a pejorative connotation. I propose that the phrase 'capacity-constrained rationality' is more neutral. If we are willing to assume that information gathering and processing takes time and that no individual can know all that there is to be known, then we need a definition of what we mean by rational behaviour where the individual is aware that his decision must be made with limited knowledge concerning the prospects he faces.

A way of reconciling capacity-constrained rationality with our model of rational behaviour under complete information is provided by an interpretation of context rational behaviour. If S_i is the largest set of prospects which can be handled by an individual, i, and S (where $S > S_i$) is the total set, then culture, society, indoctrination and professional training may serve as some of the devices which map S on to S_i. Rational behaviour is defined in reference to actions on S_i, but context has been set by the mapping of S to S_i. Thus, for individuals with limited capacity, rational behaviour can only mean context rational behaviour.

The work of Harsanyi on games with incomplete information takes the initial prior subjective probabilities as given with no explanation as to where they come from.[8] Selten considers how to cope with structural uncertainty by considering a way to deal with unknown prospects.[9] The valuation of the unknown is a parameter in his system whose setting could be explained by context. The work of Tversky and Kahneman on 'framing' can also be interpreted as concern for context.[10] Ellsberg's paper on the distinction between uncertainty and ambiguity must be considered in terms of context.[11] An individual can choose between two urns. In one he knows that there are 50 black and 50 white balls, In the other, all that he knows is that there are 100 balls of the colours black or white. He obtains a prize if he selects a black ball. How does he frame his view of the experiment and the experimenter? If he thinks that the experimenter is saving on experimental funds, the second urn may have 100 white balls. If he is trying to reward daring needy graduate students, it may have 100 black balls.

II   GAME THEORY AND TACTICAL ANALYSIS

'In a word it is easier to make a theory for tactics than for strategy.'
                                                          Clausewitz

A rough rule of thumb is that if a conflict situation can be reasonably well modelled as a two-person zero-sum game with complete information about the rules then it is amenable to a considerable body of game theoretic mathematical analysis which covers both statics and dynamics. If the situation is not well described as a two-person zero-sum game, then an *ad hoc* justification of the realism and relevance of the model, the motivations of the players and the solution concept must be given.

There have been stimulating and insightful analyses of arms races based on differential equation models,[12,13,14] and on control theory.[15] But it must be stressed without qualification that for dynamic non-constant-sum games in general there is no generally agreed solution concept.

Although questions concerning arms races, crisis instability or the spread of nuclear weapons generally cannot be treated with great confidence by mathematical analysis, many problems at the level of tactics and weapon evaluation can be modelled with a high degree of confidence as two-person zero-sum games.

There is substantial literature on duels, a survey of which has been given by Kimeldorf.[16] This work is of direct application in weapon evaluation where the relative vulnerabilities and advantages of weapons in one-to-one combat can be investigated. There is also a considerable body of literature on search and pursuit games.[17,18] Game theoretic methods can be applied directly to the study of optimal pursuit and evasion tactics such as the search for an enemy ship or submarine in a security zone. Tactical air support for land forces has also been considered.[19,20]

Although not strictly game theory, the mathematical work on models of combat attrition may be considered as closely related to two-person zero-sum games. Many variants of the Lanchester equations have been studied and applied in weapon evaluation and force and doctrine studies of combat simulation. The work of Taylor and the survey of Karr provide an extensive overview of the Lanchester attrition processes including their applications to theatre-level combat simulations.[21,22]

Even for two-person zero-sum situations modelling problems arise. H. K. Weiss in his perceptive writing on the requirements for the theory of combat notes the problems in considering morale and the problems in characterising communication and its failure.[23]

There is a small but substantial community of those concerned with military operations research working at problems where two person zero-sum game theory provides both appropriate models and conceptually satisfactory mathematical methods for direct application and computation of relevance to military problems primarily at a tactical level. This work is characterised by a maximum-solution concept which pertains naturally to the problems under consideration. Unfortunately in the shift of concern from tactical to strategic problems neither the maximum solution nor the assumptions concerning external symmetry hold in general. An attempt to concentrate on worst-case analysis can introduce a conservative bias verging on the paranoid.

In the shift from tactical to strategic problems, the uses, limitations, modelling problems, solution concepts and appalications of
game theory change radically. The stress tends to be more upon the
clarification of concepts and the construction of adequate models
than upon computation and the exploitation of specific mathematical
structure.

III   STRATEGIC ANALYSIS AND THE THEORY OF GAMES

1   On Numbers

There are possibly four numbers which count in the study of
non-constant-sum games. They are: two, three, few and many. The
economic studies of competition have concentrated heavily on duopoly (two), competitive markets (many), oligopoly (few) and to a
lesser extent on triopoly (three). In strategic analysis where the
players are nation-states, the economist's concern for anonymous
mass competition does not appear. Two, three and few are the
numbers of concern.

The division between two and more than two players is often of
value. In particular the analyst must always be on guard against the
dangers of 'maximin, worst case or polarised opposition' thinking
about two-country strategic models.

Two person non-constant-sum games split naturally into three
classes (i) no-conflict games; (ii) games with pure opposition; and (iii)
mixed-motive games. In a Utopian world with the coincidence of
joint optimality, the problem of choice by individually rational
players is solved. Games with pure opposition need not be zero-sum.
For example, we can consider two players with strongly ordered
preferences

$$a_1 > b_1 > c_1 > d_1 \text{ and } a_2 > b_2 > c_2 > d_2$$

The game shown in Figure 4.1 is one of pure opposition, although
$a_1 + d_2$ is not defined. Mixed-motive games are the predominant
type of interest. The two parties have neither a complete community
nor opposition of interest, but an intermix of both.

When we raise the question of what we mean by a solution to a
game, the division between two-player games and those with three or
more becomes even more striking. In particular dynamic games with

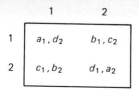

Figure 4.1

a few (more than two) players are virtually intractable to formal mathematical game theoretic analysis for two reasons. The first is that there is no consensus as to what constitutes a good-solution concept. The second is that if one selects a leading contender such as the 'perfect equilibrium',[24] it is hard to compute and, in general, is not unique; thus one cannot uniquely describe the development of play. The equilibrium concept of Kreps and Wilson is highly related to the perfect equilibrium but the equilibria are easier to compute; however, the lack of uniqueness still remains.[25]

2 The Modelling Checklist

In a previous note on the study of disarmament and escalation, seven basic considerations in modelling were raised.[26] They were:

1. Who are the players?
2. How is utility evaluated?
3. What do the pay-off matrices mean?
4. What are the moves?
5. What knowledge do players have of each other's values?
6. What is the coding problem?
7. How are coalitions, countries and institutions modelled?

Together with the first chapters of Shubik's *Game Theory in The Social Sciences*,[27] these two references provide a discussion of many of the problems in constructing formal mathematical models in 'soft subjects' such as threats and negotiations.

Although many of the items on the 1968 checklist remain, further work on the theory of games, on experimental gaming, on the analysis of war and the potential for war and on experimental psychology has suggested some modifications. In particular, more emphasis is placed here upon the modelling of utility of preferences; the description of and calculations with uncertainty; the treatment of information and communication conditions and the meaning of misperception and irrationality in the context of a dynamic game.

Before discussing the many suggestive insights to be gleaned from examining two-by-two matrix representations of various strategic problems, a brief exposition of the more important modelling problems is given.

1   Who are the players?

This poses problems in aggregation, historical context and preference representation. Although lip-service may be paid to conceptualising the USA and the USSR as players, these entities are hardly individuals with well-ordered preferences. Any theory of war or crisis control calls for a finer characterisation requiring the specification of 'games within the game'.[28] It is well known that there are considerable difficulties in constructing a completely ordered set of social or societal preferences from the ordered sets of preferences of individuals even without postulating the political parties and bureaucracies of a society which aggregate these preferences. The review of Yuen Foong Khong of Bueno de Mesquita's book, *The War Trap*, notes this particular problem.[29,30]

A glance at the command and control systems of the USA or the USSR should be enough to warn against too heavy an aggregation of players in the study of crisis control.[31,32]

Lesson   Aggregation can create players whose preferences are difficult to describe and in general will not form an ordered set. Thus what is 'rational behaviour' for a country is hardly a general operational concept.

2   How is utility evaluated?

In a weapon-evaluation exercise it is not too difficult to construct a loss-function based upon the number of tanks or aircraft knocked out on each side. The theory of duels or pursuit and evasion have natural pay-off structures. Even in economics the structure of preferences considered in consumer choice has an underlying justification in choices frequently made by many individuals over a set of reasonably well-defined goods or services. Preferences over objects of political or diplomatic choice are far more difficult to justify. Given that international relations in general and defence policy in particular are run by fiduciaries, it is unlikely that the public even perceives the choices seen by its fiduciaries; thus, while the latter may have preferences defined over moves, the former may have preferences defined only over the few outcomes they perceive.

When we move to the evaluation of megadeaths, the meaning of 'acceptable casualties' becomes a topic for Jesuitical debate. Even thinking about the concept depends upon how the question is framed. For example, can we think about a war in which the percentage of world population killed equals that inflicted upon the world of Ghengiz Khan? It is estimated that his invasions may have wiped out between 8 and 12 per cent of the world population. In modern terms this is about the combined population of the USA and the USSR.

3 How is uncertainty treated?

Since the seminal work of von Neumann and Morgenstern,[33] the conceptualisation of risk and preference for risky outcomes has been radically changed. Their key observation was logical, but with empirical overtones. If you are willing to believe the economists' assumptions concerning complete ordering or preferences over certain prospects, then all you have to do is to swallow an extra couple of innocent-looking axioms and you arrive at a utility scale or a utility function defined up to a linear transformation.

This observation provided a fundamentally new view of how to consider decision-making under uncertainty. The theory raised experimental, empirical and mathematical problems. Some forty years later it appears that the original assumptions concerning preference and the added assumptions concerning uncertainty were not as innocent as they might have seemed to be. In particular it is precisely in the domain of the problems faced in control of crises and the limiting of international political tension where many of the difficulties appear. What utilities are to be attached to one's own death, or the death of others? How are these values influenced by context? In the psychological literature it is well known that the way in which a question is framed may have considerable influence on the response. Tversky and Kahneman present an example of a question concerning the treatment of a disease.[34] It was framed once in terms of individuals probably saved and once in terms of individuals who might die. The two questionnaires evoked considerably different responses. Another phenomenon observed by the psychologists is that the treatment of extremely low- and high-probability events does not appear to fit the expected utility hypothesis. Tversky and

Kahneman offer a prospect theory to explain the divergence from expected utility theory.[35] Einhorn and Hogarth offer a different explanation based upon Ellsberg's distinction between ambiguity and uncertainty.[36,37] In the early literature on insurance and lotteries, Friedman and Savage distinguished between attitudes towards risk of loss and risk of gain.[38] Tied in with the possibility of loss is the individual's attitude towards survival. Perhaps as the risk of failure to survive is increased there comes a point of discontinuity in behaviour. Jarvis has applied the observations on small probabilities to international politics.[39]

Virtually every one of these problems concerning risk behaviour is central to the control of nuclear forces during a time of crisis. If defence budgets are to be in tens and hundreds of billions, it would appear that a major research programme on risk behaviour would be of considerable value.

The foregoing comments are all concerned with individual risk behaviour; yet in major crises involving large bureaucracies, group behaviour may be of even greater importance. The comments of Janis on 'group think' raise a new set of problems in crisis control.[40]

4 Information and communication; and coding

Information and communication, and the somewhat cryptic heading of coding, are placed together here. Even though they are separate topics, the link between them is at the nexus of many of the major difficulties in understanding threats and behaviour in crises. In game theory, information has an extremely precise context-free meaning. There are a number of states which can be distinguished by an individual. An information set portrays the set of the states among which an individual is unable to distinguish. If A's information is a refinement of B's, A has more information, he is more perceptive.

But crises between nations invariably take place in a context. The words and deeds must be interpreted in the context of the history and institutions involved. Game theory, or for that matter any other formal decision theory, has little to contribute to how one is satisfied that the appropriate context has been reflected in the model and its analysis. Information is not the mere receipt of a signal but its interpretation.

One type of problem involving information in a more or less context-free mode is the inspection problem which can be formulated in several variations dealing with attempts to verify limits on testing, numbers or locations of weapons.[41]

Another problem involving information and communication is retargeting. We may represent a defence command and control network as a graph with arcs being communication lines and nodes standing for missile sites or command centres. An attack removes some nodes and arcs. After the attack an individual commander located at some node may only have limited knowledge of how much of the system has survived. How should his optimum response policy depend upon the state of the system? Bracken, Havir, Shubik and Tulowitsky have examined some simple models and a far more extensive treatment has been given by Weiss.[42,43]

For the mathematical game theorist, military operations research analyst or technical systems designer, once values have been assigned to arrays of surviving targets, several interesting and difficult mathematical problems can be formulated. But the understanding of damage-exchange rates in a first- and second-strike analysis, counting targets destroyed on both side provides only partial insight into the analysis of grand tactics in a nuclear war. I use the phrase 'grand tactics' to stress that in a strike and counterstrike analysis the time span is short and resources are fixed as in tactical analysis, yet the consequences are clearly at the strategic level. Information that a launch has taken place is referred to as tactical warning.[44] This indicates that if we believe that a first strike must be punished, then damage-exchange or zero-sum thinking takes over. But it is precisely the difficulties encountered in attaching values to wiping out populations and in deciding why a threat to retaliate should be carried out that raise substantive issues in reconciling the strategic with the tactical damage-exchange view of nuclear exchange.

Of prime concern to the strategic analyst is the possibility of compounding human errors in a command and control system. Although many specific calculations are needed to estimate how much redundancy is required to keep certain types of error below some specified level, for the most part the problems are preformal. The uses of game theory and other methods are to pose questions and provide examples in order to isolate phenomena.

3 The Search for Solution Concepts

For tactical problems involving two players the saddlepoint or maximin solution provides a reasonable conservative extension of individual rational behaviour to a two-person game of opposition.

The solution extends to multi-stage games, and with appropriate qualifications to stochastic games of indefinite length.

Strategic problems have been considered primarily as games in extensive, strategic or coalitional form. The coalitional form is used as a parsimonious way to study the potentials for cooperation in a cartel or alliance. The format purposely suppresses details concerning information, process and strategy. There have been several attempts to devise a formal dynamic theory of coalition formation (for example, Shenoy[45]) but little application to defence. The various cooperative-game solutions, the core, value, nucleus and others do not yield particularly deep insights for two-player games,[46] and are essentially static solutions (although some formal connections between the core and strong non-cooperative equilibrium points have been made).[47]

Except for what might be a highly useful core analysis of alliances, cooperative game theory with its emphasis on avoiding dynamics and any explicit consideration of strategy does not appear to be particularly promising for the analysis of defence problems.

The obvious candidates for models of defence problems are games in strategic or extensive form. Figures 4.2(a) and 4.2(b) show the extensive and strategic forms of a two-move game where Player 2 is genuinely committed to a non-first-strike policy. Player 1 either instigates a first strike or not. Player 2 faces the option of a counterstrike if attacked.

How realistic or valuable these representations are depends heavily on the problem. But even assuming that they are adequate, the analyst requires a solution concept with which he can analyse the game. As is well known, the non-cooperative equilibrium, abbre-

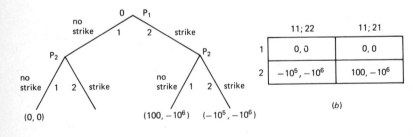

(a)

(b)

Figure 4.2

viated NE, (and several variants of the non-cooperative equilibrium) is the dominant solution used to analyse games in strategic or extensive form. The main property of the non-cooperative equilibrium is optimal response. If *A* knows *B*'s strategy, then at an equilibrium (an NE) *A* will have no desire to change his strategy as he cannot improve. The same holds for *B*. But attractive as the condition of optimal response may be, there are others such as maximin, efficiency, symmetry which have been mathematised, and still others such as honour, revenge, insecurity, fear and hate which have not yet been adequately characterised in formal models.

In Figure 4.2(b) there is a single NE, at the strategy pair (1,11;22). This is interpreted as Player 1 uses his strategy not to strike. Player 2 uses his strategy which contains the contingent plan: 'If not struck do not initiate hostilities, if struck retaliate'. Unfortunately, uniqueness of equilibria is not the rule especially for multi-move games. Consider the matrix game shown in Figure 4.3 played twice. In extensive form the game tree would have $3 + 3^2 + 3^3 + 3^4 = 120$ branches and each player has 3^4 different strategies. The matrix is the Prisoner's

	1	2	3
1	5, 5	−3, 10	−10, −10
2	10, −3	0, 0	−10, −10
3	−10, −10	−10, −10	−10, −10

Figure 4.3

Dilemma bordered by a threat alternative. The one-play game has two non-cooperative equilibria at the strategy pairs (2,2) and (3,3) with pay-offs of (0,0) and (−10,−10) respectively. But if the game is repeated twice a strategy of 'Play 1 to start, if he plays 1 then 2, otherwise play 3' is such that if both use it they obtain (5,5) in the first period (0,0) in the second and it is in equilibrium. A repetition of (2,2) or (3,3) on each play gives two more equilibria.

We now may make the distinction between an equilibrium point and a 'perfect' equilibrium point in a sequential game. Figure 4.4 shows part of the game tree (in abbreviated form) for Figure 4.5. The notation P_{12} indicates simultaneous moves as does the labelling of the branches by 1,1 to 3,3. A perfect equilibrium point is not merely an equilibrium in the game as a whole but is also an equilibrium in every subgame, where a subgame can be regarded as an independent game.[48] A subgame begins with a point of perfect information; each individual knows exactly where he is in the game tree. No information set in a subgame includes any node outside of the subgame. The broken circle in Figure 4.4 encloses a subgame.

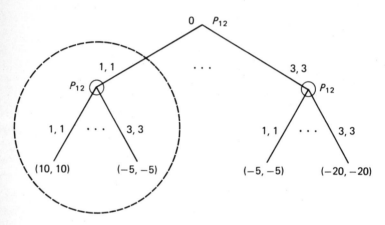

Figure 4.4

The threat-strategy pair form a perfect equilibrium because after a doublecross, even though both players would lose 10 each by the use of (3,3) in the subgame, this is an equilibrium. If we change the pay-offs slightly as is shown in Figure 4.5, then the threat strategies no longer give rise to a perfect equilibrium although they remain as an equilibrium. The key distinction involves the treatment of the plausibility of threats. The argument by those who support perfect equilibria is that the use of move 3 in the second play of the game

	1	2	3
1	5, 5	−3, 10	−10, −11
2	10, −3	0, 0	−10, −11
3	−11, −10	−11, −10	−11, −11

Figure 4.5

after being doublecrossed is plausible for the game in Figure 4.3 but not for the game in Figure 4.5. But it is likely that the difference in plausibility between accepting pay-offs of −10 and −11 is not great and the perfect equilibrium does not show this. The plausibility of a threat may depend significantly upon context.

The importance of context is nicely illustrated by an example suggested by Rosenthal.[49] Consider the game shown in Figure 4.6 and Player 2's strategy. Clearly if Player 1 plays down, both get 10 and the game is over. If he plays right, then Player 2 can end the game with pay-offs (6,7) or can give the move back to Player 1. The equilibrium should have Player 1 go down and Player 2 go right if he gets the move, followed by Player 1 going down to get (9,9). But if Player 2 ever gets the move, Player 1 by the theory is either irrational or has made a blunder of some sort. Player 2's strategy may well depend on his interpretation of the context in which he obtained the move.

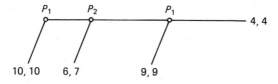

Figure 4.6

The lack of uniqueness of NE makes the backward induction a somewhat metaphysical exercise.[50] Figures 4.7(b) and 4.7(c) show two different backward inductions on the simple two-stage game shown in Figure 4.7(a). But if Player 2 were willing to commit to the

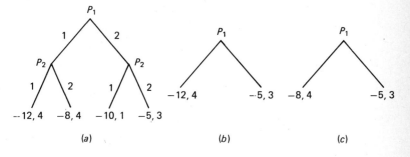

Figure 4.7

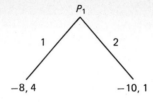

Figure 4.8

'irrational' choice of move 1 if Player 1 chose 2 and move 2 if he chose 1, then Figure 4.8 shows that this could be to his advantage.

Of the seventy-eight different 2×2 matrices with strong orderings on pay-offs, three are with pure opposition, twenty-one are no-conflict games and the remainder lead to mixed motives for cooperation. Within these games the paradox of the failure of individual rational behaviour to coincide with joint rationality appears in many different ways as is indicated. When ties or inability to distinguish between outcomes are also considered, the number of cases becomes 726 and the need for rules concerning coordination and tie-breaking procedures emerges. Many of the rogues' gallery of examples have been discussed elsewhere.[51,52] Figures 4.9(a),(b),(c),(d) and (e)

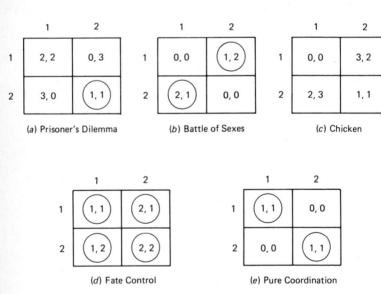

Figure 4.9

illustrate two with the NE circled. In these games in Figure 4.9(a) the equilibrium resulting from strictly dominating choices is not jointly optimal; in Figure 4.9(b) a rule to break the impasse is required; in Figure 4.9(c) there is no pure strategy equilibrium. In figure 4.9(d) and 4.9(e) coordination is a must. In Figure 4.9(d) each player controls the other's pay-offs. Each is a hostage of the other.

To Schelling, myself and others the resolution of several of these problems is in *context* or beyond the formal model or in a richer model containing traditions, conventions, cultural norms, cues, prominence or other factors.[53] If these are not added, then a way of looking at the lack of uniqueness is that the mathematical description is not rich enough to narrow down the outcomes to a single one. Harsanyi adopts the view that there should be enough there to make the selection without invoking outside factors.[54]

A promising new development which represents a considerable departure from the standard non-cooperative equilibrium analysis has been put forward by Rubinstein.[55] He considers that a matrix game is to be played by two finite automata known as Moore Machines. The players select the machines and must pay a fee for every state that is used for some percentage of the time in an indefinitely repeated game. This cost enters into the pay-offs and should be minimised (actually the pay-off he defines has to enter lexicographically into the pay-off; hence the optimisation is somewhat complicated).

An interesting point in defence studies is raised. Should one keep paying for a force that is never used (see also Downs)?[56] In Rubinstein's model the answer is 'no'. As the stockpiles of nuclear weapons grow, what constitutes use and value becomes both an academic and operational question.

For those who wish to apply formal game theory to negotiation and nuclear brinkmanship, the formal problems encountered in developing solution theories serve as a warning that calculation without context or specific *ad hoc* justification of the solution concept chosen may not be justified.

IV   BARGAINING AND THREATS, ARMS RACE AND CRISIS STABILITY

Three topics of broad application and interest to those concerned with defence at the diplomatic and strategic levels are noted.

1 Bargaining and Threats

The literature is large and diverse. A partial bibliography is provided by Shubik.[57] For the defence analyst, it is possibly worth noting three different broad sets of work: (i) the formal theory; (ii) experimental work and behavioural approaches; and (iii) an intermixture of essay analysis combined with predominantly 2 × 2 game examples.

The formal theory started essentially with Nash's analysis of a bargaining game with threats.[58] However, Zeuthen's early work predating formal game theory contained similar ideas.[59] Since Nash's work, many alternative models of bargaining and fair division have been developed. Roth gives a valuable discussion of many of the alternative axiom sets.[60] Stähl attempts to lay out a formal dynamic theory.[61] But in essence the formal work on bargaining and fair division appears to have had little direct application to strategic defence problems.

There is a growing literature on experimental gaming primarily in economics and social psychology. In some instances the relationship between theory and experimental results has begun to grow,[62,63] but the perceptive book on the art and science of negotiation by Howard Raiffa shows how wide the gap is between formal theory and application.[64] Context, socio-psychological and organisational factors, all of which are usually carefully excluded from the economic and game theory models, appear to play important roles.

Policy-makers do not have the luxury of being able to wait for theory to take a decade to justify or explain what they may have to do tomorrow morning. They tend to be more literate than numerate. Thus although massive calculations may have little impact, game theoretic reasoning and simple but striking examples such as the Prisoner's Dilemma matrix have much to teach. The intellectual basis for Mutually Assured Destruction (MAD) is clearly game theoretic but the problem of how well it might work is heavily an empirical one concerning how well the simple game theoretic model fits the facts. This is even true of 2 × 2 matrix analogies as is shown in Figure 4.10 (a more detailed discussion is given in Shubik, see also Strauch).[65,66]

Figure 4.10 shows a simple situation in which Blue can retaliate Red's strike and guarantee to inflict a damage level of −100 (Problem: What do the −200 and −100 really mean and who evaluates them?). If Blue fails to retaliate, the pay-offs are −200 and +100. We evaluate the *status quo* at 0,0. The only equilibrium is at

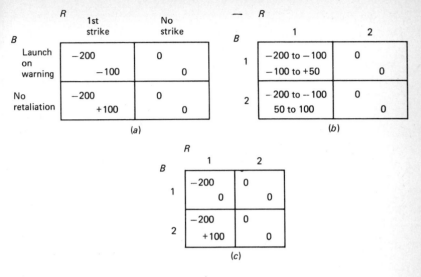

Figure 4.10

(1,2) or launch on warning and no strike. A similar analysis with a Blue first-strike completes a picture of a simple MAD world.

The numbers in the matrices have to be calculated or estimated from somewhere. This calls for evaluating one's view of the worth of targets destroyed, megadeaths, victory, defeats, Armageddon, or however else one wishes to portray the consequences of nuclear war.

Even if we assume that we have a measure for the consequences of war, another important problem concerning the representation of pay-offs in the matrices is: Do we wish to display expected values or should we indicate the degree of uncertainty separately? In Figure 4.10(a) and 4.10(c) we intrepret the outcomes as certain. In Figure 4.10(b) rather than indicate expected pay-offs, the ranges have been indicated. We can see that in cell (1,1) there is a range of 100 in the estimates of the damage caused by a first strike. Furthermore, there is a swing in the effectiveness of the counterstrike from −100 to 50. But with these shifts in values, the risk assessment could be such that for some evaluating Figure 4.10(b) a first strike is worth the gamble and for others it is not. In Figure 4.10(c), with outcomes as certain, a first-strike pay-off as the counterstrike fails.

The concentration on the 2 × 2 analogy leaves out the important possibility that nuclear threat is used to achieve moderate political goals; thus, although the dichotomous choice presented by a simple MAD analysis may serve to illustrate what is required to deter a first strike, it cannot be used to study the important interfacing between nuclear threat and limited aggression.

The intermix of essay form with examples requiring little or no mathematics can be attributed first to Schelling;[67] this type of analysis has been continued with somewhat more formality by Brams and Wittman,[68] Brams and Hessel,[69] Zaggore,[70] Moulin,[71] and others. Brams and Hessel apply their analysis to the Polish internal crisis of 1980–1.

In a perceptive article Strauch has suggested that 'It is this *transfer of understanding* which should be considered as the *primary product of planning'*.[72] His observation applies to this form of analysis. The models may be perceptive and the conjectured chains of action and reaction raise interesting questions. For transmitting ideas, advice and *ad hoc* knowledge to aid in policy-making, this approach appears to be valuable. But as a research tool it is limited. Schelling and others have raised many interesting questions but after twenty-five years few if any answers have been supplied by this mode of analysis.[73]

2 Arms Race and Escalation

The work of Richardson and Rapoport on arms races has already been noted.[74,75] Intriligator[76] provides further references and the Intriligator and Brito model of arms races shows the close analogy between certain economic models of duopolistic competition and war outbreak in armament build-up or build-down.[77] Without going into mathematical detail, the driving observation behind the Intriligator and Brito analyses and the Shubik and Thompson model of duopoly as a game of economic survival is that there can be too little armament or investment in the firm as well as too much.[78] An arms race takes away from the productive use of assets elsewhere. However, in a world with complete or little armament, the relative advantage given to the nation with a few extra arms becomes considerable. Thus in the zone near-zero instability increases as, given a slight advantage, it may be worth the risk to start a fight. At the other end of the spectrum there is an upper bound at which the overkill possessed by each side is so great that even a large accidental fluctuation does not disturb stability.

Differential or stochastic game models that can be explicitly analysed, like business cycle models in economics of Lanchester attrition models, tend to be narrow in terms of the number of variables which can be handled and the lack of qualification concerning qualitative events which may change the dynamics of a model (an example is provided by the difficulty in modelling the 'breaking-point' phenomenon in a battle when one side becomes demoralised). However, there are still valuable lessons to be learned. If one is willing to accept the assumptions, then the conclusions that there can be too little as well as too much armament are of interest.

A recurrent theme in arms-race modelling has already been noted in a discussion of Rubinstein's work. If all nations stockpile weapons, will they be used? If they are not to be used, will they be kept? The theory of taking precaution postulates that an optimal outcome is one in which disaster equipment is never used. But before the event the optimal policy requires that the equipment be procured. A completely different view is that supply creates its own demand. The debate ranges from nuclear war down to individual crime prevention. Does the banning of the possession of privately-owned lethal weapons improve or lower the level of safety? The answer is not clear and appears to depend on context. Does the banning of the possesion of nuclear weapons by nation-states improve or lower the level of safety? Who is going to do the banning and how is it to be enforced?

A simple game which can be played at parties with amusing and paradoxical consequences is the dollar auction.[79] A dollar is auctioned with bids in units of 5 cents. The high bidder wins the dollar and pays his bid, but the second highest bidder also pays. It is easy to see that a dollar may be sold for considerably more than a dollar when individuals keep bidding in order to cut losses.

This game has been considered both in terms of addiction and escalation. Teger has used the game experimentally to study the phenomenon of 'too much invested to quit'.[80] O'Neill provides an analysis based upon both players having limited resources and each knowing the resource limitations of the other.[81] He then contrasts his 'rational perfect equilibrium solution' with twelve basic items as they appear to be handled in the solution he proposes, in experimentation and in international escalation. Table 4.1 is a reproduction of O'Neill's Table 1.

The contrast between the pure game theoretic model and the list of extra considerations noted by O'Neill serves to indicate the need for

Table 4.1 Features promoting escalation in the dollar auction played by rational, real opponents and in international escalation

	Ideal dollar auction	Real dollar auction	Inter-national escalation
Entrapment	*Non-entrapping*	*Often entrapping*	*Often entrapping*
Limited ability to look ahead	–	X*	X
Desire to win for the sake of winning	–	X	X
Investment made passively	–	–	X
Verbal self-commitment to future moves	–	–	X
Uncertainty above objective consequences	–	–	X
Crisis instability	–	X	X
Expectation of future interaction	–	–	X
Informational component in moves	–	X	X
Misperception of current state of escalation	–	–	X
No third-party intervention	X	X	–
No withdrawing resources once invested	X	X	–
No dropping out on equal terms	X	X	–

*The X indicates that the property noted is present.
Source: B. O'Neill 'International Escalation and the Dollar Auction', Discussion Paper 650 (Evanston, Illinois: Dept. of Industrial Engineering, North-western University, 1985) Table 1.

considerable investigation into both the psychological and bureaucratic aspects of escalation.

3   Crisis Stability

Crisis stability or instability is possibly one of the most important problems of societal concern at this time. An early formal somewhat game theoretic analysis was provided by Ellsberg.[82] Grotte and O'Neill provides references to many of the game theoretic models developed in the past twenty years.[83,84] O'Neill using a set of five axioms,[85,86] derives a crisis instability index which he applies to the

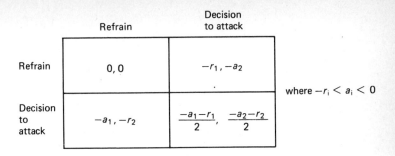

	Refrain	Decision to attack
Refrain	$0, 0$	$-r_1, -a_2$
Decision to attack	$-a_1, -r_2$	$\dfrac{-a_1 - r_1}{2}, \dfrac{-a_2 - r_2}{2}$

where $-r_i < a_i < 0$

Figure 4.11

2×2 model in which both sides can either attack or refrain from attack (see Figure 4.11).

The lower right cell has pay-offs which are a 50:50 mix of the two adjacent cells take into account the possibility, not of simultaneous attack, but of simultaneous decision to attack and chance determining who gets the first blow. The index developed is:

$$P(\text{war}) = 1/[1 + \{4a_1a_2/(r_1 - a_1)(r_2 - a_2)\}^g]$$

where g is a responsiveness factor to the pay-offs. If $g = 0$, then the index is independent of pay-offs and has a value of $1/2$. Low values of g indicate concern about factors outside of the formal pay-off description. When r_i approaches a_i, the index goes to zero as there is no advantage in first strike.

One way of viewing the index is in terms of damage exchange and regret. Figures 4.12(a),(b) and (c) illustrate this. The first matrix has an index of $1/(1 + 4/10^6)$ with $g = 1$ or 0.999. War is virtually certain. The matrix in Figure 4.12(b) provides a minimise regret argument and Figure 4.12(c) a minimin difference in pay-offs.

O'Neill, adopting a nuclear exchange model developed by Grotte, carries out a computation of his index calculated by evaluating the entries in Figure 4.11.[87,88] He then performs a sensitivity analysis on various forms of arms control and draws conclusions that space defences could be destabilising unless they were very effective.

The O'Neill papers are a nice supplement and well-reasoned operations research game theoretic addition to the writings of Bracken and Blair who are more concerned with the proneness to error and the difficulties of control of each side's politico-military-bureaucratic delivery systems than with simplified computational

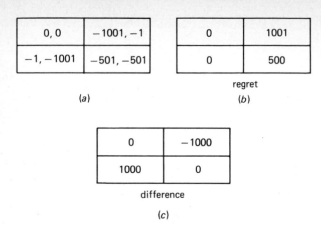

0, 0	−1001, −1
−1, −1001	−501, −501

(a)

0	1001
0	500

regret

(b)

0	−1000
1000	0

difference

(c)

Figure 4.12

models where the error factors have been implicitly assumed or avoided.[89,90,91]

Crisis control is not one problem, but many. Formal game theory possibly does more to illustrate where our knowledge of individual and institutional crisis behaviour is lacking than it does to provide a dynamics of crisis control. Under behavioural assumptions concerning risk, some of the implications of changes in force structure can be evaluated. But the essence of many of our current problems is in the dynamics and no adequate dynamic theory exists. Informal game theoretic reasoning and examples help to point out the difficulties and paradoxes in threat behaviour and 'brinkmanship'. But the questions raised far outnumber the answers supplied.

V FUTURE DIRECTIONS

The growth of the applications of game theory in many of the behavioural sciences in the past forty years has more than fulfilled its early promise.[92] Yet is is by no means a panacea. By providing better tools for analyses, more questions as well as answers are found.

The meaning of relevance and value in application depends upon purpose and priority. The applications of game theory and closely-related topics to defence problems have been and will remain diverse. There are at least seven distinctions which merit note in application. They involve various blends of policy advice-giving, mathematical analysis and operations research, human factors analysis, bureaucracy and social systems understanding, and history and political science. They are:

1. General operational advice-giving at a high policy level – this involves an intermix of conversational game theory, gamesmanship and uncommon sense. The works of Ellsberg, Schelling and Herman Kahn provide examples.[93,94,95]
2. Specific operational advice-giving is harder as it involves not only setting up a context of discourse but operationalising the examples used to illustrate paradoxes, threats and ploys.
3. The bread-and-butter direct uses of operations research and calculation come in the setting-up of problems which can be described with reasonable accuracy as two-person zero-sum games.
4. There is room for calculation and formal models if they are used in an *ad hoc* manner with extreme care. Examples are provided by Dalkey's nuclear war model;[96] Grotte on nuclear stability;[97] Shubik and Weber on systems defence,[98] and Grotte and Brooks on measuring naval presence.[99] (See also Brewer and Shubik for a coverage of the links among models, games and simulations).[100]

The four items noted above may all be viewed primarily from an operational viewpoint at some level; the remaining three call for an emphasis on basic research and theory development. They are:

5. The understanding of individual principal-party and fiduciary-agent risk behaviour under normal conditions and under stress. The psychologists have raised many questions which challenge our views of a 'rational decision' theory. But at this time we appear to be far from having a satisfactory substitute.
6. The functioning of man–machine systems both under normal pressures and under stress was recognised in the 1950s as a key area of study. The Systems Development Corporation and the Rand logistics laboratory provide examples of a large commitment to the investigation of function and failure to function in warning systems. In the past twenty years, the 'disconnect' between technical systems analysis and the human, bureaucratic, sociological and political control systems appears to have increased. Yet the need to understand the control of error in massive command and control systems has become more important in this time span. It is my firm belief that expenditures in the

range of hundreds of millions, if not billions of dollars are called for in the study of individual and systems risk behaviour.

7. The last item is the most challenging and difficult. In spite of the attractiveness of the slogan 'satisficing man' where many of us feel that we know intuitively what is meant, it has been extremely difficult to operationalise in a satisfactory manner the meaning of capacity-constrained rational behaviour. Some advances have been made in computer science in artificial intelligence. But it may be that the future development of relevance to the problems of defence calls for emphasis on models of 'context rationality'. Gaming experiments are needed to study the differences and causes of differences in situations where the game theoretic model is the same, but the briefing or setting of context, the players (their training and background), and organisational structure and time pressures are varied.

The models of man of the general, politician and bureaucrat, the game theorist, political scientist, social psychologist, psychologist, historian and artificial intelligence expert are far apart. Both the operational needs of the time and the scientific challenge call for increased understanding and resolution of these differences in view.

Notes and References

1. The US Government has a royalty-free, non-exclusive and irrevocable licence throughout the world for Government purposes to publish, translate, reproduce, deliver, perform, dispose of, and to authorise others to do so, all or any portion of this work.
2. Von Neumann, J. and Morgenstern, O., *Theory of Games and Economic Behaviour* (Princeton, New Jersey: Princeton University Press, 1944).
3. Schelling, T. C., *The Strategy of Conflict* (New York: Oxford University Press, 1960).
4. Sun Tzu, 'The Art of War' (translated from Chinese *circa* 500 BC) in Philips, T. R. (ed.) *The Roots of Strategy* (Harrisburg, Pennsylvania: Military Service Press, 1940).
5. Xenophon, *The Persian Expedition* (translated from Greek by Rex Warner) (New York: Penguin, 1949).
6. Shubik, M., *Game Theory in the Social Sciences*, vol. I (Cambridge, Massachusetts: MIT Press, 1982).
7. Shubik, M., *Game Theory in the Social Sciences*, vol. II (Cambridge, Massachusetts: MIT Press, 1984).
8. Harsanyi, J. C., 'Games with Incomplete Information Played by "Bayesian Players"' Parts I–III, *Management Science* (1967–68) pp. 14, 159–82, 320–34, and 486–502.

9. Selten, R., 'Limited Rationality and Structural Uncertainty', Working Paper no. 70 (Bielefeld, FRG: Institution of Mathematical Economics, University of Bielefeld, 1978).
10. Tversky, A. and Kahneman, D., 'The Framing of Decisions and the Psychology of Choice', *Science*, vol. 211 (1981) pp. 453–8.
11. Ellsberg, D., 'Risk Ambiguity and the Savage Axioms', *Quarterly Journal of Economics*, vol. 75 (1961) pp. 643–69.
12. Richardson, L. F., *Arms and Insecurity* (Pittsburgh, Pennsylvania: The Boxwood Press, 1960).
13. Rapoport, A., *Fights, Games and Debates* (Ann Arbor, Michigan: University of Michigan Press, 1961).
14. Intriligator, M. D. and Brito, D. L., 'Can Arms Races Lead to the Outbreak of War?' *Journal of Conflict Resolution*, vol. 28, no. 1 (1984) pp. 63–84.
15. Ho, Y. C. and Olsder, G. L., 'Differential Games Concepts and Applications', in Shubik, M. (ed.) *Mathematics of Conflict* (Amsterdam: Elsevier, 1983) pp. 127–86.
16. Kimeldorf, G., 'Duels: An Overview', in Shubik, M. (ed.) *Mathematics of Conflict* (Amsterdam: Elsevier, 1983).
17. Dresher, M., *Games Strategy* (Englewood Cliffs, New Jersey: Prentice Hall, 1961).
18. Ho and Olsder (see note 15).
19. Berkovitz, L. D. and Dresher, M., 'Allocation of Two Types of Aircraft in Tactical Air War: A Game Theorectic Analysis', *Operations Research*, vol. 8 (1960) pp. 694–706.
20. Berkovitz, L. D., 'The Tactical Air Game: A Multimove Game with Mixed Strategy Solution', in Grote, J. D. (ed.) *The Theory and Application of Differential Games* (Hingham, Massachusetts: Riedl, 1975) pp. 169–78.
21. Taylor, J. G., *Lanchester-type Models of Warfare* (Monterey, California: Naval Postgraduate School, 1981).
22. Karr, A. F., 'Lanchester Attrition Processes and Theater Level Combat Models', in Shubik (ed.) *Mathematics of Conflict* (Amsterdam: Elsevier, 1983).
23. Weiss, H. K., 'Requirements for the Theory of Combat', in Shubik, M. (ed.) *Mathematics of Conflict* (Amsterdam: Elsevier, 1983) pp. 73–88.
24. Selten, R., 'Re-examination of the Perfectness Concept of Equilibrium Points in Extensive Games', *International Journal of Game Theory* vol. 4 (1975) pp. 25–55.
25. Kreps, D. M. and Wilson, R., 'Sequential Equilibria', *Econometrica*, vol. 50 (1982) pp. 863–94.
26. Shubik, M., 'On The Study of Disarmament and Escalation', *Journal of Conflict Resolution*, vol. 12, no. 1 (1968) pp. 83–101.
27. Shubik (see note 6).
28. Shubik (see note 7).
29. Yuen Foong Khong, 'War and International Theory: A Commentary on the State of the Art', *Review of International Studies*, vol. 10 (1984) pp. 41–63.

30.   Bueno de Mesquita, B., *The War Trap* (New Haven, Connecticut: Yale University Press, 1981).

31.   Bracken, P., *The Command and Control of Nuclear Forces* (New Haven, Connecticut: Yale University Press, 1985).

32.   Blair, B. G., *Strategic Command and Control* (Washington, DC: Brookings, 1985).

33.   von Neumann and Morgenstern (see note 2).

34.   Tversky and Kahneman (see note 10).

35.   Tversky and Kahneman (see note 10).

36.   Einhorn, H. J. and Hogarth, R. M., *Ambiguity and Uncertainty in Probabilistic Inference* (Chicago, Illinois: Center for Decision Research Graduate School of Business, University of Chicago, 1984).

37.   Ellsberg (note 11).

38.   Friedman, M. and Savage, L. J., 'The Utility Analysis of Choices Involving Risk', *Journal of Political Economy*, vol. 56 (1948) pp. 279–304.

39.   Jarvis, R., *Perception and Misperception in International Politics* (Princeton, New Jersey, Princeton University Press, 1976).

40.   Janis, I. L., *Victims of Group Think* (Boston, Massachusetts: Houghton Mifflin, 1972).

41.   Aumann, R. J. and Maschler, M., 'Game and Theoretic Aspects of Gradual Disarmament', MATHEMATICA Report, Contract no. ACDA/ST-80, (June 1966).

42.   Bracken, P., Havir, S., Shubik, M. and Tulowitsky, U., 'Nuclear Warfare, C^3I and First and Second Strike Scenarios (A Sensitivity Analysis)', *Proceedings of the Seventh MIT/ONR Workshop on C^3 Systems*.

43.   Weiss, M. P., *Two Game Theoretic Studies of Military Command and Control*, dissertation (Evanston, Illinois: North-western University, 1983).

44.   Bracken, P., *The Command and Control of Nuclear Forces* (New Haven, C.T.: Yale University Press, 1983).

45.   Shenoy, P. P., 'On Coalition Formation: A Game Theoretical Approach', *International Journal of Game Theory*, vol. 8 (1979) pp. 133–64.

46.   Shubik (note 6).

47.   Aumann, R. J., 'Acceptable Points in General Cooperative N–Person Games', in *Annals of Mathematics Studies*, vol. 40 (Princeton, New Jersey: Princeton University Press, 1959) pp. 287–324.

48.   Selten (see note 24).

49.   Rosenthal verbal communication.

50.   Harsanyi, and Selten (Harsanyi, J. C., 'Solutions for Some Bargaining Games under the Harsanyi–Selten Solution Theory, Part 1', *Mathematical Social Sciences*, vol. 3 (1982) pp. 179–91) have recognised the difficulties posed by multiple equilibria and have proposed a solution concept which selects a unique equilibrium. Justice cannot be done to its intricate reasoning here.

51.   Schelling (see note 3).

52.   Shubik (see note 6), chapter 10.

53.   Schelling, (see note 3), Shubik (see note 65), Harsanyi (see note 50).
54.   Harsanyi (see note 50).
55.   Rubinstein, A., 'Finite Automata Play the Repeated Prisoner's Dilemma', (Jerusalem: Department of Economics, Hebrew University, 1985).
56.   Downs, A., *The Value of Unchosen Alternatives* (Santa Monica, California: Rand Corporation, 1964) p. 3017.
57.   Shubik (see note 6) chapter 12.
58.   Nash, J. F., 'Two-person Cooperative Games', *Econometrica*, vol. 21 (1953) pp. 128–40.
59.   Zeuthen, F., *Problems of Monopoly and Economic Warfare* (London: G. Routledge & Sons, 1930).
60.   Roth, A. E., *Axiomatic Models of Bargaining*, Lecture Notes in Economics and Mathematics Systems 170 (Berlin: Springer–Verlag, 1979).
61.   Stähl, I., *Bargaining Theory* (Stockholm: Economics Research Institute, 1972).
62.   Smith, V. L., *Research in Experimental Economics, Vol. 1* (Greenwich, Connecticut: JAI Press, 1970).
63.   Sauermann, H., *Contributions to Experimental Economics*, vol. 1 (Tübingen: Mohr, 1967).
64.   Raiffa, H., *The Art and Science of Negotiation* (Cambridge, Massachusetts: Harvard University Press, 1982).
65.   Shubik, M., 'Game Theory: The Language of Strategy', in Shubik, M. (ed.) *Mathematics of Conflict* (Amsterdam: Elsevier, 1983) pp. 1–27.
66.   Strauch, R., 'A Critical Assessment of Quantitative Methodology as a Policy Analysis Tool', in Shubik, M. (ed.) *Mathematics of Conflict* (Amsterdam: Elsevier, 1983) pp. 29–54.
67.   Schelling (see note 3).
68.   Brams, S. J. and Wittman, D., 'Non-myopic Equilibria in 2×2 Games', *Conflict Management and Peace Science*, vol. 6 (1981) pp. 39–62.
69.   Brams, S. J. and Hessel, M. P., 'Threat Power in Sequential Games', *International Studies Quarterly*, vol. 28 (1984) pp. 23–44.
70.   Zaggore, F. C., 'Non-myopic Equilibria and the Middle East Crisis of 1967', *Conflict Management and Peace Science*, vol. 5 (1981) pp. 139–62.
71.   Moulin, H., 'Deterrence and Cooperation: A Classification of Two-Person Games', *European Economic Review*, vol. 15 (1981) pp. 179–93.
72.   Strauch, R., 'Strategic Planning as a Perceptual Process', (Santa Monica, California: Rand Corporation, 1981) p. 6595.
73.   Schelling (see note 3).
74.   Richardson (see note 12).
75.   Rapoport (see note 13).
76.   Intriligator, M. D., 'Research on Conflict Theory: Analytic Approaches and Areas of Application', *Journal of Conflict Resolution*, vol. 26, no. 3 (1982) pp. 307–27.

77.   Intriligator and Brito (see note 14).
78.   Shubik, M. and Thompson, G. L., 'Games of Economics Survival', *Naval Research Logistics Quarterly*, vol. 6 (1959) pp. 111–23.
79.   Shubik, M., 'The Dollar Auction Game: A Paradox in Non-cooperative Behavior and Escalation', *Journal of Conflict Resolution*, vol. 15 (1971) pp. 545–7.
80.   Teger, A., *Too Much Invested to Quit* (New York: Pergamon Press, 1980.
81.   O'Neill, B., 'International Escalation and the Dollar Auction,' Discussion Paper 650 (Evanston, Illinois: Department of Industrial Engineering, North-western University, 1985).
82.   Ellsberg, D., 'The Crude Analysis of Strategic Choices', *American Economic Review Proceedings*, vol. 51 (1961) pp. 471–8.
83.   Grotte, J. H., 'Measuring Strategic Stability with a Two-Sided Nuclear Exchange Model', *Journal of Conflict Resolution*, vol. 24 (1980) pp. 213–39.
84.   O'Neill, B., 'A Measure for Crisis Instability', Discussion paper 652 (Evanston, Illinois: Department of Industrial Engineering, North-western University, 1985).
85.   O'Neill (see note 86).
86.   O'Neill, B., 'Applications of a Crisis Stability Index: Arms Control Agreements and Space-based Missile Defenses', Discussion Paper 651 (Evanston, Illinois: Department of Industrial Engineering, North-western University, 1985).
87.   Ibid.
88.   Grotte, J. H., 'An Optimizing Nuclear Exchange Model for the Analysis of Nuclear War and Deterrence', *Operations Research*, vol. 30 (1982) pp. 428–45.
89.   O'Neill (see notes 81, 84 and 86).
90.   Bracken (see note 31).
91.   Blair (see note 32).
92.   Shubik (see note 6) chapter 12.
93.   Ellsberg (see notes 11 and 82).
94.   Schelling (see note 3).
95.   Kahn, H. *On Thermo Nuclear War* (Princeton, New Jersey: Princeton University Press, 1960).
96.   Dalkey, N., 'Solvable Nuclear War Models', *Management Science*, vol. 11 (1965) pp. 783–91.
97.   Grotte (see note 83).
98.   Shubik, M. and Weber, R. J., 'Colonel Blotto, Command and Control', *Naval Research Logistics Quarterly*, vol. 28 (1981) pp. 281–7.
99.   Grotte, J. H. and Brooks, P. S., 'Measuring Naval Presence Using Blotto Games', *International Journal of Game Theory*, vol. 12 (1983) pp. 225–36.
100. Brewer, G. and Shubik, M., *The War Game* (Cambridge, Massachusetts: Harvard University Press, 1979).

5 Conflicts, Arms Races and War: A Synthetic Approach

Jean-Christian Lambelet
UNIVERSITY OF LAUSANNE
and Urs Luterbacher
GRADUATE INSTITUTE OF INTERNATIONAL
STUDIES, GENEVA

This chapter elaborates basic elements for an integrated formal approach to conflicts, arms races, and war in an attempt to remedy the inadequacies we see in similar theoretical efforts. Starting from a rational actor perspective in international politics, the paper presents three interconnected models of arms races or resource allocation processes, diplomatic conflict and war initiation by nations that are based upon either general optimising principles through time or differential game theoretic considerations. All these principles are defined as adjustments between actual and target values of key variables of resources devoted to defence, diplomatic conflictual efforts, and evaluations of each side's deterrent capabilities by the other. In addition, time constraints play a crucial role in the representation of the war initiation submodel. An analysis of these three interconnected formulations shows that our conception can account for several types of war initiation. On the one hand, we can emphasise a situation that we label the *paradox of the weak* where the nation with the least effective deterrent has an incentive to attack first. On the other hand, our model can also represent more classical types of confrontations where either deterrence works or where the strong attacks the weak.

I INTRODUCTION

In this chapter we are emphasising the fact that so far there are very few synthetic formal approaches which try to model conflicts, arms races and war *together*, even though these three aspects of international behaviour are obviously connected, but not necessarily in a straightforward way. Some conflicts are accompanied by arms races; some are not. Some conflicts end up in war; others do not. Some arms races turn into wars; some other ones merely produce enough mutual deterrence to prevent an armed confrontation.

To our knowledge, the only formal attempts to link at least two of these three elements have been made by Allan who examines the interaction between diplomatic conflict and arms races;[1] by Intriligator and Brito,[2] and by Brito and Intriligator.[3]

Allan's work does not include an explanation of wars, but the linkages made within it between conflict theory and arms race theory are novel and very interesting. Brito and Intriligator in their 1984 and especially 1985 papers try to tackle the delicate problem of war, and particularly the outbreak of war, within a rational-actor decision-making model. While their solutions are quite provocative and very stimulating, there are three reasons why we are not entirely satisfied with them:

1. They conceive war as avoidable through some redistribution of wealth.[4] In our view, quite a few wars cannot possibly be analysed in these terms. A classical example is ancient Rome's policy *vis-à-vis* Carthage: *Delenda est Carthago*! That is, the Romans were not interested in a share of Carthage's wealth, but rather in destroying their foe altogether. (Eventually, as one knows, the city was ploughed under.) A closely connected policy posture is epitomised by the famous (or notorious) aphorism: 'The only good Indian is a dead Indian.' The Franco-Prussian War (1870–1) affords another example of a war which could not have been averted by wealth or income redistribution: Bismarck's goal in initiating this war (or rather in making it unavoidable) was primarily to use it as a catalyst for Germany's unification under the Hohenzollern Dynasty. The annexation of Alsace-Lorraine and the Frankfurt Treaty indemnity were really by-products of Prussia's exhilarating victory – thought up, as it were, in the flush of that victory – and there is evidence that they were forced on France against Bismarck's own better judgement.[5]
2. The investigations of Brito–Intriligator result in overemphasising the importance of errors (that is, incomplete information) in explaining why wars break out.[6] In our view, quite a few wars are deliberately planned by one side. To start again with a classical

example, there is Thucydides' celebrated account of the dialogue between the delegates of Athens and those of Melos during the Peloponnesian War, with the former openly telling the latter that they would be conquered by force (as eventually they were) unless they agreed to surrender peacefully.[7] Other examples – listed at random – include: England's war against the Boers (1899–1902); the Opium War (1842); the war of the Austrian succession (1741–8); most of Louis XIV's wars; the Hundred-Year War; the US–Spanish War (1898); the war between Japan and Russia (1904–5); the Korean War (1950–3); Italy's war on Ethiopia (1935–36); the war between China and India (1962); the Yom Kippur (or Ramadan) War (1973); the war in Afghanistan (1978); and so on.[8]

3.   The model of Brito-Intriligator cannot be said to be truly dynamic since it allows for two successive periods only.

II OUTLINE

Therefore, in our view, a model linking conflicts, arms races and war must first also be able to account for wars which result from long-term strategic considerations and consequently preclude any 'buying-off' possibility on the part of the more vulnerable or exposed side. Of course, this does not mean that the buying-off option must be ruled out altogether since there is good historical evidence that it does exist – for example, the basic policy postures of both the Golden Horde and the Ottoman Turks; or (perhaps more controversially) Finland's status *vis-á-vis* the Soviet Union since 1944. In other words, the buying-off option must be one of the model's outcomes, but not the only one.

Second, such a theoretical construction has to allow for wars that are deliberately planned as well as wars occurring by accident. Of course we do not deny that wars may also break out because of deficient information, miscalculations and other accidental errors – for example, in July 1914, 'The Austrians had believed that vigorous action against Serbia and a promise of German support would deter Russia. The Russians had believed that a show of strength against Austria would both check the Austrians and deter Germany. In both cases the bluff had been called, and the three countries were faced with the military consequences of their actions'.[9]

Third, such a model should be fully dynamic: war breaks out, or peace is preserved, depending on the evolution over time of a conflict and arms race configuration.

Finally, it is also possible, as we shall see presently, that the perception of time itself plays a crucial role in this context, meaning that the parties set themselves some time horizon in order to accomplish certain things. To illustrate: Germany's pre-1914 Schlieffen plan was explicitly posited on a binding time constraint, in the sense that it gave the German armies six weeks to defeat France and its allies in the West before taking on the (supposedly sluggish) Russian 'steamroller' in the East. It can also be argued that President Lyndon B. Johnson's decision, taken in the spring–summer of 1965, to intervene massively with US ground forces in South Vietnam made (political) sense only if the Vietcong-North Vietnamese opponents could thereby be defeated thoroughly within a fairly short time-span – say, one year.

Our conception will accordingly be expressed in the form of a general conflict and war formulation which will be divided into three subcomponents: an arms race (or, to be more general, a resource allocation) model; a conflict model; and a war decision-making model. Similarly to Bueno de Mesquita,[10] Allan,[11] and Brito–Intriligator,[12] our model will be based on the rational-actor paradigm. Our conception should therefore be understood as a rational theory of conflict, arms races and war. Since our construction seeks to be dynamic, the optimising principles which characterise rational decision-making will be expressed either as variational problems or differential games (of which variational problems are special instances, according to Isaacs).[13] We shall examine these three submodels in sequence. For the moment, bilateral conflict will be considered.

III   THE RESOURCE ALLOCATION SUBMODEL

Our resource allocation or arms race submodel is derived from the Lambelet–Luterbacher model,[14] as modified in Allan by the addition of a diplomatic climate term.[15]

$$darma/dt = ka\{[exp(c - d/gnpa - e/armbp - f/clda \\ - g/confab)] - arma\} \qquad (5.1)$$

$$darmb/dt = kb\{[exp(c' - d'/gnpb - e'/armap - f'/cldb \\ - g'/confba)] - armb\}$$
(5.2)

where $arma$ = some measure of A's defence efforts (in real terms)
ka, c, d, f, g = parameters (all positive)
$gnpa$ = A's real *GNP*
$armbp$ = A's perception of B's defence effort
$clda$ = Allan's diplomatic climate (as perceived by A);
      $clda$ can also be defined more precisely as A's perception of B's attitude and intentions *vis-à-vis* itself, on a scale going from fully peaceful (zero level) to utterly aggressive
$confab$ = A's 'true' attitude and intentions *vis-à-vis* B, on a scale similar to that of *clda*
and symmetrically for the variables and parameters in (5.2).

The functional form of (5.1) and (5.2) can be justified on three grounds. First, as discussed at length in a previous paper of ours,[16] semi-log reciprocal functions exhibit a number of properties which are highly attractive in an arms-race context. For example, one notices in the equations' exponential part, which determines the desired level of, for example, A's defence effort, that for this level to be zero it is enough that any one among the explanatory variables ($gnpa$, $armbp$, and so on) be zero, which makes obvious sense: if A had no resources at all ($gnpa = 0$), it evidently could not start arming; if B is not armed at all (as perceived by A, that is, $armbp = 0$), there is no reason why A should arm; and similarly if A perceives B as fully peaceful *vis-à-vis* itself ($clda = 0$), or if A truly nourishes only peaceful designs *vis-à-vis* B ($confab = 0$).

A second justification for the functional form of (5.1) and (5.2) is to notice that they can be rewritten as follows:

$$darma/dt = ka\{exp(c_1 - d/gnpa)\ (exp(c_2 - e/armbp)\ (. . .$$

(5.1′)

where $c_1 + c_2 + . . . = c$

and similarly for (5.2).

In other words, (5.1) and (5.2) can also be viewed as *arbitrage* functions, in the sense that each actor decides to increase or decrease its desired defence effort by comparing its *GNP* with some critical level as defined by c_1; and similarly for the other explanatory variables.

Third, and most generally, the differential equations (5.1) and (5.2) can be derived from variational maximisation or minimisation principles. Suppose each country is minimising over time the logarithm of the sum of the actual amount of its defence effort, that is, *arma* in the case of country A, and its increase over time, that is, *darma/dt*, with respect to some constant target value which we will call '*arma* star' (i.e. *arma**). Such a logarithmic form can be explained in terms of decreasing marginal utilities of defence efforts. We will therefore have the minimisation of:

$$[ln(arma + darma/dt) - ln\ arma^*]^2 \quad \text{(over time)} \qquad (5.3)$$

The only feature of this expression which may be found unusual is that it includes the time derivative *darma/dt*. Suppose that at some point in time, the actual defence effort of A is less than the desired one; that is *ln arma* < *ln arma**. If, on top of that, the actual defence effort happens to be decreasing at that same point in time (that is, if *darma/dt* < 0), which means that *arma* is actually moving farther away from its target value, country A is hypothesised – according to expression (5.3) – to react more strongly and face a tougher minimisation task, as it were, than if the time derivative were either positive or zero.

At the same time, country A is constrained by the arbitrage function (5.1′) while in addition having to take into account its response, that is, the logarithm of the divergence between level and increase in defence potential:

$$[ln(arma + darma/dt) - ln\ arma^*](c1 - d/gnpa)$$
$$(c2 - e/armbp)(. . . \qquad (5.4)$$
$$\text{(again over time)}$$

If we call the log of the divergence u' and F the remaining arbitrage terms $(c_1 - . . .)\ (c_2 - . . .) . . .$, the following functional is to be minimised by country A:

$$H = (u' - ln\ arma^*)^2 + \lambda\ (u^. - ln\ arma^*)\ F \qquad (5.5)$$

where λ is an arbitrary constant. Applying the Euler condition to this function, and rearranging terms, leads to the above resource allocation or arms race dynamic equation for country A – and symmetrically for B. (For a full derivation, see the *mathematical appendix*).

We have shown previously that the dynamic system determined by equations (5.1) and (5.2) can have three equilibrium points,[17] two stable ones and an unstable one. The two stable points are located respectively at the origin and at an exhaustion of resources frontier. The point in between is unstable and determines an arms race zone which extends from it to the exhaustion of resources frontier (where 'exhaustion of resources' does not mean that the entire *GNP* goes to defence, but that each country has reached an equilibrium where it spends on defence exactly the amount of resources which it considers optimal).

Equations (1) and (2) differ from the Allan equations because they include an extra term (that is, $-g/confab$), and because *clda* is defined more precisely as A's perception of B's attitude and intentions *vis-à-vis* itself. There are two reasons for these modifications.

First, it is not obvious why an autonomous change (a 'shock') in A's perception of B's attitude should necessarily have the same effect on A's defence effort as an autonomous change of the same magnitude in A's own attitude *vis-à-vis* B – as it is implicitly the case if functions like (1) and (2) include only one general term standing for 'the diplomatic climate.'

Second, it will be seen presently that *confab* (that is, A's true attitude *vis-à-vis* B) will itself be affected by the arms race. This reflects a dynamic notion discussed at some length by one of us in a previous paper,[18] and elaborated in a subsequent contribution by Mayer,[19] namely: '[The parties'] fundamental posture (aggressive or peaceful) may and usually does evolve over time, not necessarily in some autonomous fashion, but conceivably and partly, as a result of the arms race itself'.[20] Clearly, if these feedback effects exist and are sufficiently strong, they amount to a potentially very dangerous feature of the conflict–arms-race–war nexus. This will particularly be the case if the dynamics of the whole model are such that they produce an increasing gap between *confab* (A's true attitude and intentions *vis-à-vis* B), on the one hand, and *cldb* (B's perception of A's attitude and intentions *vis-à-vis* itself), on the other hand. Notice that the divergence between *confab* and *cldb*, and similarly for country B, can be interpreted as measures of the degree of mutual paranoia (as it were) which may characterise a given arms race. Should such divergences between reality and perception actually occur, they might result – via the rest of the model and particularly via the war submodel below – in increasing the odds that a war will eventually break out. In this sense, our construction includes the possibility of a war occurring because of poor information (but not necessary because of asymmetric information). Note, however, that in our model war can also break out for other reasons, as will be seen presently.

At the same time, the existence and strength of these feedback effects are of the essence when evaluating the possibility that a unilateral initiative by one side (such as partial disarmament, a freeze on new weapon acquisition) will bring about a de-escalation of the arms race and a lessening of tensions between the two sides, without its creating an unacceptable risk for the party which is embarking on this unilateral course.[21]

As a last comment on (5.1) and (5.2), one notices that *armbp* – and not *armb* – is included on the right-hand side of (5.1), and symmetrically for (5.2). This feature was already part of our 1979 model where equations (24) and (25) on p. 58 indicate how *armbp* and *armba* are determined. These equations are also part of the present model but, to save space, they are not reproduced here.[22]

IV THE DIPLOMATIC CONFLICT SUBMODEL

The first two equations in our conflict submodel are similar to the ones presented in a recent paper by Luterbacher and Allan:[23]

$$dconfab/dt = \{[clda - U(c)ab][U(d)ab - clda] - confab\} \quad (5.6)$$

$$dconfba/dt = \{[cldb - U(c)ba][U(d)ba - cldb] - confba\} \quad (5.7)$$

The difference between these two equations and the original ones in the aforementioned paper (by Luterbacher and Allan)[24] is that in the latter no distinction was made between, for example, *confab* – that is *A*'s true attitude *vis-à-vis B* – and *clda* – that is *A*'s attitude *vis-à-vis B* as perceived by *B*. *U(c)ab* and *U(c)ba* are the respective utilities of cooperation between *A* and *B* for each country, that is thresholds up to which either *A* or *B* is prepared to accept conflictual moves by the other without escalating, psychologically speaking. On the other hand, *U(d)ab* and *U(d)ba* represent thresholds beyond which neither *A* nor *B* is willing to continue escalating psychologically.

While $U(c)ab$ and $U(c)ba$ can be measured in terms of past conflict levels between the two countries – they express the 'history' of their relations – the variations in $u(d)ab$ and $U(d)ba$ can be assessed in terms of anticipated costs of conflict. In our view, such costs are dependent essentially on two elements emphasised by Allan;[25] namely: resolve, and power capabilities. Resolve expresses the willingness of an actor to carry out a threat or to pursue conflict; power capabilities represent the possibilities of effectively carrying out threats or continuing the conflict. While resolve is a psychological element which to an extent is dependent on past successes or failures by either side (that is, again on the 'history' of the conflict itself), power capabilities evidently result from the resource allocation process described above. The $U(d)ab$ and $U(d)ba$ variables are thus first links between the conflict and resources allocation submodels. In our view, they depend on the difference (1 – balance of resolves and armaments resources), that is:

$$G[1 - (Ra.arma)/(Rb.armb)] \qquad (5.8)$$

In other words, the closer one is to equality, the higher the anticipated cost of conflict, and thus the lower $U(d)ab$ or $U(d)ba$ respectively.

The dynamic equations (5.6) and (5.7) also result from optimising processes which are similar to the ones described previously for the resource allocation model. If again each country attempts to mini-mise a sum in terms of the conflict level and the change thereof, for country *A* one obtains:

$$Min[(confab + dconfab/dt) - confab^*]^2 \qquad (5.9)$$

where *confab** is some target level or innate basic attitude, which can possibly take on the value zero if the country has a fundamentally peaceful inner drive.

On the other hand, a constraint is given by arbitraging between an adequate response and the levels of conflict which *A* is prepared to accept from *B* within the $U(c)ab$ and $U(d)ab$ limits. We thus have the constraint:

$$[(confab + dconfab/dt) - confab^*][clda - U(c)ab]$$
$$[U(d)ab - clda] \qquad (5.10)$$

Expressing these two relations as a function, just as in the resource allocation submodel, and applying the Euler conditions for an extremum, one gets the foregoing conflict equation (5.6) for A. The case for B is of course symmetric. (Again, see the *mathematical appendix*).

Notice that stable rational behaviour and arbitration principles are thus central to our whole construction.

An equation system very close to (5.6)–(5.7) has been analysed in Luterbacher and Allan;[26] and also by Allan,[27] in a slightly different form. It leads to four equilibrium points which can be either stable or unstable for given values of the $U(c)$s and the $U(d)$s. Stable equilibria occur when some asymmetries between countries are present. Otherwise, mutual psychological escalation or de-escalation is present.

There are two more variables which are endogenous to our diplomatic conflict submodel, that is *clda* (A's perception of B's attitude and intention *vis-à-vis* itself) and *cldb* which is symmetrically defined. For the time being, we will explain these variables, not by means of two extra differential equations, but by two simple linear relations, that is, in the case of A:

$$clda = a + r.armbp + s.confba \qquad (5.11)$$

where r and s are partial derivatives which are either zero or positive. The parameter r measures the extent to which A's perception of B's attitude *vis-à-vis* itself is influenced by B's objective, measurable or visible behaviour as expressed by the latter's ('permanent') defence effort. The parameter s, on the other hand, indicates to what extent A is cognisant of and influenced by B's true attitude *vis-à-vis* itself as it may be revealed by (or 'read into') such signals as official or semi-official policy statements, speeches, diplomatic notes, and other forms of communication.

Notice that the interplay between the parameters s, r and the constant term allows for a wide range of possible attitudes on the part of A. Suppose for example that s is equal to zero and r is 'large': A would then be a hard-nosed, 'no-nonsense' type of power which, like St Thomas, only believes what it sees, and which is badly informed about its opposite number's true attitude and does not trust whatever signals it gets from it. On the other hand, if r were equal to zero and s were 'large', A would be genuinely well-informed about the other side's true intentions and hence would trust whatever signals it gets from B, even though the 'observable facts' (such as B's permanent defence effort) might suggest otherwise. As to the constant term, it can only be positive. (Since *clda* is either zero – *B* is viewed as fully peaceful – or positive, a negative constant would mean a negative value for *clda* when both *armbp* and *confba* are zero). A positive constant would then mean that *A* tends to be fundamentally inward-looking and distrustful.[28]

To illustrate: in the case of England at the time of Chamberlain's appeasement policy *vis-à-vis* Nazi Germany, *r*, *s* and the constant were all three likely to be close to zero, if not actually zero. In the case of the USSR under Stalin, both *r* and the constant were probably large while *s* was likely to be close to zero.

In our conflict model as it now stands, the parameters *r*, *s* and *a* are of course time invariant. This is questionable: suppose, for example, that *B* were actually to start disarming unilaterally; or suppose that successful negotiations get under way. It is arguable that, as a result, all parameters in (5.11) – but particularly *r* and the constant – would be lower. The reason, then, why we so far have to treat these parameters as time invariant is that so little is known in today's social sciences about the reasons for, and the circumstances conducive to confidence rather than distrust, cooperation rather than confrontation, and so on.

Finally, the equation for *B* is symmetric to that for *A*:

$$cldb = a' + r'armba + s \cdot confab \qquad (5.12)$$

V THE WAR SUBMODEL

The war submodel is a differential game where actors have the choice between continuing to deter or engaging in war. It is similar to a game described by Isaacs and due to Arnold Mengel.[29] The game is defined by two kinematic equations expressing the evolution of security levels for *A* and *B*:

$$dsla/dt = ma - d_1 \cdot q \cdot slb \text{ (or: } d_1 \cdot q \cdot sla \cdot slb) \qquad (5.13)$$

$$dslb/dt = mb - d_2 \cdot p \cdot sla \text{ (or: } d_2 \cdot p \cdot slb \cdot sla) \qquad (5.14)$$

where *sla* is *A*'s security level and *ma* is *A*'s security resources, both *as perceived by B*; and symmetrically for *slb* and *mb*. Notice that (5.13) therefore describes the behaviour of country *B* and (14) that of country *A*, and not the other way around.

Kinematic equations in differential game theory are constraints on the behaviour of each player. Therefore A sees the evolution of B's security level as a limiting condition that will influence its decision to commit resources to deterrence or to war. Consequently the equation system has to be interpreted in such a way that the evolution of the security level, of, say, B, is relevant for A's decision while the evolution of the security level of A is relevant for B's decision. In a situation of incomplete information, sla and slb would be estimates of respectively A's strength by B and B's strength by A. For the moment we will consider here a situation of perfect information.

The variables ma and mb depend on A's and B's conflict resources. In this sense they can be represented by the products $Ra.armap$ and $Rb.armbp$. These expressions which combine the effects of resolve and defence capabilities constitute the links between the war model and the conflict and resource allocation models.

The control variables p and q represent the degree to which A and B are willing either to deter the other or to go to war. They vary between zero and one. The parameters d_1 and d_2 express how effective B's deterrent is *vis-à-vis* A, and vice-versa. As said, sla and slb are simple functions of $Ra.armap$ and $Rb.armbp$. As to the kinematic equations themselves, we consider two possible specifications – see (5.13) and (5.14) above. The first is a simple linear one where fixed amounts of security resources of, say, A, are deterred by a given amount of B's security level. The second one (included in the parentheses) is perhaps more realistic, in the sense that fractional rather than fixed amounts of security resources are deterred: in other words, deterrence depends on the quantity (or effective power) of the other side's security resources as well.

We consider that this security game is only possible over a limited period of time T. This reflects our idea that decision-makers see themselves constrained by time in the actions they can undertake – compare the 'outline'. A third kinematic equation is therefore necessary:

$$dT/dt = -1 \quad \text{(available time diminishes)} \tag{5.15}$$

In contrast to the control variables p and q, sla, slb and T are called state variables.

In our present war game, deterrence with respect to security levels is a zero-sum situation. A's security level is diminished by an increase in *B*'s, and the other way around. We can therefore define a minimax-type pay-off function which takes the following form:

$$Payoff = V = min_p max_q {}_0\!\int^T [(1 - q)slb - (1 - p)sla]dt \quad (5.16)$$

Solutions to the game show that if time *T* is finite, either party at some point will have an incentive to stop deterring and to attack. Solutions are calculated by establishing partial derivatives of *V* with respect to all state variables (*sla*, *slb*, *T*) and taking into account the general constraints of the pay-off function. This leads to the determination of optimal path equations for the state variables. These optimal paths will cross transition surfaces at some point. Such crossings will involve changes in the values of the control variables – from 0 to 1 or vice-versa, for instance, which corresponds to full-scale war breaking out or peace being concluded: note however that there also exists a limited region where a measure of deterrence can coexist with small-scale military action. To determine the location of the crossings, a standard procedure is to examine solutions for the optimal path equations in reverse time, that is when *T*=0, through what Isaacs calls retrogressive path equations (*RPE*).[30]

Setting up these equations and looking at their solutions leads to transition surfaces at:

$$T = 1/d_1 \text{ for } B \qquad\qquad\qquad (5.17)$$

and

$$T = (1/d_1)[2(d_1/d_2) - 1]^{1/2} \quad \text{for } A \qquad\qquad (5.18)$$

in the case of the linear formulation of *sla* and *slb*. It is clear from this result that if $d_1 > d_2$, the least effective player *A* has an incentive to switch from deterrence to war *before* the more effective player *B*. (The situation is symmetric if one assumes $d_1 < d_2$, as can easily be verified.) In other words, this situation which could be called *the paradox of the weak* shows that if a country is an ineffective deterrer it has an incentive to switch to war if it wants to accomplish some goals in a limited amount of time.

The non-linear formulation for *sla* and *slb* leads to the result that *B* reaches a transition surface at $T = 1/d_1.sla$, and symmetrically for *A* at $T = 1/d_2.slb$. In this case deterrence pays: *T* can get arbitrarily small if *sla* or *slb* are large enough. Nobody has an incentive to attack unless there is some asymmetry or some pause by one party in the development of its security level which, in some way, transforms the non-linear formulation into the linear one. Then, the strong has an incentive to attack the weak – a not uncommon event, as we argued in the introduction.

Of course, effectiveness can also evolve with time and as a result of the arms race itself. If quantities of armaments play a smaller role than the effectiveness of the deterrent (as in the linear model), or if a country suddenly loses effectiveness or sees itself as losing effectiveness as a result of the arms race itself, it also has an incentive to start a war.

VI   CONCLUSION

As is the case with short stories, but not with novels, this chapter's conclusion is open-ended. We have described the properties of our model in a sequential manner, that is taking each block of equations in turn. The next step obviously is to determine the behaviour and properties of the entire system of equations itself. However, given that our construction is relatively complex, it is unlikely that a general solution of our model can be found analytically. Consequently, numerical methods or, if one prefers, simulation will have to be used, based on estimated values for the parameters and/or on a range of plausible values. But this is another story, which we hope will be the subject of future research.

Mathematical Appendix

We want to show that equations (5.1) and (5.2) can be deduced from variational principles such as:

$$[ln(arma + darma/dt) - ln\ arma^*]^2 \quad \text{(over time)} \tag{5.3}$$

and

$$[ln(arma + darma/dt) - ln\ arma^*](c_1 - d/gnpa)(. . . \tag{5.4}$$
(also over time)

We will show how equation (5.1) can be deduced; the steps for equation (5.2) are entirely symmetrical.

Variational principle (5.3) can be expressed as:

$$I = {_0}{\int}^r[ln(arma + darma/dt) - ln\ arma^*]^2dt \tag{5A.i}$$

Function I has to be minimised over time subject to the constraint by the other side and one's own response, so that we have the constraint j:

$$J = {}_0\int^t [ln(arma + darma/dt) - ln\ arma^*](c_1 - d/gnpa)$$
$$(c_2 - e/armbp)(\ldots)dt \qquad (5A.ii)$$

A Hamiltonian can now be defined as:

$$H = [ln(arma + darma/dt) - ln\ arma^*]^2 + \lambda\ [ln(arma +$$
$$darma/dt) - ln\ arma^*](c_1 - d/gnpa)(c_2 - e/armbp)(\ldots)$$
$$(5A.iii)$$

This expression has to be minimised. The Euler first-order condition for this problem is:

$$(\partial H)/(\partial u) - (d/dt)'(\partial H/\partial u') = 0 \qquad (5A.iv)$$

Let us define

$$ln\ arma + darma/dt = u'\ \text{and}\ (c1 - d/gnpa)$$
$$(c_2 - e/armbp)(\ldots) = F$$

H then can be written as:

$$H = (u' - ln\ arma^*)^2 + \lambda\ u'\ F - \lambda(ln\ arma^*)F \qquad (5A.v)$$

and the Euler condition becomes:

$$- (d/dt)\cdot(\partial H/\partial u') = 0 \qquad (5A.vi)$$

or

$$- (d/dt).\{[\partial u'^2 - 2\ u'\ ln\ arma^* + ln\ arma^{*2} + \lambda\ u'F$$
$$-\lambda\ (ln\ arma^*)F]/\partial u'\} = 0 \qquad (5A.vii)$$

This expression leads to:

$$(d/dt)[2u' - 2(ln\ arma^*) + \lambda\ F] = 0 \qquad (5A.viii)$$

or

$$2\ u' + d(\lambda\ F)/dt = 0 \qquad (5A.ix)$$

A first integral of this equation is:

$$2\ u' + \lambda\ F = c \qquad (5A.x)$$

Assuming $c = 0$ and $\lambda = -2$, we get:

$$u' = F \qquad (5A.xi)$$

or

$$ln(arma + darma/dt) = (c1 - d/gnpa)(c2 - e/armbp)(...) \qquad (5A.xii)$$

or

$$arma + darma/dt = exp((c1 - d/gnpa)(c2 - e/armbp)(...)) \quad (5A.xiii)$$

or

$$darma/dt = exp[(c1 - d/gnpa)(c2 - e/armbp)(...)] - arma \quad (5A.xiv)$$

which is equation (5.1).

Second-order conditions are more difficult to establish. Relation (5A.v) is a particular form of the Jacobi equation.[31] The sign of the second variation is determined by the sign of the coefficient of u'^2 in (5A.v), which is always positive by definition. Hence it can be concluded that the extremal equation (5.1) indeed minimises (5.3) and (5.4).

Deriving equation (5.2) is entirely symmetrical.

Equations (5.6) and (5.7) can be deduced in a similar way. For equation (5.6), assume in (5.9):

$$(confab + dconfab/dt) = u' \qquad (5A.xv)$$

and in (5.10):

$$[clda - U(c)ab][U(d)ab - clda] = F \qquad (5A.xvi)$$

(5.9) is then:

$$Min\ (u' - confab^*)^2 \quad over\ time \qquad (5A.xvii)$$

and (5.10):

$$(u' - confab^*)F \qquad (5A.xviii)$$

We can also define a Hamiltonian of the form:

$$H = (u' - confab^*)^2 + \lambda\, u'\, F - \lambda\, confab^*\, F \qquad (5A.xix)$$

Notice the similarity of this expression with expression (5A.v). Hence we can proceed in similar ways and deduce equation (5.6). The case of equation (5.7) of course is entirely symmetrical.

Notes and References

1. Allan, P., *Crisis Bargaining and the Arms Race* (Cambridge, Massachusetts: Ballinger, 1983).
2. Intriligator, M. D. and Brito, D. L., 'Heuristic Decision Rules, The Dynamics of the Arms Race, and War Initiation', In U. Luterbacher and M. D. Ward (eds), *Dynamic Approaches to International Conflict* (Boulder, Colorado: Rienner, 1985).
3. Brito, D. L. and Intriligator, M. D., 'Conflict, War and Redistribution', *American Political Science Review*, vol. 79(2) December 1985, pp. 943–57.
4. For example, Brito and Intriligator (1985) on p. 5: 'We show, using this model, that if both countries are fully informed as to the parameters of the model, then, in fact, there will be no redistribution by actual war. Rather there will be a *voluntary* redistribution of resources, with neither side having an incentive to fight' (emphasis added). The question may hinge on whether 'voluntary redistribution' is synonymous with 'voluntary exchange' as the term is used in economics – that is, an exchange that takes place in the absence of all threat or pressure, explicit or implicit. If that is the case, then our comments in the text apply. But if 'voluntary redistribution' occurs under threat of one sort or another (for example, the threat of going to war) then it is indeed conceivable that it may avoid war – for example, in the sense that the threatened party could then offer to 'surrender peacefully' and hand over everything to the other side (where 'everything' includes the people themselves who would voluntarily go into slavery).
5. On this and other related matters, see Joachim Remak's marvellous little 1967 book (*The Origins of World War I, 1871–1914*, Hinsdale, Illinois: Dryden Press), especially pp. 2–5.
6. Again, on p. 5: 'War can occur, however, in a situation of asymmetric information, where one country is informed of all parameters of the problem, and the other is not informed as to the parameter characterizing the first country's aversion to war (or willingness to fight).'
7. See Thucydides, *History of the Peloponnesian War*, book V, chapters LXXXIV to CXVI.
8. For a useful survey of the historical evidence, see Ruloff, D., *Wie Kriege beginnen*, (Munich: Beck, 1985).
9. Joll, J., *The Origins of the First World War* (London and New York: Longman, 1984). p. 21.
10. Bueno de Mesquita, B., *The War Trap* (New Haven: Yale University Press, 1981).
11. Allan (see note 1).
12. Brito and Intriligator (see note 3).
13. Isaacs, R., *Differential Games* (New York: Wiley, 1967).

14. Lambelet, J. C. and Luterbacher, U., 'Dynamics of Arms Races: Mutual Stimulation *vs* Self-Stimulation', *Journal of Peace Science*, 1979, vol. 4, no. 1, pp. 49–67.
15. Allan (see note 1).
16. Lambelet and Luterbacher (see note 14).
17. Lambelet and Luterbacher (see note 14).
18. Lambelet, J. C. (1984), 'Arms Races as Good Things?'; (see note 2); also available (in a more complete version) as *Cahier de recherches économiques* 8501, *Départment d'économétrie et d'économie politique* (DEEP), University of Lausanne, Switzerland, January 1985, mimeo.
19. Mayer, T. F., 'Images of the Enemy and the Initiation of Nuclear War' (Boulder, Colorado: Department of Sociology and Institute of Behavioral Science, University of Colorado, 1985) mimeo.
20. Lambelet (see note 18) pp. 7 *et seq*. There is also good historical evidence to this effect – for example: 'The [pre-1914] arms race in which all the major powers were involved had contributed to the sense that war was bound to come, and sooner rather than later', Joll (see note 9) p. 202.
21. This is discussed and illustrated in Lambelet (see note 18) pp. 11 *et seq*.
22. Basically, *armbp* is a measure of *B*'s 'permanent' defence effort as seen by *A*, in the sense of Milton Friedman's permanent income hypothesis. This means that our construction eschews the possibility that expectations are formed rationally (in the sense which 'rational expectations' have in economics). This is not to say that the rational expectations hypothesis has no place in the analysis of arms races. Actually, one of us has shown that, in the 1905–14 Anglo-German naval race, the German side (but not the English side) behaved in a way which is strikingly consistent with the rational expectations hypothesis – see: Lambelet, J. C., 'The Anglo-German Dreadnought Race, 1905–1914', *Papers of the Peace Science Society (International)* vol. 22, 1974, pp. 1–45; 'A Numerical Model of the Anglo-German Dreadnought Race', *Papers of the Peace Science Society (International)*, vol. 24, 1975, pp. 29–48; 'A Complementary Analysis of the Anglo-German Dreadnought Race, 1905–1916', *Papers of the Peace Science Society (International)* 1976, pp. 49–66.
23. Luterbacher, U. and Allan, P., 'Toward a Dynamic Theory of Conflict and Coalition Formation' (see note 2).
24. Luterbacher and Allan (see note 23).
25. Allan (see note 1).
26. Luterbacher and Allan (see note 23).
27. Allan (see note 1).
28. The constant in equation (5.11) should possiblity be related to *confab** in equation (5.9). Also note in (5.11) that as *armbp* and *confba* increase – and hence *clda* too – the elasticities of *clda* with respect to *armbp* and *confba* will eventually become larger than one (as long,

that is, as *r* and *s* are non-zero); this could be interpreted as a zone of hysterical overreactions.

29. Isaacs (see note 13), pp. 96 *et seq.*; pp. 330 *et seq.*
30. On all this, see Isaacs (note 13), pp.25–43 and 64–85.
31. See: Davis, H. *Introduction to Non Linear Differential and Integral Equations* (New York: Dover, 1962) p. 449.

6 Arms Races and the Outbreak of War: Application of Principal-agent Relationships and Asymmetric Information

D. L. Brito
RICE UNIVERSITY

and M. D. Intriligator
UNIVERSITY OF CALIFORNIA

Some recent developments in principal-agent theory and asymmetric information are used to study, in the context of a formal model, both when and under what circumstances arms races lead to the outbreak of war and whether wars can be explained as the result of rational behaviour and thus subject to analysis by social scientists. In the formal model countries act as rational agents concerned with the economic right to consumption in a two-period model in which conflict, war and redistribution may all occur. The first period is one of a potential arms race, with countries choosing between consumption and investment in arms, while the second period is one of a potential crisis, with the countries bargaining and possibly using the threat of force ('conflict') or the use of force ('war') to reallocate resources. In certain circumstances arms races do lead to war, while in other well-defined cases they can result in a stable equilibrium in which each side deters the other. Some key factors in distinguishing between these two cases are the level of resources in both countries, the possibilities for redistributing resources, and the possibility that in a situation of asymmetric information the uninformed country will adopt a pooling rather than a separating equilibrium.

I INTRODUCTION; ARMS RACES AND THE OUTBREAK OF WAR

When and under what circumstances do arms races lead to the outbreak of war? This is a question of international relations that has been only partly answered by political theorists and it leads to another question of clear significance. Can wars be explained as the result of rational behaviour and thus be subject to analysis by social scientists?[1]

The purpose of this paper is to analyse the relations between arms races and the outbreak of war using a formal model that incorporates some recent developments in principal-agent theory and asymmetric information. We develop a formal model of countries acting as rational agents in which conflict, war, and redistribution may all occur. The countries are concerned with economic rights to consumption in a two-period model in which force can be used to redistribute these rights. The first period of the model represents an arms race in which countries choose between consumption and investment in arms. The second period is one of potential crisis as countries bargain and possibly use force or the threat of force in order to reallocate resources.

The model builds on recent work on bargaining with asymmetric information and employs some recent developments in models of self-selection and of sequential equilibria. In such models, two equilbrium concepts have been introduced. The first is that of a *separating equilibrium* in which the uninformed agent attempts to induce the other party to reveal the pertinent characteristic; the second is that of a *pooling equilibrium* in which the uninformed agent does not attempt to induce the other party to reveal the pertinent characteristic. In our model, agents are nation-states which can arm, redistribute resources voluntarily, or initiate a war, while the pertinent characteristic is each state's degree of aversion to war as measured by its trade-off between the utility of consumption and the disutility of war.

We distinguish between the threatened use of force in attempting to reallocate resources, which we will call 'conflict', and the actual use of weapons, which we will call 'war'. The principal question is when does conflict lead to the implementation of force and, hence, result in actual war, as opposed to the threat of war?

Section II summarises some empirical regularities that have been discovered by researchers who have investigated the outbreak of war and that should be connected with a formal model of the outbreak of war. Section III then develops the basic model; section IV treats the asymmetric information case in which only one agent is fully informed. Conclusions and some potential extensions of the model and its applications are reported in section V.

II EMPIRICAL STUDIES OF THE OUTBREAK OF WAR

Empirical studies of arms races and the outbreak of war have revealed certain regularities that should be consistent with or explained by formal theoretical models. The model to be presented in the next section is consistent with, and explains, many of these regularities.

Bueno de Mesquita used expected utility analysis to study the determinants of war.[2] The details of this study have been controversial, but, it is persuasive in arguing that wars are consistent with rational decision-making. Of the fifty-eight wars that have been fought since the Congress of Vienna, the initiator won forty-two. Bueno de Mesquita stated that if wars were non-rational events, then there should not be any systematic relationship between the initiator of a war and the victor. He computed cost–benefit ratios and found that when wars occur it was usually in the interest of one party. He did not, however, explain *why* wars occur. Wars are usually Pareto-inferior outcomes of a conflict in that both parties would be better off if the expected loser compensated the expected victor by means of a transfer of resources without actually going to war. Thus, while the Bueno de Mesquita model demonstrates that wars are usually consistent with rational behaviour on the part of the aggressor, it does not explain why wars actually occur, since it does not explain why the loser fought.

Wallace studied the outbreak of war using data on ninety-nine serious great power disputes occurring since 1815.[3,4] He was particularly concerned with whether arms races lead to the outbreak of war and concluded that conflicts and disputes accompanied by arms races are much more likely to result in war than those in which an arms race does not occur. Of the twenty-six cases that led to war, twenty-three involved an arms race, while of the seventy-three cases in which there was no war, sixty-eight did not involved an arms race. Conversely, of the twenty-eight cases in which there was an arms race, twenty-three resulted in war, while of the seventy-one cases in which there was no arms race, sixty-eight resulted in no war. In addition, Wallace found that the probability of escalating to war depends on whether the 'revisionist' power during the period prior to the crisis either wins or does not win the arms race. Of the thirty cases in which the revisionist power won, twelve resulted in war; of the sixty-five cases in which the revisionist power did not win, twelve resulted in war. These results suggest that there is an asymmetric relationship between the winner of the arms race and the probability that a crisis will escalate to war.

Siverson and Tennefoss studied the outbreak of war from 1815 to 1965.[5] They divided conflict situations into three levels: threats, unreciprocated military action, and reciprocated military action. They divided nations into four categories: allied major powers, unallied major powers, allied minor powers, and unallied minor powers. They found that major powers and allied minor powers seem to be involved in less hostility than unallied minor powers, while conflict between major powers is limited. One possible explanation is that they are stronger and hence less likely to be attacked; however, this explanation is not consistent with the observations that unallied minor powers initiated 19.1 per cent of the conflicts with major powers and that there is no case where an allied minor power initiated a conflict.

Using statistical methods, Smith attempted to identify arms races that are particularly war-prone.[6] She estimated the Richardson model and inferred stability from the estimated coefficients. She demonstrated that arms races do not always lead to war and showed that the probability of war could be predicted by the coefficients of the Richardson model. She did not explain what factors led to this result, but she noted the importance of risk factors and uncertainties that are not treated in the Richardson model and in subsequent deterministic models. These factors are, however, treated in the model below.

From this research, a pattern of the following empirical regularities appears to emerge: first, wars are usually consistent with rational decision-making on the part of the initiator; second, an arms race is less likely to lead to war if the *status quo* power 'loses' the arms race; third, conflict between major powers is limited and is less likely to escalate into war than is conflict between major and minor powers; fourth, major powers and allied powers seem to be involved in less hostility than unallied minor powers; and fifth, unallied minor powers initiated conflicts with major powers, but there is no case where an allied minor power initiated conflict. None of these results is yet carved in stone; however, they do form a reasonable starting-point for a set of 'Stylised facts' that should be consistent with or explained by formal models of arms races and outbreak of war. We now develop such a model.

III   A TWO-PERIOD MODEL

This section introduces a two-period model in which there are two countries in conflict for the rights to a flow of a single homogeneous good. For example, they may be in contention for a territory that yields a fungible resource, such as oil or the right to a market that yields income. In the first period, this good may be consumed or used to produce weapons, as in the usual guns or butter trade-off. This process is irreversible, so weapons cannot be converted back into goods during the second period. In the second period, the distribution of the good can be altered either by war or negotiation. The outcome of war depends on the amount of fighting engaged in by either country, which in turn is limited by its weapon stocks as determined by its choices during the first period. War produces an externality which is a public bad and offsets the utility of consumption in the second period. Countries are assumed to be rational and non-altruistic, and they will choose to fight if the expected value of such a strategy is greater than that of not fighting. If they do not fight, then they can negotiate a redistribution of resources in the second period.

We assume that each country has a utility function of the form

$$u\left[x(i), y(i), \frac{C}{n(i)}\right] = a[x(i)] + a[y(i)] - \frac{C}{n(i)}, \quad i = 1, 2 \quad (6.1)$$

Here $x(i)$ is first period consumption for the ith country; $a[.]$ is a strictly concave utility of consumption function such that $a'[.] > 0$ and $a'[0]$ is finite;[7] $y(i)$ is second-period consumption; C is public bad that is produced by war and that reduces utility, such as nuclear fall-out or the loss of trade due to wartime disruption of commerce; and $n(i)$ is a parameter that determines the disutility of war to the ith country. For simplicity, utility is assumed to be separable and linear in the externality. (This assumption could be easily generalised.) The value of the parameter $n(i)$ may or may not be known to the jth country; however, if not known, we assume that each country believes that the parameter characterising the other country's disutility of war takes one of two values: $n(i) = n_1$ with probability p or $n(i) = n_2$ with probability $(1 - p)$. Without loss of generality $n_1 < n_2$, so the disutility of war is greater for an n_1 country than it is for an n_2 country as measured by the amount of utility of consumption needed to offset a particular level of the externality.[8]

In the first period, each country faces a resource constraint of the form

$$K(i) = x(i) + w(i) \tag{6.2}$$

where $K(i)$ represents the total goods available to the ith country in the first period and $w(i)$ is the ith country's investment in weapons. It is assumed that total resources $K(i) + K(j) = K$ are fixed; thus, $K(i)$ is sufficient to describe the allocation of wealth.

By the second period, both countries have chosen weapon stocks $w(i)$ and $w(j)$ respectively, and there are then three possibilities. First, both countries could choose to behave passively and preserve the *status quo*. Second, one country could propose a redistribution agreed to by the second country. Third, one or both countries could propose a redistribution not agreed to by the other side that could lead to conflict and possibly to the outbreak of war.

We define as the *war allocation* the distribution of resources and the externality that results from the war described by the game

$$C = v(i) + v(j) \tag{6.3}$$

$$Y(i) = K(i) + f[v(i), v(j)] \tag{6.4}$$

$$v(i) < w(i) \tag{6.5}$$

$$v(j) < w(j) \tag{6.6}$$

Here $v(i)$ is the amount of fighting by the ith country, as measured by the amount of weapons the countries commit to the war. It is assumed that committing more weapons shifts the redistribution, measured in (6.4) by $f[v(i), v(j)]$, in that country's favour and that[9]

$$\frac{\partial f}{\partial v(i)} > 0, \quad \frac{\partial f}{\partial v(j)} < 0$$

Note that the amount of fighting a country is able to do is limited by its level of weapons, which was determined, in part, by the initial distribution of resources in the first period and that the redistribution is from one to the other so

$$f[v(i), v(j)] = -f[v(j), v(i)]$$

The value of this game for possible values of the parameters $n(i)$ together with the proposed redistribution define a game which will have an equilibrium in mixed strategies.

Setting aside for the moment the second possibility of a proposed redistribution, the complete game can now be described. In the first period, each country chooses between goods and investment in weapons. This investment has two implications: first, it provides the countries with the ability to fight in the second period; and, second, it may reveal information about the value of parameter $n(i)$.

Countries can choose two possible strategies for investing in weapons. First, they can adopt a *war arms investment strategy* in which they invest in weapons as if they planned to engage in fighting in the second period. Second, they can adopt a *deterrence arms investment strategy* in which they invest in a sufficient level of weapons so as to deter the other country from initiating a war in the second period.

Since our model is very different from models that have traditionally been used to address similar problems, it would be useful to discuss the assumptions that we have made. A basic assumption is that of rational agents maximising utility. Another basic assumption is that of a two-period model; such models are routine in economics but have not, to our knowledge, been previously applied in political science or international relations. These two assumptions probably bias the model in the direction of no outbreak of war. The assumption of rationality leads to agents adopting a cooperative solution. It has been very difficult to develop models in which rational agents carry out threats ex-post. The assumption of two time periods precludes early belligerent behaviour to establish a reputation for toughness. The special assumptions of the model – specifically that there exists a mechanism for reallocating resources and that war produces a negative externality that affects the countries in different ways – appear to be reasonable ones, consistent with the reality of conflict between nations. The technical assumptions of differentiability, continuity, and compactness are relatively harmless, and most formal models in international relations make even stronger assumptions in which these properties are implicit.

IV   ASYMMETRIC INFORMATION

This section treats the asymmetric information case in which only one country knows the utility function of the other. While this is not the most general case, it is nonetheless an important one. It is not unheard of for established powers, particularly major powers, to test the determination of new governments, particularly minor powers, in strategic confrontations.

In this case, both informed and uninformed countries maximise expected utility. The informed country has the option of bluffing so as to increase the transfer made to it by the uninformed country. The uninformed country may call the bluff by offering the informed country a choice that involves a non-zero probability of war (a 'separating equilibrium'). Alternatively, it can simply assume that the other country is not bluffing and not run the risk of war (a 'pooling equilibrium'). Whatever equilibrium is chosen depends on the relative wealth of the two countries and the underlying distribution of types. If either country is very weak, or if the distribution of wealth falls within a certain critical range (the stable set), then there is a zero probability. In the first instance, the poor country cannot afford to arm for war; in the second case, the pooling equilibrium dominates the separating equilibrium. A separating equilibrium, with a positive probability of war, may exist between these two extremes. These results are consistent with the empirical regularities discussed in section II.

The key assumption that is being made is that the uninformed country has the ability to impose on the informed country the structure of the game that is played in the second period. Thus it can choose a game in which it is optimal for the informed country to reveal its characteristics by its actions. Such a game results in a separating equilibrium. It can also choose a game in which it does not attempt to infer the characteristics of the other country. Such a game results in a pooling equilibrium. Which game is played depends on the relative costs. It is also important to note that the optimisation by the uninformed player involves backwards induction. The uninformed player computes the optimal strategy in the second period as a function of his weapon stocks and then computes the optimal investment in weapons. He then choses the dominant strategy.

Without loss of generality, it will be assumed that the jth country is informed and knows the value of the war aversion parameter of the ith country, $n(i)$. However, $n(j)$ is not known to the ith country, which knows only that $n(j) = n_1$ with probability p and $n(j) = n_2$ with probability $(1 - p)$, as introduced in section III. The ith (uninformed) country's first-period maximisation problem for the war investment strategy can then be written as one of expected utility maximisation

$$max\ p\{a[K(i) - w(i)] + V[w(i), w(n_1), n(i)]\}$$
$$+ (1 - p)\ \{a[K(i) - w(i)]] + V[w(i), w(n_2), n(i)]\} \qquad (6.7)$$

where $w(n_1)$ is the level of weapons adopted by the jth country if it is of type n_1, and where $w(n_2)$ is the level adopted by the jth country if it is of type n_2. Let the reaction function:

$$w(i) = \alpha[w(n_1), w(n_2); p, n(i), K(i)] \qquad (6.8)$$

be the solution to this maximisation problem. The jth (informed) country's problem can then be written

$$max\ a[K(j) - w(j)] + V[w(j), w(i), n(j)], \qquad (6.9)$$

as in (8.2). the solution to this maximisation problem yields the reaction function:

$$w(j) = \beta[w(i); n(i), n(j), K(i)], \qquad n(j) = n_1, n_2 \qquad (6.10)$$

The fixed point defined by these reaction functions is the war investment strategy if the jth country does not behave in a strategic manner. It may, however, pay the jth country to behave strategically.

In Figure 6.1, the distribution of wealth is on the vertical axis and the cost of war is on the horizontal axis. We can see that the war investment strategy allocation at a point like b would be preferred to the *status quo* at point a by the jth country if it were of type n_2, but not if it were of type n_1. Thus, if the ith country adopted the deterrence arms investment strategy, the jth country would receive a positive transfer if it were of type n_2 but nothing if it were of type n_1.[10] The uninformed country's problem is to pick both a level of invest-

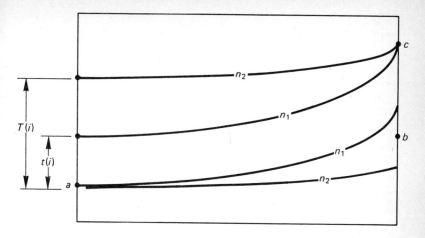

Figure 6.1   War investment allocation and the status quo in the asymmetric information case

ment in weapons in the first period and a transfer in the second period that will maximise its expected utility, given its prior belief p concerning the informed country's utility function and its wealth $K(i)$.

Define $w_d(n_1)$ as the optimal weapons level acquired by an n_1 country if it does not attempt to bluff to make the ith country believe it is of type n_2. Define $w_d(n_2)$ similarly as the optimal weapons level acquired by an n_2 country. The ith country wants to induce the jth country not to fight, and it will attempt to do so by offering a transfer to it of $T(i)$, increasing the country's resources in the second period to $K(j) + T(i)$. There is a probability p, however, that the jth country may bluff, claiming to be of type n_2 in order to receive this transfer.[11]

To prevent this type of bluffing behaviour by the jth country, the ith country will choose a probability q of fighting and a probability $1-q$ of making the transfer $T(i)$. If the conflict allocation is at a point like c, then the lottery would involve a transfer of $T(i)$ to an n_2 country and a transfer of $t(i) < T(i)$ to an n_1 country.

The ith country, knowing that $w_d(n_2)$ is optimal if the jth country is of type n_2, will propose a lottery such that it will give the jth country $T(i)$ with probability $1-q$ and fight with probability q if the jth country chooses $w_d(n_2)$ and will give no transfer if the jth country chooses $w_d(n_1)$. This lottery is chosen so that if the jth country is of type n_2 it will choose the lottery, while if the jth country is of type n_1 it will optimally choose $w_d(n_1)$.

The choice of the lottery, with a probability q of fighting, is intended to prevent bluffing by the opponent, while the choice of the level of weapons is intended to deter the opponent. The equilibrium obtained if the ith (uninformed) country uses this strategy is called a *separating equilibrium*, since it prevents bluffing by separating the n_1 from n_2 countries. Given this strategy, the jth country will choose $w_d(n_1)$ if it is of type n_1 and $w_d(n_2)$ if it is of type n_2. An alternative equilibrium that has been treated in the literature on sequential games is a *pooling equilibrium* where the jth country will choose $w_d(n_2)$ regardless of whether it is of type n_1 or n_2. Country i will choose a strategy leading to a pooling equilibrium if the costs of discriminating between the two types of countries are too high relative to the potential gains from such a separating equilibrium.

If war occurs, the outcome for the ith country is defined as

$$V[w_d(i), w_d(j), n(i)] = a[K(i) + f[w_d(i), w_d(j)]]$$

$$- \frac{[w_d(i) + w_d(j)]}{n(i)} \tag{6.11}$$

Define $V(1)$ to be the outcome of war for the jth country if $n(i) = n_1$ in (11.5) and $V(2)$ to be the outcome of war if $n(i) = n_2$. If the ith country wants to solve for the separating equilibrium, it maximises expected utility, given as:

$$a[x(i)] + p\{a[K(i)]\} + (1 - p)$$
$$\{qV[i] + (1 - q)a[[K(i) - T(i)]]\}, \tag{6.12}$$

that is, the utility of first-period consumption plus the probability of consuming $K(i)$ if the other country is of type n_1, plus the probability of the lottery involving either conflict with probability q or transfers with probability $1 - q$. This maximisation is subject to the incentive constraint that if country j is of type n_2 then it is indifferent between redistribution $T(i)$ and the outcome of a conflict

$$a[K(j) + T(i)] - V[2] = 0 \tag{6.13}$$

while if country j is of type n_1 then it is indifferent between the initial allocation and the lottery

$$a[K(j)] - \{qa[K(j) + T(i) + (1 - q)V[1]\} = 0 \tag{6.14}$$

The maximisation is also subject to the resource constraint

$$K(i) - w_d(i) - x(i) = 0 \qquad (6.15)$$

Let $\psi\,[K(i), n_1, n_2, p]$ be the value of the separating equilibrium solution of the problem.

It should be noted that *the separating equilibrium is not sub-game perfect* and requires pre-commitment on the part of the ith agent, that is to say, after the jth agent reveals that it is (or claims to be) of type n_2, it is no longer optimal for the uninformed country to carry out its declared intentions.[12] Thus the strategy that was optimal in the first period is no longer optimal in the second period, so some form of pre-commitment technology is necessary. We believe, however, that pre-commitment is not just a theoretical problem but is one that occurs in the real world. For example, there are practical alternatives to the deployment of intermediate-range nuclear missiles in Europe, but these alternatives do not pre-commit the USA to defend Europe.

If the ith country wants to compute a pooling equilibrium it maximises

$$a[x(i) + a[K(i) - T(i)] \qquad (6.16)$$

subject to the same incentive constraint as (6.13) and the resource constraint (6.15). Let $\pi\,[K(i), n_1, n_2]$ be the value of the pooling equilibrium solution of the problem.

The difference between the values of the separating and pooling equilibrium is

$$\Delta \equiv \Delta[K(i), n_1, n_2\,p] = \psi\,[K(i), n_1, n_2, p] - \pi\,[K(i), n_1, n_2] \qquad (6.17)$$

If $\Delta > 0$, then the ith country prefers a separating equilibrium to a pooling equilibrium, while if $\Delta < 0$, the ith country prefers a pooling equilibrium to a separating equilibrium.

Theorem 6.1:

$$\frac{d\Delta}{dp} = a[K(i) - \{qV(i) + (1 - q)a[K(i) - T(i)]\} > 0 \qquad (6.18)$$

So the relative value of a separating equilibrium increases as the probability that the other agent is of type n_1 increases.

It should be noted that it is possible that the separating equilibrium may never dominate the pooling equilibrium. Examples can be constructed by scaling the amount of the externality created by the conflict such that for all $K(i)$ the conflict solution is dominated by the *status quo* for both countries regardless of type. In that case, the separating equilibrium would involve no transfers for all $K(i)$ and would thus trivially be a pooling equilibrium. It is possible, however, to show that there always exists a set with positive measure such that the pooling equilibrium will dominate the separating equilibrium for all values of p. This implies that there exist distributions of wealth that are stable and that will not lead to war.

Theorem 6.2: There exists an interval of positive measure, $[k_1, K_2]$, the *stable set*, in the interval $[0, K]$ such that the pooling equilibrium will dominate the separating equilibrium for all values of p.

Theorems 6.1 and 6.2 enable us to characterise the configuration of possible equilibria. We know from theorem 6.2 that p in the stable set results in a pooling equilibrium. Further, for all $K(i)$, the locus of

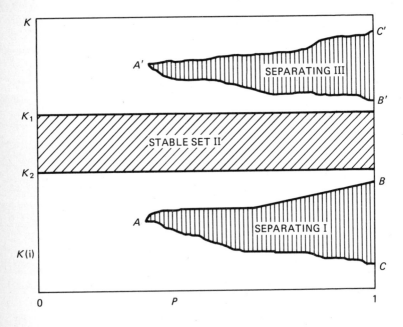

Figure 6.2   Pooling and separating equilibria

points for which $p = 0$ has the property $\Delta < 0$. Thus, if there exist regions in Γ where $\Delta > 0$, the configuration of equilibria is represented as in Figure 6.2. (Note that the variable on the horizontal axis here is p rather than C.) Examining the locus of points such that

$$\Delta[K(i), n_1, n_2, p] = 0 \qquad\qquad (6.19)$$

we find that the boundary between the pooling and separating equilibria is the locus of points illustrated as A–B–C in Figure 6.2. Points above the A–B locus involve a pooling equilibrium, while those below this locus involve a separating equilibrium.

Since $\Delta[K(i), n_1, n_2, 0] < 0$, the point A must lie in the strict interior of the set Γ. Theorem 6.1 implies that the boundaries of A–B and A–C must be monotonic.

Figure 6.2 also shows a locus A–C below which there is no game. If country i has very few resources $K(i)$, then it will allocate all its resources to first-period consumption, leaving nothing for weapon accumulation and thus entailing no conflict with country j. Such a country is, in effect, not wealthy enough to engage in conflict. The locus A–C is downward-sloping, since, as the opponent has a higher probability of the smaller parameter n_1, the expected value of participating in the game in the second period increases because of a lower expected cost of deterrence. The points $A\cdot$, $B\cdot$, and $C\cdot$ refer to comparable points except that the ith country is extracting transfer from the jth country.

For most fixed levels of p, Figure 6.2 shows that an increase in the ith country's resources as measured by $K(i)$ may lead to three distinct types of equilibria. The first, for low values of $K(i)$, is one in which country i does not accumulate weapons at all. The second, for intermediate levels of $K(i)$, is one of a separating equilibrium in which country i accumulates weapons and uses them to deter country j in such a way that there is a probability that war will occur. The third, for levels of $K(i)$ in the stable set, is one of a pooling equilibrium in which i accumulates weapons but has enough weapons so that there is a zero probability that war will occur. At yet higher levels of $K(i)$, the ith country has enough weapons so that it can extract resources from the jth. Finally, when $K(i)$ is large enough, country j does not accumulate weapons at all since $K(j)$ is so small. It is important to note that transfers are from the weak to the strong, the strong nation extracting transfers from the weaker nation.

An unallied minor power is more likely to be uninformed about the characteristics of the other country or, alternatively, that other countries will be uninformed as to its own characteristics. Thus, it is more likely to be involved in situations that result in separating equilibria than established participants. The bottom region I in Figure 6.2 characterises the situation in which a minor power would initiate conflict with a major power, while region III characterises a situation in which a major power would initiate conflict with a minor power. Thus, this theory is consistent with the Siverson–Tennefoss observations that unallied minor powers initiate conflict with major powers with a relatively high frequency.

V CONCLUSIONS AND POTENTIAL EXTENSIONS

We have developed in this paper a formal model in which conflict, war and redistribution may occur. Countries are assumed to behave as rational actors concerned with economic rights to consumption within a two-period model in which force can be used to redistribute these rights.

Using this model we have shown that war can occur, given the structure of this model, in a situation of asymmetric information – where one agent is informed of all parameters of the problem while the other is not informed as to the parameter characterising the utility function of the first agent. In such a situation, war can occur if the uninformed agent adopts a separating equilibrium strategy – in which it pre-commits itself to a positive probability of war in order to prevent bluffing by the informed agent. However, there would be no war if the uninformed agent finds it optimal to adopt a pooling equilibrium strategy, in which it does not attempt to prevent bluffing. This can occur if the distribution of resources is such that it is not in the interest of either country to engage in conflict or if the uninformed country has enough resources to 'bribe' the other country via a transfer of part of its wealth. There would also be no war if either agent has very few resources. The probability of an actual war outcome is greatest when the uninformed agent has sufficient wealth to adopt a separating equilibrium strategy but not sufficient wealth to adopt a pooling equilibrium strategy or when it has sufficient wealth to attempt to extract resources from the other.

These results can be used to address the question as to whether arms races can lead to the outbreak of war. An arms race that leads to a separating equilibrium – in which threats are part of the process of deterrence – has a positive probability of resulting in war. Other things being equal, such an outcome becomes less likely as the distribution of wealth approaches the stable set or as the probability that the opponent will bluff becomes smaller. In such cases, the uninformed agent would adopt a pooling equilibrium, which does not involve threats. The pooling equilibrium is sometimes characterised by a higher level of weapons than the separating equilibrium. In such cases, arms races that do not lead to war but rather to a situation of deterrence are characterised by higher levels of weapon expenditures than arms races that do lead to war.

The model and its results open up a new approach to the study of outbreak of war. The model will, in subsequent work, be extended to the case of symmetric uncertainty, uncertainty over technology and resources as well as uncertainty over preferences, private as well as public 'bads' resulting from war, and other similar considerations. By extending the basic model, it will be possible to address such issues as technological change and the qualitative arms race and cooperative solutions to the arms race in the form of arms limitation agreements and other arms control measures.

Notes and References

1. For a review of formal research on conflict theory see Intriligator, M. D., 'Research on Conflict Theory: Analytic Approaches and Kreps Areas of Application', *Journal of Conflict Resolution* (1982) 26, pp. 307, 327.
2. Bueno de Mesquita, B., *The War Trap*, (New Haven, Connecticut: Yale University Press, 1981).
3. Wallace, M. D., 'Arms Races and Escalation: Some New Evidence', *Journal of Conflict Resolution* (1979) 23, pp. 3–16.
4. Wallace, M. D., 'Armaments and Escalation: Two Competing Hypotheses', *International Studies Quarterly* (1982) 26, pp. 37–56.
5. Siverson, R. and Tennefoss, M., 'Power, Alliances and the International Conflict, 1815–1965', *American Political Science Review* (1983) 78, pp. 1057–69.
6. Smith, T. C., 'Arms Race Instability and War', *Journal of Conflict Resolution* (1980) 24, pp. 253–84.
7. This assumption is made so that the game is such that an agent has the option of not participating. The utility level of zero (0) can be thought of as the utility of staying home as opposed to engaging in adventures abroad in order to acquire a right to a share of total goods available, K, which, in turn, could be thought of as representing gains from international trade and diplomacy.

8.   This particular basis for uncertainty is not crucial to the properties of the model. For example, we could have modelled the problem as one of uncertainty in the technology of conflict, where the jth agent is uncertain as to the ith agent's effectiveness. What is crucial is that there is uncertainty for the jth agent about the cost and/or outcome of conflict. Also we could have formulated the uncertainty in other ways, for example, a continuous distribution over the parameter $n(i)$ reflecting the beliefs of agent j.

9.   The redistribution function $f[v(i), v(j)]$ plays a role similar to that of the threat-point in an earlier work on the Nash bargaining problem, see Brito, D. L., Buoncristiani, A. M., and Intriligator, M. D., 'A New Approach to the Nash Bargaining Problem', *Econometrica* (1977) 45, pp. 1163–72.

10.   We realise that we are avoiding the problem of determining how the surplus created by not fighting is distributed in a bargaining situation. For the sake of simplicity, we are assigning the entire surplus to the party making the transfer. Clearly any rule from axiomatic bargaining theory could also be used.

11.   The idea that the threats could be used as a screening mechanism was, to our knowledge, first used by Sanford Morton in a 1979 informal working paper at Carnegie-Mellon University, which later appeared in a revised form (see Morton, S., 'The Optimality of Strikes in Labor Negotiations', Murphy Institute of Political Economy Discussion Paper, Tulane University, New Orleans, Los Angeles, (1983)) and independently by Beth Hayes in her thesis at the University of Pennsylvania.

12.   For a discussion of perfectness, see Kreps, D. and Wilson, R., 'Sequential Equilibria', *Econometrica* (1982) 50, pp. 863–94.

COMMENT

Walter Isard
PENNSYLVANIA UNIVERSITY

The authors set out the model in which Nation *I* uses some of its resources for military purposes, and some for consumption – the consumption giving it a certain flow of utility: and Nation *J* likewise. To that analysis is added a further refinement. Each nation has a certain measure of the disutility of warfare – it maybe a high disutility or a low disutility. However, neither nation knows how the other nation regards warfare – whether it gives it a high or low disutility. So probabilities have to be attached to these alternative possibilities. To this must be further added another probability – the relative probability of war or no-war. So this model can generate a situation, for instance, in which Nation *I* has the choice of either giving up some of its resources for consumption to Nation *J*, and losing utility in that way, but avoiding war; or alternatively it can accept the disutility of war in defending its flow of consumable resources.

The model is an attractive one – not least because the authors make their assumptions clear. But of course there are a great many other models. For example, an alternative arms race model is one in which there is collusion between the military–industrial complexes of the USA and the USSR. Each side will overstate its military capability, and this in turn will enable the other side to put in a claim for more resources in order to match that overstated capability. Defence bureaucracies have of course their own utility function which depends heavily on their budgets.

It is also possible to have a model determining the level of military expenditure which depends entirely on the bureaucratic processes in one country. In the USA it would cover for example, an attempt to model something of the relationship between the President and Congress; it could use the concept of adaptive expectations. When the President put in a request for an increase in military expenditure over the previous year, the size of the increase requested would be heavily influenced by the percentage increase requested, and the percentage increase agreed by Congress, in the previous fiscal year.

7 Economic Considerations in the Comparison Between Assured Destruction and Assured Survival

Martin C. McGuire*
UNIVERSITY OF MARYLAND

One consequence of the Reagan Administration's intensified R & D efforts on strategic defence has been to re-enliven debate over Assured Destruction versus Assured Survival as alternative strategies for managing the nuclear threat of humanity. As between these two doctrines clarification of the issues is to be achieved by investigating the *incentives* each side might confront under alternative assumptions as to the outcome of SDI research including (i) incentives to deploy various strategic systems and (ii) incentives to utilise them. This chapter will utilise the concepts of *goods, preferences, technology*, and cost to investigate (i) how an assured survival strategy might come to rival an assured destruction strategy; (ii) how new, defensive-oriented cost and technology might influence the stability of the arms race; and (iii) how new cost and technology structures might influence strategic doctrines or objectives including incentives to refrain from striking first. Emphasis is placed on the relative costs of deterrence versus defence plus the degree of technological jointness in the production of these two capabilities as crucial determinants of the incentive structure of interest. Costs matter, both as positive predictors of potential future behaviour of great powers, and as normative criteria for strategic decision. The paper derives alternative cost measures for comparing offensive *vs* defensive effectiveness.

In exploring these incentives structures, we distinguish defence budget competition from allocative interaction between deterrence and defence within fixed budgets. This distinction points to several important results. One is to identify possibilities for instability in reciprocal defence–offence allocation processes. Another is to illuminate how the effects of arms-budget competition between adversaries depends on the jointness of production of defensive and offensive strength. If defensive and offensive outcomes can be chosen independent of each other, a higher strategic budget will generally attenuate the effects of allocative competition. However, if deterrence and defence are jointly produced – more or less in fixed proportions – competitive budget increases will cause hypothetical war outcomes to evolve toward extreme corner solutions. But on balance, an ascendancy of defence – that is, of the capability to support an Assured Survival strategy at a relative cost advantage – does not appear necessarily to threaten pernicious or destabilising incentives for the arms race.

I believe we can all agree that the cornerstone of our strategic policy must continue to be the deterrence of a deliberate nuclear attack against either the USA or its allies . . . I am convinced that our forces must be sufficiently large to possess an 'Assured Destruction' capability – an ability to inflict at all times and under all foreseeable conditions an unacceptable degree of damage upon any single aggressor, or combination of aggressors – even after absorbing a surprise attack. One can add many refinements to this basic concept, but the fundamental principle involved is simply this: it is the clear and present ability to destroy the attacker as a viable twentieth century nation and an unwavering will to use these forces in retaliation to a nuclear attack upon ourselves or our allies that provides the deterrent, and not the ability partially to limit damage to ourselves.[1]

We seek to render obsolete the balance of terror – or 'Mutual Assured Destruction', as it is called – and replace it with a system incapable of initiating armed conflict or causing mass destruction, yet effective in preventing war. Now, this is not and should never be misconstrued as just another method of protecting missile silos:

- The means to intercept ballistic missiles during their early boost-phase of trajectory would enable us fundamentally to change our strategic assumptions, permitting us to shift our emphasis from offence to defence.
- We are not discussing a concept just to enhance deterrence, but rather a new kind of deterrence; not just an addition to our offensive forces, but research to determine the feasibility of a comprehensive non-nuclear defensive system – a shield that could prevent nuclear weapons from reaching their targets.[2]

I INTRODUCTION

Here are two quotes which fairly stake out the territory of dispute as between advocates of assured destruction and advocates of assured survival. As between these two doctrines disagreement may arise along many dimensions, moral, political, economic, strategic, etc. This chapter is written in the conviction that irrespective of such differences clarification of the issues is to be achieved by investigating the *incentives* which each side might control under alternative assumptions as to the outcome of SDI research. The economic incentives to be explored fall into two categories: (i) incentives to deploy various strategic systems and (ii) incentives to utilise them. This essay will utilise the concepts of *goods*, *preferences*, *technology*, and *cost* to investigate (a) how an assured survival strategy might come to rival an assured destruction strategy; (b) how new, defensive oriented cost and technology might influence the stability of the arms race; and (c) how new cost and technology structures might influence strategic doctrine/objectives including incentives to refrain from striking first.

The strategic and political stakes in the research context over 'star wars' are extremely – fantastically – high and it would be imprudent to assume that a multi-billion SDI research programme will never identify a feasible, cheap, cost-effective defence technology. Careful specification of the economic structure of competition between assured destruction and survival is essential in clarifying the values, costs, and risks of SDI.[3] Costs matter, both as positive predictors of potential future behaviour of great powers, and as normative criteria for strategic decision. When resources of the magnitude in question here are devoted to defensive research, new incentive relations may emerge.

1 Preliminary Analytics: Relative Costs and Production Complementarities between Deterrence and Defence

Since McNamara's foresightful statements some twenty years ago, the momentum of the arms race has led us to a situation of total reliance on 'Mutual Assured Destruction' for essentially two reasons. First, the relative costs of population protection have remained high and correspondingly those of population destruction have become ever more cheap. It has been so much cheaper to overwhelm defensive measures than to incur the costs of the defence that both sides have essentially abandoned hope of population protection (although less decisively in the Soviet Union). Second, (and somewhat paradoxically), there has been a convergence of defensive/ offensive technologies such that *if* a country could pursue defence of its own population unilaterally, it would necessarily threaten even greater damage to an adversary. The reason for this is that when missiles become more and more accurate – as early studies demonstrated[4] – pre-emptive attack or even delayed response against unused enemy missiles is the cheapest way to save the first X-million lives in nuclear war.[5] Accordingly, even a deterrent strategy with emphasis on reliable second-strike punishment of an aggressor tends to produce a strong component of damage limitation. Analogously a defensive strategy, cost-effectively pursued, tends to generate a strong deterrent or retaliatory component as a by-product.

Figure 7.1 summarises the interplay between technology, cost, strategic objectives, and preferences which have produced these trends. From an economic perspective, decisions to procure and deploy strategic nuclear forces should be viewed (no matter how distasteful or depressing this might be to the analyst) as decisions to purchase a particular range of potential nuclear war outcomes, a range which depends on how the war might start, and the targeting patterns and restraint exercised by each side throughout the war as well as force levels and characteristics.[6] Implicitly or explicitly, the combined evaluations of these factors by the various hierarchies of government are all based on how much damage arms threaten an enemy (D_j; $j = 2, 1$) in the event of war, and how much survival they offer their possessors (D_i; $i = 1, 2$). Such evaluations will be represented here by a function of the variables D_1 and D_2.[7] Figure 7.1 shows two indifference curves taken from a single preference function for side 1, V_1^0 and V_2^0.

The technological environment as reflected in the opposing forces determines the defence and deterrent options open to each side for a certain expenditure. The options allowed by two such budget levels for side 1 are shown as $B_1 < B_2$ in the figure. The choice of level and mix of arms may then be represented as the selection of a point such as 'a', where the total expenditure on arms is balanced against other wants, and the particular deterrent or defence strategy is indicated by the relative concentration on threatening damage to the adversary versus protecting own population.[8] Evidently, the choice of strategy – whether the basic objective is to deter nuclear attack, or to protect own population from nuclear attack – depends on prefe-

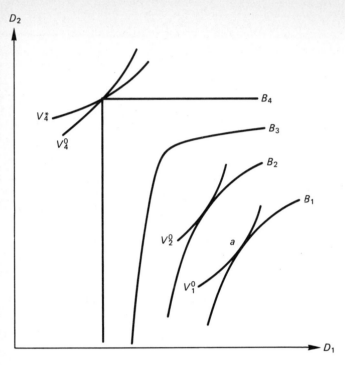

Figure 7.1   The choice between damage-inflicting and damage-averting strategies as determined by technology, costs, and preferences. If D_1 and D_2 are joint products of the same technology, strategic preferences between deterrence and defence matter less

rences and on technology. When technology is such as to make deterrence much cheaper than defence, outcomes in the north-east part of the figure are likely. If relative costs strongly favoured defence, outcomes closer to the origin would be likely. The actual evolution of technology having favoured deterrence in recent history has produced the first kind of outcome.

The second important cumulative development over recent years has been the convergence of offensive and defensive technologies. The two capabilities of deterrence and defence have increasingly become joint products of one single complex missile and anti-missile system. The physical and economic differences between systems which deter and those which defence has diminished. The effect of this development is illustrated by comparison of B_2 to B_3. With budget B_3 the technology has shifted so that the *trade-off* possibilities between D_1 and D_2 are very slight, compared with the wider range under B_2. This second feature, convergence of offensive and defensive technologies, has another result; as systems become multipurpose, the choice of preferred combinations of population protection and retaliatory capability will appear more and more dominated by technology and less by strategic preference. An extreme case of this is illustrated by B_4. Complete convergence of offensive and defensive systems results in the effective elimination of choice between deterrence and defence (for any single budget level) – an effect illustrated in the diagram by the fact the V_4^0 and V_4^* representing *different* strategic preferences generate the *same* choice of (D_1, D_2). This result has a further implication; the introduction of new, technically superior systems which are dual purpose, that is, both offensive and defensive, means that when arguing for the purchase of the new system, one need not decide in advance which strategy, deterrence or defence, should be elected. This ambiguity fairly characterises the arguments once advanced for ABM and the MIRV, and sometimes now made for SDI to the effect that SDI discoveries can be used to protect *missiles*.

II HISTORICAL ILLUSTRATION OF THE EFFECTS OF RELATIVE COSTS AND JOINT PRODUCTS: THE DETERRENT STRATEGY, THE MIRV, AND BALLISTIC MISSILE DEFENCE

With despairing remarks on the mad momentum of the arms race Robert McNamara announced the last major armaments decision of his tenure, namely the decision to recommend a limited Anti-Ballistic Missile System (ABM).[9] Earlier the more significant, if less publicised decision to deploy Multiple Independently Targetable Re-entry Vehicles (MIRVs) on US strategic land- and sea-based missiles had been announced. The demise of the ABM further illustrates how the evolution of strategic weapons, the doctrines for their hypothetical employment, and treaties for their control, have all exclusively endorsed the primacy of assured destruction. As argued above, hindsight now suggests two major economic factors in the choice of assured destruction as the primary great power strategy. First and most important, relative costs favoured this strategy. During the early years of the arms race (until the later 1960s) because of the relative invulnerability of strategic *weapons* both sides would have preferred to be the *target* of counterforce attack rather than to strike first themselves. That is, early in the nuclear era relative costs produced the following order of preference for both sides (where '>' means 'is preferred to').

No nuclear exchange	>	'Ride out' counterforce attack then retaliate or threaten to do so	>	Attack the adversary's strategic weapons and 'ride out' his retaliation

Figure 7.2(a) illustrates the war outcome options open to the two great powers until about 1968; outcome α represents 'No War'; β_1 represents '1 strikes first with maximum counterforce attack'; β_2 represents '2 strikes first with maximum counterforce attack'; γ represents all-out counter-city exchange. Evidently $U_1(\alpha) > U_1(\beta_2) > U_1(\beta_1)$; this generalises to $U_i(\alpha) > U_i(\beta_i)$.

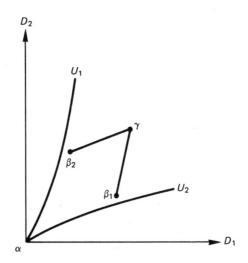

Note U_1 and U_2 are indifference curves for side 1 and 2 respectively, indicating preferences between inflicting and preventing damage. Line β_2–γ indicates the range of possible war outcomes if side 2 strikes first; and line β_1–γ indicates the range of possible war outcomes if side 1 strikes first. In each case the range arises from alternative targetting strategies by the side initiating the war. As shown, no damage (point α) is preferred to war, and both sides prefer retaliation to war initiation.

Figure 7.2(a)   War damage outcome configurations which make retaliation preferable to initiation

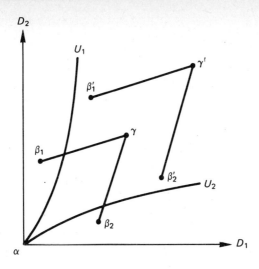

Note Lines β_1–γ and β_2–γ indicate the range of war damage outcomes if sides 1 and 2 respectively initiate. Initiation may be preferred to peace (point α) and is definitely preferred to retaliation. The cone β'_1 –γ'–β'_2 shows that an increase in overall armaments on both sides shifts the range of war outcomes so that point α is most preferred by both sides.

Figure 7.2(b)   War damage outcome configurations which make initiation preferable to retaliation

Since the late 1960s and the introduction of the MIRV technology, however, there has been a slow but cumulative shift toward the situation portrayed by Figure 7.2(b). The relative desirability of being attacked over attacking first has reversed. Because of the dramatic improvements in missile accuracy, either side can virtually disarm the other of its fixed land-based ICBMs. Given roughly symmetry of preferences, shown by the indifference curves U_1 and U_2 drawn in Figure 7.2(b), it is not at all certain that at the old force levels it would have remained true that both sides prefer peace. It seems quite feasible that $U_1(\beta_i) > U_i(\alpha) > U_i(\beta_j)$. However, this perilous combination has been forestalled through increases in overall weapons inventories on both sides, so that the present situation can be roughly illustrated by the points γ'_1, β'_1, β'_2. The overall destructive power at the disposal of both sides has increased by so much that the minimum 'residual' damage to populations and societies must make peace the rationally preferred outcome, that is,

$U_i(\alpha) > U_i(\beta_i) > U_i(\beta_j)$ despite the reversal in preferences as between being victim and aggressor.

The cause of this ominous reversal has been not merely a change in relative costs, but also a convergence of technologies for deterrence and defence. This convergence is strikingly illustrated if we consider the interaction between local ballistic missile defence (BMD) and highly accurate multiple warhead missiles. These illustrations fall into four categories: (1) MIRVs considered in isolation, (2) MIRVs against an enemy BMD, (3) BMD in isolation, (4) BMD against enemy MIRVs.

1 Multiple Warheads

The specific impact of MIRVs on deterrence versus defence incentives is best evaluated in two contexts: first against an enemy who has not deployed a BMD system; and second, against one who has. In both cases the underlying technical fact is that with every improvement in accuracy, missile forces acquire greater potential for limiting the possible damage to their owner by destroying the enemy's missiles before they are launched. Hence, missiles initially purchased for their deterrence value come to have a defensive capability once they are fitted with MIRVs.

(a) MIRVs against an adversary with no BMD

Were there any incentives for a nuclear power which faced an adversary not possessed of ballistic missile defence to make a substitution of MIRVs for single warheads within its strategic forces? To the extent that some value attached to greater population survival, an incentive existed: *for the MIRV, considered in isolation*, is primarily a weapon to limit damage. MIRVs allow the number of accurate ICBM warheads to be increased more than in proportion to total ICBM cost increase. That is, employed against an enemy with neither BMD nor MIRVs they significantly raised his cost of deterrence relative to defence. Hence, one would expect some pressure to substitute the cheaper for the more expensive capability. In other words, this new technology provided an incentive to convert a hitherto deterrent weapon to a deterrent/defensive weapon. One consequence of these incentives – as explained above – is to reverse the order of preference between striking first and second. These destabilising implications of MIRVs were drowned out only by successive increases in force levels.

It should be noted that MIRVs change the relative costs for *both* parties even if only one side deploys them. Just as they make it relatively cheap for one side to destroy another's missiles, so they raise the costs of maintaining a secure retaliatory force to that other side.[10] And the cheapest, most cost-effective response to the threat of MIRVs is itself to fit the existing force with MIRVs.

(b) MIRVs against BMD

Suppose next that the adversary does possess an ABM/BMD system. Now the incentives for deploying MIRVs are rather different. In this case, the convergence of defensive and deterrent technologies is crucial. For the same technology is required to penetrate an enemy BMD system (that is, maintain deterrence) as to deliver multiple independently targetable weapons against enemy weapons (that is, increase damage limitation. A conservative nuclear power, therefore, desiring solely to maintain assured destruction will see incentives to deploy a MIRV force to penetrate the enemy BMD. This deterrent force, as argued above, will have a significant defensive potential. But, even if no value is attached to the added defensive capability gained, there would be great incentives for the development of such a MIRV force because, for securing deterrence in the face of an ABM, MIRV-penetration-aid technology, while expensive, is much cheaper than other available systems (for example, building a great many more single-warhead boosters). In short, MIRVs may appear to be a necessary ingredient to a conservative deterrent strategy yet, at the same time, a powerful inducement – because of their joint product character – to shift strategy in favour of defence. *Hence, those who argued for the deployment of MIRVs never had to state or even decide if they meant to be altering US strategy*, and in fact they never did so state or decide (just the case illustrated by V_4^0, V_4^* and B_4 in Figure 7.1).

2 Missile Defence

Now consider why a power might develop and procure an anti-missile system. Again two contexts deserve analysis: where an adversary has and has not deployed MIRVs.

(c) BMD against Single Warheads

Had the Soviets not deployed MIRVs or other penetration aids, then a US ABM system could have bought substantial population protection at a considerably lower cost than was available under the old blast-fall-out-shelter formula. And with MIRVs in the USA inventory, ABM defence should have looked even more cost-effective. One important characteristic of BMD systems is that their damage-limiting performance is much higher when they face a missile force already partially depleted by ICBM attack, than when they must absorb a full undepleted missile force. Hence, MIRVs and ABM in combination – against an adversary with no MIRVs – reinforce still further the arguments already made as to the influence of relative costs on deterrence/defence strategy. In the event, however, the Soviets did in fact deploy MIRVs, demonstrating a capacity to undercut the viability of ABM.

(d)   BMD against MIRVs

Lastly, what is the value of BMD system when an adversary does deploy MIRVs? In the Nixon era the ABM was advertised as a *deterrent* or retaliatory weapon, which is a back-up argument not unheard in the debates over SDI – namely, that at a minimum SDI will maintain a secure, reliable, retaliatory, assured-destruction capability. One of the many methods for protecting one's retaliatory capability when challenged by MIRVs is an active, anti-missile defence of one's own retaliatory missile force. If this latter method is advocated, *proponents of SDI need not even decide whether they mean to alter US strategy in favour of damage limitation*. Evidently President Reagan's introductory quotation seems meant to preclude this type of ambiguity (see note 2).

III   THE ECONOMIC COMPETITION BETWEEN ATTACK AND DEFENCE

In addition to technical discoveries and developments attributable to the colossal expenditures on ABM research, we now have a sophisticated set of analytic tools and models available for estimating the course of strategic battles over a wide range of defence–offence combinations. Since the earliest studies, it has been known that the most cost-effective deterrent forces will usually consist of a combination of various arms, that is, missiles, bombers, submarines, surface ships, and so on. Similarly, the most cost-effective defence against strategic attack will almost always combine passive defences such as sheltering and evacuation with active defences such as air defence, ballistic missile terminal defence (and conjecturally given SDI development, mis-course and boost-phase missile defence) plus defence against SLBMs, cruise missiles, and so on. The optimal mix by attacker and defender will depend strongly on the opponent's force combination, on the information available to either side during a war and abilities to use such information (for example, missile reprogramming capabilities), on the sequence of actions (who moves first, second, and so on), on the degree of restraint and bargaining pursued during crises including exchange of fire, and on many other factors.

With so many ingredients and so much uncertainty, it is impossible to represent the entire problem as consisting of a few variables. Nevertheless, a great deal of insight regarding trends can be summarised in a picture such as Figure 7.3, which plots isoquants or constant outcome contours for one party to a strategic nuclear exchange as a function of attacker's and defender's budgetary outlays on attack and defence forces respectively. Attack expenditures are denoted a_j, and defence expenditures are denoted d_i. Each combination (a_j, d_i) generates a loss or damage D_i for the defender, according to $d_i = \phi(a_j, d_i)$. As shown, the rate at which defence and offence expenditures cancel each other out will typically depend on the level of each expenditure. That rate can be written:

$$f_i = \left. \frac{\partial d_i}{\partial a_j} \right/ \overline{D_i} = -\frac{\partial \phi_i / \partial a_j}{\partial \phi_i / \partial d_i} \tag{7.1}$$

This marginal rate of technical substitution between offensive and defensive effort can also be written $f_i = f_i(a_j, d_i)$ or $f_i = F_i(D_i, d_i)$, to indicate that relative marginal productivities will depend on the isodamage contours and on defensive budgetary effort.[11]

How these relative marginal productivities vary systematically for different values of a_k, d_k and D_k, $(k = i, j)$ is of the upmost importance for the viability of deterrence over defence, or of defence over deterrence, and, therefore, for the direction in which the arms competition between the superpowers evolves, including its stability. The shape and location of such isodamage contours will vary with the assumed scenario the war takes. For example, if based on the assumption that j shoots first, the contours D_i may all be shifted to the right compared with a scenario in which i shoots first. Notice also

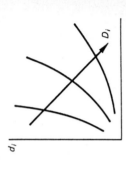

Figure 7.3(c)   Constant attack advantage at low damage levels; constant defence advantage at high damages

Figure 7.3(a)   Uniform advantage to the defence

Figure 7.3(b)   Uniform advantage to the offence

Figure 7.3(d)   Attack advantage at high damage levels; defence advantage at low damages

Figure 7.3(e)   Increasing advantage to defence at higher budget damage and higher levels

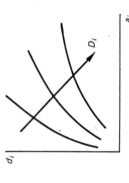

Figure 7.3(f)   Increasing advantage to defence at lower damage and lower budget levels

d_i :   Strategic defensive expenditures by side i
a_j :   Strategic offensive expenditures by side j
D_i :   Equal damage contours for side i ; higher damage contours in the direction of the arrow

that there may be systematic variation in the shapes and locations of these D_i contours. Figure 7.3 shows a variety of possible configurations.

Our purpose now is to understand better how underlying technology and economics as reflected in such maps of isoquants may induce alternative patterns of behaviour as between two adversaries in a bipolar system. Could some of the configurations in Figure 7.3 lead to insurmountable advantage for the offence and others for defence? What are the implications of alternative defence/offence combinations for stability in arms competition? for stability of peace?

1 Production Relationships between Deterrence and Defence: Are They Substitutes or Joint Products?

We have conjectured that one explanation for the evolution of mutual assured destruction over the past three decades derives from production complementarities between deterrence and defence. Here, we want to consider further the implications of such complementarities. To begin, we must be clear about the meaning of 'complementarity' in this context and in particular that we refer to complementarities *in production*. It may be true that deterrence (which requires an ability to punish others) can complement or substitute for defence (the ability to defeat or avoid punishment by others) in so far as each influences a nation's geopolitical power. For some purposes these two capabilities may reinforce each other, and for others conflict. This type of complementarity or substitutability, however, is not what we mean to identify here. The relationship at issue here is the connection between the *production* of the abilities (a) to threaten retaliation against others on the one hand and (b) to defeat such threats of the other. Our argument is that when both capabilities are produced as joint products of the same weapon systems, the evolution of the point (D_1, D_2) as in Figure 7.1 will be in the direction of one corner (north-east, that is potential mutual annihilation or south-west, that is mutual survival). By contrast, when deterrence and defence employ different technologies so that *within* a given budget resources can be allocated to generate more defence at the expense of less deterrence (and *vice versa*), then the evolution of such a point will be more likely to occupy a middle ground in the *interior* of the diagram depending on the relative costs of deterrence over defence.

These inferences can be derived in a straightforward manner by combining damage contour maps for two rivals. Figure 7.4 shows equal-damage contours for side 1 and side 2 as a function of offensive expenditure and defensive expenditure. Notation is defined as:

a_1 = 1's strategic offensive budget
d_1 = 1's strategic defensive budget
a_2 = 2's strategic offensive budget
d_2 = 2's strategic defensive budget

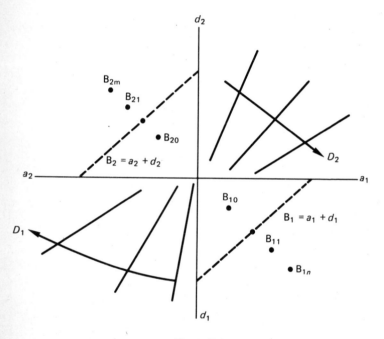

Figure 7.4

with damage D_1 and D_2 increasing in the direction of the arrows. If for a given overall strategic budget, resources could be allocated *between* defensive and offensive capabilities, then with totals $B_1 = a_1 + d_1$ and $B_2 = a_2 + d_2$, each side could pick one point on its budget line – shown as a broken line in the figure. However, when no trade-offs between a_i and d_i are possible, or when only very limited trade-offs are allowed, the dashed lines collapse to points, with larger or smaller overall budget combinations shown by points

$B_{10} < B_{11} < B_{12} \ldots B_{1n}$ and by $B_{20} < B_{21} < B_{22} \ldots B_{2m}$ and so on.

Now each combination (B_{1k}, B_{2l}), $(k = 1 \ldots n; l = 1 \ldots m)$ produces a specific outcome in the space D_1, D_2. If we map the points $D_1^{k,l}$ and $D_2^{k,l}$ into a single diagram, we will obtain a pattern for Figure 7.4 as depending on (a) the locations of equal-damage contours (b) the relative proportions in which budget outlays produce defensive and offensive capabilities and (c) the relative budgets of the two adversaries. Figure 7.5 shows the two alternative basic patterns derived from Figure 7.4. Point α shows an initial configuration of defence budgets together with implied deterrence–defence postures.

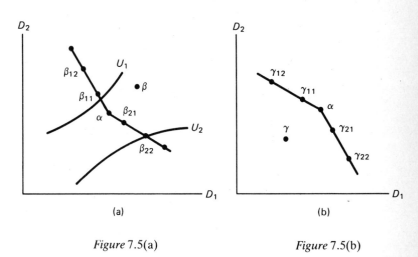

Figure 7.5(a)   Figure 7.5(b)

Assuming that both sides pursue an arms-budget competition, the figure illustrates two generic outcomes. Suppose first that the proportionate deterrence–defence components in each sides' technology are strongly weighted toward deterrence capability; then as budgets expand, the point α will drift towards β. Budget increments from side 1 only will produce points along the line α, β_{11}, β_{12}, . . . Similarly, budget increments by side 2 only will produce the points along the line α, β_{21}, β_{22}, . . . If either side assumed that the other would not react to its budget challenge, it would perceive its deterrence–defence opportunities to lie along the relevant opportunity set $\alpha \ldots B_{i,j}$ $(i = 1,2\ j = k,l)$. Next note that if side 1 never reaches satiation for D_1 or D_2, its indifference curves will always display a positive slope – that is, it will always be willing to trade some defence for deterrence. In this case side 1 would want to move along $\alpha. . .B_{1k}$ *indefinitely* or until its defence budget pinches off further provision. Since side 1's preference function does not reach a maximum along $\alpha - B_{1k}$ (that is, the indifference map is nowhere tangent to the opportunity curve) it follows that movement along that curve will tend to continue indefinitely until the marginal utility of resources foregone terminates such expansion. Moreover, economic growth will reduce the restraining influence of budget constraint on ever-increasing allocations to deterrence–defence. This analysis implies that, if deterrence and defence are produced as joint products in both countries and deterrent components predominate, the evolution of weapon configurations will lead towards the north-east corner in Figure 7.5 – that is, towards a world of 100 per cent mutual assured destruction and specifically away from interior points such as one might conjecture lay along the contract curve of mutual tangencies between U_1 and U_2.

What is the outcome of such joint-product allocation processes if the *defence* predominates? again neither side will find an interior solution along its opportunity set $\alpha. . .\gamma$ (see Figure 7.5(b)) and competitive arms configuration will drift toward the south-west corner of the figure (that is, minimal risk of population loss). Since it is commonly argued that very low damage outcomes may generate incentives for one or both sides to pre-empt,[12] this second sequence of events where defence dominates might be thought to be more dangerous than the first where deterrence dominates and the disincentive to pre-empt becomes increasingly greater as budgets grow. Judgement on this question ought to be reserved, however, until the effect of a reliable defensive capability on the stability of no-first-use is better understood.

2   Trade-offs between Attack and Defence: Relative Cost Considerations

For some elements of strategic-weapon systems, essentially no trade-offs exist between their offensive and defensive components. An ABM which necessarily protects both people and weapons is a good example. However, for other elements, weapons systems may be more defence- or attack-specific. For example, resources allocated to air defence against bombers have very slight value for protecting weapons, they only engage weapons which have already been committed to destruction of population (or of other values). The same distinction applies to passive defence measures such as sheltering and evacuation. And one can readily imagine missile defence systems which in no way threaten destruction of an adversary's weapons before they are used and therefore provide him with no incentive to use those weapons in a hurry before they are destroyed. Bubbles over cities, continental-wide electromagnetic atmospheric jamming, shrapnel in space, and space-based exo-atmospheric interceptors would seem to fall into this category.[13]

When weapons can be categorised into offensive and defensive in this manner, for any total budget b_i the allocation *between* offensive and defensive capabilities becomes a crucial choice – that is, the choice of which allocation to choose *along* the line $b_i = a_i + d_i$ becomes crucial. We can now show how this choice depends on the relative cost of increasing the enemy's damage in the event of war versus reducing own damage. Figures 7.6 and 7.7 illustrate the supreme importance of the relative costs of protection versus destruction for this choice. In each figure panel (a) indicates gross trade-offs between resources expended and damage, combining two figures similar to Figure 7.3. Figure 7.6 pictures a case where defence is more expensive than destruction and moreover becomes increasingly expensive the lower the damage level. (For instance to limit population loss to 60 per cent a defender might have to outspend an attacker 2:1 at the margin, while a marginal ratio of 4:1 obtained at 40 per cent damage and eight to one at 20 per cent.) Contrariwise, Figure 7.7 pictures the opposite case where defence is cheaper than destruction, although less cheap at very low damage levels. (Now for example the defence:offence marginal cost ratio required to limit damage to 60 per cent might be 1:8, while 40 per cent destruction would require 1:4 and 20 per cent would require1:2.)[14] In all these cases the damage functions for sides 1 and 2 will be written as:

$$D_1 = \phi_1(a_2, d_1)$$
$$D_2 = \phi_2(a_1, d_2) \tag{7.2}$$

where as before D_i indicates damage suffered by country i, and a_i, d_i indicate resources devoted by country 1 or 2 to attack and defence respectively. Thus, the slope of damage contours in panel (a) of either figure is given by expressions as in equation 7.1. Constant-output contour D_i has as its slope, f_i, the ratio of marginal productivities of a unit of resources devoted to the attack or defence. Evidently, these trade-off functions themselves depend upon (a) the level of

140

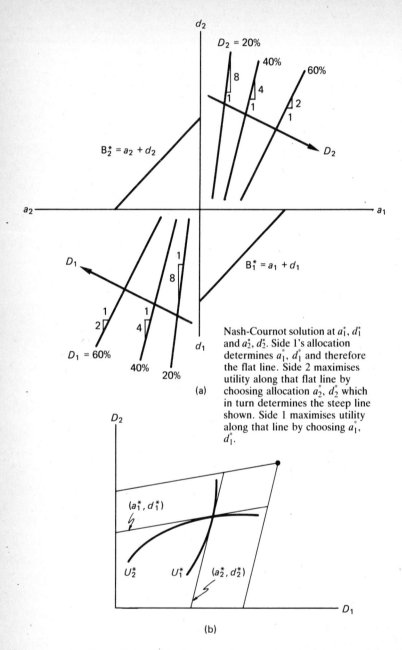

Figure 7.6   Cost advantage favours offence

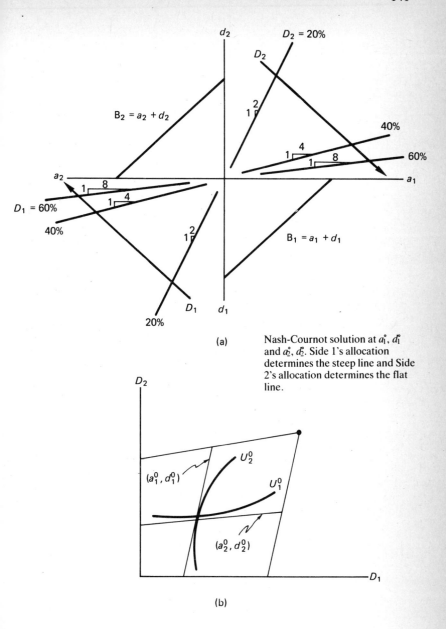

(a)

Nash-Cournot solution at a_1°, d_1° and a_2°, d_2°. Side 1's allocation determines the steep line and Side 2's allocation determines the flat line.

(b)

Figure 7.7   Cost advantage favours protection

damage at which they are to be evaluated, (b) which type of general
competition exists between offence and defence as pictures in Figure
7.4, and (c) whether it is the defence or offence which has a general
technical advantage. In general, however, for all contingencies we
would expect:

$$\phi_a^1 = \partial\phi_1/\partial a_2 > 0$$
$$\phi_d^1 = \partial\phi_1/\partial d_1 < 0$$
$$\partial_a^2 = \partial\phi_2/\partial a_1 > 0 \tag{7.3}$$
$$\phi_d^2 = \partial\phi_2/\partial d_2 < 0$$

The second panel (b) in each of Figures 7.6 and 7.7 translates a part
of the information contained in the first panel (a) into more compact
form to indicate how the functions ϕ_2 and ϕ_2, the budget constraints,
and the strategic preferences of both sides interact when trade-offs
are possible between offence and defence. Panel (b) plots alternative
feasible damage outcomes, D_1 and D_2, which a particular budget
combination B_1^*, B_2^* can produce. In each figure the set of feasible war
outcomes is represented by the diamond-shaped area. In Figure
7.6(b), side 1 through its choice of budget allocation a_1^*, d_1^* determines
one particular *flat* line. Side 2 chooses a point on that line by its
decision as to how to allocate B_2^* between attack and defence.
Similarly, side 2 determines which *steep* line is available to side 1; by
choosing particular values a_2^* and d_2^*, side 2 limits 1's choice to one
particular steep line. The criterion for the line determined by (a_1^*, d_1^*)
to be flatter or steeper than the line determined by (a_2^*, d_2^*) can now
be employed to give an operational meaning to the idea that defence
is relatively more costly than offence or *vice versa*. A simple raw
criterion for cost-competitive superiority of offence over defence
would be as follows:

Raw criterion

$$\phi_a^2 > -\phi_d^2 \text{ or } 1 > \frac{-\phi_d^2}{\phi_a^2}$$
$$\tag{7.4}$$
$$\phi_a^1 > -\phi_d^1 : \text{ or } \frac{\phi_a^1}{-\phi_d^1} > 1$$

Under this criterion a marginal dollar of side 2's attack budget produces more damage than a marginal dollar of side 1's defence budget would defeat or avert. Similarly a marginal dollar of side 1's attack budget would cause more damage than a marginal dollar of side 2's defence budget prevents. Thus a raw criterion for the ascendancy of the offence (defence) over the defence (offence) requires inter-country resource comaprisons. A less demanding, more operational criterion only requires intra-country cost comparisons. This is a criterion based on the *comparative* slopes of each side's budget lines. Thus, if as pictured in Figure 7.6(b), it is cheaper at the margin for both sides to injure an enemy than to reduce own damage, the slope of side 1's budget line must be flat *in comparison* with the slope of side 2's budget constraint. Accordingly this slope or comparative-advantage criterion for the ascendancy of offence requires:

Comparative advantage in destruction

$$\frac{\partial D_2}{\partial D_1}(a_1, d_1, a_2^*, d_2^*)\bigg/_{\bar{B}_1} > \frac{\partial D_2}{\partial D_1}(a_1^*, d_1^*, a_2, d_2)\bigg/_{\bar{B}_2} \tag{7.5}$$

where the bar-notation, a, d indicates variables are held constant at value a^*, d^*. That is:

$$\frac{\phi_a^2}{-\phi_d^1} > \frac{-\phi_d^2}{\phi_a^1}; \quad \text{or} \quad \frac{\phi_a^1}{-\phi_d^1} > \frac{-\phi_d^2}{\phi_a^2} \tag{7.6}$$

Examination of equations (7.4) and (7.6) indicates that (7.4) is a lesser included category of (7.6). Next, in contrast with (7.6) and (7.8) ascendancy of the defence requires a reversal of slopes as in Figure 7.7. The general criterion is:

Comparative Advantage in Defence

$$\frac{\partial D_2}{\partial D_1}\bigg/_{\bar{B}_1} < \frac{\partial D_2}{\partial D_1}\bigg/_{\bar{B}_2} \tag{7.7}$$

that is:

$$\frac{\phi_a^2}{-\phi_d^1} < \frac{-\phi_d^2}{\phi_a^1}; \quad \text{or} \quad \frac{\phi_a^1}{-\phi_d^1} > \frac{-\phi_d^2}{\phi_a^2} \tag{7.8}$$

IV OFFENSIVE AND DEFENSIVE ARMS RACE PROCESSES

Given that assured destruction is cheap and assured survival dear, and given that major SDI breakthroughs just might reverse the relative costs, what difference does it or would it make in the continuing process of weapons accumulation? We will use the analytics developed above to discuss three important elements of this question; (a) whether the incentive to spend on arms is inherently more stimulated by one technology or the other; (b) whether a qualitative difference in the allocation *between* defence and offence can be attributed to the different technologies (for instance, defence-favouring and offence-favouring cost-relationships; (c) whether the stability of armament processes changes in a systematic fashion when destruction or protection is cheaper.

To help with these questions – in a preliminary way at least – reference is made again to Figures 7.6 and 7.7 – which were drawn to contrast the implications of offensive versus defensive superiority. First, each figure shows that where there is scope for choice *between* deterrence and defence an interior solution with indifference curves tangent to opportunity lines is plausible, and less extreme solutions closer to the diagonal of the box are to be expected. Moreover, when cost conditions favour the offence, Nash-Cournot outcomes in the allocation game between offence and defence will produce higher damage levels than on the contract curve of Pareto-optimal combinations. On the other hand, when cost conditions favour the defence, Nash-Cournot outcomes will lie inside the contract curve of Pareto-optimal combinations. Evidently the allocation between deterrence and defence within fixed budgets is a duopoly-type game for both adversaries; as such, Stackelberg leader/follower and other non-zero-conjectural-variation reaction functions are available to describe alternative modes of behaviour and resulting equilibria solutions among arms race competitors. Thus allocation games between destruction and protection may constitute an important part of the analysis leading to decisions to deploy.

Another difference to follow from a comparative cost advantage for offence or defence relates to the consequences of *budget competition* by the two adversaries, that is competitive expansions of arms-race budgets in contrast to competitive allocations of a given total budget between offence and defence. If cost and technology favour destruction then strategic budget growth will enlarge the proportion of allocative outcomes in the north-east region of the picture, whereas if costs favour protection, the proportion of allocative outcomes near the origin will increase. This rather qualitative analysis, however, in no way suggests that one cost/technology configuration is inherently more likely to lead to greater overall arms-budget competition.

1 Stability of Allocation Outcomes

Other things being equal, a smaller range of outcomes involving very high damage levels is arguably more desirable from a world perspective. More germane to the analysis of offensive versus defensive arms races, however, is how protection-favouring cost and technology might affect the incentives to accumulate arms. Exhaustive analyses of arms races suggest that those driven essentially by deterrence motives tend toward a stable equilibrium solution while those driven by a motives to survive generate unstable 'solutions'.[15] Such analyses have uniformly assumed, however, that each side's strategic weapons produce higher deterrence *and* defence as joint products, as in Figure 7.1. The relevant question in our context, therefore, becomes whether protection-favouring technology/cost will also generate similar instability in the arms acquistion competition.

It appears that such instability should not generally carry over to the defensive arms race context for several reasons. First, the source of the instability of assured survival under joint-product technology is precisely that with defence and offence produced in fixed proportions increasing one side's protection will necessarily reduce the other's survival. If this joint-product linkage is broken, the basic cause of the instability disappears. Second, the relative cost advantage which destruction yields over protection is itself a function of arms-budget levels; in which event either adversary can influence which portion of the 'Damage-Space' diagram (for example, Figure 7.6(b) or 7.7(b)) obtains by selection of its budget.

Limited analysis at this stage suggests that the interaction between subjective preferences and objective opportunities might direct an offensive–defensive arms race towards a stable compromise, towards progressively higher potential damage levels, towards minimal potential damage in both sides, or just possibly towards one-sided asymmetry with one country concentrating on offensive and the other on defensive weapons. Of particular interest, is the outcome of Nash-Cournot allocation behaviour under such diverse circumstances and how these naive, myopic, utility-maximising choices for each side interact with overall budget decisions.

2   Assured Destruction, Assured Survival and Stability of No-First-Use

In a world where populations are helplessly vulnerable to annihilation from strategic nuclear weapons, it is supremely important that both adversaries with weapons of mass destruction be reassured that the *weapons* of both are safe. In the world today it is in the USA's (USSR's) interest that the USSR (USA) know their weapons are safe and invulnerable. Otherwise the tragic, possibly undeniable, temptation arises to use weapons before they are destroyed. Such has been the situation over the past three decades up to the present day. Since strategic weapons can cause losses of immense value – the loss of entire societies – destroying those weapons would remove an effective instrument of threat, punishment, vengeance, and so on from their owner's arsenal.

Although it is fairly obvious, it should nevertheless be most strongly emphasised that the instability produced by a threat to the security of another's *weapons* derives entirely from the fact that those weapons *are effective* at causing damage. There is temptation to use weapons before they might be destroyed only if they can be used for something. Accordingly it follows that the more a particular type of offensive weapon can be rendered *ineffective no matter whenever it is used*, the less is the temptation to use the weapon early just because its security is at risk.[16] It follows that a technically effective and cost-effective defensive technology will not necessarily exacerbate the temptation to initiate usage. A comprehensive picture of the effects of defence requires knowledge of how the mechanics and structure of force characteristics influence incentives to refrain from attack. An important ingredient in such structure relates to how war outcomes are moulded by three components: (i) whether side 1 designs its forces on the assumption that it will initiate a war with a first strike and its adversary will only strike second in retaliation, or instead designs its forces on the assumption the enemy will strike first; (ii) whether side 2 designs for a first or second strike; and (iii) which side in fact initiates a war.[17] Evidently many other factors influence outcomes; such factors as target choice, restraints on forces, as well as threats and bargaining during a war may be the most important. Still, technology and costs of strategic defence may work either way to stabilise or destabilise the reciprocal decision to refrain from or merely postpone attack. Under some cost and technology assumptions, if war occurs, the side to initiate it would come out ahead. There it is the utterly disastrous consequences of the *best* war outcome compared with peace which provides each side with the incentive to refrain from attack. These configurations, nevertheless, generate cascading instabilities if either adversary forms the opinion that war is imminently inevitable. Such, to a rough approximation, is the present situation marked as it is by many times more MIRV warheads than launchers (SLBMs and aircraft provides some measure of stability but fixed ICBM forces are essentially vulnerable to complete elimination). Under other cost and technology assumptions it can be genuinely preferable to defend, so that retaliation dominates war initiation. An important element in the first set of assumptions (although not the only one) will be that technology and costs favour destruction, while an important element in the second set is just the opposite.

V SUMMARY AND CONCLUSION

This chapter has been motivated by two presuppositions. The first is that reasonable appraisal of assured survival as an alternative to assured destruction will be advanced by an understanding of the incentive structure which a successful SDI research outcome would create. The second is that relative costs of deterrence versus defence plus the degree of technological jointness in the production of these two goods are crucial determinants of the incentive structure of interest.

In exploring these incentive structures, we have distinguished defence budget competition from allocative interaction between deterrence and defence within fixed budgets. This distinction points to several important results. One is the number of possibilities for instability in reciprocal defence–offence allocation processes. Second, the effects of budget competition can depend on the joint production issue. If defensive and offensive outcomes can be chosen independent of each other, a higher strategic budget will generally attenuate the effects of allocative competition. However, if deterrence and defence are jointly produced – more or less in fixed proportions – competitive-budget increases will cause the hypothetical war outcomes to evolve toward extreme corner solutions. But on balance, an ascendancy of defence – that is of the capability to support an assured survival strategy at a relative cost advantage – does not appear necessarily to create pernicious or destabilising incentives for the arms race.

Notes and References

* Department of Economics University of Maryland. This was written while the author was Visiting Professor, Osaka University. Support from the Department of Economics, Osaka University, and from the Japanese Fulbright Commission is gratefully acknowledged.

1. *Statement by Secretary of Defense, Robert S. McNamara on the Fiscal Year 1969–73 Defense Program and the 1969 Defense Budget*, p. 47.
2. Speech by President Ronald M. Reagan to the National Space Club, 29 March 1985.
3. Without some further clarification along such lines, it is unclear whether critics of SDI regard it as undesirable because it may succeed or because it may fail.
4. See Office of the Director of Defense Research and Engineering, *Damage Limiting – A Rationale for the Allocation of Resources by the US and the USSR*, May 1964.
5. Depending on assumptions, X may range from 10 to 100.
6. These hypothetical war outcomes figure in the evaluation of strategic security in three ways: first, they influence the underlying incentives to avoid nuclear war and provocations which may lead to nuclear exchange. Second, they influence the stability of the mutual restraint which leads both sides to avoid attack even if they think that an attack might be imminent. Last, the (virtually unimaginable) amount of destruction which actually would occur in a nuclear war is of intrinsic importance.
7. Apart from the likelihood that such preferences are very complex, their general character will depend critically on side i's perception of the adversary (j), to what degree he is an enemy, the rationality or irrationality of his leadership, the degree to which i's and j's national interests or world ambitions conflict, the character of communication between adversaries and consequently the level of trust and suspicion. All these factors and others determine each side's perception of the threat posed by the other.
8. The interactive character of the arms race stems from the fact that the other side (side 2) must make parallel choices, which, in turn, influence the options open to side 1. For a choice such as point 'a' to represent an equilibrium, therefore, it must be made in reaction to an equilibrium choice of strategy by the opposite side.
9. 'There is a kind of mad momentum intrinsic to the development of nuclear weaponry. If a weapon system works – and works well – there is a strong pressure from many directions to procure and deploy the

weapon out of all proportion to the prudent level required' (Speech to UPI Editors and Publishers, Fairmount Hotel, San Francisco, California: 18 September 1967).

10.   In evaluating MIRVs as a damage-limiting device, US planners had to allow for the fact that the greater the delay in using them, the more their cost-effectiveness is degraded. From the Soviet viewpoint US MIRVs unambiguously raise the cost of maintaining a secure reliable Soviet deterrent force, since that capability must be calculated as surviving a US attack. The Soviet alternatives for maintaining deterrence have all been very expensive, for example, changing to SLBM, hardening their missile sites, multiplying the number of sites, and so on, *except for a response of retro-fitting with* MIRVs.

11.   Of course the functional relationships compressed into equations such as ϕ_i or f_i assume the appropriate level of engineering optimisation in the background.

12.   Michael Intriligator, 'Strategic Considerations in the Richardson Model of Arms Races', *Journal of Political Economy*, 1975, pp. 339–54.

13.   In general a passive defence system which blocks increasing numbers of enemy re-entry vehicles without proportionate cost increases will confer a cost-advantage on the defence. Generally such an advantage to the defence will exploit some natural protective resource. One such may be an advantage in communication and intelligence. And a defence system which is effective or becomes activated only *after* and attacker launches his force will eliminate the incentive to launch *in a hurry*.

14.   In this chapter we assume symmetry with regard to these relative costs for comparison between side 1 and side 2. In reality, however, the US population and industrial structure is more concentrated than that of the USSR. For some imaginable defensive systems such concentration would be an advantage for the defence, and for other imaginable defensive configurations it would be a disadvantage. The interaction relative defensive–offensive costs and the geographical–physical configuration of population and industry should be significant for both positive and normative analyses of how various countries might react to SDI or actual defence deployments.

15.   See, for example, Martin C. McGuire, *Secrecy and the Arms Race* (Cambridge, Massachusetts: Harvard University Press, 1965).

16.   And the less rationale for acquiring the weapon in the first place, it might be added.

17.   There is no assumption that war will, in fact, break out. This is a heuristic calculation to determine the incentives which can preclude its outbreak. Naturally, both sides can design for the same or for different assumptions; both may prove to be right, both wrong, or either are right and the other wrong.

COMMENT

Kurt W. Rothschild
VIENNA

Professor McGuire's interesting chapter contains a lot of material for discussion both with regard to factual content and to methodology. Even if I were fully at home in his field of studies (which I am not) I could not hope to do full justice to his essay in this short contribution. All I can do is to raise some questions and express some doubts which might give rise to further discussions.

McGuire's chapter deals with the vital problem of possible threats and chances in a world of nuclear armaments and SDI proposals. A central idea in this chapter is that these weapon systems and their deployment can be oriented especially towards deterrence or especially towards defence, but that normally the two effects cannot be completely separated so that deterrence and defence are necessarily joint products. There is a certain vagueness in the paper as to the extent of this complementarity on the production side. At the beginning McGuire stresses the complementarity aspect and sees a 'cumulative development over recent years [for the] convergence of offensive and defensive technologies'. It would be interesting to discuss whether this is so and whether one can expect this to be a continuing trend; but the main point here is that in the later parts of his paper McGuire does assume a considerable flexibility in the combination of deterrence and defence, and this provides the basis for his central theme: the analysis of incentives and choices between different military technologies, and their possible effects with regard to war prevention or war results.

The choice process is pictured as a decision regarding the allocation of a given budget (the size of which is not explained) between offensive and defensive capabilities so as to maximise a utility function in which the expected damage (in terms of lives?) of the adversary in case of war enters with a positive sign and the damage suffered by one's own side with a negative sign. The choice problem is thus equivalent to the traditional choice problems in economic theory (in consumption and production) with 'costs' being given by the technologically determined trade-offs between defensive allocations (reducing one's own damage) and offensive allocations (increasing the adversary's damage).

Before I turn to some methodological questions I want to mention a few difficulties I have with the basic framework. One concerns the choice variables. The possible outcomes of strategies (underlying the utility and production choices) are points in the D_1 D_2-plane (where D_1 is damage suffered by the decision maker and D_2 damage suffered by the adversary). Now, the corner points of this setting have a clear meaning. $D_1 = D_2 = 0$ means that peace is preserved; $D_1 = D_2 = 100$ per cent means complete destruction of both sides. But what about intermediate points? Is the combination of certain D_1-D_2 values a basis for strategic choices? Does it make sense to compare damage combinations of $D_1 = 30$, $D_2 = 40$ per cent with $D_1 = 35$ and $D_2 = 42$? Surely, the target function of military strategy is to gain victory in case of war at the lowest possible cost in lives and material to oneself. A high D_2 cannot compensate for losing a war. And I doubt whether a reliable relationship can be established between D_1 and D_2 on the one hand and victory on the other, though a certain correlation will obviously exist.

My second point is more of a political nature. While I recognise that theoretical analyses have to be restrictive and that a two-dimensional presentation has many advantages, I find it dangerous – at the present moment more than ever – to create the impression that the question of a nuclear holocaust depends mainly on the way nuclear technologies develop and on a 'proper' choice between their defensive and offensive aspects. The question of assured destruction or assured survival – which gives the essay its dramatic quality – will most likely depend on the capacity of the actors to bring in *other* determinants for choice, in particular political parameters which – like verification procedures, improved communication in a political and technical sense, confidence-building activities, etc. – could not only provide new chances in themselves but could also change the offensive–defensive mix of existing weapon systems. The whole idea of Geneva and other conferences is directed towards this possibility.

I now turn to the methodological side of the paper. It is here that I have serious doubts. In order to avoid misunderstandings let me – to begin with – stress two points. First, there is no doubt that McGuire has used the tools of traditional economic analysis – of production theory, duopoly theory, game theory – in a very circumspective and imaginative manner and has derived from them some interesting and valuable insights. Second, I am fully aware that it is always easy to attack a theoretical paper for its 'unrealistic' assumptions or for neglecting this or that point. This is a mistake I shall try to avoid. I fully admit that an economic theoretical analysis has to introduce drastic simplifications if it is to be feasible at all. My doubts are not directed against the 'reductionism' as such but are concerned with the question whether the traditional economic tools are adequate for the present problem.

As we know, economic analysis has developed a powerful structure to deal with problems of rational choice and decision-making on the individual level. This structure has proved extremely successful when dealing with some central problems of a market economy. This in turn has provided a great temptation to treat a large number of semi-economic and non-economic themes with similar tools in a similar manner. Gary Becker's attempts to shed light on our love affairs with the aid of the economic tool-kit are a telling example of this tendency. Sometimes it can yield valuable results but it also runs into the danger of missing the special qualities of a special subject.

I believe that in the present case this danger is a very real one. McGuire adapts the cost-preference decision model of traditional consumption and production theory to the choice and incentive problems of nuclear strategy. I want to suggest that this analogy suffers from fundamental differences in the two cases both with regard to the preference (utility) side and to the 'cost' side.

Let me start with the preference (utility) structure. To get definite results McGuire needs stable and continuous preference structures as we know them in consumption theory. Now we know that indifference curves are strictly speaking an instrument for picturing individual preferences, and that we run into considerable conceptual difficulties when we try to construct aggregated social indifference curves. Still, such social preference curves can be accepted as an approximation for behaviour in stable groups. But when McGuire speaks of the utility functions of 'Side 1' or 'Side 2' he refers to very special complex groups with very complex decision processes where differing interests of armament firms, of military leaders from different service branches, of a small group of politicians, and of a small group of scientists clash with each other and are resolved in a complicated interplay which cannot be captured – with the best of will – by smooth and twice differentiable indifference curves and D_1 and D_2 as arguments. If we have to look to economics for help in shedding light on the decision processes in the world of the military–industrial establishment we should turn towards the attempts of organisation theory and of some contemporary theories of the firm and of corporations which try to grapple with such complicated and changing interactions of different interests.

The situation is just as critical when we turn to the 'production' side. Quite apart from the principal difficulties of giving concrete content to D_1 and D_2 (that is, to the trade-off between damage at home and damage abroad) there is the decisive fact that in the field of nuclear armaments (and military strategy in general) conditions are so different from normal production surfaces that the application of normal production theory becomes very questionable indeed.

The latter is designed to deal with the choice of technique in a static environment where a large number of alternative blueprints are available and a cost-efficient process is selected. In the military case the situation is completely different. It is characterised by an extremely dynamic setting where new technologies are constantly turning up, with little time and few opportunities for testing and learning processes. Change and uncertainty are the dominating features; the idea of stable and continuous production functions and clear trade-offs can hardly be relevant for such a situation. Rather, a few focal alternatives will be under discussion from which one has to be selected on a basis which ranges from incomplete information to wild speculations. Again, if it has to be economic theory to which we turn it should not be the traditional production and duopoly theory with their clear-cut results. We should try to take some cues from approaches in investment and/or planning theory (where similar problems arise), even if they have no very definite results to offer so far.

In addition to these difficulties of thinking in terms of reliable and continuous production surfaces (producing attack and defence) there is a further serious problem. In the military field the allocation of a *given* budget to *existing* technological alternatives does not seem to be the main mechanism which charts the course towards survival or destruction. I would suggest that what we see today is a well-funded, fairly autonomous technological development which constantly throws up *new* military applications which do not so much lead to a very careful selection process aiming at allocational efficiency but to a considerable pressure for ever higher budgets.[1] An analysis of the forces which determine the size of military budgets and their development may, therefore, be a decisive element in any study of further trends towards militarisation or arms reduction and the strategies connected with them. Certain parallels could perhaps be found in the economics of health services where we also find an overriding target (saving lives), a stream of new and expensive technologies, and a constant quest for higher budgets with allocation taking second place.

In conclusion I would, therefore, submit that while the chapter certainly throws up important questions and indicates an interesting taxonomy of possible developments it would be important to investigate very carefully the limitations of the traditional tools and to experiment with alternative approaches.

Note

1.   The amount of waste and obsolescence in the military sphere seems to be considerable.

8 Economic Warfare between the Superpowers

Murray Wolfson
OREGON STATE UNIVERSITY

and John P. Farrell
OREGON STATE UNIVERSITY

Open-ended arms races subject to the constraints of production possibility frontiers become an instrument of economic warfare in which one country can force reduced consumption and investment on its opponent by requiring them to keep in step. In the presence of differing factor endowments both nations may wage economic war against each other. War must be understood as the projection of national power through means that are economic and political as well as military. The danger to peace is that a power losing the economic war might undertake a preventive military war while it still has a chance.

Our calculations suggest a linear Soviet arms growth and a parabolic US trend since the Vietnam War. Were these trends to continue the USA would soon overtake the USSR and by 1990 would present them with the three alternatives of submission, abandonment of acceleration of capital formation rates and improvement in consumption per capita, or launching a pre-emptive war as weaker nations may do when they see the tide running against them.

It is to be hoped that policy-makers will manage the economic war, so as to achieve a reduction in arms acquisition in the context of a general political settlement.

I INTRODUCTION

It is a commonplace of history that wars and preparations for wars have decisively altered the course of national economies for the worse – or the better. Yet the economic cost of war is more than a simple consequence to one's own country of the expenses of military

155

exigency; costs can be projected on to an opponent by his need to stay in step militarily. Hence, the arms race itself becomes an instrument of conflict which we call economic warfare. Political, military and economic instruments all enter as arguments into that function which projects national power.

Economic war fulfils all the classic functions of war. It destroys the capacity to resist, inflicts unacceptable costs, and imposes the political will of the victor. We will show how the expenditure forced upon each other by both the superpowers in the arms race shape the economic warfare between them. We conclude that the greatest danger to peace is that a nation losing war in the economic dimension may choose to substitute the military instrument if that seems to yield even a small positive probability of success. We show that it is impossible narrowly to define military deterrence separately from the economics of the arms race. The arms race is not a harmless, though somewhat expensive form of aggressive display in which both parties can assure the destruction of the other, and both are deterred from doing so. Rather, it is an economic war that runs the risk of becoming military warfare.

Our point of departure is a paper by Wolfson which developed as a criticism of the well-known Intriligator–Brito deterrence model of the arms race.[1,2] It showed that in the presence of scarce resources arms races between countries with differing absolute or relative factor endowments cannot continue escalating in their open-ended rough parity as Intriligator–Brito suggest, without imposing intolerable economic costs. Included in those costs is the loss of capacity to produce armaments in the future.

Intriligator and Brito have stressed that their model refers to the nuclear-missile arms race which is only a relatively small part of the defence budget. In the USA in 1983, $9.3 bn was spent on missiles out of a total defence budget of $207.2 bn.[3] Yet, since the delivery and protection systems of the armed forces are either complementary to nuclear missiles or substitutes for them, the Intriligator–Brito pure-deterrence account of the arms race is plausible only to the degree that: (1) strictly nuclear-missile deterrence can be isolated from other dimensions of the long-term military–economic–political conflict; and (2) increases in expenditures on missile systems such as the Strategic Defence Initiative (SDI) and its Soviet counterparts do not change in order of magnitude.

Our concern in studying the US–Soviet antagonism is the danger of the outbreak of any war between them – nuclear or conventional.

Therefore we analyse total military activity in its economic aspects. Nevertheless, it will prove convenient to adapt the Intriligator–Brito model to our purposes by broadening its specifically nuclear missile aspects into a generalised military-power arms race.

For our purposes, we schematise the USSR as a fully employed although inefficient and sluggish labour-intensive economy; and the USA as a capital-intensive economy with greater productive capacity which experiences intermittent periods of slack resources. By comparing the impact of military expenditures on these two systems, we show how the arms race is related to the economic warfare between them.

II   THE INTRILIGATOR–BRITO MODEL OF THE ARMS RACE

The Intriligator–Brito model consists of a system of differential equations that relate missile stocks at the outset of war to their use and destruction in the course of missile war itself. The dynamic and specifically missile-related aspect of the model concerns the process of war once initiated. Since we are not concerned with the progress of the war, but its initiation, these terms (which are of negative exponential form and tend rapidly to zero) do not concern us.[4] We are left with the boundaries between war initiation and the maintenance of peace through mutual deterrence.

The boundaries of deterrence are given in terms of the following variables: M_a and M_b stand for the missile stock; f_a and f_b are the efficiency of missiles in destroying other missiles; and K_a and K_b equal the minimum unacceptable level of casualties of each country in terms of the efficiency of opponents' missiles in inflicting casualties. Then A deters B when $M_a \geq f_b M_b + K_b$ and B deters A when $M_b \geq f_a M_a + K_a$. Regions of attack by one or both countries are bounded by these relations where inequalities are reversed. Roughly translated, the first equation says that the number of missiles belonging to A is greater than or equal to B's capacity to destroy A's missiles, and still leave A with enough missiles to inflict unacceptable casualties on B. Symmetry gives us the second equation.[5] Clearly the definition of deterrence given above is not limited to missiles, but applies to any military interaction. The missile stock variables can be generalised as military power which can be directed toward destroying other military power with given efficiency, or toward inflicting casualties on the opposing population.

Intriligator and Brito partition the arms race into regions shown in Figure 8.1. They come to the conclusion that there exist regions of mutual deterrence where both countries are capable of inflicting unacceptable casualties on each other in retaliatory strikes; there are regions of war initiation where neither country fears that it will be the victim of unacceptable retaliation, and either may strike; and there are unstable regions where war may be initiated by one of the parties but not by the other.

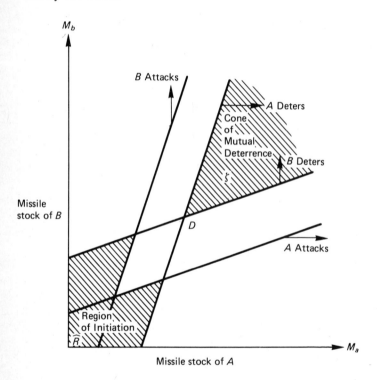

Figure 8.1   Deterring and initiating regions in the weapons plane

III   A MODEL OF ECONOMIC WARFARE

Let us now construct a highly simplified static model of an economy of a country B which is engaged in an arms race with A. We present a general model first, and then specify the characteristics of the Soviet and US economies.

1. Deterrence

Country B takes the military power acquisition of its opponent as exogenous. That means that it must at least deter A from attacking it, but in this model it does not consider bargaining or otherwise inducing A to lower its level of armaments. By deterrence B modifies the behaviour of A in *using* its military power. Then:

$$M_b \geq f_a M_a + K_a \tag{8.1}$$

2. Production Possibilities

Country B must decide whether to produce military power M or civilian goods C_b with its scarce resources. It operates on or within its production possibility frontier which is taken as convex and downward sloping. Equality in (8.2) implies full employment of all factors.

$$H(M_b, C_b) \leq 0 \tag{8.2}$$

3. Saving and Investment in the Civilian Economy

By identity, the civilian output is either consumed, Eb, or saved. We will assume macroeconomic equilibrium and equate savings with gross investment, I_b^g, so we can write the identity:

$$E_b + I_b^g \equiv C_b \tag{8.3}$$

If we permit ourselves to express this physical relationship in money terms, as we will have to do when we attempt to measure these magnitudes:

$$E_b + I_b^g + M_b \equiv GNP_b \tag{8.3'}$$

The *behavioural* decision to save a portion of the civilian product depends on the nature of the country involved. In a capitalist country savings out of civilian income depends on the level of disposable income (not the same as civilian income due to tax finance of public civilian goods), interest rates and the array of individual preferences and distributions of wealth that economists usually impound in *ceteris paribus*. Despite the complexities of government fiscal policy and individual choice, it would seem reasonable to construct a simple constant average propensity to save out of civilian income as a first approximation.

$$I_b^g = S \ C_b \tag{8.4}$$

In a communist economy matters are not nearly as clear since the decision whether to save or consume is taken primarily from the supply side in terms of the central planning authorities' decision to produce capital, military or consumer goods. At the same time, these decisions cannot be made in total disregard of the willingness of the population to accept the division, since work incentives, not to speak of public order, must be considered.

Qualitatively speaking there is a mixture of individual and public choice involved in both social systems. Clearly the Soviet government has reacted to a perceived military threat by increasing its propensity to save as well as direct production of armaments. We will try to place some empirical and historical flesh on this statement. For the purposes of setting out our model, however, let us take equations (8.1)–(8.4) as our point of departure.

These four equations permit us to make a static model of the impact of the arms race on B, treating A as exogenous. That is as far as we will go in this paper. Clearly it would be possible to construct a model for country A given the military preparations of B. If B did more than minimally deter A, then A would at least have to deter the enlarged expenditures of B. To solve the equations simultaneously we would need to know the reaction of each country to the other's preparations, in a Richardson-style representation that may or may not have equilibrium points. Instead, let us assume at first that equation (8.1) is satisfied with equality, and that B simply attempts to deter A. Where appropriate, we will relax this assumption.

The mapping from M_a to I_b^g is given in Figure 8.2, where we will take it that all the equations are met with equality implying minimum deterrence, full employment and constant average propensity to save. Since the slope of this mapping is the composition of the slopes of the positive slope of (8.1) and (8.4) and the negative slope of (8.2), gross investment in B is negatively related to the military expenditures of A which determines it. Thus, even though the capital markets

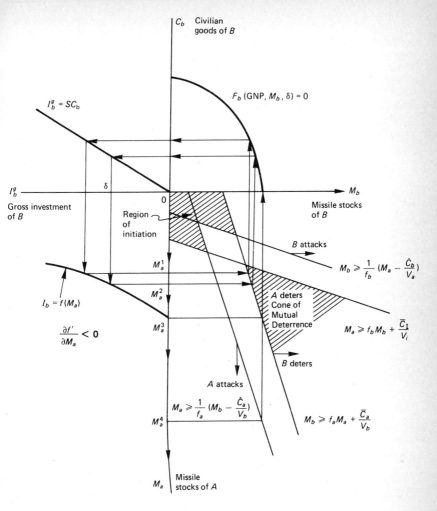

Figure 8.2   Levels of economic warfare

of these two countries may be separated by social systems, they are nonetheless linked by the arms race between them.

Now we can distinguish degrees of intensity of economic warfare waged by A against B:

(1)   *Crowding out.*   For any positive M_a a cost is imposed on the civilian sector of B. The matching increased M_b is paid for through

reduced civilian income by reduced consumption or by reduced capital accumulation.

(2) *Destruction of capital.*   Take it that the rate of depreciation of capital per annum is given by δ shown on the investment axis. If A goes beyond M_a^2 the level of gross investment falls below this amount, the capital stock is destroyed and with it the capacity to produce military as well as civilian goods. B is losing the war.

(3) *Negotiation from strength.*   If the military strength of A exceeds M_a^3, B does not have the capacity to inflict unacceptable casualties on A in response to A's initial attack even if it were to devote *all* it resources to military production. A can impose its terms on B.

(4) *Initiation of war.*   If A achieves M_a^4, it can destroy all the military power which B can muster, and suffer only an acceptable number of casualties itself. A may go further than imposing its political will on B, and may destroy it.

This very simple model may be extended in ways that add realism and relevance to present circumstances. Each of these could be formalised with profit, but that is beyond the scope of the present paper.

1.   We have already mentioned the presumption that the opponent's arms procurement is exogenous to the planning of each antagonist. Deterrence refers to the use or threat to use arms rather than their acquisition. In reality there is a strategic game afoot in which each party attempts – by threat or inducement – to deter the other from *acquiring* the arms with which to attack or deter. Clearly this is part of the process of debate over the Strategic Defense Initiative as well as less exotic weaponry.

2.   This static representation of the arms race can be broadened as a process to consider the dynamics of economic growth on one hand and the development of military power over time on the other. Even in the absence of a variational formalism, it is immediately obvious that the diversion of resources from the civilian sector today reduces the investment and consumption return to labour and other factors which is the basis for military power tomorrow.[6]

3. The resource base for economic warfare transcends national lines. Both contending parties have access to the labour and capital resources of other countries so that a more complete model would include these sources and the nature of their linkage to the superpowers.

One means of using foreign resources is the fighting of proxy military and economic wars by client-states such as has taken place in Korea, Indo-China, the Middle East, and Central America since the Second World War. In many of these situations, the USA has found itself combating a labour-intensive opponent.

Less obvious is the ability of the USA to mobilise world resources through international capital markets in its capital-intensive economic war. The present arms build-up is carried on under an international regime of floating exchange rates and relatively restrictive monetary policy in the USA. The resulting interest rate squeeze of deficit-financed military expansion has resulted in unilateral transfers of funds to the USA which is the counterpart of the balance-of-trade deficit which brings net real foreign resources into the country.

IV CAN BOTH PARTIES WAGE EFFECTIVE ECONOMIC WARFARE AGAINST EACH OTHER?

To answer this question, we must study the military power function. At least at first, let us think of military power as a single-valued function of the various human and material implements of war. We divide these into 'high-technology' (H) and 'low-technology' (S) instruments. Presumably, H represents capital-intensive and S represents labour-intensive means of war.

$$M_i = f_i(H, S), \quad i = A, B \tag{8.5}$$

Clearly the amount of military power is constrained by the resources which each country possesses, and is willing to divert from the civilian economy. For any C, we have a *military production possibility frontier* of S and H producible with the remaining resources.

$$G_i(H, S; C) = 0, \quad i = A, B \tag{8.6}$$

We assume that these functions possess the usual slopes and convexities assigned to them by economic theory.

Now fix the minimum size of the civilian economy C_o which A is willing to endure. Then for any civilian economy of A greater than or equal to that level $(C > C_o)$,[7] country A *absolutely dominates* B, if for *any* civilian economy of B, and for any combination of S and H on A's military-production possibility frontier, A attains military-power superiority $M_a > M_b$. That is essentially the model of economic warfare we presented initially where A could drive all the way to war initiation, M_a^4, and destroy B if it so desired. A exerts *limited domination* over B if in the A economy there exists $C > C_o$ compared with *some* current attainable civilian economy of B such that the inequality in military power holds for all S and H. In the presence of the threat from A, B will contract its civilian economy and enlarge its military to keep A from expanding to the critical value M_a^4 of war initiation.

Since the present arms race has obviously not – yet – achieved a state of absolute domination – and probably not limited domination – by either party, and since both the USA and USSR have different factor endowments, it must be that for the relevant choice of C the military-production possibility frontiers intersect as shown in Figure 8.3 where they are labelled T_a and T_b. Even though there is no domination for *all* combinations of S and H, it must be the case that each nation *can* dominate the other for those combination of instruments in which it has a 'comparative advantage', and for the given levels of C for both parties.

That means that deterrence has two aspects, adjusting the instrument-mix in the military-power function and changing the level of resources diverted from the civilian to the military sector.

The first is if country A were to match the military power of B by adjusting the combination of instruments in which A has the comparative advantage. Under the static circumstances portrayed in this diagram, a sufficient condition for mutual deterrence is perfect information, identical military-power functions, and the existence of suitable slopes for both military-power and military-production possibility frontiers. Then each country could deter the other by moving to a common 'isoquant' labelled M, producing the same level of military power by different means in accordance with their own factor endowments at points α and β respectively. If it were not physically or politically possible to deter B, even waging war with its optimal instrument mix, then it must do so by decreasing its civilian economy.

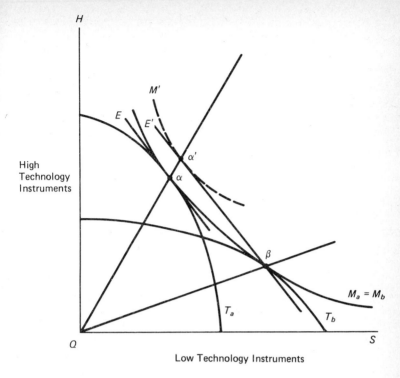

Figure 8.3   Economic war with different factor endowments

In this way, *A* might successfully wage economic warfare against *B* by enlarging its capital-intensive, high-technology instruments. But since the military-production possibility frontiers are presumed to cross, *B* might successfully wage economic war against *A* by enlarging its labour-intensive, low-technology instruments forcing it to contract its civilian economy to meet the threat.

While the USA is likely to be able to wage capital-intensive economic warfare against the USSR, it may be that the USSR can simultaneously wage labour-intensive war against the USA. This might be done directly or through proxies. In the Korean and Vietnam conflicts the USA found itself fighting a labour-intensive war which imposed social costs too great to be accommodated voluntarily by market forces. The impossibility of using an 'all-volunteer' army in conflicts of this sort is testimony to the high opportunity costs of labour-intensive war to an economy such as that of the USA.

The significance of General Eisenhower's dictum that the USA should never allow itself to become involved in a land war in Asia, is not so much a statement about the geography of the region as its factor endowments. The danger of labour-intensive war in, say, Central America, is a threat to the USA just as the Star Wars programme is a threat to the USSR in space. The point is not so much where the conflict is, but the nature of its relative factor utilisation.

Now even where mutual deterrence is possible, the sufficient condition of perfect information is obviously hard to satisfy.[8] Not only would there have to be no military secrets, but each nation would have to evaluate the other's military power correctly in terms of the opponent's military power function and how it compared with one's own.

If military expenditures were used as a proxy to estimate the military power of one's opponent, then the classic index number problem illustrated in Figure 8.3 will serve to destabilise the situation. General Bissell says, 'The dollar measure of Soviet defense programs used by the Intelligence Community is an estimate of what it would cost, using prevailing US prices and wages, to produce and man a military force of the same size and with the same weapons as that of the USSR, and to operate that force as the Soviets do'.[9] In that case, the Soviet choice of β, would be valued in US prices as E' in Figure 8.3. Even though US expenditures at E would be sufficient to deter the Soviets, it would appear that the USA was being outspent, and there would be grounds for expanding military power to α' with necessarily reduced civilian production and a shift in the military-production possibility frontier. The corresponding misperception on the other side gives grounds for their reaction aggravating the arms race. One must understand this process not just as a military intelligence matter, but as part of the budgetary evidence adduced by the military in the internal political struggle for resources that goes on within both nations.

An additional destabilising element may arise from the very nature of military power. Thus far we have been assuming that there exists a well-defined quasi-concave function which embodies military capabilities with different inputs. This might not be the case. There may be no high-technology means of combating masses of low-technology troops; at the same time it may be that masses of soldiers cannot defeat an atomic attack. That is to say, these instruments are not substitutes for one another in a military-power function which can be adjusted to meet the conditions for deterrence.

If it is simply not possible to carry out the deterrence then the relationship is 'lexicographic', like the letters of the alphabet in the dictionary in which no second letter of an alphabetised word can move it to a position other than that indicated by the first letter. Less extreme assumptions include regions of quasi-convexity or discontinuity in an otherwise quasi-concave military-power function. As a result, each nation may end up fighting the kind of war which does not reflect its comparative advantage. The US experience with the Korean and Vietnam wars are cases in point.

The fear of such a circumstance requires enhanced military expenditures. But these funds will be spent in accordance with the comparative advantage of each country. Then each opponent, fearing a war on the terms dictated by the enemy, will have to further enlarge his preparation, and the arms race will continue.

The danger arises from the dynamic situation. Either through design, or misinformation, or the absence of well-defined relationships in military power, the arms race has a tendency to escalate. As it absorbs resources, it drives us closer to the point where the threat of domination prompts one of the parties to make a military move while they think they still have time.

V TRENDS IN ECONOMIC WAR BETWEEN THE USA AND THE USSR

We now turn our attention to past trends in the conflict between the superpowers in the hope of quantifying the alternatives they face.

The long-term history of real US military expenditures since 1950 shows two basic characteristics. First, they have shown no overall secular trend, but are dominated by dramatic but temporary surges associated with the Korean and Vietnam wars as well as the current rearmament programme.[10] Second, the real burden of military expenditures in the USA has declined dramatically over the long run, despite the build-up of the past years. Military expenditures as a percentage of GNP reached 13 per cent during the height of the Korean War and 9 per cent during the height of the Vietnam War. In 1984 military expenditures were only about 6 per cent of GNP.[11]

The USSR shows a different pattern (Figure 8.4). For 1966–83, the longest period for which we have data ostensibly comparable to that of the USA, Soviet military expenditures exhibited steady, almost linear growth, while US military expenditures dipped sharply after

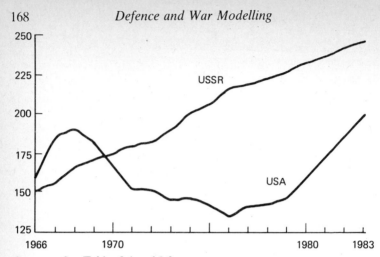

Source: See Tables 8.1 and 8.2.

Figure 8.4   Soviet and US military expenditures, 1966–83
(billions of constant 1981 dollars)

Table 8.1   Soviet real consumption(C), investment(I), GNP and military
expenditures(M) 1951–83

Years	C		GNP	C/GNP	I/GNP
		(average % growth)		*(average ratio)*	
1951–5	4.9	12.6	4.6	58.9	17.2
1956–60	5.7	10.5	5.9	57.3	22.7
1961–5	3.7	8.0	5.1	56.1	25.7
1966–70	5.3	6.1	5.3	55.4	26.7
1971–5	3.6	5.4	3.7	53.5	29.7
1976–80	2.8	3.9	2.5	52.9	32.0
1980–3	1.8	3.9	3.2	52.0	33.3
1951–83	4.1	7.5	4.6	55.0	26.0
	M	*GNP*	*M/GNP*		
1967–83	2.9	3.5	15.3		
1972–83	3.1	2.6	15.0		
1977–83	2.0	2.4	14.9		

Sources: (upper panel) Joint Economic Committee of the US Congress,
USSR: Measures of Economic Growth and Development, 1950–1980, US
Government Printing Office, 1982: *USSR: Facts and Figures Annual*, vol.
9, 1985; underlying data are 1970 roubles; (lower panel) US Arms Control
and Disarmament Agency, *World Military Expenditures and Arms
Transfers*, various years; *SIPRI Yearbook, 1984*; underlying data are 1981
dollars.

the Vietnam war only to start an upward spiral toward the close of the Carter administration in 1979. Despite declining Soviet GNP growth rates, Soviet military expenditures always grew in real terms, whereas US military expenditures declined absolutely in seven of the seventeen years between 1966 and 1983 and increased in the others.

Dollar estimates for the USA and the USSR, which suffer from the distorting effects of the index number problem, show the USSR outspending the USA. Since the Soviet GNP is substantially smaller than the US GNP, the Soviet burden (military expenditures/GNP) is correspondingly higher than that of the USA.

Do these contrasting trends in total military expenditures constitute an arms race? Taken over the period for which we have comparable data, it would appear that the Soviet military gets its steady increase in expenditures in a manner that is not systematically related to the wide fluctuations of the USA. Yet a closer look at Figure 8.5 suggests a systematic relationship between US and Soviet military spending, though the relationship is neither simple nor contemporaneous and is certainly not linear. The core relationship is masked because not all gross military expenditure is mutually deter-

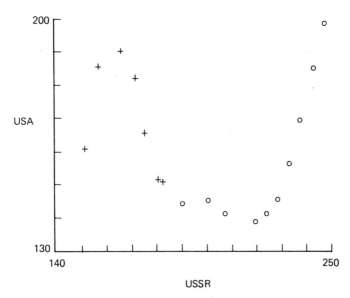

Source: See Table 8.1; circles indicate years 1974–83

Figure 8.5   Soviet and US military expenditures, 1966–83
(billions of constant 1981 dollars)

mined. Thus the Vietnam war and, to a lesser extent, the Korean war involved US expenditures to which the USSR did not feel compelled to make an immediate response. At the most these wars were directed at the Soviet periphery. In addition as we have explained, these conflicts were also labour-intensive and hence were extremely expensive in real terms, given the US factor endowment. The USSR could afford to pursue its steady course, reacting if at all to such subcomponents of the arms budget which might more proximately be directed toward it.

It is reasonable to assume that since the Vietnam war military expenditures in the USA and the USSR have been closely related. Indeed, for 1974–83 it turns out that there is a very close parabolic relationship between the two which is undoubtedly statistically significant despite the small sample of years, as the F statistic makes clear. US military expenditure (MILUS) increased at a constant rate and were substantially related to the *square* of the Soviet leve? (MILSU).

$$\text{MILUS} = 2\ 808\ 702 - 25.04\ (\text{MILSU}) + 5.867\ (10\text{-}05) \ (\text{MILSU})^2 \tag{8.7}$$

t ratios (17.67) (−17.56) (18.40)
$R^2 = 99.3$ DW $= 3.02$ $N = 10$ $F = 526.34$

There is a problem of overestimation of Soviet expenditure inherent in the method of evaluation in terms of US equivalent, but Figure 8.4 shows that Soviet expenditure still exceeds that of the USA in spite of the constant acceleration of US expenditure since 1974. Nor does the acceleration model imply that US arms have always been increasing. On the contrary, this period starts with the end of the Vietnam expenditures, when the decrease in expenditure given by the negative linear term dominated. However, this decrease became smaller and was dominated by the positive squared term as US expenditure rose more rapidly than that of the USSR. It is interesting, therefore, to see that the acceleration process began before the Reagan administration although most of the positive slope is associated with his presidency.

Without claiming too much for this exercise as a forecasting device, it does characterise recent trends in relative Soviet–US military spending. It can be used to explore the hypothetical macroeconomic implications of alternative economic military policies facing policy-makers. What would happen, for instance, if the USA continued its present course? What would be the result if the USSR continued their present course and allowed themselves to be overtaken? What would happen if they abandoned their past policies and attempted to match or surpass the USA? Before we can answer these questions we need to study the differing macroeconomic processes of the two nations involved.

VI MACROECONOMIC MECHANISMS

The costs of economic warfare, and the means of meeting these costs are different in the USA and in the USSR. Certain modifications must be made in our basic model to account for system-specific features of these two countries.

1 The Costs of Economic Warfare

As a market economy, the USA does not necessarily operate on its transformation curve because of its inherent cycles of unemployment and slack resources. If the USA were country *B* in Figure 8.2, an observed point in the upper right quadrant might lie within the frontier. If so, increments in military expenditures (indeed, any exogenous expenditures) might be considered 'free' in that they appear to carry no opportunity cost in terms of the sacrifices of goods currently produced. Output is produced simply by mobilising otherwise idle resources. Of course, there is an opportunity cost in the sense that the fiscal stimulus of military expenses could have been directed to other public uses.

Such zero opportunity cost is possible only in the extreme case where resources are fully mobile, so that if they are not employed in the civilian sector they can in short order be transferred to the military. In practice, even in recessionary times, it is widely believed that high military-expenditures deficit financed under restrictive monetary policies have crowded out civilian investment, construction, agriculture and interest-sensitive consumption industries. Regions supplying these sectors have experienced unemployment even while rapid expansion has taken place in military-related industries elsewhere. These civilian activities are, so to speak, casualties of economic warfare.[12]

Instead of comparing military expenditures with GNP, it is more reasonable to assume that the opportunity cost of military expenditures varies inversely with the gap between actual and full-employment GNP. The GNP gap, however, has been substantial in relation to total military expenditure in the USA, ranging from 50 to 83 per cent between 1966 and 1983 (Table 8.2). While there are undoubtedly real costs associated with military expenditures in the USA, they are less than the ratio of military expenses to GNP. The degree to which the ratio to GNP overstates the real cost depends on the state of the business cycle.

Table 8.2   US military expenditures and the GNP gap, 1974–83

Year	US military expenditures		GNP gap	
	Billions of 1981 dollars	*% of potential GNP*	*Billions of 1981 dollars*	*% of US military expenditures*
1974	145.5	0.8	19.7	13.5
1975	141.2	4.6	116.5	82.5
1976	133.7	2.3	59.7	44.6
1977	140.0	−0.2	−5.3	−3.8
1978	141.1	−2.5	−68.1	−48.3
1979	145.6	−2.6	−73.1	−50.1
1980	157.4	0.4	11.6	7.4
1981	169.9	0.5	14.8	8.7
1982	185.2	4.7	142.9	77.1
1983	198.5	3.9	121.9	61.4

Source: *Survey of Current Business*, December 1983.

There is always an opportunity cost to increase military output in the Soviet economy. The USSR may be regarded as a full-employment, albeit relatively inefficient, economy. This means that there are no idle resources which can be mustered to produce military (or other) goods without foregoing others. The USA is therefore able to impose a cost on the USSR which it has to bear only partially itself.

2 Meeting the Cost of Economic War

While the military burden has the effect of reducing the civilian economy in both the USA and the USSR, the means whereby it is divided into consumption and savings (= investment) differs between them.

For the USA one might roughly consider Disposable Personal Income to be a proxy for the civilian economy, on the simplifying grounds that the military sector is approximately the same as the tax burden. Fundamentally, the decision to save or consume is an individual choice, made in the light of time preferences and the real market rate of interest. Whether this real rate is subject to control by the monetary authorities is a vexed question into which we will not inquire here.

Matters are quite different in the Soviet economy where central planners operate on the supply side to decide the rate of savings and in general the division of GNP into its major components. Ostensibly, the division between investment and consumption depends on planners' preferences, but it is not unconstrained. Too much investment means too little consumption, forced savings and an erosion of work incentives, a decrease in effective labour supply and ultimately in output. These savings–labour-supply linkages have been stressed recently in models of disequilibria macroeconomic regimes developed by Portes and others.[13]

The trend of the Soviet propensity to save out of the civilian national income cannot be determined directly with available data. We can approximate this ratio by dividing investment by the sum of investment and consumption.[14] Figure 8.6 shows the steady rise in this ratio from 19 per cent in 1950 to 39 per cent in 1983, so that a given level of civilian GNP corresponds to a higher rate of investment. For the Soviets, higher savings rates are a possible response to the arms race as well as to their need for capital deepening.

In the face of a slowing growth in GNP, the Soviets have attempted to maintain their linear growth in military expenditures at the price of restricted growth in consumption and investment. Of the latter two, it has been consumption that has been squeezed. This is implicit in Figure 8.6.

Table 8.1 shows the average growth rates by five-year periods, as well as the relevant ratios. Notice that the slower percentage growth rates in military expenditure are consistent with the linear expansion

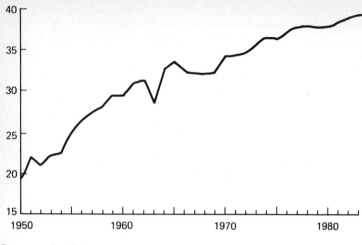

Source: See Table 8.1

Figure 8.6   Soviet investment/(investment + consumption)
1950–1983 (%)

of those expenditures as GNP grows. The investment rate continues to rise in order to achieve something like the accustomed growth in GNP at the cost of a squeeze on consumption.

It is important to stress, however, that this squeeze on consumption is relative. In absolute amount, consumption has steadily increased since 1950. The Soviet government has been unwilling or unable to reduce consumption absolutely in order to pay for its large investment and armaments programme. This long-run progress in consumption, one can argue, sets up expectations of future progress, however, moderate. Stagnation or absolute decline in material living standards in any system is steadfastly resisted by the populace and unwelcome to the leadership. The implication is that macroeconomic choices for the Soviet leadership are getting harder. With flagging economic growth and serious popular resistance to relative, let alone absolute, cuts in consumption, the costs to the USSR of matching or surpassing the USA build-up will indeed be large.

VII MACROECONOMIC PROJECTIONS

The macroeconomic implications of military expenditures for the Soviet economy can be illustrated on the basis of some simple numerical projections. Needless to say, the highly aggregated nature of the underlying statistics and the simplicity of the model restrict the valid use of these results to gross orders of magnitude.

1. In the first projection (Figure 8.7) we assume that Soviet military expenditure continues after 1983 at the 1977–83 trend rate of about 2 per cent per annum. US military expenditures are generated according to the parabola fitted to the data in equation (8.7).

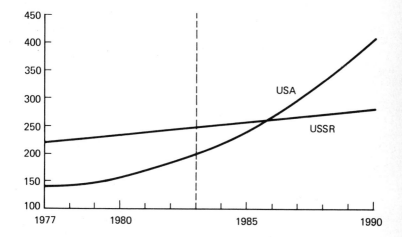

Note: Soviet military expenditures are projected at the 1977–83 trend rate (2 per cent). US expenditures are based on the parabola estimated in the text.

Figure 8.7   Projected Soviet and US military expenditures, 1974–90 (billions of constant (1981) dollars)

As a result, the USSR maintains historical growth rates in consumption, investment and GNP, but at the cost of falling behind in the arms race. If in 1983 the Soviet military expenditure exceeded those of the USA by 26 per cent, by 1986 expenditures would be approximately the same, and by 1990 the USA would lead Soviet spending by 44 per cent. According to this picture, the unperturbed Soviets do not react to continued US military spending which makes it impossible for them to deter the USA. On the Intriligator–Brito hypothesis, they would allow the USA to achieve a level of armaments such that US political domination or war initiation would result. This is an implausible outcome.

2. A more conservative forecast replaces the parabolic form of the US arms build-up with a constant rate of growth. In Figure 8.8 Soviet and US military expenditures are projected using their 1977–83 time trends, 2 per cent and 6.2 per cent per annum respectively.

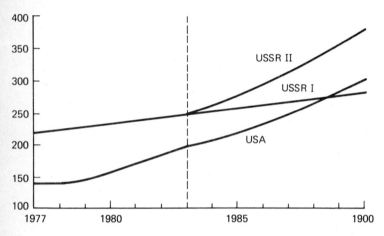

Note: USSR II military expenditures are projected at a 6.2 per cent rate, the same rate as the US projection. 6.2 per cent is the trend growth rate for US military expenditures for 1977–83. USSR I is Soviet military expenditures projected at their 1977–83 trend (2 per cent).

Figure 8.8   Projected Soviet and US military expenditures, 1974–90 (billions of constant (1981) dollars)

Again US spending overtakes Soviet spending, shown as USSR I, although this time in 1989 instead of 1986. The US advantage in spending in 1990 is 6 per cent rather than 44 per cent.

3. The more likely future is an acceleration in the Soviet response to the USA which continues on the conservative constant 6.2 per cent path. In Figure 8.8, USSR II depicts a possible Soviet militarisation programme in which they decide to maintain their

relative position of 1983 where they exceeded the USA by 26 per cent. This 26 per cent is maintained until 1990, the terminal year of the projection. In this case, the USSR has not 'lost' the arms race. It has maintained parity in military spending, but at a cost in forgone consumption and investment. Soviet military expenditures as a percentage of GNP climbs from 14 per cent in 1983 to nearly 20 per cent in 1990.[15] Compared with the scenario of USSR I, where Soviet military expenditures increase at the 1977–83 trend, by 1990 an additional $97 bn must be taken from other uses and sacrificed to the arms race.

If the Soviets choose to pursue USSR II, what is given up is naturally a matter of policy choice. If GNP grows at the historical 2.6 per cent trend, but military expenditures mimic the US 6.2 per cent rate, GNP minus military expenditures must grow at 1.9 per cent rather than 2.3 per cent. If it is assumed that the Soviets abandon their historical policy of a secular rise in the ratio of investment to GNP, allowing the ratio to remain at its 1983 level, and optimistically, that GNP grows at its secular rate despite the slower rate of capital accumulation, even then consumption, as the residual, can grow at only 1.4 per cent instead of the trend rate of 2.3 per cent.

Thus on a conservative view of the Soviet matching of US military growth, investment and consumption would both grow more slowly than the historical trend while military expenditures would grow faster (Table 8.3). With consumption from 1983 to 90 growing at 1.4 per cent per annum, and assuming a population growth rate of 0.9 per cent as in the previous decade, per capita consumption would increase by a minuscule 0.5 per cent. If any of the conservative assumptions do not hold – for example, if the USA continues its parabolic military spending path, if Soviet GNP fails to grow because of the deceleration in investment or because the reduction in consumption leads to lesser labour efficiency – the secular trend in per capita consumption in the USSR could become negative.

While it is the most likely course, this last alternative involves a deterioration of performance by historical standards which would have a substantial effect on the Soviet economy's efficiency, growth potential, consumer welfare – and, ultimately, its military power. At the same time, a continuation of the US military build-up would impose costs on the US economy, but they are not likely to be of the order of magnitude of those imposed on the Soviet system.

Table 8.3   Soviet GNP, military expenditure(M), investment(I) and consumption(C) 1983–90

| | Year | | Projection (1983–1990) | Past Trend (1977–1983) |
| | 1983 | 1990 | | |
	(billions of 1981 dollars)		(growth rate as %)	
GNP	1668.8	2001.9	2.6	2.6
GNP-M	1422.6	1621.2	1.9	2.3
M	246.2	380.7	6.2	1.9
I	561.2	673.2	2.6	3.6
C	861.3	948.0	1.4	2.3

Sources: See Table 8.1. Assumptions: GNP grows at its historical rate (2.6 per cent); the share of *I* in GNP is the same in 1990 as in 1983; *M* grows at a rate that matches the US build-up, 6.2 per cent (USSR II); 1983 *I* in dollars is derived by multiplying *I*/GNP (roubles, CIA data) by GNP (dollars, US ACDA data). *C* is approximated as GNP − (*C* + *I*).

VIII   CONCLUSIONS

1. We have shown theoretically that the arms race is not an exercise in mutual deterrence, but constitutes a weapon of economic warfare. Each nation can force its opponent to keep up its military expenditures, and if countries have different production possibilities either in size or kind, they can inflict economic damage on the other. This economic damage takes the immediate form of reduction in consumption and investment, and ultimately in military potential. Thus the distinction between economic, political and military war is eroded, as nations choose one or the other combination of these instruments.

2. We have examined the orders of magnitude of the economic war between the USA and the USSR. It is apparent that the USA suffers economic casualties in this war in the form of crowded-out civilian industries. At the same time, the cyclical slack in resource use reduces the economic costs of the conflict to the USA; and, the availability to it of world resources added to its greater overall GNP give it an added advantage. The USSR appears to be vulnerable to economic warfare. On conservative assumptions, extremely difficult choices would be imposed upon it by

1990 under present trends. It would either have to accept American military superiority, or impose costs on its consumption and investment programme which would ultimately erode its military potential even further.

3.   An economic model – certainly one as simple and aggregated as this one – captures only a slice of reality. This is not said to hedge our conclusions, but simply to say that forces other than those we have displayed operate and hence present trends may not continue. Consider some of the alternatives:

(a)   The economic war continues unabated.The USA strikes blows at Soviet capital formation and through it, at its consumption and military potential, say to the point of zero growth. The USSR attempts to acquire the capital-intensive parts of the world, wars and preparations for wars, say to the point of requiring a reinstitution of the draft. Other countries are drawn in as the USSR attempts to acquire the capital-intensive parts of theworld, or at least deny them to the USA. The USA attempts to involve China and other labour-intensive nations to counter the Soviet comparative advantage. It is hard to imagine that process continuing for very long without an explosion. The danger is that the loser in the economic war will resort to the military option rather than accept defeat.

(b)   The countries agree to limit the economic war tacitly or by agreement. That requires a change from present trends. The refusal of the US Congress to accelerate the defence budget in real terms in 1985 holds out a hope that given the costs, the USA will not drive further. At the same time, the arms budget in real terms is not a simple number but a vector of resources of different scarcity. A limited budget with a large 'Star Wars' component will still exert considerable leverage and this appears to be the bone of Soviet contention. The Soviet *quid pro quo* for a relaxation of the arms race is unknown at this point. It is unknown whether that would be acceptable either to its own military establishment or to the USA.

Wars end. Economic war is no exception. The question is whether it will end in compromise and limited continuing hostility or whether it will escalate out of control.

Notes and References

1. Wolfson, M., 'Notes on Economic Warfare', *Working Paper 84–9*, Department of Economics, University of Adelaide, Australia, and *Conflict Management and Peace Science* Vol 8, no. 2, Spring 1985, pp. 1–19.
2. Intriligator, Michael D., 'Strategic Considerations in the Richardson Model of Arms Races', *Journal of Political Economy*, 1975, pp. 339–53; Intriligator, M. D. and Brito, D. L., 'Can Arms Races lead to the Outbreak of War?', *Journal of Conflict Resolution*, 28, 1 March 1984, pp. 63–84.
3. *Survey of Current Business*, February 1985, p. 9.
4. Wolfson, 'Notes on Economic Warfare' (see note 1), p. 2.
5. Elsewhere we have studied the impact of changing attitudes toward casualties and its relation to the size of existence of zones of initiation (Wolfson, see Note 1). We have also shown that the proliferation of missiles among more nations contradicts the existence of positive regions of mutual deterrence and enlarges the region of war initiation under plausible assumptions. Wolfson, M., 'A Theorem on the Existence of Zones of Initiation and Deterrence in Intriligator–Brito Arms Race Models', *Working Paper 84–10*, Department of Economics, University of Adelaide. Cf. Intriligator, M. and Brito, D., 'Nuclear Proliferation and the Probability of Nuclear War', *Public Choice*, XXVII, 2, 1982, pp. 247–60.
6. In discussing this point before the Joint Economic Committee, General Schuyler Bissell, Deputy Director of the Defense Intelligence Agency, agreed with the assessment of the situation of the USSR by some of his Soviet counterparts:

    > Soviet leaders have acknowledged the negative effects of the high military spending on the economy and on the USSR's standard of living but to date have been consistently willing to pay the price. Some also realise that the Soviet military in the long run is only as strong as the rest of the economy. 'The sharpening of the international situation compels the socialist state to increase military production and consumption. Easing of the tension permits a decrease, a full utilization of economic might for raising the standard of living of the workers and the development of the national economy. *It is impossible to allow, on the one hand, a reduction of military–economic might, for in this case the defense capability of the country would be threatened; on the other hand, an excessive increase in military–economic might cannot be allowed because in the final analysis this could slow the development of the very foundation of military power – the economy – and do irreparable harm to defense capacity* (emphasis added). Pozharov, A. I. *The Economic Foundations of the Defense Might of the Socialist State*, Moscow 1981, p. 116'. Hearings Before the Subcommittee in International Trade, Finance and Security Economics of the Joint Economic Committee Congress of the United States. Ninety-Eighth Congress, First Session, Executive Session, 28 June and 20 September 1983, pp. 95–7.

7. We could represent this civilian economy constraint as a social utility function whose arguments would be consumption, investment in future growth and defence. The present simpler formalism seems sufficient for our present purposes.

8. Our concern for sufficient conditions for a peaceful outcome rather than necessary ones reflects more than a logical distinction. The cost of war is so high that we are concerned to find those 'sufficient' policies which guarantee peace, as well as to identify 'necessary' policies without which peace is impossible.

9. Wolfson, M., 'Note on Economic Warfare'.

10. US national defence expenditures in 1953, 1958 and 1984 were 91, 101, and 90 billion constant (1972) dollars, *Economic Report of the President, 1985*, pp. 233, 237.

11. Ibid, pp. 233–4.

12. An estimate of the effect of military expenditures on Britian and France is given in Chapter 6.

13. Portes, R., 'Internal and External Balance in a Centrally Planned Economy', *Journal of Comparative Economics 3*, 1979, pp. 325–45.

14. The data cited in Table 8.1 do not separate I into its military (I_m) and civilian (I_c) components. Hence we use $I/(C + I)$ to approximate $I_c/(C + I_c)$. (Here C stands for consumption, and is not to be confused with the civilian sector of a national economy which we designate by C_a and C_b).

15. Assuming Soviet GNP grows at its 1977–83 trend rate (2.6 per cent).

Part III

Macroeconomics in an International Political Framework

9 Economic Change as a Cause of International Conflict[1]

Bruce Russett
YALE UNIVERSITY

This chapter reviews various hypotheses about the relation between economic change and governments' readiness to participate in international conflict. It develops a theoretical model with hypothesised linkages from economic difficulty, to governments' efforts to contain domestic political discontent stemming from that difficulty, through militarisation to participation in militarised international disputes. It also develops a hypothesis that democratic governments may respond to economic difficulty in a way that is systematically different from that of non-democratic governments. It then tests these hypotheses on two large bodies of cross-temporal and cross-national political and economic data. The results suggest some tendency for democratic governments to engage in international conflict more often after economic downturn, and for non-democratic governments to do so after economic expansion.

The effects of economic recession and depression are enduring matters of concern. One of the most serious and least examined is the possible effect of economic downturns on the incidence of serious diplomatic disputes and armed conflict between nations. But despite the plausibility of many arguments, and the dire consequences if they are correct, the relationship of economic downturn to international conflict has yet to be examined in a sufficiently rigorous fashion. What exists is a voluminous speculative literature reflecting a range of ideological and theoretical positions on economics and international politics, and a few inconclusive data-based investigations. This chapter makes no effort to summarise all the merely speculative work, but does review some of the major theoretical perspectives, provides a brief overview of the systematic empirical efforts, and presents some new preliminary empirical analyses.

I WHY ECONOMIC CONDITIONS MAY PROMOTE INTERNATIONAL CONFLICT

First for review are empirical studies which examine the effects of very long economic cycles with a view to establishing that major wars are more frequent in the *upswing* phase of those cycles that last about a half-century. Kondratieff, the major figure in this 'long-cycle' literature, himself concluded that the most destructive wars have historically occurred on the upswing.[2] Kondratieff's work was long ignored by 'mainstream' social scientists. His data were rather primitive; at most they extended over a century and a half, thus presenting no more than three possible long cycles; he had no convincing causal explanation for his alleged cycles; and many analysts even doubted that such cycles actually existed. But with the experience of another fifty years, better data, and a renewed interest in the possible course of long economic cycles we find mounting evidence for the existence of such cycles.[3] The data now provide some basis for trying to link long cycles to international conflict.

One empirical analysis of the post-Napoleonic period appears to confirm a positive relationship between long-wave upswings and major wars but the authors are unable to determine the direction of any causal relationship; that is, whether from economy to war or vice versa. Another study going back as far as 1495 seems to have found confirmation of war-stimulating effects of long-cycle upswings, but the economic data to document the cycles so far back in time are not fully satisfactory.[4]

Other investigations have looked at the expansion phase of shorter-term business cycles and their association with war. Among these are work by Macfie who claimed to have found that during the period 1853–1914 twelve of the most destructive wars all began in the final part of the business upswing, and Blainey who made a similar claim.[5] But a more rigorous analysis covering the UK, France, Germany, and the USA over the period 1793–1962 found 'very little empirical support' for any relationship between short cycles and war.[6]

A counter-hypothesis, however, is perhaps more plausible; that is, that the *downswing* frequently brings international conflict in its wake. Several causal mechanisms may be operative. When the economy begins to falter, national governments come under increasing pressure to 'do something', among which trade protectionism typically looms large. To the extent that tariffs, import quotas, and other exclusionary measures are instituted the effects on other countries are usually contagious, and conflictful. The consequence may be a marked decline in international trade, followed by further deterioration in domestic economies and further exacerbation of interational political conflicts. The 1930s are widely thought to typify this process.[7]

More important is a chain that progresses through militarisation. Another variant of 'do something', is 'pump-priming' to stimulate the domestic economy. Military spending is a relatively easy means of promoting economic activity; indeed military spending and tax-cutting (rather than increasing expenditure for civil government functions) may be the only forms of pump-priming acceptable to conservative administrations.[8] Similarly, unemployment may be cut directly by expanding the size of the armed forces.

These types of military-preparedness measures may or may not slow down or reverse the *economic* decline, but they can be expected to produce some definite *political* consequences. On the one hand, they reinforce the *domestic* arguments for similar policies in other nations by generating an *external* stimulus; that is, they tend to generate higher levels of threat-perception among the political élites in neighbouring countries, especially in the case of traditional rivals. What may have begun as a purely internal measure for economic renewal can end up as an international provocation. The more widespread and vigorous these measures, the greater the likely rise in international tension levels. Furthermore, increases in military spending and recruitments also exercise a dangerous effect at *home*: with each increment in the allocation of economic and demographic resources to the military, there is some associated increment in the political influence of the beneficiaries. The net effect of these domestic and international processes is therefore an increased militarisation of the separate nations' foreign policies, and an increased level of international tension as the world economy is fragmented and states feel threatened by others' militarisation. From this lethal combination, an increase in the frequency or severity of international disputes would come as no surprise. Finally, of course, militarisation may be an intermediate rather than a causal variable in a chain leading to international conflict. That is, governmental élites may build up their military establishments for the express purpose of using them in conflict with other states, perhaps seeking that conflict as a means of diverting popular attention away from domestic economic difficulties and toward a common external enemy. We will have more to say about this last phenomenon shortly.

This is not meant to imply that economic hard times will always result in either militarisation or international conflict. Those who govern states may respond in many ways to economic privation, with only some of those responses culminating in external conflict, just as many kinds of non-economic influences will affect the existence and timing of acts in the international area.[9] Sometimes a government will embody a great deal of good will and legitimacy in the eyes of its people. If so, economic hard times may not be soon or strongly met by protests, demonstrations, or other political acts manifesting popular dissatisfaction. Or a government may have its population so cowed that protest is effectively suppressed even without acts of overt government coercion. And surely militarisation itself need not be directed toward external enemies, but rather domestic dissidents. Military forces can be built up as an instrument of suppressing domestic dissent. In fact, a government with its hands full trying to put down acts of civil rebellion may go to substantial lengths to *avoid* becoming embroiled also in an international conflict.[10]

Thus we can hypothesise the following possible government policies being adopted to deal with the political consequences of economic downturn: First, if domestic discontent is slight and serious discontent is not anticipated, there may be *no* actions that affect the likelihood of international conflict. (Pump-priming, if it exists, may be confined to tax-cutting and increased civil spending.) Second, domestic discontent may be handled by strengthening military and security forces, but directing those forces solely toward domestic opponents. In this instance, the likelihood of international conflict may actually *decrease*. Third, a state's militarisation may unintentionally stimulate international tensions, other states' perception of threat, and the likelihood that the first state will thus find itself the *target* of hostile acts. Finally, a state's militarisation may lead to a greater probability that the same state will initiate conflictful international action, either as a result of strengthening jingoistic and militaristic political forces within its own system or as a result of a deliberate policy of diverting domestic discontent toward a foreign enemy. In these various chains the extent of domestic discontent and of militarisation (including the form of militarisation) assume the role of crucial mediating variables.

Systematic evidence for a causal linkage from economic downturn to subsequent international conflict is fragmentary. Some support can be found in Bernstein's early study of major-power wars, and in Gochman's report that the USA has been more prone to involvement in conflict in periods when its military–industrial capabilities have been declining, but these findings are far from compelling.[11] One of the reasons for inconclusive and competing empirical results is doubtless a common one: different empirical domains (different countries or sets of countries and different time-periods), and different measures of the variables.

A more fundamental reason, however, is probably to be found in the specification of the temporal character of the relationship. International conflicts are not likely to follow immediately on the heels of an economic downturn, especially if the relationship runs through an intermediary process of domestic militarisation and international threat-perception. It takes time for the downturn to be recognised as such by the political authorities, and more time for its impact to be felt in the political consciousness of the populace. If the authorities decide to try to cushion the impact by pump-priming in the military sector, plans must be drawn up and funds appropriated and spent. Further lags are in store before the newly-augmented military forces will be ready for active use. It takes time to build and design the weapons that military commanders will require, and it takes time to train the troops that are to use them. Military bureaucracies must prepare and obtain some consensus on war plans. The populace in general must be prepared, with clear images of who their enemies are and of the cause that will justify war with them. In short, preparations for war take time. Just how long a lag we should expect to find between economic downturn and subsequent war initiation is unclear. It may be somewhat shorter for an authoritarian government operating a command economy than for a democratic government working in a largely free-market economy. But surely it will require more than a year or two. The expectation of a significant time lag remains, though in modified form, even if we specify a causal link to less extreme forms of international conflict such as diplomatic disputes.

If the process occupies a period of several years, one implication for empirical analysis is obvious. The lag from downturn to conflict may well take so long that the conflict may occur only when the economy has already begun to recover. This will be the case particularly if the pump-priming exercise of militarisation is successful. If militarisation produces a kind of prosperity, as intended, of course the conflict will occur during a period of (perhaps recent and relative) prosperity. Thus an empirical analysis that looks at simultaneous relationships between economic conditions and the initiation of international conflict will find one between economic upturns and conflict, whereas a properly specified analysis, built on a lagged relationship, would find our hypothesised relationship between economic downturns and conflict. Hints of this can be found in some of the foregoing analyses.

Other factors may be at work in a linkage between economic downturns and international conflict. One can be found in studies of the electoral and policy cycles in modern industrial democracies, best documented in the USA, but also in Europe. It is well known that the electorate responds closely to recent changes in economic conditions. Of all forms of government, it is in democracies that the state's leadership will be held accountable. The change in economic conditions (for example, the change in real personal income, or in inflation and unemployment) in the quarters immediately preceding an election is an excellent indication of the likely size of the vote that will be obtained by the party in power.[12] Voters react negatively to poor economic conditions, and they have relatively short memories. They will respond quickly to adversity, and similarly will respond favourably to a government that has 'done something for them lately', in the form of engineering an economic recovery even if the recovery follows a recession induced not so long ago by that same government. An electoral cycle is thus linked to the business cycle. Furthermore, governmental élites are aware of this electoral response, and therefore move to induce a favourable one. The idea of a policy cycle implies that governments deliberately stimulate the economy, by cutting taxes and by increasing spending and transfer payments, in the months and quarters immediately preceding an election. And as we noted, one form of spending particularly susceptible to such motivations, is for the military. Here then is a hypothesis of military pump-priming as a policy cycle especially found in democratic political systems. It has not been conclusively supported as has been that of an electoral cycle, but it is at least highly plausible.[13]

Another set of relevant phenomena concerns the familiar frustration–aggression hypothesis, resting here on the premise that economic downturn, coming after a period of prosperity, growth, and rising expectations, can easily generate high levels of frustration for élites and public alike. If frustration leads to aggressive behaviour at the level of the mass public, one might expect the leaders of national societies to show similar tendencies both as they respond to populace moods and as their own political fortunes are endangered by the economic decline. A related line of reasoning is that as economic downturn leads to public discontent and partisan opposition to the regime, one response by national leaders is to engage in efforts to divert attention from domestic problems. Foreign adventure is often the policy of choice, making disputes and war more likely.[14]

A reason to believe that governments may deliberately respond to economic adversity with steps that may lead to international crisis is the now widely recognised 'rally round the flag' effect.[15] Governments routinely achieve a temporary burst of popular support in response to international crisis. This phenomenon is by now so familiar and well documented that government leaders can anticipate and perhaps deliberately invoke it. It is but a short step of reasoning to hypothesise that governments may be especially likely to invoke the 'rally round the flag' effect of international crisis at times when their popularity is impaired by economic adversity. In fact, international crisis may be a surer 'fix' for electoral unpopularity in the short run than stimulating the economy, which takes more time. Recent work on American presidents' popularity in opinion polls indicates that when an international crisis occurs, or when a president directs some form of conflict toward the USSR, his approval rating typically jumps by 4 or 5 percentage points. Moreover, Presidents Eisenhower and Kennedy both seem to have gained popularity by taking conflictual acts towards the USSR at a time when those acts diverted attention from domestic economic problems. Long wars clearly hurt presidents' popular standing – but shorter, lower-level and possibly more controllable conflicts may be just the answer for a democratic leader beleaguered by a poorly-performing economy.[16]

All these arguments suggest not only that economic downturns may set in motion a variety of political forces that lead to international conflict, but that the strength and character of these effects may be different for different kinds of political systems. It is a commonplace to argue that authoritarian, and especially military, regimes are especially likely to engage in foreign adventure and conflict. Authoritarian governments are likely to have an advantage in the early preparations for war. They can make plans, purchases, and deployments in secret. At least in the short run they can impose sacrifices on their population. Even during a period of stagnation they can, through repression, divert some resources to preparation for war. Relevant examples, including some linked to adverse economic conditions, are not hard to find. In recent history, one can quickly recall the case of the Argentine military dictatorship and its attempted seizure of the Falkland Malvinas Islands in the spring of 1982, a time of deepening economic and political crisis at home. The Falkland dispute of course had a history of well over a century, but the time the Argentine generals chose to activate it – and so, they hoped, to shore up their fading popularity – was no coincidence. A somewhat different example is from Germany of the 1930s. Adolf Hitler surely owed his accession to power largely to the frustrations of voters during the great German Depression. Those frustrations were readily vented on foreign 'enemies' as well as on domestic scape-goats. Furthermore, Hitler revived the German economy largely through a vigorous programme of rearmament. The consequence, several years later, was the combination of a virulent ideology and a power-mad dictator with a people prepared to avenge previous national humiliations and a military machine capable of activating expansionist policies.

We therefore have the basis, drawing on these examples, for a hypothesis that the link from economic downturn to subsequent international conflict is likely to be intensified under authoritarian governments. Nevertheless, we should not endorse that hypothesis too uncritically in the light of the points above about the responses which democratic governments are likely to make to economic adversity. It may well be that even if democratic governments lack some of the aggressive impulses of authoritarian regimes, they may be under more immediate pressures, because of their vulnerability to the periodic electoral process, to do *something* in the face of any significant economic reversal, and that something may include induc-ing or at least risking foreign conflict. Thus we can hypothesise that the type of political system makes a difference without committing ourselves to a position as to whether democratic or authoritarian regimes will be more conflict-prone.

A further complication, implicit in the preceding discussion, is that there may be a link between domestic conflict and international conflict, especially under particular types of political regimes. An even fuller specification, therefore, would call for an interaction among economic downturn, domestic political conflict, and regime type, with some combination of these being most lethal in inducing international conflict. And the fact is that a systematic investigation of such a complex *interactive* relationship has never been undertaken.[17]

II ELEMENTS OF AN EMPIRICAL TEST

Speculative theorising and selective examples do not, of course, suffice to establish the reality of a general relationship. This chapter marks the beginning of an effort to specify some of the relevant hypotheses and to test them on a large cross-national and cross-temporal data base. This report will be purely preliminary. Nevertheless, we can outline some procedures for a systematic empirical test, and report some simple findings and non-findings.

Hypotheses about the relation between economic downturn and war can be interpreted at various levels of analysis. In the most general sense they can be interpreted as applying to the international economic and political system; that is, periods in which the global economy as a whole is in recession or depression will be followed by periods of intensified or more frequent international conflict. To test that sort of hypothesis we would measure the ups and downs in the world economy and relate them to data on subsequent conflict. But we would be surprised if such a test gave very satisfactory results. First, it loses all the subtleties and interactive effects inherent in our discussion of different modes of reaction to economic adversity by different kinds of political systems. Second, and equally serious, it assumes that most countries experience ups and downs in the international economy to roughly the same degree. In other words, it assumes a fully interdependent world economy. But we know this assumption to be heroic, even for the contemporary system. The economies of some industrialised countries were in a vigorous upswing during 1983 and 1984 (for example, the USA) while others (for example, most of Western Europe) remained stagnant; many less-developed countries suffered stagnation or serious recession (for example, much of Latin America) while some of the Asian newly-industrialising countries like Singapore and Taiwan continued a lively expansion. Whereas one could make some meaningful generalisation about 'the world economy', all national economies were far from synchronised. Lack of synchronisation is more pronounced for less-developed countries (particularly subject to vagaries of weather or specialised commodity-market conditions) than for industrialised and economically diversified countries, and the further back one goes in time and into periods of substantial protectionism or mercantilism.[18]

Tests at the level of the individual nation-state seem much more appropriate. We can be sure that the nation itself has experienced economic fluctuation and, moreover, can in theory introduce controls for type of political system and militarisation. For this analysis we work with the set of countries for which reliable data on per capita gross domestic product (GDP) exist over a long time period, in many cases well back into the nineteenth century and in several instances as far back as 1850. These data are for twenty-three countries, including the USA, Canada, Australia, Japan, most of Western Europe, and some of Eastern Europe.[19] Data for some countries are missing for years immediately before or after major wars. We use a per capita version because we assume that changes in individual well-being are more relevant than simply aggregate national product, changes which may come as much from demographic growth as from individual prosperity. As our chief independent variable we will use the change in per capita *GDP*, lagged from one to three years behind the year for international conflict. Also, in anticipation that accumulated changes over preceding periods may be more politically relevant, we can, for example, include change in GDP per capita for *each* of two years preceding the year in which we hypothesise conflict to occur. Both of these procedures reflect our expectation that the initiation of international conflict will not be set in motion immediately by short-term economic adversity.

Note that the form of our economic data permits us to investigate both our primary hypothesis that international conflict will be more likely after economic downturns and at the same time the alternative hypothesis that conflict is more likely following years of relative prosperity. Note too that this procedure is not keyed specifically to phases of a business *cycle*, whether of the long-wave (Kondratieff) variety or shorter-term cycles, such as 'Juglars', the existence of which has long been recognised. That is, our analysis will look for cases of conflict after economic downturn, whether or not the economy has moved into an expansionary phase by the time of conflict. Finally, since our hypotheses concern acts taken by sovereign governments, the analysis omits the country-years before a state achieved full independence or years when, as a result of the Second World War, the state was not an independent actor.[20]

Since we have hypothesised that authoritarian and democratic regimes may have different incentives – in kind and degree – to move from economic change to international conflict, we also introduce a control for regime-type. Basic coding of this variable is on the principle laid down in earlier work on the relation between regime-type and war involvement. That is, we code a government as democratic if it:

(a) held periodically scheduled elections in which opposition parties were as free to run as governmental parties, and in which (b) at least 10 per cent of the adult population was allowed to vote either directly or indirectly for (c) a parliament that either controlled or enjoyed parity with the executive branch of government.

By these standards the UK becomes democratic with the Second Reform Bill of 1867; some states are listed as democratic from the (later) time at which we begin to have adequate economic data; and others, such as Germany and Japan, are identified as democratic only for brief periods before the Second World War and then again after the war. For most states and years we are also able to include an indicator for militarisation. Data on military spending in constant currency values are still not adequate, but we do have data from the Correlates of War project on military personnel, and use the percentage change from the year immediately prior to the year of possible international conflict.

For the dependent variable we use the occurrence of a militarised international dispute involving the country. A militarised dispute is defined here as a confrontation between two or more members of the international system, in which at least one of them engaged in one or more of the following acts: (a) the use of military force in war or (b) short of war; (c) the redeployment of existing military forces; (d) the mobilisation of reserve forces; or (e) the explicit threat to use force.[22] For the countries and years included here we have more than 400 disputes, with the data-set ending with the year 1976. We will also be able to distinguish between simple participation in a dispute and *initiation* of a dispute. (We use the codings of Gochman and Maoz, who identify an initiator as the first state to take an action codable on their scale of conflict, not necessarily the first to use force.)[23] The reasoning behind a hypothesis that economic adversity would often lead a state to initiate an international dispute should be apparent from our previous discussion. But there can also be a reasonable hypothesis that a state that has experienced a serious economic downturn – and perhaps domestic political discontent as well – may seem a tempting target, inviting a traditional rival to feed on its weakness or attempt to settle an old score. Possibly an example of this phenomenon would be Iraq's attack on Iran in 1980, as being triggered partly by Iran's economic disorder. Thus our analysis will first be addressed merely to participation in disputes, and will then discriminate between initiator and target.

A subsequent analysis – more than we are able to undertake in this report – will deal with the relation between economic changes and the likelihood that militarised disputes (whether or not they are more frequent after economic downturn than otherwise) are more likely, if they do occur, to escalate into war in times following economic adversity. We are inclined to believe that the circumstances that produce serious militarised disputes are not the same as those which determine whether disputes will escalate into war. It may well be that the matter of escalation is determined much more by decision-makers' perceptions and decision-making procedures in crisis than by underlying economic or social conditions. Rather, leaders may decide to pursue adventurous or aggressive foreign policies, such as the initiation of a militarised dispute, which will carry an increased *risk* of war. If so, economic downturns would indeed produce greater frequency of war, but only through the mechanism of producing more frequent militarised disputes (a serious proportion of which, in turn and for other reasons, escalate to war). But it is also plausible that economic downturn would make decision-makers less willing or able to compromise with their counterparts in adversary states, and hence would increase not only the frequency of militarised disputes, but the likelihood that any particular dispute would escalate to war. Thus eventually a more complete causal chain must be investigated.

The statistical method we employ is therefore a pooled time-series analysis with nation-year as the unit. The analytical procedure is 'probit analysis', a version of regression analysis suited to circumstances like this one where the dependent variable is dichotomous (dispute or no dispute) rather than continuous.

III   RESULTS

The analysis produced several statistically significant, if sometimes substantively modest, results. First (and no surprise), in all the equations major-power status was strongly associated with dispute involvement. Major-power status did not, however, interact with militarisation, political system, or economic change to produce large or consistent differences in the way those variables were associated with dispute involvement. (Equations were run separately for major and minor powers, but the results are not shown here.) Second, militarisation modestly increased the likelihood that democratic states would be involved in conflict. Most important from the perspective of this chapter, economic change is significantly associated with the likelihood of involvement in international disputes, but in opposite directions for democracies and non-democracies. That is, for democracies economic *downturn* is more likely to lead to subsequent involvement in conflict. They seem somewhat prone to the temptation to engage in militarised disputes (not necessarily war, however) following, and perhaps because of, deterioration of economic conditions in their countries. They may resort to policies to encourage a 'rally round the flag', especially if they have also expanded their military forces over the immediately preceding year. This may not come as particularly pleasant news to partisans of democratic government though it does suggest, ironically, that the reality of pressures is responsive to demands of the electorate, diverting popular attention from economic woes if adequate means to correct those woes are not available. For non-democratic countries the result is the opposite; economic *expansion* is more likely to lead to involvement in conflict, and the relationship is stronger.

Table 9.1 displays the probit analysis for dispute participation with two-year and three-year time-lags from economic change, no lag for change in militarisation, and major power status, controlling for type of political system. The negative sign preceding the first number (the constant) in each equation indicates that the normal condition is for a country not to experience a dispute in any given year. Since *GDP* per capita change in one year is only moderately correlated with change in the subsequent year, it is appropriate to include two lagged years in the second equation for each political system.

Variations on this analysis produced no improvement in explanatory power. For example, using a lag of only one year usually resulted in non-significant results, suggesting – as we expected – that it takes time for the effects of economic change to result in decisions for international conflict. The effects are cumulative, not transitory. Deleting the major power variable usually raised the significance level of economic change, but not in any way that would compensate for the poorer model specification. Finally, the results for initiation of

Table 9.1 Probit-analysis results, 1853–1976

Democratic countries

Dispute participation =   − 1.361**** − 0.017** *GDP* change two yrs
                                   (0.082)   (0.010)

                                   + 1.198**** major + 0.450*** military change
n = 871   (0.107)   (0.181)

Dispute participation =   − 1.339**** − 0.015** *GDP* change two yrs
                                   (0.087)   (0.010)

                                   − 0.016* *GDP* change three yrs + 1.203****
                                                                          major
                                   (0.011)   (0.109)

                                   + 0.451*** military change
n = 853   (0.182)

Non-democratic countries

Dispute participation =   − 1.543**** + 0.029** *GDP* change two yrs
                                   (0.124)   (0.013)

                                   +1.253**** major − 0.763* military change
n = 509   (0.143)   (0.379)

Dispute participation =   1.699**** + 0.036*** *GDP* change two yrs
                                   (0.124)   (0.013)

                                   + 0.031*** *GDP* change three yrs + 1.331***
                                                                          major
                                   (0.012)   (0.152)

                                   − 584* military change
n = 490   (0.384)

---

*   statistically significant at 0.10 level.
**   statistically significant at 0.05 level.
*** statistically significant at 0.01 level.
****statistically significant at 0.001 level.

All tests are one-tailed.

First number is the coefficient for the constant; subsequent numbers are for the independent variables. Standard errors of coefficients are given in parentheses.

international conflict (rather than mere participation in conflict) were slightly weaker. This was not anticipated by most of the theoretical perspectives we reviewed, but may merely reflect difficulties in adequately deciding, for coding purposes, who initiates a given international crisis.

These results, though statistically significant, are not overwhelming from a substantive point of view.[24] With a large data base, it is not difficult to obtain statistically significant results that nevertheless account for little variance. The results do not improve greatly upon a 'naive' model that predicts that any particular year, regardless of preceding economic conditions, will not be characterised by a militarised dispute. (The model correctly predicts some disputes, but incorrectly predicts almost as many disputes in years that were in fact peaceable.) Also, the fact that results are weak for a shorter time lag should caution us, given the lack of strong theoretical reasoning for the particular time lags that proved most powerful.

In probit analysis the coefficients from Table 9.1 are not readily interpretable in substantive terms, and the most familiar measure of strength of association for the whole equation (R^2) has little meaning. But it is possible to calculate the contribution that a given change in an independent variable makes to the probability that a state will be involved in an international dispute, holding the other independent variables constant. Table 9.2 presents these contributions for the second equation for each type of political system. Thus among democracies, a two-year lagged increase of 10 per cent in per capita *GDP* is associated with a 0.87 probability of no dispute involvement, but a 10 per cent drop in *GDP* is associated with only a 0.79 probability of no dispute involvement.

While these results are intriguing, and basically support my theoretical perspective, we should not make too much of them at this point in the investigation. One way to strengthen or weaken our confidence would be to try to replicate this investigation on a much larger data set. After doing the preceding analysis, I was able to obtain economic data that covered most independent states from 1950.[25] This new data base has several advantages. First is simply the largely independent check on the results from the first set. (I say largely because the post-1950 twenty-three-nation data from the first data set are incorporated into the second, creating an overlap of about 25 per cent.) Second, the larger data set provides far more instances of non-democratic regimes and some instances of centralised non-market economies. In so doing it also includes more truly non-democratic

Table 9.2   Probability of 'no-dispute'

	Value %	Probability of 'no-dispute'		Value %	Probability of 'no-dispute'
Democratic countries					
GDP change	+10	0.868	*GDP* change	+10	0.865
two yrs	+5	0.851	three yrs	+5	0.847
	0	0.832		0	0.827
	−5	0.813		−5	0.806
	−10	0.792		−10	0.784
Military change	+10	0.834	Minor power		0.924
three yrs	+5	0.839	Major power		0.587
	0	0.844			
	−5	0.850			
	−10	0.856			
Non-democratic countries					
GDP change	+10	0.769	*GDP* change	+10	0.755
two yrs	+5	0.812	three yrs	+5	0.808
	0	0.850		0	0.854
	−5	0.882		−5	0.891
	−10	0.909		−10	0.921
Military change	+10	0.839	Minor power		0.937
three yrs	+5	0.832	Major power		0.581
	0	0.824			
	−5	0.816			
	−10	0.808			

states, of which there are plenty in recent years, as contrasted with the perhaps oligarchic but not truly authoritarian nineteenth-century European regimes that constitute many of the non-democratic states in the first analysis. Third, it is possible that the link between economic decline and war is particularly a modern phenomenon, resulting from the demands of modern mass democracy and the expectations for control of the business cycle introduced by the macroeconomic policies of post-Keynesian economics. If so, concentration on a large data set limited to the period 1950–76 might produce stronger results, and perhaps different results for non-democratic states.

Table 9.3 shows the results for those equations that were most powerful in Table 9.1. These results clearly are disappointing. The coefficients generally point in the same directions as did those from the long-term historical data set, but only one of those for economic change even approaches statistical significance. The three-year lag is especially weak, perhaps suggesting a speed-up in the pace of political expectations. That they point in the same direction, and continue to suggest a systematic difference between the behaviour of democratic and non-democratic states, is intriguing, and useful as mild confirmation. So too is the fact that the two-year lag again works best, as does participation in, rather than initiation of, disputes. But such suggestions are hardly overwhelming. Possibly the weak results in this table are because the theoretical perspective of this chapter applies primarily to states with some real independence of action, and who have some real points of contention with other states. For very many countries in the post-Second World War international system

Table 9.3 'Probit analysis' results, 1953–76

Democratic countries

Dispute participation = $- 1.137^{****} - 0.017^* \ GDP$ change two yrs
                          $\quad (0.094) \quad\quad (0.014)$

   $- 0.011 \ GDP$ change three yrs $+ 0.971^{****}$
   $\qquad\qquad\qquad\qquad\qquad\qquad\qquad\qquad$ major
   $\quad (0.016) \qquad\qquad\qquad\qquad (0.169)$

   $+ 0.022$ military change
$n = 657$ $\quad (0.347)$

Non-democratic countries

Dispute participation = $- 0.863^{****} + 0.006 \ GDP$ change two yrs
                          $\quad (0.048) \quad\quad (0.006)$

   $- 0.000 \ GDP$ change three yrs $+ 1.294^{****}$
   $\qquad\qquad\qquad\qquad\qquad\qquad\qquad\qquad$ major
   $\quad (0.006) \qquad\qquad\qquad\qquad (0.191)$

   $- 0.060$ military change
$n = 1315$ $\quad (0.103)$

---

*   Just short of statistically significant at 0.10 level.
****Statistically significant at 0.001 level.

neither of these conditions may apply. Their 'normal' condition of 'no-dispute' – whatever their short-term economic condition – may simply be overwhelming the relatively few instances of conflict in this large-scale statistical analysis.

This chapter represents a report on work in progress. Though certainly inconclusive, it shows some reason to believe that international conflict may, in part, be explicable as the acts of decision-makers when faced with the domestic political consequences of economic change. It is one of the very few research reports indicating a systematic difference in international behaviour between democratic and non-democratic political systems. Several subsequent lines of investigation need to be pursued. Some mediating variables which we initially mentioned have not been included because of incomplete or unsatisfactory data, notably indicators of domestic political conflict and of military spending; these would be much superior to simply the number of military personnel. If leaders of democratic states resort often to the 'rally round the flag' effect, they may be especially likely to do it shortly before elections. Thus a variable for election year should be included. Extension of the analysis into the process by which disputes escalate to higher levels, including war, is definitely in order. So too is analysis of a model of simultaneous equations from economic downturn to war both directly and through steps for militarisation and disputes. Models that distinguish differential rates of downturn between initiator and target are also promising. Finally, intensive studies of appropriate cases might help to generate more complex and multivariate hypotheses.

These preliminary results are promising enough, and the problem important enough, to justify further effort. We certainly cannot expect to explain all or even most cases of international conflict from this perspective; the variance accounted for by these models may never be large. We may be able to say something, from historical experience, about the probabilities that under contemporary conditions states may be more aggressive or risk-prone following economic setbacks. Major powers may be more likely to initiate conflicts under such conditions, or to be drawn in when smaller powers do so. If so we will have something useful to say in a world which lacks neither international conflict nor periodic economic adversity.

Notes and References

1. Work on this topic was begun when I was a Fellow at the Netherlands Institute for Advanced Study in 1984, and has been supported by the World Society Foundation in Switzerland. It owes much to conversations with Marc Blaug, Paul Kennedy, and J. David Singer. John Bailey, James Lindsay, Céleste Wallander and Yagil Weinberg provided valuable research assistance.

2. Kondratieff, N., 'Die Langen Wellen der Konjunktur', *Archiv fur Sozialwissenschaft und Sozialpolitik*, 56: 1926, pp. 573–600.

3. van Duijn, J. J., *The Long Wave in Economic Life* (London: Allen & Unwin, 1983). See also the articles by Glismann, Rodemer and Wolter, and by Cleary and Hobbs, in Freeman, Christopher (ed.) *Long Waves in the World Economy* (London: Butterworth, 1983).

4. Thompson, William R. and Zuk, Gary, 'War, Inflation, and the Kondratieff Long Wave', *Journal of Conflict Resolution* 26, 4: 1982, pp. 621–44; and Goldstein, Joshua S., 'Kondratieff Waves as War Cycles', *International Studies Quarterly*, 29, 4: 1985, pp. 375–402.

5. Macfie, A. L., 'The Outbreak of War and the Trade Cycle', *Economic History*, 3, 1938, pp. 89–97; Blainey, Geoffrey, *The Causes of War* (New York: Free Press, 1973).

6. Thompson, William R., 'Phases of the Business Cycle and the Outbreak of War', *International Studies Quarterly*, vol. 26, no. 2, June 1982, pp. 301–11.

7. For a vigorous dissent see Strange, Susan, 'Protectionism and World Politics', *International Organization*, 39, 2; 1985, pp. 233–59.

8. Baran, Paul, and Sweezy, P. M., *Monopoly Capital*, (Baltimore: Penguin, 1969).

9. For the general point, see Most, Benjamin, and Starr, Harvey, 'International Relations Theory, Foreign Policy Substitutability, and "Nice" Laws', *World Politics*, 363, 1984, pp. 383–406.

10. Kegley, Charles, Richardson, Neil and Richter, Gunter, 'Conflict at Home and Abroad: An Empirical Extension', *Journal of Politics*, 40, 1978, pp. 742–52.

11. Bernstein, E. M., 'War and the Pattern of Business Cycles', *American Economic Review*, 30, 3, 1940, pp. 524–35; Gochman, Charles, 'Status, Capabilities, and Major Power Conflict', in J. David Singer (ed.) *The Correlates of War II: Testing Some Realpolitik Models* (New York: Free Press, 1980).

12. Kramer, G. H., 'Short-term Fluctuations in US Voting Behaviour', *American Political Science Review*, 65, 1971, pp. 131–43; Nordhaus, W. D., 'The Political Business Cycle', *Review of Economic Studies*, 42, 1975, pp. 169–89; Hibbs, D. A., Jr, 'On the Demand for Economic Outcomes: Macroeconomic Performance and Mass Support in the United States, Great Britain, and Germany', *Journal of Politics*, 44, 1982, pp. 426–62; and Hibbs, D. A., and Vasilatos, N., 'Macroeconomic Performance and Mass Political Support in the United States and Great Britain', in Hibbs, D. A., Jr, and Fassbender, H. (eds) *Contemporary Political Economy* (New York: North Holland, 1981).

13.   See Tufte, Edward, *Political Control of the Economy* (Princeton: Princeton University Press, 1979); Brown, T. A., and Stein, A. A., 'Review of Tufte (1978)', in *Comparative Politics*, 14, 4, 1982, pp. 479–97; and Thompson, William R. and Zuk, Gary, 'American Elections and the International Economic Cycle', *American Journal of Political Science*, 27, 3, 1983, pp. 464–84 for critiques of Tufte; Nincic, Miroslav, and Cusack, Thomas, 'The Political Economy of US Military Spending', *Journal of Peace Research*, 16, 2, 1979, pp. 101–15, for suggestions that military spending is especially manipulable for this purpose; and Krell, Gert, 'Capitalism and Armaments: Business Cycles and Defense Spending in the United States 1945–79', *Journal of Peace Research*, 18, 3, 1981, pp. 221–40, for a critique of Nincic and Cusack.

14.   A vigorous if controversial assertion of this proposition as applicable to various phases of modern European history is Meyer, Arno, 'Interval Crisis and War Since 1870', in Bertrand, C. L. (ed.), *Revolutionary Situations in Europe, 1917–1922* (Montreal: McGill University Press, 1977).

15.   Muller, John, *War, Presidents, and Public Opinion* (New York: Wiley, 1973); Brody, Richard A., 'International Crises: A Rallying Point for the President?' *Public Opinion*, 6, 6, 1984, pp. 43, 40.

16.   Ostrom, Charles, and Simon, Dennis, 'Promise and Performance: A Dynamic Model of Presidential Popularity', *American Political Science Review*, 79, 2, 1985, pp. 334–58.

17.   The systematic empirical literature of these relationships individually (that is, in bivariate form) is both voluminous and largely inconclusive. Despite some dissent – for example, Rummel, R. J., 'Libertarianism and International Violence', *Journal of Conflict Resolution*, 27, 1983, pp. 27–72 – I believe the predominant evidence is that neither a democratic nor an authoritarian regime, as such, is significantly more likely than the other to engage in conflict. See, for example, Singer, J. David and Small, Melvin, 'The War-Proneness of Democratic Regimes', *Jerusalem Journal of International Relations*, 1, 1, 1976, pp. 50–69; Chan, Steve, 'Mirror, Mirror, on the Wall. . .: Are the Free Countries More Pacific?' *Journal of Conflict Resolution*, 28, 4, 1984, pp. 617–48; and Erich Weede, 'Democracy and War Involvement', *Journal of Conflict Resolution*, 28, 4, 1984, pp. 649–64. On the relation – or, more correctly, the lack of it – between domestic conflict and foreign conflict see Rummel, R. J., 'Dimensions of Foreign and Domestic Conflict Behavior: A Review of the Empirical Findings', in Pruitt, Dean and Synder, Richard (eds), *Theory and Research on the Causes of War*, (Englewood Cliffs, New Jersey: Prentice-Hall, 1969); Stohl, Michael, 'The Nexus of Civil and International Conflict', in Ted Gurr (ed.) *Handbook of Political Conflict* (New York: Free Press, 1980); Eberwein, Wolf-Dieter, 'The Quantitative Study of International Conflict: Quantity or Quality? An Assessment of Empirical Research', *Journal of Peace Research*, 18, 1, 1981, pp. 19–38; Singer, J. David, 'Accounting for International War: The State of the Discipline', *Journal of Peace Research*, 18, 1, 1981, pp. 1–18; and

Ward, Michael, and Widmaier, Ulrich, 'The Domestic–International Conflict Nexus: New Evidence and Old Hypothesis', *International Interactions*, 9, 1, 1982, pp. 75–101.

18. For example, van Duijn (see note 3) reports a lack of synchronisation between the apparent timing of long waves for France and those for the other big industrial countries.

19. Maddison, Angus, 'Per Capita Output in the Long Run', *Kyklos*, 32, 1/2, 1979, pp. 412–29; supplemented by Mitchell, B. R., *European Historical Statistics, 1750–1975* (New York: Facts on File, 1979, 2nd edn).

20. For the relevant dates see Russett, Bruce, Singer, J. David, and Small, Melvin, 'A Standardized List of National Political Entities in the Twentieth Century', *American Political Science Review*, 62, 3, 1968, pp. 932–51.

21. Singer, J. David, and Small, Melvin, 'The War-Proneness of Democratic Regimes', *Jerusalem Journal of International Relations*, 1, 1, 1976, pp. 50–69 (esp. p. 55). These codings are virtually identical to those used by Chan (see note 17). I am grateful to Professor Chan for providing me with them in correspondence.

22. The coding procedures, rationale, and resulting patterns are found in Gochman, Charles and Maoz, Zeev, 'Militarised Interstate Disputes, 1816–1976: Procedures, Patterns, and Insights', *Journal of Conflict Resolution*, 28, 4, 1984, pp. 585–616.

23. Our codings modify the Gochman and Maoz set in several respects. We are interested only in the year a dispute began, not in subsequent years when it may continue. Also, we do not count disputes initiated when a country was already involved in another dispute at the same or higher level; such subsequent disputes are more likely to result from horizontal expansion of the initial dispute than from any changes in economic conditions. All wartime years after the first are excluded from the analysis. Finally, since we were looking for relatively autonomous decisions we did not want to include cases where smaller powers were likely to have been brought into an ongoing dispute, not entirely voluntarily, by pressure from large powers. Hence we excluded instances of subsequent involvement (1850–99, two weeks or more from the dispute beginning; 1900–76, one week).

24. Statistical significance levels are given as a guide to strength of association, not because we are generalising from a random sample. Because of heterogeneity across countries in the data set, the standard errors are likely to be exaggerated, in which case the levels of statistical significance would be low, and hence our report is likely to be, if anything, conservative.

25. Summers, Robert, and Heston, Alan, 'Improved International Comparisons of Real Product and Its Composition', *The Review of Income and Wealth*, 30, June 1984, pp. 207–62; United Nations, Projections and Perspective Studies Branch, *Handbook of World Development Statistics, 1982* (New York: UN Department of International Economic and Social Affairs, 1982).

10 Whither Modernisation and Militarisation? Implications for International Security and Arms Control*

Edward A. Kolodziej
UNIVERSITY OF ILLINOIS

Modernisation and militarisation are closely associated. Militarisation responds to the imperatives arising from the global modernising process begun five centuries ago with the rise of the territorial state and with the destruction of the European feudalism and its gradual replacement by capitalist-based economy.[1] To establish this association – and the direct and indirect causal connection between them – the discussion below first defines the principal characteristics of modernisation as a global process of socio-economic change and political transformation and defines militarisation in terms that can be linked to key characteristics of modernisation. Some of the implications of this argument for global arms control accords are subsequently outlined in the concluding section. Aims of modernisation will have to be redirected and the means used by the world community in this pursuit will have to be redefined if militarisation is to remain the servant, not master, of modernisation.

I PRINCIPAL CHARACTERISTICS OF MODERNISATION

1 Search for Global Order and Legitimacy

As a social process, modernisation has four characteristics that can be associated with militarisation. First, it is the search of peoples everywhere for a global order based on a claim of universal legiti-

206

macy. The nation-state has emerged as the provisional answer to this aspiration. The destruction of Christian unity and the eruption of internecine religious wars between Catholics and Protestants generated the need for an arbiter, independent of these communal struggles, to resolve differences and to protect both persons and property within territorially defined states and to provide for the collective security of populations – progressively defined as national entities – against foreign opponents. Thomas Hobbes' *Leviathan* became the model for Western Europe. The modern secular state crystallised around hereditary monarchs who, basing their authority on divine right and blood, monopolised the functions of internal order and external security. Religious and hereditary tests were eroded eventually as determining principles of legitimate rule. While political regimes today differ with respect to their claims to exercise legitimately the state's monopoly of violence, they almost all rest on some secular principle of legitimacy whether defined along liberal republican, democratic, socialist, or autocratic lines of rule. The Iranian revolution and reactionary movements like Islamic fundamentalism, ironically, are evidence of modernity's ascendancy.

The nation-state triumphed for several key reasons. Its appeal was more broadly based than the personal loyalties underlying feudalism. It elicited the support of rising entrepreneurial classes; appealed increasingly to artisans and small landowners and peasants; and absorbed the energies and talents of those elements of the old aristocracy, like France's de Tocqueville or the Prussian *Junkers*, who sensed the irresistible force of the new social and economic movements sweeping Europe.[2] Under the centralising control of monarchical rule, the nation-state proved more successful than its opponents at mobilising the material and human resources of the realm for war and economic growth.[3]

The victory of the nation-state in Europe was simultaneous with its extension to the globe as the principal vehicle for organising the world community.[4] The struggle among European states for continental dominion was widened to a global scale, encompassing peoples everywhere. National survival, prosperity, and greatness justified empire and legitimated the manipulation of alien peoples and their exploitation for the benefit of Europe's ruling classes and populations. Rival European states projected their local struggles to the world environment with the result that through colonisation the modern world system became an extension of European politics. Over five centuries to the present era, first Spain and Portugal, then

Holland, Britain and France, and finally Germany and Italy successively entered the competition for European hegemony resting partially on empire abroad. Europe's quarrels defined the world's
political agenda. The Euro-centric system prevailed until its collapse
in 1945 with its temporary replacement by a bipolar system, polarised
between the USA and the USSR.

Since 1945, the world community has been in the grip of two
movements, both rooted in the nation-state. The first has been the
pursuit of competing imperial systems by the superpowers. They may
be viewed as just the latest in a long succession of nation-state
contestants bent on fashioning a world order to suit their aims and
interests. The superpowers, like their predecessors, have so far been
frustrated in their quest for dominion by their counterbalancing
rivalry. The superpowers also confront scores of new nation-states in
the decolonised southern hemisphere as well as the old but still
vigorous states of Europe and Japan, strong regional powers with a
global political and economic reach. This network of nation-states
limits the hegemonic pretensions of Moscow and Washington. The
centripetal force of the superpower struggle and the centrifugal
tendencies of third-state rivalries around the globe obscure the
victory of the nation-state as the provisional answer to the imperative
underlying modernisation: the search for a more inclusive and
reliable order than that afforded by inherited or traditional forms of
political organisation.

2   Search for Welfare

The demand for ever greater levels of prosperity is the second
distinguishing feature of modernisation. Populations around the
world refuse to accept the low and deprived material standards of life
to which they were born. Emulated is the example of developed
states, located principally in the northern hemisphere, which have
enjoyed progressive and accumulating economic expansion since the
fifteenth century. Commercial capitalism followed by state-led mercantilist practices induced the search for raw materials, the internal
development of European markets, and the expansion of trade first
to the Mediterranean littoral, then to the New World, and, subsequently, to Asia and Africa. Beginning with the eighteenth century,
commercial and mercantilist capitalism gradually gave way to industrial and finance capitalism. The process of constructing a world
capitalist economy on which the wealth of the European states

increasingly depended was completed by the end of the nineteenth century. While a European centred global order collapsed as a consequence of the destruction wrought by the First and Second World Wars, liberal Western capitalism survived as a consequence of a strong and expansionist American economy and the defeat of the protectionist imperial regimes of Germany, Italy and Japan.

Even before the emergence of the USA as capitalism's champion, perceived inequities of the capitalist system led to political movements and revolutionary forces that created Socialist and Communist regimes, committed to state ownership of the means of production as an antidote to the real and alleged excesses of capitalist market practices. It was not so much industrialisation itself that was rejected but the mechanisms by which its productive fruits were to be distributed and future investment priorities determined. In place of the market, distributive decisions on profits, wages, and investments were assumed by state officials, exercising power through mass-based parties. With decolonisation, collectivist solutions to economic growth gained additional force. The Western, capitalist states were challenged in the north by the Communist bloc and by developing states of the south which often preferred a Soviet to an American model of modernisation.

3 Search for Scientific Discovery and Technological Progress

The search for greater world security and wealth is associated with a third characteristic of modernisation: the unique prestige enjoyed by scientific discovery and technological advancement. Traditional man expected little or no change in nature or society. He accepted his fate as a product of God's will, blind force or social inheritance. There existed few widely accepted objective tests for physical or social truth. Traditional explanations of the physical universe reinforced social and political controls exercised by religious leaders or rulers claiming divine investment. Once scientific knowledge established itself as an independent source of truth, it challenged traditional and social authority and undermined the legitimacy of these institutions relying on these principles of rule. In applying scientific knowledge to technological innovation, modernising societies created a powerful instrument for change, physical and social, whose limits have yet to be fully exploited.

With scientific knowledge and technological progress, man could control and shape physical nature to his liking. He also had access to an unprecedented array of powerful instruments to shape his socio-economic conditions and political destiny. What could not be anticipated, as discussed below, was the extent to which the principal beneficiary of this new knowledge and know-how would be the nation-state. Science and technology have proved critical in assisting nation-states to respond to the security dilemma underlying the global nation-state system and to the welfare demands of populations who either consent or are coerced to pledge loyalty to them.

4 Search for Personal Worth

Modernisation, defined by the globalised nation-state, industrialisation, and the spread of science and technology, has produced new institutions to ensure its ascendancy and spread. These institutions of governance, of economic productivity, and of knowledge acquisition and application confer power, privileges, and position on the élites who command and control them. Status is determined, not as before, through inheritance, blood, or ascription, but through talent, performance, or societally defined tests or criteria of utility. As Samuel P. Huntington and Robert Dahl observe, 'The traditional distribution of status along a single bifurcated structure characterised by "dispersed inequalities gives way to pluralistic status structures characterized by dispersed inequalities".'[5]

At the same time modernisation implies a conception of personal merit that is radically egalitarian. Talent and performance, as tests of individual worth, compete with the conflicting claim that equality, unmixed by qualifications of national origin or ethnic, religious tribal or racial background, should alone be a proper measure of personal value. This levelling process, as de Tocqueville recognised,[6] unleashes pressures for socio-economic improvement and expectations of popular participation in the domestic politics of states. While mass participation has become a common feature of modern rule, participation variously manifests itself, often in contradictory fashions: for example, in authoritarian regimes, through mass mobilisation by élites, operating through nationally-based parties or bureaucracies, or in liberal democracies, through public opinion expressed through open elections, media representations, or private associations and pressure groups.

II MILITARISATION AND MODERNISATION

How is modernisation associated with militarisation? How are its four characteristics – the rise of the globalised nation-state, world-wide demands for welfare, the spread of science and technology, and the redefinition of personal worth based on talent, performance, and equality – linked to militarisation? Some notion of what is meant by militarisation is essential if a relation is to be established between these two powerful forces that shape the world community.

Militarisation refers to all forms of social activity which are directly or indirectly related to the organisation of violence for the purpose of deterring, defending against, or defeating an opponent. The need for organised violence initially arises from the conflict of political units which are unable to resolve their differences by mutual consent, by accepting rules for non-coercive competition, or by an appeal to universally applicable moral principles or laws. The opponents rely on violence or its threat to impose their demands on each other. They are thus locked, as Schelling suggests,[7] in a bargaining process where killing, maiming, hurting, and damaging are the instruments by which they seek to have their way. Carried to the extreme, with no other limitation on their struggle than the competition of opposing will with force as the arbiter, the clash approaches what Clausewitz has termed 'pure war'.[8] Clausewitz's 'pure war' may be extended to what Kenneth Boulding terms a 'pure theory of threat systems', wherein political communities devote all of their time, energy, and resources to preparation for war and do so in the pursuit of what is perceived as a social good.[9] The Napoleonic Wars, the First and Second World Wars, the religious wars of the seventeenth century, the Punic Wars, and the struggles between the Greek city-states provide examples of conflicts that enveloped and absorbed almost all social relations within and between political units. Militarisation thus includes not only the preparations for warfare and its execution but 'an emphasis', as Alfred Vagts observes, 'on military considerations, spirit, ideals, and scales of value, in the life of states'.[10] National human and material resources are oriented toward activities associated with expenditures for military forces and arms as well as for industrialisation, research, and development dedicated primarily to armaments. Conversely, opportunity costs are incurred in terms of civil pursuits defined by the production of consumer goods and services, education, welfare, the arts, and leisure.

1   Response to Order and Legitimacy: The Nation-State and the Permanent War System

Analysts of modernisation have generally excluded the nation-state from their consideration as a vehicle of modernisation of the global community. They have preferred instead to view modernisation as a phenomenon occurring principally *within* the borders of the territorial state.[11] Consequently, the distinguishing feature of the nation-state system – war – is excluded from examination. The nation-state is fundamentally different from all other social groupings because it monopolises the legitimate use of organised violence.[12] If this critical feature of global relations is excluded from an analysis and evaluation of the modernisation process, internal or domestic socio-economic and political institutions which respond to the conflict-producing sources of inter-state relations appear alien and exogenous to the modernisation process rather than a response to it. Forgotten is the historical lesson that the success of the nation-state, as a modernising force within the global political community, was due precisely to its capacity to wage war better than alternative forms of social organisation. Michael Howard reminds us that:

> the growing capacity of European governments to control, or at least to tap, the wealth of the community, and from it to create mechanisms – bureaucracies, fiscal systems, armed forces – which enable them yet further to extend their control over the community, is one of the central developments in the historical era which, opening in the latter part of the seventeenth century, has continued to our own time.[13]

The nation-state, first within Europe and, later, in the developing world, reflected an expectation, translated into a demand during the decolonisation era, that the global community be based on a principle of order and legitimacy that transcended religious, ethnic or class origin and even cultural and linguistic differences. The success of the nation-state was testimony to the quest for a unit that could function as the vehicle for an enlarging consciousness of unity in organising political affairs in opposition to restrictive, parochial, or non-secular principles of organisation.

Excluding the nation-state from an analysis of modernisation also simplifies the problems that must be resolved if the needs and demands animating the modernisation process are to be satisfied.[14] Controlling violence as a problem is narrowed to control *within* the state although the issue facing the global community is limiting violence simultaneously *within* and *between* states. The possibility of total militarisation, defined along lines suggested by Clausewitz's conception of 'pure war' or Boulding's notion of 'pure threat systems', arises today from nation-state conflicts that currently revolve, interdependently, around East–West and North–South axes. The superpower power conflict is as intrinsic to the global modernisation process as is the process of nation-state building in the countries lying largely in the southern hemisphere. Viewed from an historical perspective, encompassing over five centuries of evolution, the distinction between developing and developed nations loses much of its force if one views them as different elements of a single, if hetergeneous, political community confronting, as a collectivity, the overriding issue of establishing a stable and what is perceived as a legitimate global order. While each unit may well differ for the foreseeable future with respect to its internal definition of modernity, all face the issue of order as a common problem to be resolved together if a workable international political system is to be progressively formulated and instituted.

Even if nuclear war had not raised the prospect of total war, one would still be obliged to address the problem of the militarisation of the modernisation process. If one examines various measures of militarisation the trends are markedly upward. Table 10.1 indicates that between 1973 and 1983 there were increases in world military expenditures for developed and developing states, armed forces, the ratio of military expenditures to *GNP* (accompanied by an increase in the rate of *GNP* growth), and military spending per capita. Only the ratio of military expenditures to central government expenditures and armed forces per 1000 of population declined.

Arms deliveries and agreements also climbed in this period. In current dollars, world totals rose in current dollars from $56.9 bn in 1973–6 to $147.3 bn in a comparable three-year period from 1981–4. The corresponding totals for developed states in these two time-periods are respectively $15.1 bn and $27.6 bn. Those for developing states show an even steeper ascent from $41.9 bn to $119.7 bn.[15]

What seems clear is that the security dilemma, endemic first to the evolution of the nation-state system within Europe which led to successively larger wars in the nineteenth and twentieth century, now absorbs the world community. The spread of the security dilemma has three distinctive but mutually reinforcing features which institutionalise regional and global conflict and instability and militarises

214

Table 10.1   Measures of militarisation

		1973	1983
1.	Military expenditures (*in billions of constant 1982 dollars*)		
	World	564.9	778.9
	Developed states	469.7	616.3
	Developing states	95.3	162.6
2.	Armed forces (*in thousands*)		
	World	25580	28355
	Developed states	10484	10827
	Developing states	15096	17528
3.	Ratio of military expenditures to *GNP*		
	World	5.7	6.1
	Developed states	5.8	6.2
	Developing states	5.4	5.8
4.	Military expenditures per capita		
	World	144	166
	Developed states	458	557
	Developing states	32	45
5.	Ratio of military expenditures to central government expenditures		
	World	24.1	19.2
	Developed states	24.5	19.5
	Developing states	22.5	18.5
6.	Armed forces per 1000 people		
	World	6.5	6.1
	Developed states	10.2	9.8
	Developing states	5.2	4.9

Source: US, Arms Control and Disarmament Agency, *World Military Expenditures and Arms Transfers, 1985* (Washington, D.C.: US Government Printing Office, 1985) p. 47.

international relations. First, the superpower conflict draws third states into its vortex. The superpower conflict replaced the struggles among the European states as the principal axis around which world politics revolves. These two competitors, with military means capable of being speedily directed to any part of the globe, advance fundamentally different visions of how the modernisation process should proceed. These two secular religions clash over the principles of world order, economic solutions to material plenty and equity, and conceptions of personal worth and social status. Whatever the merits of these ideological stances, they still serve, as Charles de Gaulle never ceased to contend,[16] the parochial national needs and interests of their superpower proponents.

The superpower competition and arms race that has motored world conflict since the Second World War penetrates regional disputes arising from the same security dilemma underlying the Cold War. The East–West blocs testify to this process. The superpower struggle in the developing world provides additional evidence. The battlegrounds today are Central America, the Middle East, south-west Asia, and southern Africa whereas the Balkans, Korea, and Vietnam were the cockpits of conflict a decade or more earlier. Even the all-but-defunct non-aligned movement can be viewed as essentially spawned by the superpower conflict since it sought to preserve some measure of independence for the newly emerging states of the south from superpower depredations and the risk of nuclear conflict.

Conversely, local rivalries risk assuming a global significance as regional opponents seek superpower assistance in resolving their quarrel on favourable terms. During the era of colonial empires, the European states performed this policing role. The dismantling of the Eurocentric system left few effective international agencies to fill the vacuum left by the withdrawal of European forces. The United Nations, divided against itself, has failed to perform this role, notwithstanding some successes in minor peacekeeping roles. Its effectiveness has been progressively narrowed and marginalised by superpower discord and the intransigence of local states which reject its edicts or advice. What is left to preserve peace is the precarious counterbalancing military power of local rivalries. International security leans on a weak reed. Regional arms races in Europe, the Middle East, Africa, and Asia deepen the superpower global arms competition. The military requirements of superpower intervention, in turn, must be valued upward as local resistance is strengthened by the growth in the size and sophistication of national armed forces, the development of indigenous arms production facilities, and easier access to multilateral supply sources for weapons, equipment and material.

Third, the strength of the delicately woven cloth of security arrangements defining inter-state conflicts is further tested by the rending impact of modernisation on traditional societies. Since the Second World War these societies have unravelled at a faster rate than the new classes and élites produced by modernisation could be woven together into a cohesive fabric to replace *anciens régimes*. The worst of both worlds is visited on the world community, as in Lebanon, where inherited communal rivalries clash with new secular forces within an international environment driven by irreconcilable regional rivalries and the superpower conflict. At stake is the future of modernisation; at issue is the heightened militarisation of the international system between *and* within states.

2   Response of Militarisation to Welfare

The security dilemma confronting modern states has also generated a requirement for the creation of military industrial–scientific–technological complexes (MISTs) to develop and produce weapons. The quest for political independence prompts states to pursue, within their resource possibilities, autarchic weapons acquisition policies, preferring indigenous production to external dependency. The state's claimed monopoly of the legitimate exercise of violence would have little effect if it did not simultaneously seek a corresponding control over the means of arms production. The rise of the modern state has been almost synchronous, if not synonymous, with its weapon-making capability. The superpowers are almost totally independent of other states in weapon-production. Both also supply most of the arms sold or transferred to third states. The developed states of the north also meet much of their own arms needs. France, as the world's third arms supplier, is essentially autonomous in meeting its military requirements. The other major states of East and West Europe, measured by arms sales, also possess impressive arms production capabilities. Between 1979 and 1983, seven East- and West-European states delivered $46.5 bn in weapons to third states. The superpowers transferred weapons valued near $97 bn during the same period. The Europeans controlled approximately 27 per cent of a $170 bn market; the USA and the USSR accounted, respectively, for 33.3 and 23.7 per cent of world trade in arms.[17]

One particularly striking feature of the post-colonial period is the growth in the number and sophistication of weapons production centres in the developing world. In 1950, there were only five countries producing one or more major weapon systems, including ships, armour, aircraft, or missiles. In successive decades, this number rose from 14 (1960) to 21 (1970), and, finally, 26 (1980).[18] Over this period the number of states producing one or more systems within one of the four major weapons categories also increased.

Table 10.2 outlines the enlarging capabilities of developing states to manufacture a wide array of systems. In 1960, only seven countries in the developing world had entered the aircraft industry. They turned out fifteen different systems. Twenty years later eighteen countries produced sixty-seven types of equipment. In 1960 no developing state produced ground armour; a generation later six countries produced seventeen systems, ranging from tanks to armoured bridgelayers. The same upward trends are visible for missiles and naval vessels. By 1980, nine states were producing twenty-six different kinds of missiles, and twenty-five countries were constructing forty-five naval systems within six ship categories. Six countries (Argentina, Brazil, China, India, Israel, and South Africa) maintained production lines for all major weapons systems.[19] Some, like Israel and Brazil, succeeded in developing their own research and development base for some arms. Depending on the system or state, one can discern a progressive expansion among developing states of weapons-development capability defined at the lowest level of capability as licensed component production to – in succeeding orders of sophistication – licensed system production, system modification and reverse engineering, dependent R & D and production, and independent R & D.[20]

Once in place, these MISTs tend to make claims on internal investment resources that progressively enlarge their impact on their national economies and, collectively, on the world economy. In its initial stages, the MIST complex of a state responds primarily to security imperatives. The historic growth of weapon-producing centres in the developed world appear to fit such a pattern of development. Set in motion, the MIST complex tends to perpetuate and enlarge its hold on a state's economy and welfare-producing policies.[21] The MIST complex can claim to produce a useful public service and product – security. Added justification for an autarchic weapons policy is also found in the claim that the independence of the nation-state and the maintenance of the domestic regime are preconditions for the material development of the society.

Table 10.2   Arms production in developing countries, 1960, 1970, 1980

	1960		1970		1980	
	Number of countries	Number of systems	Number of countries	Number of systems	Number of countries	Number of systems
Aircraft						
Fighters	1	2	3	4	6	10
Trainers (jet)	3	3	4	4	3	5
Trainers (basic)	6	7	5	6	11	13
Maritime (reconnaissance)	–	–	–	–	2	2
Transports	1	1	4	6	8	11
Aircraft (engines)	1	1	2	2	6	8
Helicopters	1	1	2	2	11	15
Avionics	–	–	–	–	3	3
Total	7	15	8	24	18	67
Ground equipment						
Tanks	–	–	3	3	5	6
APC	–	–	1	2	5	6
Armoured cars	–	–	2	2	2	2
Reconnaissance vehicles	–	–	–	–	2	2
Armoured bridgelayers	–	–	–	–	1	1
Total	–	–	5	7	6	17
Missiles						
Surface-to-air	–	–	–	–	5	6
Air-to-ground	–	–	1	1	5	6
Air-to-air	1	1	2	2	5	5
Surface-to-surface	1	1	1	1	3	4
Anti-tank	–	–	1	1	7	8
Total	1	2	5	5	9	26
Naval vessels						
Frigates	1	1	1	1	4	5
Corvettes	2	2	2	2	1	1
Patrol craft	8	8	13	13	20	25
Submarines	–	–	–	–	3	3
Amphibious craft	1	1	2	2	4	4
Support craft	6	6	4	4	7	7
Total	13	18	15	22	25	45

Sources: Andrew L. Ross, *Arms Production in Developing Countries: The Continuing Proliferation of Conventional Weapons*, no. N-1615-AF, Rand Corporation Note (Santa Monica, California, 1981) pp. 16–19 and Stockholm International Peace Research Insititute, *World Armament and Disarmament Yearbook, 1974*, pp. 230–58, and ibid, 1980, pp. 168–73 (Cambridge: Oelgeschlager, Gunn & Hain).

As their resource and bureaucratic base expands, MIST complexes gradually gain increasing control over their demand function. Not only military but civilian goods and services are offered as evidence of the welfare producing capability of the MIST system. These are defined in terms of import-substitution policies to preserve scarce foreign reserves, increased exports to lower unit costs, stimulation of R & D, and high employment, especially of skilled workers, technicians, and scientific personnel. The privileged access of the MIST complex to policy circles and its central bureaucratic position enlarge its capacity to create and stimulate demand for its products and services. Its power derives from its manipulation of the symbols of security and welfare, fundamental societal values; from its self-serving interpretation, circulated in the media, of its contribution to social well-being; from its unique importance in the national decision-making process; and from its control over the participants *within* the MIST system. In the latter case, the processes of recruitment, promotion, worker and professional socialisation, and punishment fall within the purview of MIST leaders.

MISTs redefine the traditionally understood trade-off between guns and butter. No choice need be made. Indeed, the leadership speaks of 'more butter (that is, welfare) because of guns (security)'. The arms complexes of the developed systems do not present themselves as burdens on the national treasury but as assets in welfare production. This same positive stance also manifests itself in developing countries, as the partisans of MIST systems in India, [22] Israel,[23] and Brazil,[24] – states producing advanced weapons – emphasise the economic and technological advantages of military weapons development.

Whether these claims are true or not is less compelling than that they are perceived as true. Conversely, and partly because MISTs control the information needed to evaluate them, it is very difficult to measure conclusively the opportunity costs of adopting a model of development dependent on military production. Arms production and sales by developing countries continues to mount. At present concentrated in nine states (excluding China), arms production in 1980 (licensed and indigenous) reached a peak of $1.2 bn in 1975 prices. An estimated 1 million workers were directly engaged in the arms industry, with India topping the list (280 000), followed by South Africa (90 000), Israel (75 000), and Egypt (75 000). From a negligible level in the 1960s, arms exports by developing states, currently representing 4 per cent of the global market, shot dramatically upward in the 1970s, reaching a peak of $250 m in 1982.[25] By contrast, in the developed world, more than 10 million workers in 1982 were engaged directly in arms production,[26] and arms deliveries by these states were roughly twenty-five times greater than their counterparts in the developing world.

MISTs are subject to what Johan Galtung characterises as an *Eigendynamik* of economic growth. The incentives to expand, defined as the continued supply of investment to keep the system operating at efficient levels, appear compelling:

> Thus, if the raw materials are there, the labour is there, researchers have done their job so that the model of what to produce exists, and the whole administrative machinery is present, there will be a tendency to try to provide the missing capital rather than to send the raw materials back, dismiss the workers, let the research findings be shelved unused, and transfer the administrators else-where.[27]

These pressures work quite independently of the security considerations that may originally have led to the organisation of a MIST complex. They have a ratchet effect on managing conflict-relations between opponents. A relaxation of tensions does not lead immediately to a reduction in arms-making capability as the arms complex resists reductions in its size or influence.

3 Response of Militarisation to Scientific and Technological Development

As nation-states and MISTs have responded to security and welfare imperatives, they have relied increasingly on scientific discovery and technological development in pursuing their aims and interests. The modern state cannot be conceived apart from the close, symbiotic relation between its spread and the development of techno-scientific establishments and the evolution of increasingly destructive war-fare.[28] It is now commonplace to note that armed struggles between rival states are fought increasingly in their respective laborato-ries. Progress in basic physics, chemistry, and mathematics opened the way to the development of new technologies. These produced a revolution in metals and materials, communications, transportation, electronics, and energy. As men and states learned to understand and control nature, not merely to adapt to its exigencies and seeming vicissitudes, they have applied techno-scientific tools of control to better their material condition and, not surprisingly, to resolve their conflictual relations. Science and technology now simultaneously serve beneficent and hostile aims. The result is a continuous, cumulative, and potentially unlimited process of new product developments and services, expanding economic growth and wealth-production, and, simultaneously, the mounting lethality of conventional and nuclear weapons measured by the rapid speed and distance of their delivery, destructiveness, and target efficiency.

The organisation of national and international scientific and technological resources has not proceeded along a defined, linear course, free of other societal needs or forces. It has not evolved as an unmixed good wherein scientific discoveries and technological advancements were mobilised and directed altruistically to mankind's socio-economic improvement. As often as not, these resources were mobilised for war and coercion. It is no accident that nuclear physics and engineering were given significant impetus by the Second World War. The same claim can be made for progress in naval and air transport, civilian communications, ground transportation, electronics, and modern computational systems. That these developments could well have occurred in the absence of the push given them by war, while certainly true, is somewhat beside the point from an historical perspective. Their synchronous evolution suggests more than a mere happenstance. As a social process, one has supported the other.

Conflicts between modern nation-states and those arising at a socio-economic level from modernising processes within states prompted and guided – as they still do today – the militarisation of global scientific and technological resources along nation-state lines. It was only to be expected that models of modernisation – the post-war Japanese case notwithstanding – would rest on the assumption of scientific and technological progress as a precondition of national security and domestic welfare. If one examines France's post-war socio-economic and political development, for example, it was explicitly patterned after the American case. The leadership of the French Fourth and Fifth Republics consciously applied an American-inspired development plan, aimed at broadening and deepening France's scientific and technological base, so that France would be propelled along the same path as the USA toward economic *and* military strength.[29] One sees the same forces operating throughout the developing world.[30]

Confidence in science and technology as the instrument of national security and welfare remains a powerful modernising and militarising force. For most modern or modernising nation-states investment in national scientific research and development skewed heavily toward military weapons. The ministries of defence are important funnels for the allocation of research and development funds often on a scale surpassing what is channelled through educational establishments and industrial programmes. Over half the R & D resources of the French government and approximately one-third of all R & D expended by the French state stems from expenditures made by the Ministry of Defence.[31] The USSR appears no less committed to an economic development strategy tied closely to sustained military modernisation. Its foreign assistance programme, not surprisingly, is consistent with this strategy in assigning priority to arms transfers and military over economic aid to developing countries.[32]

The American National Defense Education Act to foster scientific education was principally spurred by the fear of a scientific–technological breakthrough in the Cold War in the wake of the Soviet launch of the first man-made satellite in 1957. A generation after the initial passage of this legislation, the search for scientific and technological solutions to national welfare and security concerns proceeds unabated. These sentiments and expectations are at the surface of President Ronald Reagan's promotion of the idea of a Strategic Defense Initiative to reconstruct fundamentally the nuclear balance of terror defining US–Soviet strategic relations:

> Let me share with you a vision of the future which offers hope. It is that we embark on a program to counter the awesome Soviet missile threat with measures that are defensive. Let us turn to *the very strengths in technology that spawned our great industrial base and that have given us the quality of life we enjoy today.*
>
> What if free people could live secure in the knowledge that their security did not rest upon the threat of instant US retaliation to deter a Soviet attack, that we could intercept and destroy strategic ballistic missiles before they reached our own soil or that of our allies?
>
> *I know this is a formidable, technical task*, one that may not be accomplished before the end of this century. Yet, current technology has attained a level of sophistication where it's reasonable for us to begin this effort. It will take years, probably decades of effort on many fronts. There will be failures and setbacks, just as there

will be successes and breakthroughs. . . But isn't it worth every investment necessary to free the world from the threat of nuclear war?[33]

Science and technology are expected to resolve the security problems to which their own success has contributed. Societal and state resources are marshalled to modernise the military establishment and, paradoxically, to perpetuate the modernisation process.

4   Response of Militarisation to Personal Worth and Social Status

A final function served by militarisation is its response to the rising expectation of populations everywhere for a differential definition of personal worth based on talent and performance and, conversely, on a notion of fundamental equality. While both reject birth and blood as well as religious, ethnic, linguistic or racial tests of individual merit, modern military organisations and MISTs complexes are built on differential professional standards that rest ostensibly on objective performance criteria. Those who rise to ranks of importance are accorded access to power and special privileges that distinguish them from their peers. In the modern state, high position in the military establishment and in those structures castellated around it must normally be earned through advanced educational degrees, long apprenticeship within a military or civilian bureaucracy, and tested loyalty to the professional code and organisational needs of the military system. The benefits of loyalty and performance – power, position and privilege – may, of course, be enjoyed through service in other valued socio-economic and political structures – in industry, finance, education, or the media. But to the degree that militarisation responds to the personal needs of the modernising individual, its hold on the modernisation process is tightened and the state's resources are deflected to lethal concerns.

MISTs and military structures recruit society's best and brightest. Talent that might otherwise fill non-coercive roles is siphoned off into activities intimately tied to organised coercion and violence. In the absence of other outlets for ambition and talent, military establishments and their supporting MISTs discharge what are perceived as an indispensable role in discovering new talent, in socialising new generations to the norms of modernity, and in investing high social value in the activities of a significant segment of a nation's leadership classes.[34]

As the French Revolution demonstrated, the military also respond to egalitarian compulsions within modern society. Since the French Revolution, the citizen has been defined as a soldier. Together, they are valued facets of what is posited as one integrated national personality. The destitute and deprived, as well as the gifted and advantaged, find outlets for social acceptance in the armed forces. New possibilities for personal satisfaction and advancement are available for those from even the lowest rungs of the social ladder. Note, for example, the disproportionate number of blacks in the US armed forces relative to their number in the American population, a circumstance partly explicable by the blockages to personal betterment operating within American society.[35] Observe, too, the number of governmental leaders, particularly those holding positions of power in the developing world, who rise from modest circumstances to high position after a long incubation within the military bureaucracy. The rise of military officers, like Gamal Nasser and Anwar Sadat in Egypt, Mengistu Haile Mariam in Ethopia, John Doe in Liberia, and Muammar Qadhafi in Libya, to national political leadership are symptomatic of tendencies within modernisation that respond as much to the personal expectations and needs of modern man as to military requirements of national security.

The personal satisfactions accorded by the military and its ancillary support mechanisms – for differentiation and equality – are complemented by the discharge of critical socio-political roles. For many nation-states, particularly those in the developing world, the army is the nation. In some instances it is the primary vehicle in building a nation to replace the local, familial, tribal, or communal bonds broken by the march of modernity. It infuses a sense of national consciousness and central authority within societies in the throes of rapid and disruptive social change. This national integrative function is hardly unique to the twentieth century. Prussia was first an army before it was a nation. Using the military to enforce integration can also be costly; witness civil strife in Nigeria in the 1960s, the decimation of Cambodian society a decade later, and the pursuit of a revolutionary reconstruction of the Ethiopian nation with little attention devoted to the basic care and nurturing of the population. On the other hand, when civilian rule breaks down, as in Turkey, the army may act as the self-styled guardian of the state until societal conflict can be brought under control, but inevitably at a cost to personal freedom and, as often as not, to socio-economic development.[36]

III SYSTEMIC IMPLICATIONS OF MODERNISATION AND MILITARISATION ON ARMS CONTROL

The implications of the preceding analysis are sobering. First, modernisation is no automatic answer to militarisation. It is part of the problem since its imperatives, as these have been historically recorded, have directly and indirectly contributed to the militarisation of relations between states and that of socio-economic and political development within states. This dilemma is most acutely confronted when one examines the war-prone tendencies of the nation-state system. The nation-state provisionally resolved the need for personal and collective security. Possessing a monopoly over organised violence, it could arbitrate internal differences between clashing factions and impose an order backed by courts and coercion. Against foreign enemies, it could wage war more efficiently and effectively than city-states or feudal lords. As Hobbes made clear, much of its claim to legitimacy rested on its ability to provide internal and external security. War, too, was legitimated since it authoritatively settled differences between states when other modes of resolution failed. It served as a useful medium of exchange in estimating the power of states, much as the free market settled accounts between buyers and sellers.

So long as the nation-state could wage war effectively, its authority to rule those pledging loyalty to it remained essentially intact. Now that war, especially global nuclear war, threatens the nation-state and the incipiently anarchical system on which the tenuous governance of the world community has been built, the claim of the nation-state to legitimacy is seriously impaired. Total war threatens to rend the tie between function – successful war-making as the prerequisite of security – and the legitimacy of the state flowing from the discharge of this function. The right of the state to monopolise organised violence is fundamentally challenged. In this light, there is a kernel of truth in the argument, advanced by Kenneth Boulding and others, that the war-system and national security establishments are *in*security systems since they cannot guarantee security and their arms competition threatens the security that they claim to accord.

The growing measures and modes of lethality at the disposal of a world of nation-states erode the viability of the nation-state and the war system on which it is based. The very effectiveness of the nation-state is waging wars – once a solution to personal and collective security during the long breakdown of the feudal system – is now a major threat to world order. The security dilemma, intrinsic to the nation-state system, drives the militarisation of the modernisation process. In attempting to address one issue – security – the modern state, in competition with itself, threatens the world community. The ironic consequence is that modernisation is itself its own enemy since it is a primary source of potentially destabilising militarisation. How the world community will extricate itself from this self-imposed impasse is not clear, for the nation-state has never been more ascendant, *faute de mieux*, over other conceivable social alternatives in organising the world community, yet never has it been as vulnerable to its own potentially self-destructive tendencies.

Second, if the world community insists on modernisation and yet is threatened by its lethal elements and if there exists no arbiter, as before, in the form of a powerful monarch to resolve the quarrels of feudal lords, then one must primarily count on the imperfect, self-regulating mechanisms of the system itself until more stable and less coercive mechanisms for global social control are in place. A premium must, therefore, be placed on arms control and on buying time until such mechanisms can be fashioned, their implementation negotiated, and their institutionalisation ensured.

As for arms control, the growth of centres of organised violence around the globe establishes an objective condition advising the extension of the concept of arms control to the entire global security system.[37] In its simplest form, arms control may be understood as the definition of rules for the use or threat of force between adversaries by which they mutually regulate their competition. Since the world security system is increasingly interdependent, wherein the eruption of violence is one part of the globe affects others, rule-making in conducting war and in manipulating threats between states cannot be confined only to the superpowers. Such a narrow approach has several drawbacks. States whose interests are affected by superpower conflict or condominium have few avenues to promote their views and to act, implicitly, as counterbalances to the superpower arms race. On the other hand, the damaging impact of local conflicts is not easily confined to a region. Long distances and poor communications no longer separate areas of the globe as before. Because opponents at regional and global levels possess such destructive military capabilities, potentially damaging to each other and to third states, they exercise as a matter of fact and circumstance a *droit de regard* – a right to take and give notice of each other's preparations for war. Mutual recognition of these opponent and third-state rights, implicitly acknowledged in the superpower SALT and START processes, prepares the way not only for mutual acceptance and legitimation of military modernisation but also the institutionalisation of regional and global arms control processes as prerequisites for the creation and maintenance of order-bearing regimes between states.

If arms control accords can limit the size of national arsenals, reduce the pace of weapons development, and stabilise arms competition by mutual legitimation by opponents of their modernising programmes, then another major purpose of such accords is served: they buy time. Tension-less time is needed to afford the opportunity to construct alternative structures and institutions, primarily within states, to satisfy the welfare, acquisition and application of knowledge, and personal needs of populations. Unless these imperatives of modernisation are addressed, the world community will be perpetually condemned to revolve in a vicious circle of its own making. Conflict and arms races will compel increases in defence spending, the expansion of military establishments, and the growth of MISTs; correspondingly, élites and mass needs will be met through an increasingly militarised modernisation process.

Creating alternatives for personal and collective satisfaction will take time, resources, and the mobilization of political will to withstand the resistance to change of those whose personal stake is rooted in the curent military environment. A less war-prone world implies not only the construction of international regimes to regulate and resolve inter-state differences but also, and of equal importance, the erection of domestic supports to uphold the inevitably fragile arms control arrangements that one currently expects from nation-states which are jealous of their independence and prerogatives. To build arms-control constituencies across nation-state boundaries implies non-governmental contacts based on professional and personal contacts that promise to have a long-term impact on moderating the deep and genuine differences currently splitting governments and political regimes. Since modernisation generates global interdependence in welfare creation, in techno-scientific development, and in defining human rights and personal worth, one can conceivably build on these elements of modernity – and on élite and mass sentiment associated with them – in checking the damaging and and debilitating tendencies of unbridled militarisation.

From a global perspective, slowing arms races, buying time, and legitimating the continual modernisation of national arsenals can serve to relax, if not transform, the urgency to build more and better arms. To assist in regulating these processes there is a corresponding need for independent international agencies to monitor and measure the militarisation process to determine whether it is getting out of hand and engulfing the non-coercive and civil forces of modernisation. Governments, as biased observers, are not always credible observers. Regional security organisations – NATO or the Warsaw Pact – are similarly defective. Their assessments are principally designed to magnify the threat posed by their opponents and to minimise the menace of their own military preparations, characterised with unfailing consistency as non-aggressive and defensive. The United Nations is also flawed since it is currently more the battleground of nation-state conflicts than an arbiter.

Notwithstanding this pessimistic assessment, the global political community has made headway in creating institutions capable of objectively determining the real and potential costs of militarisation. Universities, their research centres, and professional academic associations, like the International Economics Association and the International Political Science Association, can play a useful role in developing the data and measures needed to know whether the trend toward militarisation is increasing or decreasing. They can usefully supplement the work of such international bodies as the Stockholm International Peace Research Institute (SIPRI) and the International Institute for Strategic Studies (IISS). All these instrumentalities are critical components of a world-wide network of independent centres dedicated to measuring militarisation and to evaluating its impact on modernisation.

International efforts to build a body of reliable facts and measures of militarisation cannot be expected to resolve the dilemmas of militarisation and modernisation. They can be expected to produce a more revealing mirror than exists now of the flaws and fissures of the world community. Accurate diagnosis of the sources of conflict and their institutionalisation and reinforcement within military establishments and MISTs is a necessary, if not sufficient, condition of remedy. Unless states and their societies know where they are in modernising themselves and where they have been, it will be impossible, except by chance or force, to direct the global community down less destructive paths than those it has already stumbled along. To be consistent with itself, modernity implies control: over physical nature and over the instruments, including organised violence, that will fashion and fabricate a viable world community.

Only a modernisation process attentive to the global forces driving it will possess the guiding vision and capacity to mobilise world resources to discipline militarisation to the conflicting imperatives of modernisation: the search for global order and legitimacy based on universally accepted principles of authoritative rule; increased prosperity and the equitable distribution of expanding global wealth; access to scientific knowledge and technological advancement; and a definition of personal worth that harmonises, on the one hand, the competing notions of merit as a function of talent and performance and, on the other, the contesting demands of equality and personal freedom.

Notes and References

*I should like to thank Andrew Ross for helpful criticism of this chapter.

1. These beginning-points of modernisation are widely held in the scholarly community although there is a wide disparity of views about the causal relation between capitalism and the state. Marxists see the two phenomena as causally related, with capitalism as the motor force of the modern state. See Wallerstein, Immanuel, *The Modern World System, I* (New York: Academic Press, 1974) and *The Modern World System II* (New York: Academic Press, 1980). For a similar interpretation of contemporary international relations, consult Kaldor, Mary and Eide, Ashborn (eds) *The World Military Order* (London: Macmillan, 1979). The classical statement is, of course, of V. I. Lenin, *Imperialism, the Highest Stage of Capitalism* (New York: International Publishers, 1939).

    Other writers see the state arising from primordial concerns tied to personal and collective security. The territorial nation-state met those needs more satisfactorily than the feudal system. See Herz, John H., *The Nation-State and the Crisis of World Politics* (New York: McKay, 1976). Herz's theme of the conflict-prone character of the nation-state system is elaborated in Waltz, Kenneth, *A Theory of International Relations* (Reading, Massachusetts: Addison-Wesley, 1979). One of the most penetrating rejoinders to the Marxist analysis of the state remains Schumpeter, Joseph, *Imperialism* (New York: Meridian Books, 1955).

    This discussion treats the nation-state and capitalism as separate but interdependent instruments of modernisation responding to two fundamentally different, but universally experienced, human needs and demands: security and welfare to which the nation-state and capitalism are, respectively, provisional solutions.

2. De Tocqueville, Alexis, *De la Démocratie en Amérique* (Paris: Pagnerre, 1850) 2 vols; Craig, Gordon A., *The Politics of the Prussian Army, 1640–1945* (London: Clarendon Press, 1955).

3.   Michael Howard briefly but brilliantly traces this success in his *War in European History* (Oxford: Oxford University Press, 1976).
4.   The notion of world community used here is drawn from Hedley Bull's essay 'Society and Anarchy in International Relations', in Butterfield, Herbert and Wight, Martin (eds) *Diplomatic Investigations* (Cambridge: Harvard University Press, 1966) pp. 35–50; see also his 'War and International Order', in James, Alan (ed.) *The Bases of International Order* (Oxford: Oxford University Press, 1973) pp. 116–32. Bull's notion of the world community, when compared with the political arrangements within a nation-state, implies an imperfect global system composed of rival nation-states which share a common, if weakly defined and fragilely maintained, interest in the preservation and extension of a world order.
5.   Huntingdon, Samuel P., *Political Order in Changing Societies* (New Haven: Yale University Press, 1968) p. 32, partially quoting Robert Dahl, *Who Governs?* (New Haven: Yale University Press, 1961) pp. 85–6.
6.   See note 2, De Tocqueville.
7.   Schelling, Thomas C., *The Strategy of Conflict* (New York: Galaxy Books, 1963) and *Arms and Influence* (New Haven: Yale University Press, 1966).
8.   Clausewitz, Carl von, *On War*, translated by Graham, J. J. (London: Routledge & Kegan Paul, 1962) vol. I, pp. 1–45.
9.   Boulding, Kenneth, 'Toward a Pure Theory of Threat Systems', *American Economic Review*, LIII, no. 2 (May 1963) pp. 424–34.
10.   Vagts, Alfred, *A History of Militarism* (New York: Meridian Books, 1959) 2nd edn, p. 14. This chapter seeks not only to associate militarisation and modernisation but also, as a secondary objective, to contribute to efforts aimed at establishing the conceptual and epistemological basis for the measurement of militarisation. Analysts should be able to narrow their differences over these measures without necessarily being obliged to agree on what might be considered, viewed from divergent valuational systems and priorities, appropriate and justifiable levels of militarisation for a particular nation-state or for the global system.
11.   See note 5, Huntington and Apter, David, *The Politics of Modernization* (Chicago: University of Chicago Press, 1969). For an exception see, Morse, Edward, *Modernization and the Transformation of International Politics* (New York: Free Press, 1976). Dependency theorists are also concerned about the impact of the international system on internal modernisation, but they narrow their focus to effects of capitalist economic practices on development rather than on the global system, including the nation-state and multinational corporations as independent actors. Representative of this school are the views of Cockcroft, James D., Frank, André Gunder and Johnson, Dale L., in *Dependency and Underdevelopment* (New York: Doubleday, 1972). For an alternative view consult Gilpin, Robert, *The Multinational Corporation and the National Interest* (Princeton: Princeton University Press, 1974).

12.   Following traditional realist thinking, Raymond Aron defines international relations precisely in terms of this characteristic. Aron, Raymond, *Peace and War: A Theory of International Relations*, translated by Howard, Richard and Fox, Annette Baker (New York: Doubleday, 1966).

13.   Ibid, p. 49.

14.   An exception is Wallensteen, Peter, Galtung, Johan, and Portales, Carlos (eds), *Global Militarization* (Boulder, Colorado: Westview, 1985). While the discussion focuses on militarisation, it is compatible with the meaning of modernisation used in this analysis.

15.   US, Arms Control and Disarmament Association, *Military Expenditures and Arms Transfers, 1985* (Washington, D.C.: Government Printing Office, 1985), p. 4.

16.   See Kolodziej, Edward A., *French International Policy under de Gaulle and Pompidou: The Politics of Grandeur* (Ithaca: Cornell Univesity Press, 1974).

17.   See note 15, US, Arms Control and Disarmament Agency, p. 131.

18.   Neuman, Stephanie, G., 'International Stratification and Third World Military Industries', *International Organization* XXXVIII, no. 1 (Winter 1984), pp. 172–3.

19.   Ibid, p. 178. See also Neuman's 'Third World Arms Production and the Global Arms Transfer, System', in Katz, Everett James (ed.), *Arms Production in Developing Countries* (Lexington: Lexington Books, 1984) pp. 15–38.

20.   For these definitions, see Ross, Andrew L., *Arms Production in Developing Countries: The Continuing Proliferation of Conventional Weapons*, no. N–1615–AF, Rand Corporation Note (Santa Monica, California: Rand Corporation 1981) pp. 16–19.

21.   For example, examine Klare, Michael T., *American Arms Supermarket* (Austin: University of Texas Press, 1984); Pearson, Frederic S., 'Of Leopards and Cheetahs: West Germany's Role as a Mid-Sized Arms Supplier', *Orbis*, XXVIX, no. 1 (Spring 1985) pp. 165–82; Freedman, Lawrence, *Arms Production in the United Kingdom: Problems and Prospects* (London: Royal Institute for International Affairs, 1978); and Kolodziej, *Making and Marketing of Arms: The French Experience and its Implications for the International System* (Princeton: Princeton University Press, 1987).

22.   For India, see Subrahmanyam, K., *Defence and Development* (Calcutta: Minerva 1973) and Thomas, Raju, *The Defence of India: A Budgetary Perspective of Strategy and Politics* (Columbia, Missouri: South Asia Books, 1978).

23.   For Israel, see Klieman, Aaron S., *Israel's Global Reach: Arms Sales as Diplomacy* (Washington, D.C.: Pergamon-Brassey, 1985); and Mintz, Alex, 'Military–Industrial Linkages in Israel', *Armed Forces and Society*, XII, no. 1 (Fall 1988) pp. 9–28; and Harkavy, Robert E. and Neumann, Stephanie G. 'Israel', in Katz (see note 19) pp. 193–224.

24.   Fro Brazil, see Myers, David, 'Brazil' in Kolodziej, Edward A. and Harkavy, Robert E., (eds) *Security Politics of Developing Countries* (Lexington, Lexington Books, 1982) pp. 53–72.

25.   Brzoska, Michael and Ohlson, Thomas, *Arms Production in the Third World* (London: Taylor & Francis, 1985) chap. 1. See also Ross, Andrew 'World Order and Arms Production in the Third World', in Katz, James E. (ed.) *Sowing the Serpent's Teeth: The Implications of Third World Military Industrialization* (Lexington: Lexington Books, 1986).

26.   Leitenberg, Milton and Ball, Nicole, *The Structure of the Defence Industry* (London: Croom Helm, 1983).

27.   Galtung, 'Military Formations and Social Transformation: A Structural Analysis', in *Global Militarization*, (see note 14) p. 4.

28.   See McNeill, William H., *The Pursuit of Power* (Chicago: University of Chicago Press, 1982); Pearton, Maurice, *Diplomacy, War, and Technology Since 1830* (Lawrence, Kansas: University of Kansas Press, 1984); and Howard (see note 3).

29.   Gilpin, Robert, *France in the Age of the Scientific State* (Princeton: Princeton Unversity Press, 1968).

30.   Katz (see note 19); Kolodziej and Harkavy (see note 24), and Leitenberg and Ball (see note 26).

31.   Kolodziej (see note 21) Chapter 3.

32.   See, for example, Kanet, Roger E. and Metzger, Clair A., 'NATO–Warsaw Pact Rivalry in the Third World Arms Market', in Clawson, Robert W. (ed.) *East–West Rivalry in the Third World: Security Issues and Regional Perspectives* (Wilmington, Delaware: Scholarly Resources, 1986) pp. 133–48.

33.   Quoted in a symposium on space weaponry sponsored by *Daedalus, Weapons in Space, II: Implications for Security*, Summer 1985, p. 370 (emphasis added).

34.   Galtung (see note 27) p. 14.

35.   Moskos, Charles C., 'Race and the Military', *Armed Forces and Society*, VI, no. 4 (Summer, 1980) pp. 587–94.

36.   See Nordlinger, Eric, *Soldiers in Politics: Military Coups and Governments* (Englewood Cliffs, New Jersey: Prentice-Hill, 1977) for an evaluation of the mixed contribution of military regimes to economic development.

37.   This is the argument of Mehta, Jagat S. (ed.) *Third World Militarization: A Challenge to Third World Diplomacy* (Austin, Texas: Lyndon B. Johnson School of Public Affairs, 1985).

11 The Current Warfare/Welfare Alternative and the Evidence from Technology*

Ulrich Albrecht
FREE UNIVERSITY OF BERLIN

This chapter consists of four parts. The first deals in a principal manner with the past limitations of the dialogue between economic science and peace research. The reasons for this are seen, both in the Smithian and Marxist tradition, in the continued dominance over social science of traditions of social thought which have their origin in the past when military activities were less significant for economic life than they are today. Second, the old 'bread vs guns' dichotomy is examined in relation to military spending and economic growth and productivity in countries with different systems and levels of development. This point is substantiated by scrutinising in part III the evidence on the economic dividend of military R & D funding, and by deriving conclusions about demands on future economic analysis of the matter. Fourth, and most importantly, with a view to the unsatisfactory results of economic research into the priority which military programmes enjoy, an argument is submitted about the intertwining of forces of industrialism and militarism, and the oscillation between private enterprises and government establishments in running R & D projects.

I   ECONOMICS AND PEACE RESEARCH

The old 'bread *versus* guns' dichotomy appears to move into new regions of controversy. In any modern society 'defence expenditure' (they do not officially call it military spending) and spending for social purposes constitute the two main categories of public spending. Most politicians of the West would subscribe to the general formula that general public welfare, as expressed by fair distribution of economic growth, needed to be safeguarded by appropriate spending for defence. This is unlikely to continue in an era of persistent economic depression, with small or even diminutive rates of growth, significant inflation, and (at least in Europe) enormous pressures to stick to welfare state policies. Social and military security of society may become alternatives, with strong competition from ecological security. In order to assist in judging alternatives it seems that an understanding of the economics of technology becomes more and more the requirement of the day.

Economic science is not well prepared to deal with the issue. One cannot pretend that an established dialogue exists between economists and peace researchers. Yet the problem is certainly not confined to economic science. It is necessary to challenge the limitations of at least three types of existing (social) science literature. First, within the relevant texts of sociology, there is a failure to analyse the significance of war and military preparedness for other institutions of modern societies. Second, within the literature of economics, which pretends to an orientation to the subject, there is a gulf between studies of welfare provision and of the welfare state on the one hand, and of arms expenditure on the other. Third, within political theory there is an isolation of democratic theory from a concern with the place of war and of the military in the shaping of political life.

The reasons for this situation stem from the continued dominance over social sciences today of traditions of social thought which have their origin in the eighteenth and nineteenth century. In neither Smith nor Marx is there a systematic analysis of the role of military activities in the formation of modern economic life, though neither neglects it completely (see, for example, Chapter 2 of this book, by Christian Schmidt). Marx confined himself to a few sketchy observations about the role of armaments in economic life on which he never elaborated. Both Marx and Engels (especially the latter) did give attention to the role of warfare in influencing social change in modern times. However, despite their profound differences, Smith and Marx considered industrialism as essentially a non-military force. The lack of a Marxist tradition in this area is particularly puzzling because the labour movement repeatedly had to grapple with the problem.

The leading social theorists of these days were united in the view that the military was an obsolete institution, belonging to a vanishing formation of society. Spencer, and before him Durkheim, developed the thesis of 'incompatibility' between the military and an advanced capitalist society. Sombart and Schumpeter continued the argument. Weber's writings on these issues did not have the influence upon modern social science that his other writings came to enjoy.

These comments concentrate on the forerunners of modern social science. Naturally there has been progress since then in many respects, but it is relatively easy to demonstrate that the failings still remain. Marxist thought in the twentieth century has certainly not ignored the phenomenon of war, force and arms production, but it is preoccupied either with the role of the state in economic life, or with the state as the focus of 'internal oppression'. Very little attention indeed has been given to military–economic questions.

The case is the same in economics. Modern economics was shaped against the background of nineteenth-century debates concerning the expansion of exchange relationships with the development of modern industry. Both classical and neoclassical economics begin from the idea that exchange relations are the foundation upon which other forms of social relationship become based in modern societies. Since these are, in a certain sense, the sole concern of economics in a way in which they cannot be in sociology, it tends to follow that economics is much less able to find a place for war and military issues than is sociology. Theoretical economics has no concepts with which to address the relevant issues. Thus, although there is a literature dealing with the economics of the arms industry, and of military expenditure more generally, this remains essentially disconnected from the main premises of economic enquiry.

The major aim of study should therefore be to reintroduce the investigation of war, and its long-term effects, into the core of the social sciences. Modern societies are frequently labelled 'industrial', recalling the differentiation which nineteenth-century social thought drew between the military societies of the past and the supposedly specifically economic institutions of the present. Given, however, that the twentieth-century world is one in which there has been an expanding combination of industrialism and the means of waging war, we must seriously pose the question whether or not this assumed differentiation is valid. Whether or not we still live, in some sense, in 'military societies', after all, is a matter which has to be regarded as problematic. It is the main concern of Section IV of this chapter to investigate just this issue. The contrast between militarism and industrialism, embodied very generally in modern social science, is something which has to be regarded at least with considerable caution.

II   MILITARY ACTIVITIES AND THE TOTAL ECONOMY

Particularly in the view of establishment circles, high public spending for social purposes is waste, because of the low economic returns to this kind of activity. Large military budgets, on the other hand, are considered likely to reap a number of economic benefits, which in turn could lessen social problems.

Critics maintain that the 'countries with the highest military burdens compete less well in world markets'.[1] The same point is made in a study by the US Congressional Budget Office: 'International comparisons seem to support the notion that high defense spending retards economic growth'.[2] The same report, however, adds that time-series data on productivity – the economic indicator most likely to be affected by technology policies – do not support this interpretation. For a number of countries the report found that in certain phases there was a positive relationship over time between the share of military activity in the economy and growth in productivity. The report therefore concludes that 'elementary statistical tabulations provide mixed evidence on the relationship between defense spending and trends in productivity growth'.[3] It points out that most other studies do not isolate the effects of military spending from other factors, such as the accumulation of capital or the qualification of the labour force. Hence the assessment of any causal link is not possible.

Several reports prepared for the United Nations by governmental and non-governmental experts, including the three in the series on the 'Economic and Social Consequences of the Arms Race and of Military Expenditures' as well as 'The Relationship between Disarmament and Development', also argue that parallelism does not establish causality. When an economy has unutilised or underutilised resources, any kind of spending, including that on military purposes, can stimulate the economy. But when the factors of production are fully or mostly utilised, as seems to have been the case in several industrialised countries, allocations to military technology, or any other form of spending requiring a long gestation period without an immediate demand, will have a depressing long-term effect on the economy.

There are few systematic studies comparing the role of military R & D in the economies of differing social systems, and virtually none on the centrally planned economies. Though the average rate of economic growth of the Eastern European countries and of the USSR far exceeded the average rate of growth of both the developed 'market economies' and the Third World economies in the past two decades, the growth-inhibiting effect of military R & D programmes is particularly relevant to their case. In general, the supply-side constraints on their economic performance are more identifiable because, by and large, both investment and employment opportunities – and needs – tend to exceed the available capital and labour resources in these countries. Therefore military investments, research efforts and resource employment always compete with civilian ones, and imply a net reduction from the capital and labour resources available for economic growth. As Robin Luckham summed it up, 'the military competition with the West demands a higher proportion of smaller resources'.[4]

Concerning the situation in the Third World, a UN study comments:

> The release of human resources from the military sector can relieve their labour shortages and the reallocation of material resources can speed up their process of industrialization with greater prospects of maximization of consumer satisfaction in their own societies besides enabling them to compete more effectively in international trade wherein their current share is not commensurate with their share in the global industrial output'.[5]

In the Third World countries with a sizeable military industry, planners have high hopes of general benefits, especially with respect to the level of technology in their country. According to an Indian expert:

> in an industry like electronics where technological changes are rapid, and in view of the demand of strategic self-sufficiency and the current dependence on imported manufacturing technology, we just must devise ways and means of ensuring that the resources committed to domestic design and development pay off commercially.[6]

However, Third World countries generally do not have the industrial structure appropriate for the peaceful application of results of the military use of technology.

Given the specific situation of the Third World, the impact of military R & D and production activities there requires a separate effort for the evaluation of economic prospects. In his report to the seventh summit conference of non-aligned countries, its Chairman said:

> Over thirty countries of the underdeveloped world today produce weapons. In 1979, military industrial output in these countries amounted to $5 bn. . . The economic effects of military expenditures are for the underdeveloped countries even more negative than for the more advanced countries as a whole. . . It has been established that for each dollar spent on arms in the underdeveloped countries, domestic investment is reduced by 25 cents.[7]

III   THE SPIN-OFF FROM MILITARY TECHNOLOGY

For the state as an actor, the lead-sector for dealing directly with modern technology is the military one. Here the state directly administers technology and has complete control over outputs and inputs. This may have contributed in the past to the preferential treatment which the military sector enjoyed in political quarters. There is a strong belief in a 'seed' role of military technology.

Enthusiastic appreciations of spin-offs from military and space activities (which are in turn predominantly military) can be quoted in legions. 'The space program has radically altered our lives', wrote *The New York Times* in 1978.[8] Stating that 'space exploration had a recognizable impact on the way we live and think', the paper spanned the change from 'Teflon pans in the kitchen to instant global communications'. Such an assessment, however, has a very limited perspective since neither Teflon pans nor instant global communications have a direct bearing on the severe economic problems of the world. Economists remain split about the actual effects of advances in military technology for the economy in general. It has been argued, on the one hand, especially in reports submitted by the United Nations,[9] that military spending is mainly unproductive. Therefore, the conversion of resources to the civilian sector is seen as likely to improve the performance of the economy.

On the other hand, it has been claimed that military spending on R & D in particular is essential to economic growth. Despite the absence of consensus among economists on how growth is achieved, there are two main variants of this view. The one most pertinent for R & D programmes is that there are significant spin-offs as a result of research for military requirements and the kind of resulting technological advance. The other view is that lower military spending, as a consequence of reductions, would result in lower government spending altogether because there is no visible aggregate demand which would find political support to the same extent.[10]

Country assessments tend to point more to the negative range of evaluations. Britain, with a military R & D investment in the class of superpower efforts (one half of public funds for R & D) provides a striking example. The possible economic benefits from a large military R & D investment have been officially discussed in the UK. Applications such as liquid crystals, portable satellite communication links, night-vision equipment and carbon fibres are quoted as successful examples of civil 'spin-offs'. Furthermore, there are royalties from military patents.[11] The Electronics Economic Development Committee of the UK, concerned that British electronics industry was deriving too little commercial advantage from the major R & D investments of the Ministry of Defence, commissioned a former chief scientist at the Department of Industry to identify barriers to the transfer of technology from military R & D contractors to civilian industry. His conclusion was that the typical arms-manufacturing firm, with a high share of government contracts for the military use of R & D, showed the lowest rate of conversion of their research results into commercial outputs of any form.[12] The Ministry of Defence commented on the findings by comparing the benefits of British arms sales with civil 'spin-offs': 'We have become increasingly conscious that as compared with defence exports (the value of which is expected to reach £1800 m sterling in 1982/3) *the number of success stories in the field of civil exploitation is relatively few'*.[13] A committee of the House of Lords described the creation of a circle of large firms which have prospered through, and become heavily dependent on, Ministry of Defence contracts, and which have kept largely to themselves the R & D associated with this work.[14] Whatever the causes of the British experience may have been,[15] the limited success of the application of military R & D to civil technology in society as a whole seems to be typical.

The relationship between sectoral public R & D funding and the contribution of the respective sector to output in manufacturing industries in the UK and FRG are interesting. In the UK and in the FRG funds for R & D go predominantly into aerospace first and foremost, then electronics and then general engineering. The contribution of the respective sectors to output follows exactly the opposite pattern, placing the much hailed aerospace sector in the economically least significant role. In the case of Japan, the pattern of spending for public R & D funding is distinctly different; close to nil in aerospace, secondary also in electronics, but concentrated in the sector of 'other manufacturing industries'. In any case, the comparable amounts of public R & D investment are much lower in the case of Japan.

The consistency of findings about the relatively small returns of military R & D investment to the economy demands a more thorough analytical assessment than usually offered. The British approach of differentiating types of commercial applications is not quite pertinent. If not the economy as a whole, then parts of it may benefit from this approach. Vested interests in military R & D should apparently be scrutinised in order to learn why such a large amount of funds continues to flow into this activity, thus broadening the assessment to a political-science framework rather than a narrower one of economic analysis. There are vested interests, first in the supply of capital and second in qualified manpower. The military use of capital resources circumscribes economic objectives in a situation of world-wide strict public budgets, let alone the fiscal crisis in a number of states which support military R & D programmes. The economic nature of military spending adds further to the capital bottleneck. Though a redistribution of national income in favour of military activities, or an international income redistribution in favour of major arms-exporting nations if there are privileged capital returns on sales, may lead to an increase in the capital supply in the latter, yet this expansion of capital funds in the arms sector takes place at the expense of a relatively greater decrease of investment resources of the civilian sector and at the expense of the arms-importing countries.

Contradicting interests are promoted by governments when they encourage capital to engage in R & D work. Private shareholders in market economy countries enjoy a number of preferential benefits if they invest in military activities. Such incentives range from tax exemptions, government support in taking credits, supplies of capital goods (government-owned floor-space and machinery) and components bought in by the government. The type of contract for military

R & D work is usually, because of the risks involved, cost plus fixed fee. All these privileges are meant to act as incentives to induce capital to engage in this area if other motives do not suffice. The level of such subsidies varies and it appears to be especially high in Western Europe.

A second vested economic interest is that of qualified manpower. Given the notable differences in manpower demands for military and civilian products, a high concentration of national resources appears as some sort of specific 'brain drain'. In a number of cases a large share of the best qualified and innovative engineers is not available for civilian work. This competition for the skills of qualified manpower is particularly obvious in some developing countries. Here one observes a brain drain, both between and within nations. Differences of income level and the better research facilities for military R & D projects tend to widen these differences.

New technologies, which are not yet commercially or militarily viable, can be modelled as 'seed' sectors. This provides for a third kind of vested economic interest in military R & D. For private enterprises which are engaged in both civilian and military markets, government-sponsored programmes offer promising opportunities to test out new technologies which, if the whole affair were to be financed commercially, would perhaps never be brought into active R & D. The development of large by-pass jet engines for wide-body commercial aircraft can thus be seen as facilitated by military requirements for engines producing more than 6 tons thrust.

However, the approach of identifying vested interests and of denouncing particular private interests in the R & D process is far from satisfactory. More penetrating means of analysis are required, particularly in the distribution of R & D results.

First, an assessment about the general potential of the civilian 'spin-off' should be based on a better understanding of the mechanism of such transfers. The very terms 'spin-off' and 'fall-out' signal that there is no analytical insight into the ways and means of the process – and improved knowledge would certainly help to maximise transfers. Surveys made in the USA and the FRG on military R & D outputs at different stages of project cycles note a trickling out, which increases as an originally military innovation approaches commercial application.[17] One estimate suggests that not more than 20 per cent of the results of military R & D are in any way meaningful for the civilian sector of the economy of advanced industrialised countries.

Second, the pace and development of R & D in 'high technology' areas apparently leads to a process of decoupling from civilian R & D, which remains tied to cost considerations (in R & D effort as well as in terms of manufactured goods). Modern military technology appears as an island of excellence, far off the coastline of technological mediocrity which characterises the mass of industrial goods around us. The Report for the UK Electronics EDC portrays this in the following manner 'In the past several decades the level of this civil platform has been subsiding, leaving the defence peaks standing even higher relative to the national electronic engineering plateau'.[18]

The study of disarmament and development by the UN Group of Governmental Experts summarised a number of contributions to this problem and emphasised that citing evidence for positive spin-offs from military R & D in terms of employment and technological advance does not really answer the relevant question.[19] Resources used by the military have opportunity costs related to alternative uses of these resources. Thus one may point to some positive effects for the civilian sector of military R & D such as air-traffic-control devices. But the argument is only valid if it can be shown that such infrastructures were unlikely to have been established in any other way or less economically than through military activities.

The real question is 'What are the opportunity costs involved?' This question applies to the equilibrium effects and particularly to the overall programme costs.

> If military spending and employment play indeed a role in the anti-cyclical policy to maintain or restore equilibrium in a national economy, and if the military sector is not only consuming but also generating and mobilizing resources by organisaztion, training, R & D, etc. for development, then by *what alternatives* and at *what costs* could the same results be achieved?[20]

Furthermore, a somewhat obvious and striking snag in the reasoning of those who support the 'spin-off' or 'fall-out' effects of military R & D is the underlying assumption of full employment. Except for some of the centrally planned economies in Eastern Europe which face situations of labour shortage (or hidden unemployment) most other countries need to consider whether promotion or expansion of military R & D activities can refloat the economy in a situation of severe unemployment, and how the spin-off mechanism acts with respect to overall technological developments in a phase of under-utilisation of resources.

The responsiveness of the economies to the innovations offered from military R & D is certainly tied to the general state of economic affairs. In the past, phases of sustained growth – albeit at limited rates – and a greater open-mindedness towards investment in high-risk markets, the empirical findings of some actual spin-offs could well have reflected reality. In the current situation with high interest rates, diminutive or negative growth, a constant level of unemployment, the same technologies offered fifteen years ago are likely to be rejected by civilian industry on grounds of marginal relevance or exorbitant costs or a combination of both. Some authors maintain that there are additional features which limit the prospects of successful spin-offs. Szentes refers to the fact that a high number of military R & D projects have no 'realizable use-value', even for military purposes, and hence the contribution of such research to the economy will be remote.[21]

The economic spin-off of military R & D presumably also varies according to the overall size of the national R & D programme. An American study found general scepticism among Western European firms of the potential for civilian spin-off from the military sector.[22] This scepticism is shared by responsible politicians. Mr Riesenhuber, the West German minister for R & D policies, recently stressed the uncertainty as to whether spin-off takes place at all, and that where such benefits do 'occur [they are] always where nobody expects them'.[23]

R & D efforts are usually geared to 'projects', and each individual project is organised in a life-cycle, starting with basic research and ending in a manufacturable good. Commonly, the project life-cycle is subdivided into stages, and these stages are assessed with respect to their fertility for spin-off. A simple model gives, in time sequences this chain of stages:

$$\text{basic research} \longrightarrow \text{applied research} \longrightarrow \text{engineering development} \longrightarrow \text{production}$$

Such linear models are of course simplifications. Apparently they reduce the complexity of intra-sectoral technology transfers too much, and thus they will be unable to produce the necessary insights. Above all, the basic category of demand is totally neglected. If there is no demand for an innovation, then even the greatest flow of new technological ideas will disappear into thin air. Figure 11.1 would be a more appropriate model for the study of intra-sectoral technology transfers. The basic message of Figure 11.1 is that the stirring up of demand for a number of stage activities remains paramount. R & D demand is firstly inherent both for basic and for applied research in the later stages of a project itself. For technology transfers the more rewarding aspect will be to understand the potential demands from other sectors. These demands may come into being, with varying intensity, along a number of stages. In the end the demand-R-&-D spin-off relationship will be a cyclical one. For a higher spin-off output it will be crucial to learn more about the actual process.

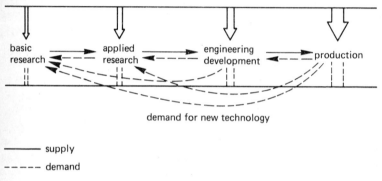

demand for new technology

———— supply

– – – – demand

Figure 11.1

IV   THE RELATIONSHIP OF MILITARISATION AND INDUSTRIALISM

There would seem to be no convincing argument which truly explains in economic terms the rationale of military activities. The conventional wisdom of economists is that military decisions are of a non-economic nature, they are external data which are given before any economic reasoning commences. These military decisions may be rational or based on irrational mechanisms, of which the most common denominator is provided by the metaphor of 'the arms race'.

A deeper understanding of the dynamism of the arms race as a race in technology – as the preceding section has demonstrated – becomes economically highly relevant. The question is whether a special relationship exists between militarism and industrialism which gives momentum to the arms race and if so, how this special relationship might be specified. The concepts of militarism of the past are often parochial and not relevant to the problem we face today. Among the phenomena which sustain contemporary militarism are the serial manufacture of weapons at large and the organisation of R & D on a large scale. Industrialism may be defined as the energetic effort to turn out – that is, to produce or reproduce – capital. Yet the militarism and industrialism of different political systems are worth looking at to see whether there are lessons to be learned.

One would hope for an explanation of why the old Marxist hope for the disappearance of militarism under socialism is frustrated. Reference to the alienation of consumer industrialised societies from militarism in mass political thinking may be sound, at least on the surface (the Falklands war would not prove such a general assertion). The real test comes to any effort to improve the understanding of the interrelationship between militarism and industrialism when one turns to Hitler's Third Reich.

The Nazis were certainly not interested in industrial mobilisation *per se*. Their objective was absolute preparation for war. This objective was not a goal for the industrialists, but the Nazi challenge offered unrivalled prospects for industrial mobilisation and modernisation. Hence the attraction which the otherwise-obscure Nazi ideology offered to these circles. National Socialism with the vision to 'rebuild Germany' provided the basis for the symbiosis between industrial capitalism and this type of militarist movement. It may well be that this very combination, a striving for industrial modernisation plus a backward-looking, non-modernist ideology pointing at the masses, provide the two pillars of the contemporary militarism–industrialism phenomenon.

In the USSR, by contrast, there does not seem to be the same specific linkage, the mutual reinforcement of militarism and industrialism, though this does not preclude the possibility that both phenomena exist there. There is indeed evidence of 'Red Militarism',[24] a special brand of militarism which is valued as a positive asset by some ideologists. There is certainly also a specific notion of industrialism in the USSR. It is not focused on consumerist approaches, but founded on infrastructures (with a high demand on the organisation of political legitimacy) as indicated by Lenin's dictum about the definition of communism being based on the electrification of the whole country. 'Red Militarism' and the Soviet kind of industrialism – that is the core of the problem on the Eastern side – simply do not intermesh in the dynamic kind known from Western militarism and private industrialism.

The fact is that private entrepreneurship has added that little amount to the arms race which was needed to create the decisive leading edge, and to give the USA the technological upper hand. It has been maintained that virtually any recent innovation in the US arsenal – the light-weight fighters F-16 and F-18, the B-1 bomber, the STEALTH technology for lowering radar cross-sections – originated from programmes in private industry, with no public funding in the beginning.[25] Such a statement may present an exaggeration by individuals, but it points to possibilities for verification.

Before such a step, a possible misunderstanding ought to be ruled out. The Pentagon runs a programme labelled 'IBD' (for Independent Bids for Development) which reimburses the costs of private programmes if the project at a later stage becomes a government activity. As Gordon Adams has demonstrated,[26] not every claim for IBD funds is successful – there remain financially high-risk projects which never recover the cost incurred.

Adams estimates this net contribution of private capital to US government military R & D spending at $1 bn (compared with some $20 bn in government outlays). Hence the private nature of innovative projects in military technology does not imply that the entrepreneur can be sure of reimbursement by public funds.

'Successful' innovations show a marked change in their 'private' and 'public' nature. The US Air Force abandoned funding for strategic missiles in 1954, because the evidence available suggested that the biggest possible throw-weight of a missile would never equal the lightest possible H-bomb warhead. Two scientists, Drs Ramo and Wooldridge, decided to pursue the project, convinced of the feasibility of their approach. They continued with private funds, and after Sputnik's spectacular launch, their private firm was able to present the necessary technology for missiles which could carry a satellite bigger than an orange or a football.

The most recent example is provided by STEALTH. The core group of scientists who actually developed this technology decided to work on a private basis. The reasons for this decision remain open to speculation, but by now all US STEALTH research is carried out by a private firm, with large government orders. This scheme differs from Drs Ramo and Wooldridge's persistence on a line of technology in the absence of public funding. But it highlights the meaning of the private element in the US military technology effort.

This aspect merits assessment. The resort to private entrepreneur-ship, even if it remains limited to small phases in the life-cycle of big R & D projects, is apparently able to squeeze out that little extra bit of ingenuity which the two huge bureacracies, the Pentagon and its Soviet counterpart, are unable to mobilise by the means available to these two competing units.

This brings us close to a real understanding of the interrelationship between militarism and industrialism. Militarism *per se*, a nihilistic exaggeration of the features of the military, does not suffice in an explanation of the current arms race. Industrialism, on the other hand, without a specific political orientation, is also an empty notion. It appears that a peculiar linkage, military–industrialism, is the combination of terms which really provides for a concept to under-stand the dynamism of the arms race, the provision of the 'leading edge'.

Notes and References

*   I benefited greatly from work as a consultant to the Governmental Group of Experts appointed by the Secretary-General of the United Nations for a study on the military use of R & D (GA Resolution 37/99J), and from a workshop at King's College, Cambridge organised by the Political Science Department of the University of Cambridge, 'The Welfare–Warfare State and the Conditions of Liberal Democracy', January 1984. The usual disclaimers apply.

1.   Sivard, Ruth L., *World Military and Social Expenditures*, (Leesburg, Va.: World Priorities, 1982) p. 23. Published by the author.
2.   Congressional Budget Office, *Defense Spending and the Economy*, (Washington, DC: GPO, 1983) pp. 38–40.
3.   Ibid, p. 38.
4.   Luckham, Robin, 'Militarism and International Dependence' in Richard Jolly (ed.) *Disarmament and World Development* (Oxford: Pergamon, 1978). Cf. also Szentes, Tamas, 'Economic Effects of Global Militarization' in *Development and Peace* (Budapest) vol. 4, no. 1 (Spring 1983).
5.   UN, ESCAR, A/32/88 (Sales Publication no. E.78.IX.1) p. 96.
6.   Parthasarathi, A., 'Development Strategy for Electronics Industry: Ensuring Success of Technological Innovation' in *Economic and Political Weekly*, vol. V, no. 48, 28 November 1978, p.M-149.
7.   Castro, Fidel, *The World Economic and Social Crisis: Its Impact on the Underdeveloped Countries, its Somber Prospects, and the Need to Struggle if we are to Survive*, Report to the Seventh Summit Confe-rence of Non-aligned Countries (Havana: Publishing Office of the Council of State, 1983) p. 204.

8. Wilford, John Noble, 'The Spin-off from Space', *The New York Times Magazine*, 29 January 1978, pp. 10, 12.

9. United Nations, *Economic and Social Consequences of the Armament Race and its Extremely Harmful Effects on World Peace and Security* (A/32/88 Add) 1977; Review of the implementations of the recommendations and decisions adopted by the General Assembly at its Tenth Special Session. (A/36/346) 1981.

10. This view has been propagated by the political left, notably the school of thought originated by Baran and Sweezy, *Monopoly Capital* (New York: Monthly Review Press, 1966) and subsequent writings.

11. Gummett, Philip (Programme of Policy Research in Engineering, Science and Technology, University of Manchester) 'Defence Research Policy' in Goldsmith, M. (ed.) *UK Research Policy: A Critical Review of Policies for Publicly-funded Science and Technology* (London: Longman, 1984).

12. Maddock, Sir Levan, *Civil Exploitation of Defence Technology*, Report to the Electronics EDC (London: NEDO, 1983) (mimeo).

13. Comment by the Ministry of Defence, Annex II to the above-mentioned Report (emphasis added). The report also informs about a number of measures taken to improve inter-industry technology transfer.

14. House of Lords, Select Committee on Science and Technology, 1982–3, *Engineering Research and Development* (London: HMSO, 1983, HL89) vol. II, paragraphs 19. 1-19-2.

15. I have to admit that this brief assessment of British R & D success has been critically commented upon by UK government experts, who stress that by now relevant measures have been taken to ensure the success of government spending (oral communication).

16. Volker, Hauff and Scharpf, Fritz W., *Modernisierung der Volkwirtschaft: Technologiepolitik als Strukturpolitik* (Frankfurt and Cologne: EVA, 1975) p. 73.

17. See the *UN Report on the Economic and Social Consequences of the Arms Race and of Military Expenditures*, Sales Publication no. 83. IX.2, and the *UN Report on the Relationship between Disarmament and Development*, Sales Publication no. 82, IX.1.

18. *Civil Exploitation of Defence Technology* (see note 12) p. 8.

19. UN Publication no. E.82.IX.1, chap. 4.

20. Szentes, T., 'East–West and North–South Relations: Disarmament and NIEO or further Negative Sum Game', *Development and Peace* (Budapest) Vol 3, Spring 1986, pp. 3–29.

21. Ibid.

22. Udis, Bernard, *From Guns to Butter: Technology Organizations and Reduced Military Spending in Western Europe* (Cambridge, Massachusetts: Ballinger, 1978) p. 255.

23. Interview with Mr Riesenhuber in *Der Spiegel*, no. 37 (9 September 1985) p. 28.

24. I have dealt with the issue in 'Red Militarism' in *Journal of Peace Research* no. 2, vol. XVIII, 1980, pp. 135–49.

25.   Paine, Christopher and Adams, Gordon, 'The R and D Slush Fund' in *The Nation*, 26 January 1980, p. 72.
26.   Adams, Gordon, *The Politics of Defense Contracting: The Iron Triangle* (New Brunswick and London: Transaction, 1982) pp. 95 and 99.

12 Military Expenditure Comparisons

Hans Christian Cars
MINISTRY OF DEFENCE, SWEDEN

and Jacques Fontanel
CEDSI, GRENOBLE

One problem in the negotiation and verification of any possible international agreement on the reduction of military expenditure is the difficulty of determining common definitions and methods of evaluation and comparison. Various alternative methods of comparison are discussed and the work of a United Nations group dealing with these matters, including particularly the purchasing power parity method, is reviewed. It is concluded that, given political will and reasonable availability of adequate and relevant information, the construction of useful instruments for international and intertemporal comparison of military expenditure is feasible.

I INTRODUCTION

An agreement between the militarily most significant powers to reduce their military expenditures would be a major political achievement. As it has often been stated that part of the resources thus released should be devoted to economic and social development, in particular to the benefit of the developing countries, such an agreement would also have important economic implications. Furthermore, unlike negotiations on most disarmament measures such as a nuclear-weapon-free zone or a comprehensive nuclear-test ban, negotiations on a reduction of military expenditures would have interesting economic aspects in addition to the obvious political ones.

II BASIC PROBLEMS

Basic problems would be to agree on common definitions and rules for the valuation, accounting and reporting of the military expenditures of negotiating parties. On that basis, generally acceptable methods would have to be applied for the assessment of each side's expenditures and for their comparison. The quality of such assessments and comparisons would of course depend very much on the availability of adequate and accurate information.

Comparisons of military expenditures would not only be of interest in the context of possible future negotiations but are also needed as a means of analysing the social costs of the current arms race. There are obviously great difficulties in estimating the real military expenditures of different states as the figures differ largely among the few well-known sources that are available in this field.[1] This is especially true with respect to the military expenditures of countries with a centrally planned economy, as reliable data – even in terms of national currencies – are hard to obtain from such countries. A further problem is to compare such data with those of other countries as given in their national currencies, bearing in mind the fact that existing exchange rates often poorly reflect the relative domestic purchasing-power of national currencies.

1. In all countries military secrecy hampers the availability of information but to an extent that varies largely among the countries. While some of them are rather open with regard to their military expenditures, others are very restrictive leaving the field open for more or less pertinent guesses.

2. Information produced and assessments made by various institutes are not easily comparable because of differing definitions with regard to the concept of military expenditures. Such components as military aid, civil defence, paramilitary forces, pensions for former military personnel, etc., are treated in different ways. In some cases they are considered as parts of the military expenditures and in other cases they are left aside. Such differences must of course be taken into account when figures from different sources are compared with one another.

3. Results from nuclear and space research efforts may have important military applications although the projects may be considered as being of a basically civilian character. It is a matter of judgement how much of the costs of such efforts should be

defined as military expenditures. This difficulty may also cause important differences when it comes to the assessment of military research expenditures of various countries.

4. For the comparison of military expenditures of freely convertible currency countries most sources use market exchange rates as a means of converting national expenditure data into US dollars. As exchange rates may change drastically in a rather short period of time, results depend heavily on the particular time for which the rates are selected. Thus, the choice of exchange rates may have an important impact on the comparisons of military expenditures among countries. A further complication is created by the fact that market exchange rates do not exist for all countries. In such cases some other rates must be used instead and for that purpose several different approaches can be adopted.

For reasons such as these the use of exchange rates for the comparison of military expenditures may produce different results and none of them *per se* may be more or less correct than any other.

In addition to this it should be noted that the use of exchange rates as a means of international expenditure comparisons is susceptible to producing arbitrary differences because of subjective choices. Moreover, exchange rates, whether they are set administratively or on an international currency market, often poorly reflect the relative purchasing-power of the respective currencies with regard to their various domestic uses. Thus, other methods or instruments are needed in order to obtain reasonably accurate comparisons of international volume.

III ALTERNATIVE METHODS OF COMPARISON

For the purpose of comparisons of international military expenditure a number of alternative methods have been elaborated and applied by various institutes and independent scientists. In addition to the budgetary approach there is, *inter alia*, the so-called hardware-method by which industrial statistics are used as a basis for various attempts to assess the size and scope of a country's military sector, including the defence industry and its production potential.

Another method is the so-called building-block method. This is used by the American Central Intelligence Agency to estimate the hypothetical dollar costs of producing in the USA the Soviet armed forces, including the training of their manpower together with the procurement and maintenance of their weapon systems and other types of equipment. One of the shortcomings of this method, however, is that it tends to overvalue the Soviet military efforts, as these are estimated at prices prevailing in the USA, where the price structure is quite different from the one existing in the USSR. This means that factors that are relatively cheap and therefore widely used in the military sector of the USSR, such as manpower, get too heavy a weight, if differences in relative prices are not properly taken into account.[2]

IV   THE WORK OF THE UNITED NATIONS

Parallel to the many efforts made by various institutes and individuals to explore the world's military expenditures a good deal of work has also been devoted to this issue by the United Nations. Ever since 1973 when it was proposed to the United Nations General Assembly that the major powers should cut their military spending, successive expert groups appointed by the Secretary-General have devoted substantial efforts to the analysis of the above-mentioned problems. In a first stage these efforts resulted, *inter alia*, in the elaboration,[3] testing,[4] and adoption,[5] by the United Nations of an international system for standardised reporting of military expenditures. Since the adoption of this system in 1980, more than thirty countries from all major geographic regions and with different economic systems have participated in the system and reported their military expenditures to the United Nations.

In a subsequent stage the problems of comparing military expenditures were examined by a group of experts with a view to finding appropriate solutions. This group pointed to the purchasing-power-parity method as an interesting approach which should provide much better results in international comparisons than those obtained through the use of prevailing exchange rates. Although purchasing power parities (PPPs) had already been constructed for the comparison of different large economic aggregates such as gross domestic product, private consumption and total government expenditures, it was still an open question whether this method could be successfully applied to comparisons of military expenditures considering their particularities and the generally limited availability of data. The group also stated the need for specific military price indices, as it was shown that general price indices in several cases poorly reflect the actual price changes in the military sector.

Based on its analysis of the problems related to international and intertemporal comparisons in general and with special regard to military expenditures the group suggested in its report to the Second Special Session on Disarmament in 1982 that a practical exercise should be undertaken with a view to assessing the feasibility of constructing military PPPs.[6] It was also suggested that such PPPs should be constructed together with military price indices for those countries that would volunteer to participate.

V   A PRACTICAL EXERCISE

The General Assembly agreed and decided that a new exercise should be started in 1983.[7] The group that was entrusted with this task worked for two years in cooperation with eight countries and presented its final report to the Secretary-General in the summer of 1985.[8] The countries participating in this exercise were Australia, Austria, Finland, Italy, Norway, Sweden, the UK and the USA.

As a result of its work, the group came to several conclusions. One of them was that the construction of 'useful instruments for intertemporal and international comparisons of military expenditures, i.e. military price indices and PPPs, is feasible, given a sufficient availability of relevant statistical information'.[9] The group also stated that the experience gained through the exercise had been limited by the fact that no developing or planned economy country had chosen to participate.

For many years military or defence price indices have been continuously constructed by several countries. As a consequence, the methods applied by the group for the purpose of intertemporal comparisons did not represent anything very new.

Concerning the international comparisons, however, the group's exercise was the first in which the PPP-method was applied to military expenditures. In addition to the technical–statistical problems which are generally related to international comparisons of different economic aggregates, the group also had to tackle a number of problems specifically related to military expenditures. Such problems for instance were caused by the secrecy surrounding military information, the difficulty in determining unit prices, the high degree of differentiation with regard to military equipment and construction, and the lack of market prices.

The general scarcity of data, particularly with regard to military hardware made it necessary for the group to proceed in stages requesting from each participant additional information that would match that previously obtained from one or more of the other countries. Efforts were also made to ascertain that the prices reported for different items were calculated in the same way by all countries. However, in spite of these efforts most of the submitted price data on procurement items could not be used, because the items were often too different to warrant meaningful price comparisons.

Because of the general scarcity of price data on procurement items and the difficulties inherent in finding matching pairs of such items the basis for the construction of procurement PPPs was rather meagre, particularly from a quantitative point of view. Thus, the results obtained and presented in the group's report might have been different, if more data had been available.[10] The primary purpose of the exercise, however, was not to obtain infallible results but to examine the feasibility of the PPP-method for the comparison of military expenditures among countries. In the group's opinion it was demonstrated through the exercise that this method is applicable to military expenditures including military hardware and that good international comparisons are possible, given reasonable availability of data and provided necessary effort is made to select and collect the information.

Furthermore, the group concluded that military price indices and PPPs reflect the real value of military expenditures better than civilian indices and other measures, and that their use is, therefore, preferable for measuring and comparing real military expenditures in the context of international negotiations on agreements to reduce such expenditures. In such a context, countries might well be more willing to exchange among themselves more information on characteristics and prices of military goods and services compared with that which they are willing to provide under present circumstances.

A special problem which the group faced was the comparison of conscripted and enlisted soldiers. On the one hand, these two categories of military personnel can be supposed to fulfil about the same functions in the case of war. On the other hand, it is clear that conscripts undergoing the first part of their basic training are less skilled and experienced than the average professional soldier. Upon careful examination of this question the group finally decided to regard conscripts with a training of six months or more as being by and large comparable to average enlisted soldiers. Thus, total subsistence costs of such conscripts, including daily pay, food charges and costs of accommodation, were compared with the average salary of enlisted soldiers. On this basis purchasing-power parities were also constructed for this category of personnel for all participating states.

VI   THE RESULTS

The results of the group's exercise as presented in its report can be described as follows:

(a) *Military price indices* were constructed for all participating states, both for their total military expenditures and for a great number of different expenditure categories and subcategories. These results as shown in Tables 12.1 and 12.2 were also compared with two types of general civilian price indices. These comparisons are presented in Table 12.3. Judging from Table 12.1 it is evident that there can be important differences among countries with regard to their rates of military price increases. In the case of the USA the strongest inflationary pressure seems to have come in the two years under consideration from the procurement sector. This was probably because of the quickly-growing demand for military goods and services at that time followed by shortages in the defence industry. As for the other countries their major cost categories did not show inflation rates that were very different from the average.

The results presented in Table 12.2 provide ample opportunity to analyse in detail the relative price increases of the different subcategories of one of the main cost categories, namely that of operating costs. For five of the eight countries prices of personnel – that is, salaries and wages – increased at a lower rate than prices of goods and services in the operating-cost category. In all but two countries salaries and wages of military personnel grew more slowly than those of civilian personnel.

As shown in Table 12.3 comparisons were made with defence price indices of some countries which are known to use a large amount of input data and very elaborate methods for the construction of such indices. As may be seen from the table some of the group's results came very close to those obtained through such national efforts. This is an interesting observation and it is worth noting that the group obtained its results by means of a simplified method using a relatively

Table 12.1 Military price indices for major cost categories constructed by the Group[a]

(Index 1980 = 100)

Countries	Operating costs		Procurement		Construction		Research and Development		Total military expenditure	
	1981	*1982*	*1981*	*1982*	*1981*	*1982*	*1981*	*1982*	*1981*	*1982*
Australia	121.9*	132.4*	109.9	120.8	(112.4)	(125.1)	112.0*	123.6*	119.0	129.8
Austria	106.5	115.7	107.9	116.6	(109.0)	(117.9)	**	**	106.9	116.0
Finland	106.8	118.0	(108.4)	(116.3)	(110.2)	(117.7)	106.5	119.6	107.4	117.4
Italy	131.9	144.8	121.0	143.3	118.6	139.6	120.6	139.1	129.3	144.2
Norway	114.5	125.4	(111.2)	(122.3)	(109.3)	(117.2)	111.8	122.0	113.4	124.1
Sweden	109.4	118.0	112.5	123.5	105.7	111.2	110.4	117.4	110.2	119.1
UK	117.6	127.9	(109.5)	(118.0)	(112.9)	(112.9)	123.0	131.7	116.7	125.2
USA	110.5	117.4	112.7	131.6	107.7	106.9	109.8	113.8	110.9	120.5

Notes

* Based exclusively on submitted salary data.

** No such expenditures reported.

[a] Bracketed index numbers are not calculated by the Group, but are either suggested by the contact, in which case they are in *italics*, or collected as substitute indices from civilian OECD statistics.

Table 12.2   Military price indices for subcategories of operating costs constructed by the Group

(*a*)   *Price indices for personnel*
(Index 1980 = 100)

Participating States	Conscripted personnel		Other military personnel		Civilian personnel		Total personnel	
	1981	1982	1981	1982	1981	1982	1981	1982
Australia	–	–	124.1	134.2	112.8	124.7	121.9	132.4
Austria	100.0	120.7	107.1	114.4	108.0	118.0	105.5	117.0
Finland	112.1	128.1	102.7	112.0	106.3	116.1	104.3	114.1
Italy	195.6	195.6	116.8	129.3	128.6	143.1	137.7	147.5
Norway	113.1	124.3	111.9	122.3	114.3	124.1	112.8	123.2
Sweden	105.4	110.9	106.3	112.5	106.7	113.6	106.3	112.5
UK	–	–	110.4	117.2	117.8	124.5	112.9	119.7
USA	–	–	108.4	119.2	109.8	115.9	108.8	118.1

(*b*)   *Price indices for operations and maintenance*
(Index 1980 = 100)

States	Materials for current use		Maintenance and repairs		Purchased services		Rent costs		Total operations and maintenance	
	1981	1982	1981	1982	1981	1982	1981	1982	1981	1982
Australia	–	–	–	–	–	–	–	–	121.9	132.8
Austria	105.0	107.3	115.9	125.0	108.1	112.9	107.5	117.4	108.5	113.3
Finland	111.4	125.6	107.8	118.4	110.5	123.3	100.0	160.0	109.4	122.0
Italy	121.8	145.8	119.7	137.1	118.7	139.7	114.7	133.3	119.9	139.2
Norway	118.0	126.3	118.2	129.5	118.3	142.1	111.5	123.8	117.9	129.7
Sweden	116.8	135.3	111.6	116.2	108.8	115.6	113.0	122.0	113.6	125.5
UK	120.2	136.6	133.6	145.9	117.7	124.9	–	–	122.8	137.0
USA	116.4	116.4	110.2	115.9	110.9	116.4	107.7	114.2	113.4	116.2

Table 12.3 Civilian and military price indices
(Index 1980 = 100)

Participating States	Civilian price indices				Military price indices			
	GDP deflators		Consumer price indexes		As calculated by participating States[a]		As calculated by the Group of Experts	
	1981	1982	1981	1982	1981	1982	1981	1982
Australia	110.3	122.5	109.7	121.9			119.0	129.8
Austria	106.3	113.3	106.8	112.6			106.9	116.0
Finland	111.7	121.7	112.0	122.5	111.2	120.7	107.4	117.4
Italy	118.3	138.9	119.5	139.2			129.3	144.2
Norway	114.0	125.2	113.6	126.5	112.1	124.4	113.4	124.1
Sweden	109.4	119.0	112.7	121.7			110.2	119.1
UK	111.6	119.6	111.9	121.5			116.7	126.2
USA	109.2	116.3	110.4	117.2	111.5	121.1	110.9	120.5

Note
[a] or by the Group on the basis of specific sets of indices and weights submitted by participating States.

limited amount of information. This may be of special interest in the light of possible future negotiations on a reduction of military expenditures as a simple method and the use of easily verifiable data might greatly facilitate such negotiations.

For five of the eight countries military prices rose faster than the corresponding civilian price indices which seems to support the widely-held viewpoint that military expenditures have an inflationary impact on the economy. This notion is, however, contradicted by the results obtained for the three other participants which happen to be the Scandinavian countries. It is hard to say whether this is a coincidence or a sustained pattern for these three countries.

(b) *Military purchasing-power parities* were constructed for all participating states, both for their total military expenditures and for some expenditure categories and subcategories. These results are shown in Table 12.4. They are also compared in Table 12.5 with exchange rates and a set of civilian purchasing-power parities as constructed by the Organisation for Economic Cooperation and Development (OECD). To achieve these results the group had to use a limited number of surrogate indices and parities, which were provided either by the participating states themselves or in some cases collected from other sources.

Concerning Table 12.4 there is one observation particularly worth mentioning and this is the very strong domestic purchasing-power of the dollar with regard to the category of procurement and construction. In view of the highly-developed US arms industry and its many technological advantages it is not surprising to find that the Americans get relatively more for their money in terms of weaponry and other types of military equipment than they get in terms of personnel and various kinds of those goods and services that fall within the operating-cost category. The extent to which this is really the case may not be accurately reflected by the results in Table 12.4 because of the limited number of comparable data mentioned earlier. However, the results strongly support the generally accepted hypothesis that the USA have a substantial cost advantage over other countries with regard to procurement items.

It may also be noted that the military personnel in Australia, Austria and the UK is relatively much more expensive than the civilian personnel, while the opposite is true for Finland. One might have expected military personnel to be relatively less expensive in countries which have conscription. However, the results presented in Table 12.4 do not give evidence of such a pattern.

Table 12.4   Military PPPs of 1982 as constructed by the Group

(*a*) *PPPs for total expenditures and major categories*

Participating States	Operating costs	Procurement and construction	Research and development	Total military expenditures
Australia	1.37	2.60	1.14	1.45
Austria	11.77	51.44	–	13.56
Finland	3.17	9.38	4.91	4.00
Italy	567.00	2302.00	673.00	679.00
Norway	6.34	13.36	6.51	7.14
Sweden	6.24	11.63	5.37	7.10
UK	0.54	1.54	0.49	0.61
USA	1.05	0.89	1.05	1.00

(*b*) *PPPs for subcategories of operating costs*

Participating States	Military personnel	Civilian personnel	Operations and maintenance	Total operating costs
Australia	2.02	1.02	0.99	1.37
Austria	13.58	7.34	12.97	11.77
Finland	2.49	4.35	4.41	3.17
Italy	493.00	552.00	906.00	567.00
Norway	5.69	5.51	8.28	6.34
Sweden	6.74	5.81	5.81	6.24
UK	0.73	0.32	0.57	0.34
USA	1.03	1.15	1.01	1.05

Note: Based on data for construction items only.

Table 12.5   Exchange rates and various PPPs for participating states (1980–2) (National currency units per dollar)

Conversion rates	Australia	Austria	Finland	Italy	Norway	Sweden	UK	USA
1982								
Exchange rates[a]	0.98	17.06	4.82	1353	6.45	6.28	0.57	1.00
PPPs for GDP[b]	1.03	16.10	5.30	983	7.30	5.97	0.54	1.00
The Group's military PPPs	1.45	13.56	4.00	679	7.14	7.10	0.61	1.00
1981								
Exchange rates[a]	0.87	15.93	4.32	1137	5.74	5.06	0.49	1.00
PPPs for GDP[b]	0.99	16.10	5.2	892	7.11	5.88	0.54	1.00
The Group's military PPPs	1.44	13.58	3.98	661	7.09	7.13	0.61	1.00
1980								
Exchange rates[a]	0.88	12.94	3.73	856	4.94	4.23	0.43	1.00
PPPs for GDP[b]	0.99	16.50	5.08	821	6.79	5.85	0.53	1.00
The Group's military PPPs	1.34	14.09	4.11	567	6.93	7.28	0.58	1.00

Sources

[a]   Exchange rates are the yearly average dollar rates as published by the International Monetary Fund; see *International Financial Statistics*, April 1985 (Washington: IMF, 1985).

[b]   For PPPs for GDP constructed by the Organisation for Economic Cooperation and Development, see *National Accounts, Main Aggregates*, 1960–83, vol. 1 (Paris: OECD, 1984) pp. 123–30.

Table 12.6 Participating States' military expenditures of 1982 as percentage of the military expenditure of the USA

Source of information / Type of conversion factor	Arms control and Disarmament Agency (USACDA) Exchange rates	Stockholm International Peace Research Institute (SIPRI) Exchange rates	International Institute for Strategic Studies (IISS) Exchange rates	Organisation for Economic Co-operation and Development (OECD) GDP PPPs	Group of Experts Military PPPs
Participating States					
Australia	2.48	2.24	2.56	2.12	1.52
Austria	0.58	0.41	0.43	0.49	0.53
Finland	0.51	0.46	0.44	0.45	0.55
Italy	6.24	4.98	4.63	5.32	7.68
Norway	1.04	0.93	0.86	0.78	0.78
Sweden	2.36	1.98	1.61	1.66	1.39
UK	15.80	13.94	12.37	15.02	13.28
USA	100.00	100.00	100.00	100.00	100.00

As shown by the results in Table 12.5 there were important differences both between military and civilian PPPs and between military PPPs and exchange rates. While the relations between military and civilian PPPs remained relatively stable over time their relations to exchange rates behaved very differently. As a result of the then-growing international value of the US dollar, exchange rates rose markedly in the years from 1980 to 1982. As the PPPs were not so much affected by the rise of the dollar, the relations between PPPs and exchange rates changed considerably in this short period, which clearly demonstrated the arbitrariness in selecting the exchange rates of one particular year as a tool for international comparisons.

The military PPPs constructed by the UN Group of Experts were used to compare the military expenditures of 1982 as reported to the United Nations by those countries which participated in the group's exercise. As shown in Table 12.6 the resulting figures were in turn compared with corresponding figures obtained from other sources. It may be noted that compared with those of other countries the US expenditure figure increased in all cases with the exception of Finland and Italy when military PPPs of 1982 were used instead of exchange rates of the same year. If the same kind of comparisons had been made a couple of years later, when the dollar rate had reached its peak, the opposite results would undoubtedly have been obtained. This again indicates that exchange rates should preferably not be used for international volume comparisons if other instruments, such as PPPs, are available.

VII   CONCLUDING REMARKS

The PPP-method is by no means an easy way out. The construction of PPPs is a time-consuming and difficult task. Furthermore, it rests on the assumption that a reasonable amount of relevant statistical data can be made available which is not at all obvious in the field of military expenditures. Given political will and a reasonable availability of adequate and relevant information, the construction of useful instruments for international and intertemporal comparisons of military expenditures is feasible.

Notes and References

1.   For further information see Jacques Fontanel: *L'économie des armes* (Paris: La Découverte, 1984).

2.   For a further presentation and analysis of these factors see Jacques Fontanel: *L'estimation des dépenses militaires soviétiques* (Grenoble et Lyons: ARES, Défense et Sécurité, 1981).

3.   *Report of the Secretary-General: Reduction of Military Budgets – Measurements and International Reporting of Military Expenditures* (New York: United Nations, 1976) A/31/222.

4.   *Report of the Secretary-General: Reduction of Military Budgets – International Reporting of Military Expenditures* (New York: United Nations, 1980) A/35/479.

5.   General Assembly resolution 35/142 B of December 1980.

6.   *Report of the Secretary-General: Reduction of Military Budgets – Refinement of International Reporting and Comparison of Military Expenditures* (New York: United Nations, 1982) A/S–12/7, paragraph 10.

7.   General Assembly resolution 37/95 B of 13 December 1982.

8.   *Report of the Secretary-General: Reduction of Military Budgets – Construction of Military Price Indexes and Purchasing-Power Parities for Comparison of Military Expenditures* (New York: United Nations, 1985) A/40/421.

9.   Ibid, paragraph 155a.

10.   Ibid, chapter IV.

13 The Economics of Military Spending: Is the Military Dollar Really Different*

G. Adams and D. A. Gold
CENTER ON BUDGET AND POLICY PRIORITIES,
WASHINGTON

The economic impact of military spending has become a subject of intense debate in the USA with the dramatic increases in US military spending of the 1980s. The Defense Department and industry argue that defence spending creates jobs and promotes economic health. Critics argue that such spending is inflationary, saps productivity and technology, and creates fewer jobs than other federal spending. This chapter reviews these claims and concludes that the economic impact of military spending is only marginally different from that of other forms of federal spending. It is not uniquely inflationary, has an unclear relationship to productivity and technological development, and does not create significantly different numbers of jobs. Military spending does, however, affect regions, sectors of industry and segments of the labour market in different ways from other federal spending. Through these effects, a 'political economy' of military spending emerges, where decisions on levels of US military spending and on specific weapons programmes are supported by microeconomic impacts. The economics of military spending involves public policy choices about the directions of national security policy and about national economic development; the macroeconomic issues are, at best, of marginal importance.

I INTRODUCTION

The economic impact of military spending has become a subject of intense debate in the USA. Since 1981, US military spending has grown to unprecedented levels. In fiscal year 1980, US 'national defence' outlays were \$134 bn; FY 1985 outlays are twice that amount, or \$248.7 bn, real growth (after inflation) of over 35 per cent. By FY 1990 US national defence outlays will reach \$354.3 bn. American defence spending will have grown 164 per cent, including inflation, over the decade of the 1980s.[1] In fact, by fiscal year 1988, US national defence outlays in constant dollars will surpass any previous year in American history since 1946.[2]

The Defense Department and its contractors often argue that the US budget has an important impact on the US economy. Secretary of Defense Caspar Weinberger, for example, has stated that cutting \$1 bn out of defence will reduce US employment by 35 000 jobs.[3] The Pentagon has created a 'Defense Economic Impact Modelling System', in part to project the economic opportunities business will encounter as military spending expands in coming years. Defence contractors use analyses of the economic impact of weapons they are building to lobby Congress on behalf of the programmes.[4]

Critics of nuclear weapons programmes and of high levels of defence spending also muster economic arguments. Military spending, they argue, spurs inflation by pumping money into the economy without adding to the supply of goods. Moreover, high levels of military research and development sap the nation's technological strength by consuming funds and personnel that could be used to enhance American competitiveness in international markets. Finally, fewer jobs are created by military spending than by almost any other form of federal spending.

Beyond their arguments over national security issues, supporters and critics of weapons programmes and the military budget also use a language of economic argument. Their competing research efforts gather data, create models and issue broadsides as part of the political conflict over such weapons as the B-1 bomber, MX missile and 'Star Wars' and as part of the debate over the distribution of the federal budget.

Despite the vociferous arguments and the mustering of facts, neither side has convinced the other on the issue and the level of US military spending remains high. Those who argue that military spending is harmful to the economy have not moved communities to reject defence industry, nor has the argument caused the media to conduct systematic exposés of the economic dangers of high levels of military spending. Economists do not treat military spending as a central issue in their work on the US economy. Few political leaders call for a shift in federal spending priorities to halt the supposed 'damage' to the economy caused by military spending.

In the 1980s, moreover, the trends in the American economy seem to suggest that the critics of military spending are not having the better part of the argument. Inflation levels have declined dramatically since the 1970s. American technology seems to be entering a new phase of expansion and jobs are being created in the US economy at a rapid rate.

A re-evaluation of the argument over the economic impact of military spending is clearly overdue. This chapter lays out such a re-evaluation. It does not describe new original research. In many of the areas in dispute, research has been ample. Instead we review this body of work, draw some conclusions about its validity, and suggest areas for further research.

Our review of the existing literature suggests that the argument over the economics of defence is, at its heart, political. Defense Department claims are exaggerated, promoting the defence budget and positive Congressional decisions on weapons proposals. The critics also overstate their views, however.

The economic impact of military spending, we conclude, is only marginally different from that of other forms of federal spending. The key difference is not at the level of macroeconomics – arguments over inflation, productivity or employment – but rather at the microeconomic level – where military spending affects regions, sections of industry and segments of the labour market. These microeconomic impacts have created a 'political economy' of military spending, where political decisions draw strength from microeconomic impacts. Fundamentally, defence economics involves public policy choices about the directions of the nation's economic development; the macroeconomic issues are, at best, of marginal importance.

II INFLATION

Military spending is often seen as a cause of inflation. Analysts point to numerous historical examples, most recently the experiences of the

Second World War, when price controls, rationing, and other restrictive devices were needed to keep inflation in check, and of Vietnam, which saw the beginning of more than a decade of high rates of inflation.

To some, military spending is inherently inflationary because it creates income and purchasing power without also creating additional goods and services for people to purchase. As described in a United Nations report 'effective demand is created without offsetting increases in immediately consumable output or in productive capacity to meet future consumption requirements. This excess demand creates an upward pressure on prices throughout the economy.[5]

This explanation, while seemingly clear and obvious, provides very little guidance as to whether military spending is a cause of inflation. Some government expenditures may have a positive long-term impact on productivity and an economy's ability to produce goods and services. At the time they are undertaken, however, practically all government outlays, whether for health, public works, police, the military or something else, increase purchasing power without expanding the quantity of products for sale on the market.

This excess demand is the reason why rising government outlays can restore an economy in recession. To treat such demand as always inflationary assumes that the economy is always near full employment. If growth in government outlays occurs when an economy is expanding or already suffering from inflationary pressures, then greater inflation could result. Here the inflationary potential of government spending can be offset if outlays are financed by taxation or forced savings, removing from the economy the amount of purchasing power equivalent to the new expenditure.

Different financing mechanisms can lead to different impacts on inflation. Wartime spending, for example, can create inflationary pressures since demand increases so rapidly, and production is diverted to the war effort. If taxes are raised and savings are stimulated, demand can be brought back into balance with available supply. If, instead, higher military expenditures are financed by deficits, and the central banks step up their buying of bonds and boost the money supply, inflation is a likely result.

Without a war, the inflationary impact of an increase in military spending will depend on the method of financing, as well as on the state of the economy as a whole.

In the case of Vietnam, the increase in US military outlays occurred as the economy was in the midst of a long boom. The

Johnson Administration made an explicit decision to allow the deficit to rise and not to seek a tax increase to finance Vietnam outlays. In this instance, higher military outlays without any compensating action on the revenue side were a direct initial cause of higher deficits. A significant increase in inflation followed as monetary policy was not restrictive enough to offset the fiscal stimulus. The transmission of inflation abroad appears to have been linked to the fact that other countries, under the fixed exchange rate system, had to absorb the dollars the USA was spending in Asia.[6]

During the Reagan Administration, an increase in military outlays has been accompanied by large tax cuts, reductions in civilian government outlays, rapid growth in federal interest payments, and large deficits. The deficits result from many changes, notably the 1981 tax cut. It is not clear that they result from the military build-up. More important, the high US deficits of the 1980s have coincided with lower inflation, thus calling into question the claim that a military build-up, combined with large deficits, is automatically inflationary.

When the Reagan build-up began, a number of critics hypothesised that the size and speed of the increase in military outlays, and its concentration in hardware would lead to inflation since there were simply not enough resources available quickly enough to satisfy both civilian and military demands. Shortages and bottlenecks in civilian and military industries would increase sectoral inflation and that could spread throughout the economy. Even the military was worried about the bottleneck problem.[7]

In reality, tight monetary policies and the deep recession of 1981–2 broke the inflationary momentum and generated substantial excess capacity. As the US recovery gained momentum, a rapid increase in imports of both capital goods and consumer goods has also kept capacity utilisation rates lower than expected. The large increase in foreign capital inflows has aided the US financial system in meeting both governmental and private credit needs.

Econometric evidence is inconclusive on the relation between military spending and inflation. Bezdek's simulation study, in which five-year, 30 per cent increases in military spending, compensated by an equal dollar-increase in non-military outlays, was compared with both a 'no change' alternative and with a 30 per cent cut in military outlays compensated by equivalent increases in non-military programmes, found that the higher level of military spending was accompanied by lower GNP and employment, and a higher price level.[8] Since the military spending changes were fully offset by other spending changes, no deficit financing was involved. Hence the link must lie somewhere else.

Studies of actual data, however, have found that military spending has essentially no effect on inflation. DeGrasse, in a crossnational study using rank correlation analysis, found that a country's rank in the sample with respect to military spending as a share of gross domestic product had no relation to its rank with respect to inflation rates. Vitaliano concluded that adding variables measuring military spending to an expectations-augmented Phillips Curve, an equation which explains current inflation in terms of unemployment and expectations of future inflation 'do[es] not support the hypothesis that defense spending exerts a separate, discernable effect on the inflation rate'.[9]

It is possible that the link between military spending and inflation occurs in a manner not made visible by traditional testing methods. Melman, Dumas, and others have argued that military spending's negative impact on productivity growth creates an inflation-prone industrial structure, which makes inflation more likely over time.[10]

The depletion view points to the large quantity of capital inputs and skilled labour used by the military sector and denied to the civilian sector as a source of declining productivity in the industrial sector as a whole. Case studies of specific industries, such as machine tools, are pointed to as evidence, and the paucity of R & D and new investment and decline in productivity in basic industries such as automobile and steel are also mentioned. Without significant productivity growth, production cannot keep pace with demand, especially when the latter is stimulated by expansionary policies. In such a situation, there will be a tendency for prices to rise.

Defence-industry contracting and pricing policies would seem to suggest that this sector is a likely source of cost–push inflationary pressures. There is very little competition within defence industries and there are significant barriers to both entry and exit. The Pentagon's long-standing insistence on high performance, state-of-the-art equipment, the growth of top-heavy administrative structures in both industry and government, and military contracting practices all tend to validate the tendency for costs to rise.[11] Drawing on Hong's econometric work, Dumas and Melman argue that military producers can be characterised by 'cost-pass-along', rather than cost-minimising behaviour.[12] Moreover, they argue, this behaviour spills over into civilian sectors and produces cost–push inflationary pressures that explain the stagflation that dominated the USA and much of the world economy after 1966.

Hong's empirical work on cost-pass-along consists of estimating an equation for prices and one for wages, with the latter including a measure of administrative overhead, a key variable cited by Melman as indicative of military industry cost–push behaviour. Hong's results indicate that cost-pass-along behaviour became dominant in the US economy after 1966, coinciding with the onset of stagflation.

If depletion has an inflationary effect, however, it would be over long periods, and in any given shorter time period might well be swamped by cyclical movements and policy changes. After 1966, for example, a number of economic variables changed. The decline and collapse of the Bretton Woods system, the Nixon Administration's failures in macroeconomic management and the international oil crisis would have generated a more inflationary environment in the USA, regardless of cost maximising defence management.

The relationship between Hong's results and these changes has not been explored. It is also not clear how cost-pass-along behaviour spills over into non-military sectors of the economy, especially when these sectors are much more subject to competition than the military sector. Does cost-pass-along characterise such industries as automobile, computers, telecommunications equipment and semi-conductors in the 1980s, where cost appears to be falling, not rising, amidst intense internal competition?

The military spending/inflation link is not so clear as sometimes supposed. Methods of financing deficits, general economic conditions and the complex realities of production in the economy all make this relationship uncertain.

III MILITARY SPENDING, TECHNOLOGY AND INVESTMENT

The impact of military outlays on new investment, technological progress, and economic growth is one of the more contentious issues in the debate over the economic impacts of military spending. A long-standing view, going back at least to Adam Smith treats military spending as an unproductive activity that draws potentially productive resources from the economy while providing little or no stimulation in return.[13] An alternative position sees the military as a source of significant technological innovation that spills over into the civilian economy while at the same time providing demand stimulation.

There is a substantial literature and some statistical evidence that suggests there is a trade-off between military spending and investment,[14] and a few case studies on the negative impacts on civilian technology of trends within military technology.[15] At the same time, there are historical studies of how military technology has stimulated civilian industries.[16]

This issue has been strongly debated in the 1980s. At the beginning of the Carter–Reagan build-up in military spending in the USA, numerous analyses were put forward suggesting how it would draw needed technological resources from the civilian economy, stimulate further inflationary pressures, and undermine the chances of a substantial recovery.[17] Instead, after a deep recession brought on by tight monetary policy, the US economy was completing the third year of a boom, in 1985, with an expansion of new investment, significantly lower inflation, and technological progress in established industries like automobile-manufacturing and telecommunications and new industries such as robotics and bioengineering. This strong recovery has occurred despite the fact that some of the critic's predictions have come true, such as a shift of engineering talent to the military sector and large federal budget deficits. The negative side of the argument seems to miss something.

A number of statistical studies show a negative relationship between military spending and investment and between military spending and the level of GNP or the rate of growth of GNP. Rank correlation analyses across countries have yielded negative correlation coefficients whereby countries with higher shares of GNP devoted to the military tend also to have lower investment shares and lower rates of growth.[18] Econometric models have yielded negative regression coefficients when military spending is related to investment.[19]

Simulation studies using econometric and input/output techniques have concluded that when the military share of the economy is projected to rise, investment and total output is lower.[20] Some of these studies have covered the USA, some other OECD countries or a pooling of data from OECD countries, which Leontief and Duchin investigated future conditions for the entire world economy. This negative conclusion is not universally accepted, however. Rank correlation analyses compare two variables with each other; the measured trade-off may, however, result from some unmeasured third variable that affects both the primary variables. When data for a number of countries are pooled, the resulting coefficients are averages, and it is not clear whether they are measuring a meaningful economic relationship within any single country.

The direction of causation between military spending and investment and economic growth, especially in a cyclical context, is also unclear. A negative relation is usually interpreted as showing that growth in military spending causes a fall, or slower growth, in investment and GNP. Some researchers have argued that military spending is used by the US government as a counter-cyclical device, so that a negative relationship would be consistent with a causal mechanism running the other way – from GNP and investment, and other measures of cyclical activity, to military outlays.[21]

Boulding's less-known study illustrates some of the problems that researchers must confront in analysing this relationship.[22] He analysed US national income data for two years – 1929 and 1969. Each year was the peak of a long-business-cycle boom. Between the two years, military spending as a share of GNP had increased dramatically. However, there was no fall off in the investment share of GNP; instead, it was the private consumption share that fell. In addition, the level of GNP was substantially higher in 1969.

Interpreting these findings, the growth in military spending may have been largely financed out of taxes on income from wages and salaries, which are the primary determinant of consumption, rather than taxes on property income, which would affect investment. Boulding's results reflect long-term relationships, while other studies measure movements confined to a shorter period of time. Thus, it is difficult to generalise about a trade-off between military spending and investment.

Boulding's results also illustrate another difficulty with such a possible trade-off; there need to be mechanisms by which it occurs. Military spending may attract investment resources via the government budget process, obtaining private funds through taxing and borrowing and obtaining a large share of those funds in competition with other government programmes. In the USA, however, taxation has tended to have more of an impact on consumption than on investment. The impact of deficit financing is uncertain; moreover, deficits have only recently made an important contribution to federal government revenues and could not account for much of the resource shifts before the mid-to-late 1970s.

It is more likely that military and civilian government expenditures move together, rather than in opposite directions. Russett, examining data on US government spending on military, health and education from 1941 to 1979 found no systematic pattern of trade-off. In his view, the Reagan Administration is an exception to a more general pattern. Domke, Eichenberg and Kelleher similarly found no statistically significant trade-off between military and welfare expenditures, except for wartime periods.[23] Even if there were a trade-off between military spending and domestic spending, it is not clear how a shift within the government budget would affect capital formation in the economy as a whole.

Another way of approaching the problem is to argue that military–industry bids key investment resources away from the private sector during a period of rising military outlays, creating bottlenecks in the private sector, stimulating inflationary pressures, raising the costs and reducing the effectiveness of private investment spending.[24] Some of this market-generated crowding out occurred during the Korean and Vietnam build-ups. There is no reason, however, why an economy operating at less than full capacity should experience such bottlenecks over a long period. The current build-up has not generated inflation nor used up available capacity, suggesting that an increase in military spending is not sufficient, by itself, to generate such a problem. Macroeconomic and specific industry and labour-market conditions may be more important. Only research on how an economy adjusts to changes in military spending over both short and long periods of time will assess the validity of such a trade-off mechanism.

It is a common piece of wisdom, however, that Japan's superior economic performance in recent decades is due to its low level of military spending, while countries with higher military burdens, such as the USA and UK have been unable to find the right formula for sustained economic growth. Some statistical analyses argue that countries that devote a small proportion of their output to military spending tend to have higher savings and investment ratios, higher productivity growth, and higher GNP growth than countries with higher ratios of military spending to GNP.[25] This argument places far too much weight on one factor. Japan's rapid economic growth is linked to several social and economic circumstances and government policies: large numbers of relatively low-paid workers ready to move into industrial and commercial activities in the 1950s and 1960s; close relationships among financial, marketing, and industrial enterprise allowing firms to weather recessions and concentrate on long-term objectives; a production strategy emphasising product quality and the continual updating of process technology allowing Japanese firms to penetrate Western markets with high quality, low-cost products; and government policies that stimulate savings and investment and reinforce technological dynamism.

Would such policies and circumstances have been as effective if military spending had been higher? For example, would the Japanese have adopted policies that financed higher military outlays by reducing consumption, or investment? Would a larger Japanese military industry have cost-control problems and could the government insulate the civilian economy from such inefficiencies? These questions need to be addressed before any conclusions can be formed about the role of low military spending in Japan's economic performance.

Similarly, while both the USA and the UK have experienced problems with respect to capital formation and economic growth, it is not clear how much of this can be attributed to military spending as opposed to other variables. In the USA, economic-growth rates have been highest when military spending has been high or rising, as in the mid-1950s, mid-to-late 1960s, and 1982–5, while the period when military outlays fell coincided with the stagflation of the 1970s. Military spending's impact on productivity could occur over a long period of time, and stagflation could be attributed to past high military outlays. However, this explanation needs to be compared with alternatives: the impact on US growth of the decline of the Bretton Woods monetary system or the impact of stop–go macroeconomic policies and the policies and the protection of British financial interests on British economic growth.

Some analysts argue that the military imposes its requirements on civilian industries, thus weakening the latter as a competitive force. For example, the relative decline of US semi-conductor and electronic products industries compared with those of Japan has been attributed to the dominance of military research and development with its emphasis on exotic requirements and its de-emphasis of cost control.[26]

On the other side, there are a number of examples of military technology and military products that spill over into civilian sectors. Weapons production appears to have been a source of significant technological innovation during the nineteenth century in the USA,[27] and during and immediately after the Second World War.[28] Moreover, such technologies as aircraft, aircraft engines, microcircuits, computers, fibre optics, lasers, composite materials and metallurgy can all be linked to military spending. Finally, while excessive costs do characterise defence production and are consistent with defence industry contracting practice, it is not clear how they are passed along to the private sector. The transfer of technology between military and civilian sectors needs to be clearly described and its costs and benefits more adequately measured.

The historical process surrounding technology transfer also needs to be explored. Kaldor has argued that 'military technology is rarely in phase with civilian developments' over the long term being 'very advanced, stimulating new civilian technology' in some periods, but being 'decadent, dragging the economy backwards' at other times. Britain at the end of the nineteenth century and the USA after the Second World War are cited to argue that military technology has become dominated by 'elaborate custom-built product improvements that are typical of industries on the decline instead of the simpler mass-market process improvememts which tend to characterise industries in their prime'.[29] It is difficult to generalise from this analysis. There are only a few examples and the concept of a long wave has been difficult to pin down both theoretically and empirically. But Kaldor's analysis strongly suggests military spending can be either 'advanced' or 'decadent'.

Further research on spin-off should analyse the conditions under which a stimulative or retarding effect occurs. Such research is expecially useful when large, research-intensive programmes are dominant, such as the Strategic Defense Initiative and Very High Speed Integrated Circuit programmes of the 1980s. Because of their size and their explicit goal of creating new technologies, such programmes could clarify the spin-off relationship.

While military spending can impinge upon investment and technical progress, there are unanswered questions about the importance and direction of this effect. While R & D is a determinant of economic growth, its importance is not clear. Future research should compare military spending with other influences on investment and technology, as well as analyse the impact of military spending in different historical periods and under different economic conditions.

IV   MILITARY SPENDING AND EMPLOYMENT

1   Implications for the Number of Jobs

The impact of military spending on employment is another highly contentious issue in the military/economy debate. Critics of military spending frequently argue that it creates fewer jobs than virtually any other form of federal spending, that a shift of federal funds from the defence budget to other parts of the federal budget or to a tax cut would create a larger number of jobs, and even that continuing to spend money on the military actually costs the economy jobs.[30]

The Defense Department and the defence industry, on the other hand, argue that military spending is labour-intensive, creating 35 000 jobs per billion dollars spent.[31] They also point to the historical experience of the Second World War, when military spending clearly mopped up an enormous reservoir of unemployment, and ask what would happen to employment in the communities where defence plants and military bases are located were military spending to be cut.

The argument is an important one. Critics of the defence budget use the employment argument to demonstrate that lower military spending will mean greater economic security. The Defense Department uses its employment argument to suggest, forcefully, that Congress should support defence spending because of the jobs at stake.

Considerable research exists on the debate over military spending and employment. The assumptions made in this literature vary and the conclusions are widely different. Depending on the source, one could conclude that defence spending makes a big difference to the number of jobs in the American economy, a little difference or virtually none at all.

The variations in the number of jobs created by military spending is the first point of disagreement. Data from the US Bureau of Labor Statistics, some critics argue, shows an enormous difference between the number of jobs generated by spending on health or education and those generated by defence purchases. Some studies using input–output models of the US economy (looking at the employment requirements generated by a given amount of final demand for military and civilian products) show similar, if less exaggerated, results. Comparing a given military product (for instance,the MX missile) to a set of alternatives, some of these studies suggest, almost any alternative expenditure of defence funds would create a larger number of direct and indirect jobs in the economy than would defence spending.[32]

The most recent input–output analysis, performed by the Congressional Budget Office in 1983, comes to the conclusion that the number of defence jobs generated per $100 bn of expenditure is not terribly different from other kinds of federal spending. Using an economic model developed by Data Resources International, Inc., The CBO concludes:

> additional spending on defense and on non-defense purchases of goods and services appear to have roughly equal expansionary effects on employment in the short run. Econometric model simulations suggest that an additional $10 billion in defense spending in the current fiscal year could create up to 250 000 additional jobs; the same $10 billion spent on non-defense purchases in the public and private sector could also create almost 250 000 jobs.[33]

The difference between these outcomes depends on the assumptions being made in the model and on what is being compared. Defence spending clearly generates a number of direct and indirect jobs, ranging roughly from the 25 000 estimated by CBO to the 35 000 cited by the Defense Department in testimony.[34] This number, however, is relatively meaningless unless one compares it with the number of jobs created by other kinds of federal or private spending.

The Defense Department clearly overstates the conclusions one might draw from its 35,000 jobs per billion figure. Cutting this amount from the budget would not necessarily mean the loss of those jobs; the outcome depends very much on what is done with the billion dollars, or the comparative use of the money. Returned to the economy in the form of deficit reduction, a billion-dollar defence cut could result in lower federal borrowing requirements, lower interest rates, increased private sector borrowing, and, consequently, significant new job-creation. Spent elsewhere in the federal budget, these funds might directly employ more people than the number of jobs lost as a result of the defence cutback. Of course, these funds might also be used on programmes that could create significantly fewer direct or indirect jobs, for instance, transfer payments, which are less stimulating to the economy than purchases of goods and services.[35]

On the other hand, the conclusion that defence spending actually *costs* the economy jobs is also overstated.[36] If alternative forms of federal spending create marginally more direct and indirect jobs than defence, the issue is not one of 'jobs lost', but, rather, of jobs one might have preferred in other sectors rather than the jobs created by defence spending.

The reason why such comparisons are unsatisfying lies in the assumptions made in these analyses of military spending and employment. One common assumption is that defence dollars come out of another slice in a fixed federal pie; if defence goes up, domestic spending goes down.[37] Another version of this assumption is that taxpayers, who might otherwise spend their tax dollars on other activities that would create more employment, are funding defence.[38]

These arguments assume that the federal budget is a zero-sum game, funded entirely out of tax dollars. With a budget deficit, however, federal spending is not zero-sum. Defence can be funded out of borrowing, not necessarily out of programmes for the poor. Moreover, depending on how such a deficit is financed, taxpayers are not denied significant disposable income because of taxes for defence. The 1981 tax cut, for example, has actually increased disposable income for private consumers.[39]

Input–output models also assume that the economy operates at full employment. This makes the jobs-impact issue difficult to resolve. It means that a shift of funds to defence automatically means taking economic resources away from other activities. Were this true, those engaged in the other activities will find they lose their jobs, unless their skills can be transferred to defence activities. At the very least, one more job in defence means more than one more job less in some other activity.

The problem here lies in the model. The American economy has scarcely ever operated anywhere near full employment since the end of the Second World War. If there is less than full employment, spare plant capacity and labour exist in the economy. An increase in military spending may use or employ this spare capacity and labour, leaving virtually no impact on employment in other areas.[40]

Existing analyses also encounter problems with the assumptions they make about the nature of the defence sector itself. Defence, it is argued, is a high technology sector; more of the funds in this industry go for materials, technology and equipment and less for labour, relative to other sectors of industry.[41] There is, however, little evidence that defence production overall is significantly more capital-intensive than other sectors. While airframes, air engines, and missiles can be highly capital-intensive, electronics assembly, ship-building, and communications equipment are far less so.[42]

Finally, the models are not always clear about whether or not all defence-related and induced jobs are being included. Defence employment estimates should be comprehensive, including the jobs in the Defense Department, as well as those in the private sector, since both sets are essential to the performance of military tasks.[43] In addition, models need to make clear whether they are including the induced jobs which result from the wages spent by those directly and indirectly employed by military spending.

The CBO analysis clearly includes all Defense Department spending, not just defence purchases and thus counts all direct and indirect jobs created in the Defense Department and in industry by military spending. Since its assumptions are the most comprehensive, the comparative outcomes from the CBO study are probably the most comprehensive and accurate. The CBO study also calculates induced employment, showing that military spending has a relatively higher ability to create induced jobs (a higher 'multiplier') than other forms of federal spending. However, CBO notes in an appendix that a different model would show a larger multiplier for non-defence spending, which would change the comparisons.[44]

If the CBO estimates are the most reliable current data, defence may not have a substantially different impact on the number of jobs in the economy from other forms of public and private spending. The *number* of jobs created by defence spending, however, may not be the most significant measure of the employment impact of defence spending. If defence dollars create jobs in some areas of the country, but not others, jobs for certain types of workers, but not others, or jobs in some sectors of industry, but not others, then defence dollars represent a choice, explicit of implicit, about the job creation effect federal spending will have on American society. The employment impact of military spending may be an issue of jobs *where* and jobs *for whom*.

2 Geographical Implications

Federal spending in general and defence spending in particular, are not distributed evenly across the population and territory of the USA. Defence spending data for 1984 show a strong concentration of spending in fifteen states (by rank): California, Texas, Virginia, New

282 Macroeconomics in an International Political Framework

York, Florida, Massachusetts, Missouri, Maryland, Connecticut, Georgia, Pennsylvania, Washington, New Jersey, Ohio, and North Carolina.[45] Weighted for the state's contribution to the federal income tax, its share of *GNP* or of population, this pattern is clearly uneven.

Moreover, the geographic distribution of defence contracting has shifted dramatically over time toward southern and western states. The north-east/mid-west regional share of prime contract dollars dropped from 71.8 per cent in 1951 to 37 per cent in 1983, while the south–west states increased their share from 28 per cent to 63 per cent. This shift has affected Indiana, Iowa, Michigan, Minnesota, Ohio and Wisconsin, whose share fell precipitously from 31 per cent in 1951 to 9.8 per cent in 1983. Michigan and Illinois actually received fewer real (after inflation) prime contract dollars in 1983 than in 1951.[46]

The loss of Pentagon investment in plant and equipment, wage-dollars paid into the local economy and orders and subcontracts to other suppliers has probably had an impact, over time, on the gradual shift of economic activity and, consequently, job creation, away from the American mid-west and toward the periphery of the country.

This relationship should not be overstated, however. Clearly defence spending shifts are not the only explanation for the larger changes in American economic geography. Changes in the productive process in industry, in the costs for labour and raw materials, in the investment climate in different areas, in domestic and overseas markets, among many other factors, have an impact on plant location, the creation of jobs and the movement of the labour force. Moreover, since the defence share of US GNP has declined since the end of the Vietnam War, regional economic changes cannot be explained solely or even principally in terms of defence spending.[47]

The impact of defence-spending choices on economic geography clearly requires further study, using data over a period of time, in the context of wider economic changes.

3 Sectoral Employment Differences

Defence spending has an immediate and pronounced impact on employment in several specific sectors of industry, as input–output models show. Defence employment is highly concentrated in such sectors as ordnance (79.7 per cent of 1982 output), missiles and space vehicles (67.5 per cent), radio and TV communications equipment

(58 per cent), aircraft engines (53.5 per cent) and aircraft (40.4 per cent).[48]

Funds for defence can encourage employment growth in these sectors or sustain existing employment when demand lags on the commercial side. Other kinds of federal spending would stimulate employment in other sectors. Transfer payments, for example, tend to have an impact widely across the economy, with particular gains in non-durable manufactures, services, and public-sector employment. Spending on health creates jobs in services and public employment. Public-works projects, infrastructure, education, energy, among many other alternatives, all create employment in construction and manufacturing.

The key issue is the choice being made. If defence spending is expanding while, at the same time, spending for other programmes is declining, employment in the sectors where defence jobs are concentrated tends to gain, while employment declines in other sectors.[49] In other words, federal spending decisions represent conscious or unconscious choices with respect to job creation in different sectors of the economy. Since US unemployment is especially concentrated among lower skilled workers, minorities, women, and teenagers – parts of the US labour force that work in the sectors of the economy stimulated by non-defence spending – defence spending, at the expense of non-defence spending, can have clear social and political consequences.

Here, too, the case should not be overstated. Defence spending is not the only thing that stimulates sectoral differences in job creation. Tax policies which stimulate private-sector-investment decisions also have an employment impact. Independent private-sector-investment decisions probably have the most important impact on employment growth and decline in different sectors of the US economy. Further research should clarify the relative role of defence spending in creating and maintaining employment in different sectors of the economy.

4 Labour Market Differences

The American labour market is segmented into different types of work. Defence spending affects some types more heavily than others. The Defense Department civilian workforce and defence industry workers tend to have more skilled machinists, metal workers, aeronautical and electronic engineers, scientists, social scientists, lawyers and managers than the American economy as a whole and it is often argued that a high proportion of total US employment in these categories is in the Defense Department and the defence industry.

This argument needs to be made with some care, however. A high proportion of total 1981 US employment in some subsets of these categories was employed by the Defense Department or the defence industry, including, for example, 61 per cent of vocational education teachers, 60.4 per cent of mathematical specialists (not otherwise classified), and 47 per cent of aero-astronautical engineers.[50]

When one combines all the subsets with the highest proportions in defence work, however, they still do not constitute a large share of the total US job market – only 1.6 per cent in 1981. The vast bulk of the US labour market is far less dependent on defence-related employment.

Even when one explores the share of such categories in total employment in the Pentagon and with its contractors, they constitute a minority of total employment: 309 000 people, or 9.2 per cent of total employment in the Pentagon and the industry in 1981. The largest number of Pentagon employees on the civilian side of the Pentagon were mechanics, repairers and installers, clerical workers, managers, secretaries, stenographers and typists, among others. Many of these are 'service' types of employment open to a wide range of workers in the labour force.

Even in the defence industry, many jobs are not extremely technical. In 1981, 43.2 per cent of all defence industry employment was in the following categories: clerical workers, crafts workers, assemblers, operatives, labourers, metal-working operatives, professional and technical workers, and food-service workers.

Although the defence labour force may not be dramatically different from the rest of the American labour force,[51] the highest rates of US unemployment occur in the less skilled parts of the labour force, not in the highly skilled parts of defence contracting. Here, too, federal-spending choices constitute an industrial policy by stealth or inadvertence.

The research and development part of the defence labour force merits separate consideration. A significant proportion of US scientists, engineers and technicians are employed in defence-related work which, some analysts argue, deprives the civilian economy of these skills, with serious consequences, for technological development in the wider economy.[52] Were a very high proportion of such personnel employed in the defence sector, this problem could be serious.

However, there is considerable disagreement on the exact size of this 'brain drain'. Estimates range from 25 per cent of scientific, technical and engineering personnel to over 50 per cent who are employed in the defence sector.[53] This disagreement makes a considerable difference in terms of the pressures on the labour market for technical personnel and the availability of such personnel for commercial work.

In the long run, this problem may be less serious than it seems. Neither the supply of such personnel nor the total US investment in R & D is static. Thus, the available jobs, civilian and commercial, for technical personnel can grow and the supply may also be able to respond, over time, to those changes in demand. The market for R & D talent is clearly rising. In 1960, the US federal government spent $8.7 bn on research and development, (64 per cent of the total national investment, public and private). This figure rose to $29.6 bn by 1980, or 47.6 per cent of total national spending on R & D.[54]

Moreover, as the government market for R & D employees rose, so did the private market. In 1960, private industry spent $4.5 bn on R & D (33.3 per cent of the national total); by 1980, this had risen to $30.4 bn, or 48.9 per cent of total national R & D. Clearly a larger number of R & D employment choices were available in 1980 than twenty years earlier.

Defence spending may have more significant impacts on employment viewed from the perspective of geography, industrial sectors and types of work than it does on the overall number of people employed. The central issue with respect to employment is one of choice. If one knows how jobs distribute across the country, among sectors of the economy and within the labour market, does defence spending constitute an industrial and labour policy by inadvertence? Conscious of the employment impacts of their spending choices, would policy-makers prefer to have different employment outcomes? How are these preferred outcomes revealed in the priorities chosen for federal spending?

V   THE POLITICAL ECONOMY OF MILITARY SPENDING

The economic impact of military spending is neither as dramatically positive as sometimes claimed by the Department of Defense, nor as uniformly negative as sometimes argued by critics. However, military spending is far from neutral. Implicitly or explicitly, military spending is an economic development policy. The local, industrial and labour force impacts of this kind of spending create a 'political economy'. The steady, even tenacious persistence of constant high dollar levels of US defence spending, with strong political support, can be explained in part because of this political economy.

Although US defence budgets arise, in part, out of a clear, detailed definition of (principally Soviet) 'threats' to the USA, there is clear disagreement about such threats and about the weapons and forces required to meet them.[55] Bureaucratic structures in the Pentagon also explain, in part, high US defence budgets.[56] Bureaucratic self-promotion, budgetary inventiveness, inter-service rivalry and 'log-rolling' in the Defense Department have lives of their own linked only indirectly to perceptions of the 'threat'.

All four US military services, for example, have air forces, each one with several different types of aircraft. There are no examples of successful, long-term joint aircraft procurement. Inside one service, weapons programmes can ensure that a particular office in that service maintains its separate mission and increases its budget. For example, despite Air Force testimony in the 1970s that the existing B-52 bomber could survive as a nuclear-cruise-missile carrier until the year 2000, the proposed B-1 bomber programme clearly maintained that service's future commitment to the manned bomber mission and dramatically increased the Air Force budget.[57]

Moreover, the military frequently manages its procurement process in a way that keeps defence budgets high.[58] The revelations of wasteful spare parts purchases and excessive overhead charges in the early 1980s are only one of the obvious symptoms of a deeper management problem.[59]

Bureaucratic self-promotion and wasteful management, however, do not fully explain why the US Congress continues to fund high levels of defence spending, despite policy disagreements and Pentagon inefficiencies. At the heart of the defence spending process lies a political economy linking national security spending decisions to the microeconomic impacts we have already analysed. To understand this microeconomy, we must examine the historical relationship between two supposed antagonists in American society: government and the defence industry.

Historically, the American defence industry and the governmental agencies which buy its goods have been involved in a close, highly cooperative relationship. The First World War brought about a

major growth in US defence manufacturing, and brought industrialists from this sector into government decision-making positions.[60]
This relationship took a more permanent form after the Second
World War.[61] Within the framework of global US commitments, a
large permanent military establishment and significantly higher
defence spending, the military services and the defence industry
developed a close self-conscious interaction. For defence contractors,
this close interaction was of crucial importance; prime contractors
found defence a stable and profitable business.[62]

For the defence bureaucracy, close interaction was also desirable.
Not only did it facilitate communication over defence needs, it also
provided different Pentagon offices with external allies in the process
of defending missions and expanding their budgets. By definition, as
this relationship grew, the Defense Department became ever more
involved in decisions which affected parts of the American economy
at the microeconomic level.

The funds to continue this relationship, however, derived from
neither party, but from the Congress. Elected representatives and
congressional committees have, thus, become a third party in the
political economy of defence. Budgetary and spending decisions on
defence have been made for some time within this policy triangle: an
intimate interaction over policy decisions between federal agency
(the Pentagon), its client group in American society (the defence
industry), and Members of Congress with a special interest in that
part of the federal budget (the members of the Armed Services
committees, the Defense Appropriations subcommittees, and
members from congressional districts and states where defence
dollars are spent).[63]

This type of 'iron triangle', or 'sub-government', is common in
American politics.[64] It has the following characteristics:

- A close working relationship, in a clearly delineated arena of
  policy between the bureaucratic agency, key committees and
  Members of Congress, and a specific, private sector interest.
- A close interpenetration between the private-sector interest and
  the bureaucratic agency. Individuals on each side move freely
  back and forth, interact formally and informally, and tend to
  develop shared values, interests, and perceptions about future
  policy.[65] Through this interaction, authority over policy comes to
  be shared; private-sector individuals become, in effect, policy-
  makers and administrators.[66]

- A slow emergence over time. Such iron triangles are not wilfully created in a single moment as a conspiracy, but grow out of constant interaction among the players. Each side seeks to maintain the structure as circumstances change; disagreements, which do happen, are reconciled within the framework.
- A strong tendency to become 'iron' – closed off from the surrounding policital arena. The key actors in Congress, in the industry, in the agency make strenuous efforts to protect the structure from external penetration.[67] This isolation means that perspectives on alternatives to the existing policies become narrow and outside proposals are rejected as threatening. Government and private actors come to share the assumption that they act not only in their own interests, but in the 'public interest', as well.[68]

This iron-triangle structure, operating within, but often independent of national security considerations, is a major source of continued high levels of US defence spending. The economic effects of military spending we have described are a crucial element in maintaining this triangle. The structure depends on a constant flow of information, access, influence, and, especially, money. Both Defense Department and industry officals are highly conscious of this flow and its economic impact, since the fiscal and economic outcomes can be translated into political support for the defence budget.

The defence industry is a crucial actor in this political–economic process. Defence is big business: the Pentagon's contract market comes to roughly $150 bn per year. It is a concentrated and stable business: most of the top twenty-five contractors to the Defense Department have been in the business for over forty years and, together, receive 50 per cent of all of the contract dollars the Defense Department awards. The business is important to the companies; many of them do over 50 per cent of their sales with the federal government.[69]

As a result, defence contractors work hard within the iron triangle to translate the economic benefits of defence spending into political support for high budgets and contracts. To a contractor, a weapon programme is not only a contribution, real or symbolic, to national security, it constitutes a significant corporate fiscal stake in the procurement part of Pentagon spending. Once underway, such programmes can be sustained, in part, by the constituencies which depend, politically or economically on the flow of contracting dollars.

This flow depends on decisions made in the Congress, which makes committees and Members of Congress important participants in the defence iron triangle. Given the fact that most major weapons programmes are already well underway, with strong bureaucratic commitment and corporate involvement, by the time they reach high levels of visibility in Congress, committees and members on Capitol Hill already have limited room for manoeuvre. This 'political space' grows even smaller as defence contracting companies (and the Pentagon) focus pressures and incentives on Congress, coordinated largely through their Washington offices.[70]

For the defence contractor, the fiscal and economic benefits of defence contracting are tools in this process of political influence. Direct lobbying, campaign contributions and the intelligent use of the local economic impacts of contracting are all parts of the lobbying effort. Congress, as an institution, is well structured to render this lobbying effort effective. Members of the Armed Services and Defense Appropriations Committees jealously guard their jurisdiction and close off the defence decision-making process in Congress from encroachment by other committees. Moreover, individual members, especially in the House of Representatives, are acutely sensitive to the local economic impacts of federal spending, including defence. Their re-election fortunes depend, in part, on remaining sensitive to the developments in the local economy.[71]

In addition to the direct lobbying and campaign contributions defence contractors make to Members of Congress, the local 'constituents' of defence spending are brought to bear in the political process.[72] Grass-roots mobilisations, based on the microeconomy of defence spending, can be an important part of the contractor's effort to ensure a favourable Congressional vote on weapons programmes. The geographic, sectoral and labour market impacts of defence spending all become an important part of the message conveyed to Congress from the grass roots. Contractors consider the communities in which they are located, subcontractors in other parts of the country, the labour force and trade unions inside their plants, and even their stockholders parts of the constituency committed to a weapon programme. Part or all of the elements in this constituency can be mobilised directly to lobby the Congress; their dependency on defence contracting is part of the lobbying pitch a company makes directly to a Member of Congress.

Contractor-mobilisation of the defence microeconomy can sometimes take the form of a full-scale campaign. In the mid-1970s, for example, Rockwell International mounted such an effort on behalf of the B-1 bomber programme, then on the brink of cancellation. The company urged its 115 000 employees and the holders of its 35 million shares of stock to write to their Congressmen. More than 3 000 subcontractors and suppliers in forty-eight states were also asked to tell their Congressmen about the adverse impact cancellation of B-1 would have in the districts they represented. Rockwell acknowledged that it spent $1.35 m on the grass-roots effort alone between 1975 and 1977. In addition, Rockwell put together district-by-district descriptions of the economic impact of the B-1 programme, which it used as part of its direct lobbying presentation to Members of Congress.[73]

Given the resources which can be mobilised on behalf of each weapon programme the constituency in Congress favouring continued high levels of procurement spending is large. Virtually every member has some kind of prime or subcontracting impact in their state or district. The rather thorough penetration of this kind of constituency-building throughout the Congress is one central element in keeping defence budgets at consistently high levels. For this reason, when Congress does reduce the Pentagon's initial budget request, cuts generally affect spending for personnel and operations and maintenance, which have far less effective supporters in the defence microeconomy. When weapons programmes themselves are cut, savings generally take the form of stretching out anticipated purchases, rather than the outright termination of a programme.[74] Hearings and legislation in Congress on spending issues which do not directly touch the budget – waste and fraud measures, for example – have little impact on the votes taken on weapons programmes or on how overall defence spending might be reduced.

While national security considerations clearly have an impact on defence budget and policy decisions, they do not fully explain the size, scope, and political clout of the iron triangle. Bureaucratic sources of defence spending also provide, at best a partial explanation of where and how weapons originate, why they are so hard to cancel and why the Congress does not make major shifts in the defence programme and budget proposed by an administration.

The microeconomy of defence spending is an important part of the puzzle. While the macroeconomic effects of military spending may not be terribly different from other government spending, the microeconomic effect is clearly of critical political importance. The regions, labour force and industries which derive employment and revenue from Defense Department spending have become an important element in keeping such spending itself at high levels. A high flow of funds continues to fuel the political machinery. The result is a net gain for some in the economy and foregone opportunities for others who might make political claim to the same federal resources.

VII   CONCLUSION

This brief analysis of the existing literature on the economic impact of military spending points in some new directions for both supporters and critics of high levels of military spending. For those who argue that defence spending is inflationary, our analysis concludes that it is not particularly more inflationary than other forms of federal spending. Instead, the impact of military spending on inflation depends on how that spending is financed and the general state of the economy in which it occurs. The links between defence and inflation are neither obvious nor simple.

The relationship between military spending, productivity and technology are also more complex than the existing debate suggests. Defence spending may actually be funded out of personal consumption, rather than investment, leaving ample room for private sector investment to grow. Here, too, movement in the wider economy has an important role in determining the relationship of military technology to investment and GNP. Moreover, it is not at all clear that military technology is either intrinsically harmful or beneficial for technological development in the American economy. Its contribution appears to depend on the kind of technology and the economic setting in which the invention is occurring.

The picture is far from unidimensional, as well, with respect to employment. Military spending clearly creates jobs; it is not clear that it creates fewer jobs than other forms of federal spending, as some critics charge. Once one has fully counted the defence labour force – public and private – and made appropriate assumptions about the economy in which jobs are being created, defence and other government programmes seem to create fairly similar numbers of jobs.

The key employment issue is not the number of jobs, but the location and nature of those jobs, as well as the sector in which they are found. Here, military spending appears to have quite a different impact from other programmes: the jobs are in certain parts of the country, for certain parts of the labour force and in certain industries.

Even here, however, the differences should not be exaggerated. There are many larger forces influencing the growth and direction of the American economy; military spending is only one of them.

In the end we conclude that perhaps the greatest significance of military spending's effect on the economy is its role in creating a 'political economy' of defence. High levels of defence spending may have far more to do with the regional, sectoral and labour market effects of that spending than with its macroeconomic impact.

Some issues require further exploration, especially the rather complicated relationship between military spending and technology. There is, however, clearly a middle ground in the debate over military economics, to which this chapter makes an initial contribution.

Notes and References

*   This study was supported by Grants from the Rockefeller Brothers Fund, the Circle Fund, the Levinson Foundation and general support funding from the Defense Budget Project.

1.   Office of Management and Budget, *Mid-session Review of the 1986 Budget* (Washington, DC: OMB, 1985) p. 26.

2.   Defense Budget Project, *The FY1986 Defense Budget: The Weapons Buildup Continues* (Washington, DC: Defense Budget Project, 1985).

3.   Department of Defense, *FY 1984 Report of the Secretary of Defense* (Washington, DC: Department of Defense, 1983) p. 68.

4.   See, for example, the case of the B-1 bomber campaign conducted by Rockwell International described in Adams, G., *The B-1 Bomber: An Analysis of Its Strategic Utility, Cost, Constituency and Economic Impact* (New York: Council on Economic Priorities, 1976).

5.   United Nations Centre for Disarmament, *Economic and Social Consequences of the Arms Race and of Military Expenditures* (New York: United Nations, 1978) p. 41.

6.   Stevens, R. W., *Vain Hopes, Grim Realities: The Economic Consequences of the Vietnam War* (New York: New Viewpoints, 1976) especially chap. 6.

7.   DeGrasse, R., Jr, *Military Expansion Economic Decline* (Armonk, New York: Sharpe, 1983) pp. 117–26; Thurow, L., 'How to Wreck the Economy', *New York Review of Books* 14 May, 1981; Gold, D. and DeGrasse, R., Jr, 'Economic Recovery *vs* Defense Spending', *New York Times* 20 February, 1981. For a contrary view see Congressional Budget Office, *Defense Spending and the Economy* (Washington, DC: US Government Printing Office, 1983).

8.   Bezdek, R., 'The 1980 Economic Impact – Regional and Occupational – of Compensated Shifts in Defense Spending', *The Journal of Regional Science*, vol. 15, no. 2 (1975).

9. DeGrasse, R., Jr, *Military Expansion* (see Note 7) chap. II; Vitaliano, D. F., 'Defense Spending and Inflation: An Empirical Analysis', *Quarterly Review of Economics and Business*, vol. 24, no. 1 (1984) pp. 22–32. Starr, Hoole, Hart, and Freeman, using statistical techniques designed to assess whether a relationship between two variables exists, concluded that the tests did not support the existence of a relation between military spending and inflation for the USA and the UK, but did suggest one for France and West Germany. The tests are not able to suggest what that relation might be, however. See Starr, H., Hoole, F. W., Hart, J. A., and Freeman, J., 'The Relationship Between Defense Spending and Inflation', *Journal of Conflict Resolution*, vol. 28, no. 1 (1984) pp. 103–22. Smith found no statistically significant relation between military spending and inflation. Smith, R. P., 'Military Expenditure and Capitalism', *Cambridge Journal of Economics*, vol. 1, no. 1 (1977) pp. 61–76.

10. Melman, S., *The Permanent War Economy* (New York: Simon & Schuster, 1974); Melman, S., *Profits Without Production* (New York: Knopf, 1983); Dumas, L. J., 'Military Spending and Economic Decay', in Dumas (ed.) *The Political Economy of Arms Reduction* (Boulder, Colorado: Westview Press, 1982).

11. Adams, G., *Controlling Weapons Costs: Can the Pentagon Reforms Work?* (New York: Council on Economic Priorities, 1983).

12. Dumas, (see note 10); Hong, B. Y. *Inflation Under Cost Pass-Along Management* (New York: Praeger, 1979).

13. Melman, S., *The Permanent War Economy* (New York: Simon & Schuster 1974); Melman, S., *Profits Without Production* (New York: Knopf, 1983).

14. Bezdek, R., 'The 1980 Economic Impact – Regional and Occupational – of Compensated Shifts in Defense Spending', *The Journal of Regional Science*, vol. 15, no. 2 (1975); DeGrasse, R., Jr, *Military Expansion Economic Decline* (New York: Sharpe, 1983); Leontief, W. and Duchin, F., *Military Spending: Facts and Figures* (New York: Oxford University Press, 1983).

15. Kaldor, M., *The Baroque Arsenal* (New York: Hill and Wang, 1981) pp. 4, 5; Melman, S. (1983) (see note 10); Noble, D., *Forces of Production* (New York: Knopf, 1984).

16. Rosenberg, N., *Perspectives on Technology* (New York: Cambridge University Press, 1976); Trebilcock, C., 'Spin-Off in British Economic History: Armaments and Industry, 1760–1914', *Economic History Review*, vol. 22, no. 3 (December 1969).

17. DeGrasse, R., Jr, *Military Expansion Economic Decline* (1983); Thurow, L., 'How to Wreck the Economy', *New York Review of Books*, 14 May 1981; Gold, D. and DeGrasse, R., Jr, 'Economic Recovery *versus* Defense Spending', *New York Times* (20 Febuary, 1981).

18. DeGrasse, R., Jr, (see Note 17) (1983); Szymanski, A., 'Military Spending and Economic Stagnation', *American Journal of Sociology*, Vol. 79, no. 1 (1973) pp. 1–14.

19.   Smith, R. P., 'Military Expenditure and Capitalism', *Cambridge Journal of Economics*, vol. 1., no. 1, (1977); Smith, R. P., 'Military Expenditure and Investment in OECD Countries, 1954–1973', *Journal of Comparative Economics*, vol. 4 (1980).

20.   Bezdek, R., (see Note 14) (1975); Leontief and Duchin, (see Note 14) 1983; Dunne, J. P. and Smith, R. P., 'The Economic Consequences of Reduced UK Military Expenditure', *Cambridge Journal of Economics*, vol. 8, no. 3, September 1984.

21.   Cypher, J., 'The Basic Economics of Rearming America', *Monthly Review*, (November 1981); Griffin, L. J., Wallace, M. and Devine, J., 'The Political Economy of Military Spending: Evidence from the United States', *Cambridge Journal of Economics*, vol. 6, no. 1, (1982).

22.   Boulding, K., 'The Impact of the Defense Industry on the Structure of the American Economy', in Udis, B. (ed.) *The Economic Consequences of Reduced Military Spending* (Lexington, Massachusetts: Lexington Books, 1973).

23.   Russett, B., 'Defense Expenditure and National Well-Being', *American Political Science Review*, vol. 76, no. 4 (1982) pp. 767–77; Domke, W. K., Eichenberg, R. C., and Kelleher, C. M., 'The Illusion of Choice: Defense and Welfare in Advanced Industial Democracies', *American Political Science Review*, vol. 77, no. 1 (1983) pp. 19–35.

24.   DeGrasse, R., (See Note 7) (1983); Thurow, L., (see Note 7) (1981); for a contrary view see Congressional Budget Office, *Defense Spending and the Economy* (Washington, DC: US Government Printing Office, 1983).

25.   De Grasse, R. (see Note 7) (1983); Szymanski (see Note 18) (1973).

26.   De Grasse, R. (see Note 7) (1983); Kaldor (see Note 15) (1981); Borrus, M., Millstein, J. E., and Zysman, J., 'Trade and Development in the Semiconductor Industry', in Zysman, J. and Tyson, L. (eds) *American Industry in International Competition* (Ithaca, New York: Cornell University Press, 1983).

27.   Rosenberg (see Note 16) (1976).

28.   Gansler, J., *The Defense Industry* (Boston, Massachusetts: MIT Press, 1980).

29.   Kaldor, M., *The Baroque Arsenal* (1981) pp. 4, 5.

30.   See Gold, D. A., *et al.*, *Misguided Expenditure: An Analysis of the Proposed MX Missile System* (New York, Council on Economic Priorities, 1981), esp. Table 5, p. 157; Bezdek, R., 'The Economic Impact – Regional and Occupational – of Compensated Shifts in Defense Spending', *Journal of Regional Science*, vol. 15, no. 2 (1975); Chase Econometric Associates, *Economic Impact of the B-1 Program on the US Economy* (Bala Cynwyd, Pennsylvania: Chase Econometrics, 1975): Brancato, C. K. and LeGrande, L., 'Impact on Employment of Defense versus Non-Defense Government Spending', *Congressional Research Service Issue Brief MB82246* (Washington, DC: Library of Congress, 1984). See also Anderson, M., *The Empty Pork Barrel* (East Lansing, Michigan: Employment Research Associates, 1982) who states (p. 1) that 'contrary to long held and popular belief, military spending is not good for the economy. It does not

create employment – it generates unemployment. . .every time the military budget went up $1 billion, 10 000 jobs disappeared in the United States.'

31. Weinberger, C., *Annual Report to the Congress, Fiscal Year 1984* (Washington, DC: Department of Defense, 1983) p. 68.

32. See, in particular, Anderson, M. (see Note 30) (1982) for a large gap and Gold, *et al.* (see Note 30); Brancato and LeGrande (see Note 30), and Bezdek (see Note 8) for smaller ones.

33. Congressional Budget Office, *Defense Spending and the Economy* (Washington DC: CBO, 1983) p. 43. The CBO study makes the reasonable assumption that defence spending includes salaries and benefits for the Defense Department's military and civilian employees. When CBO focused solely on defence purchases from industry there was some difference with non-defence purchases, the former creating 210 000 jobs per $10 bn spent.

34. Direct jobs are those employed by federal funds; indirect jobs are those that result from purchases of inputs for production.

35. Weinberger, C. (see Note 31) p. 68.

36. The job loss argument is most clearly stated in the work of M. Anderson, especially *The Empty Pork Barrel* (see Note 30). For a critique of this argument, see the CBO study; Mosley, H., *The Arms Race: Economic and Social Consequences* (Lexington, Massachusetts: Lexington Books, 1985); and Riddell, T., 'The Employment Effects of Military Spending', paper presented to the Allied Social Science Association Meetings, December, 1984.

37. See above, p. 275, where we suggest that the historical experience of federal spending does not show this trend.

38. M. Anderson, *The Empty Pork Barrel*, makes this argument: 'If people all over the country are paying high taxes, a substantial percentage of which goes to the Pentagon, they do not have control over that money. This means that they build fewer houses, buy fewer cars, take fewer vacations, and vote lower taxes for their state and local governments. . . One must also ask how that dollar would have been spent if the Pentagon had not received it – if instead it had been used by consumers to buy the goods and services which they needed or had been turned over to state and local governments to meet public needs.'

39. One might argue that federal borrowing can affect the supply of available capital for other investment purposes, and exert upward pressure on interest rates. This relationship is, at best, unclear. Even if it were true, the consequences for job creation (or presumed job loss) are far from clear.

40. Congressional Budget Office, *Defense Spending and the Economy* (Washington, DC: CBO, 1983) p. 43, note 4. The CBO study makes this point, linking the spending and employment arguments. Some research, CBO notes, assumes 'that, because a higher share of GNP spent on defense is associated with a lower share spent on other things, higher real defense spending will necessarily lead to lower real spending elsewhere. Such a conclusion follows only if the economy is

at full employment, which is hardly an accurate description of today's US economy.'

41.   See DeGrasse (see Note 7) (1983) and Anderson, M., *The Empty Pork Barrel*, who argues (p. 1) that defence production is 'technically very complex, it involves large amounts of expensive raw materials, and even more expensive equipment. Therefore, less of the money spent goes towards hiring people and more goes toward buying high priced equipment than when the money is spent on civilian purchases.'

42.   Duchin suggests that a breakdown on defence employment among the different types of defence production would probably show variations of labour and capital intensity. See Duchin, F., 'Economic Consequences of Military Spending', *Journal of Economic Issues*, Vol. XVII, No. 2 (June 1983), pp. 543–553. There is also little evidence that defence sector production equipment is more expensive than that used in other sectors of manufacturing. Despite recent Defense Department investments in computer-aided and robotic production equipment, much of the defence sector machinery is quite old, dating, in some cases, from the 1950s. See Gansler, J., *The Defense Industry* (Massachusetts: MIT Press, 1980).

43.   Department of Defense, *Atlas/State Data Abstract for the United States, Fiscal Year 1984* (Washington, DC: DOD, 1985) p. 117. Over 3.3 million people work directly for the Department of Defense. There is a curious discrepancy in one study between the researcher's estimate of jobs in the defence sector and data from Defense Department. In Anderson, M., *The Empty Pork Barrel* (1982) p. 6, military industry employment is estimated at 790 800 in 1977 and 1978. The Defense Department estimated 1977 defence-related industry employment at 1 710 000, a difference of nearly 1 million jobs, Department of Defense (1985) pp. 118–19 and Mosley, H. (see Note 36) p. 91.

44.   Congressional Budget Office (see Note 40).

45.   California, alone, received over 20 per cent of total Defense Department prime contract awards and compensation payments in FY 1984. While military and civilian pay and retirement benefits tend to be spent largely in the state in which they are paid, it can be argued that roughly half of prime contract dollars are subcontracted, some of which leaves the state. Subcontract data is difficult to obtain, making a precise estimate of its impact on the overall distribution of defence spending difficult to estimate. There is, nevertheless, some evidence that subcontracting is also highly concentrated in the prime contract states. Data calculated by the authors from Department of Defense, *Atlas/State . . .Fiscal Year 1984.*

46.   North-east–Mid-west Institute, *The Pentagon Tilt: Regional Biases in Defense Spending and Strategy* (Washington, DC: Northeast–Midwest Institute, 1984) pp. 1, 24, 26. Other analysts agree. Ann R. Markusen argues that military contracting has stimulated industrial growth, especially in high technology, from Boston to Long Island (but not the rest of New York State), Florida, Texas and California, while the old industrial heartland (Milwaukee, Chicago, Cincinnati, Buffalo, New York City, Philadelphia, Baltimore and presumably Detroit) have not

had that stimulation. See Markusen, A., 'Defense Spending and the Geography of High Tech Industries', *Working Paper No. 423* (University of California, Berkeley: Institute of Urban and Regional Development, 1984); Markusen, A., 'Defense Spending: A Successful Industrial Policy?', *Working Paper No. 424* (University of California, Berkeley: Institute of Urban and Regional Development, 1984). In 1982 the staff of the Joint Economic Committee concluded that the US defence build-up, concentrated in high technology procurement, 'is likely to exacerbate the regional imbalances in the national economy', since the mid-west, with idle plant capacity, is not the region where military equipment is purchased. See Joint Economic Committee, Subcommittee on Economic Goals and Intergovernmental Policy, *The Defense Buildup and the Economy* (Washington, DC: JEC, 1982).

47.   It is also not reasonable to examine the distortions in the American economic geography caused by federal spending by focusing solely on Defense Department spending. See Anderson, J., *Bankrupting America: The Tax Burden and Expenditures of the Pentagon by Congressional District* (Washington, DC: 1982) which makes the case on the basis of defence spending alone. In order to understand these potential distortions, one must review all federal spending and do so over a considerable period of time. Senator Daniel P. Moynihan reviews all federal taxes and federal spending in his annual report on New York State's fiscal relationship with the federal government. According to the 1985 report, in 1984 thirty states were in surplus with the federal government, while twenty states were in a deficit. See Moynihan, Senator D. P., *New York State and the Federal Fisc: IX* (Washington, DC: Office of Senator Moynihan, 1985) pp. 40–2.

48.   Markusen, A., Working Paper No. 423, p. 35.

49.   As defence spending rose in the 1980s, for example, domestic spending was also being cut. These latter cuts led to declining membership in unions that organise among public employees and service industries. See Lance Compa, 'Labor and the Military – A History' in Gordon, S. and McFadden, D., *Economic Conversion: Revitalizing America's Economy* (Cambridge, Massachusetts: Ballinger, 1984) p. 34. See also Bezdek (see Note 8) Gold *et al.* (see Note 30); Reppy, J., 'Long Term Consequences of Military Spending', paper presented to the International Studies Association meeting (Washington, DC, 8 March, 1985) p. 5; Congressional Budget Office (1983); and Department of Defense, *Symposium on the Impact of Higher Levels of Defense Expenditures on the United States Economy in the 1980s* (Washington, DC: DOD, 1980).

50.   In addition, 30.3 per cent of mathematicians, 24.7 per cent of life and physical scientists, 24.4 per cent of physicists, 21.5 per cent of engineers (not otherwise classified – NOC), 18.3 per cent of electrical engineers, 15.8 per cent of industrial technicians, 15.8 per cent of social scientists (NOC), 15.7 per cent of mechanical engineers, 14.2 per cent of lawyers, 13.1 per cent of technicians (NOC), 12.2 per cent of mechanical engineers, 11.3 per cent of computer programmers, and 10.9 per cent of electrical and electronic technicians were employed by

the Defense Department or the defence industry. See Congressional Budget Office (see Note 4) Table 6, p. 27 and Table A-11, Appendix A. See also Bezdek, R. (see Note 8); DeGrasse, R., Jr, (see Note 7) (1983) on the composition of the defence industry labour force.

51.   The specialised nature of that workforce is occasionally overstated, for example, 'the specialized nature of military employment reduces its economic usefulness. Much of the new employment generated by a military buildup goes to people who need it less', DeGrasse, R., Jr, (see Note 7) (1983) p. 32.

52.   See Hartung, W. D., DeGrasse, R., *et al.*, *The Strategic Defense Initiative: Costs, Contractors and Consequences* (New York: Council on Economic Priorities, 1985) chap. 3; as well as DeGrasse, R., Jr, (see Note 7) (1983); Hartung, W. (see Note 52) (1984); Anderson, M., *The Empty Pork Barrel*, (1982).

53.   Anderson, M., *Neither Jobs Nor Security* (1982) p. 9: argues that 'over half of the US scientists and engineers have been working on military and space contracts'. Reppy, J. (see Note 49) (1985) estimates that 42 per cent of US scientific manpower is in defence-related work. DeGrasse, R., Jr, (see Note 7) (1983), p. 102, using National Science Foundation data prepared in the late 1970s estimates that 25–35 per cent of US scientists and engineers were working on defence projects.

54.   Congressional Budget Office (see Note 40) (1983) Table A-10, for this and the data which follows.

55.   See Department of Defense, *FY 1983 Report of the Secretary of Defense* (Washington, DC: DOD, 1982); Department of Defense (see Note 00) (1983); Holzman, F., 'Are the Soviets Really Outspending the US on Defense?', *International Security*, vol. 4, no. 4 (Spring 1980) pp. 86–104; Stubbing, R., 'The Imaginary Defense Gap: We Already Outspend Them', *Washington Post* (14 February, 1982), p. C-1; Collins, J., *US–Soviet Military Balance: Concepts and Capabilities* (New York: McGraw-Hill, 1980); Levin, Senator C., 'The Other Side of the Story', monograph, May 1983; Defense Budget Project, *The FY1986 Defense Budget: The Weapons Buildup Continues* (Washington, DC: Defense Budget Project, 1985); Committee for National Security, *Spending for a Sound Defense: Alternative to the Reagan Military Budget* (Washington, DC: Committee for National Security, 1985).

56.   See, for example, Peck, M. J., and Scherer F. M., *The Weapons Acquisition Process: An Economic Analysis* (Boston, Massachusetts: Harvard School of Business Administration, 1962); Fox, R. J., *Arming America: How the US Buys Weapons* (Boston: Harvard School of Business Administration, 1974); Sapolsky, H. M., *The Polaris System Development: Bureaucratic and Programmatic Success in Government* (Boston: Harvard University Press, 1971); Fitzgerald, A. E., *The High Priest of Waste* (New York: Norton, 1972).

57.   See Adams, G., 'A Bomber for All Seasons' (New York: Council on Economic Priorities newsletter, 1982).

58.   In 1983, the presidential business commission investigating government waste pointed to roughly $30 bn a year in wasteful Pentagon

spending. See President's Private Sector Survey on Cost Control, *Task Force Report on the Office of the Secretary of Defense; Task Force Report on the Department of the Army; Task Force Report on the Department of the Navy; Task Force Report on the Department of the Air Force* (Washington, DC: Department of Commerce, 1983).

59.   See Defense Budget Project, *Nuts and Bolts at the Pentagon: A Spare Parts Catalog* (Washington DC: DBP, 1984); Adams, G. A., *Controlling Weapons Costs: Can the Pentagon's Reforms Work?* (New York: Council on Economic Priorities, 1983); and Peck and Scherer; Fox (see note 56); and Fitzgerald (see note 56).

60.   See Cuff, R. D., *The War Industries Board: Business–Government Relations During World War I* (Baltimore, Maryland: Johns Hopkins Press, 1973); Koistinen, P., *The Military Industrial Complex: A Historical Perspective* (New York: Praeger, 1980); Adams, G., 'Defense Policy-Making, Weapons Procurement, and the Reproduction of State–Industry Relations', paper presented to the American Political Science Association, (Washington, DC: 28 August, 1980).

61.   See Kaufman, R., *The War Profiteers* (Garden City, New York: Doubleday/Anchor Books, 1972) p. 248; Fox, J. R.; Peck and Scherer; Melman, S., *Pentagon Capitalism* (New York: McGraw-Hill, 1970); and Melman, S., *The Permanent War Economy* (New York: Simon & Schuster, 1974).

62.   Gansler, J., *The Defense Industry* (Boston, Massachusetts: MIT Press, 1980.)

63.   Adams, G., *The Politics of Defense Contracting: The Iron Triangle* (New Brunswick, New Jersey: Transaction Press, 1982).

64.   Adams, G., 'Disarming the Military Subgovernment', *Harvard Journal on Legislation*, vol. 14, no. 3 (April 1977) pp. 459–503; McConnell, G., *Private Power and American Democracy* (New York: Knopf, 1967); Freeman, J. L., *The Political Process* (Garden City, New York: Doubleday, 1955); Cater, D., *Power in Washington* (New York: Random House, 1964); Hayes, M. T., 'The Semi-Sovereign Pressure Groups: A Critique of Current Theory and Alternative Typology', *Journal of Politics*, vol. 40, no. 1 (1978) pp. 134–61.

65.   Zeigler, H., and Peak, W. G., *Interest Groups in American Society* (Englewood Cliffs, New Jersey: Prentice Hall, 1972) 2nd edn, p. 180.

66.   See Seidman, H., *Politics, Position and Power* (New York: Oxford University Press, 1970) p. 18; McConnell (see note 64); O'Connor, J., *The Fiscal Crisis of the State* (New York: St Martin's Press, 1973) p. 66.

67.   See Adams, G. (see Note 63) (1982); Schattschneider, E. E., *The Semi-Sovereign People* (Hinsdale, Illinois: Dryden Press, 1975) 2nd edn; and Hayes

68.   Neustadt, R., *Presidential Power* (New York: Wiley, 1976) p. 172.

69.   Adams, G. (see Note 63) (1982) chaps. 6, 7, 9, 11, 13 and company profiles.

70.   Adams, G. (see Note 63) (1982) (company profiles section). From 1977 to 1979, the eight leading defence contractors employed 200 people in their Washington offices, and forty-eight registered lobbyists. According to audits by the Defense Contract Audit Agency,

Boeing, General Dynamics, Grumman, Lockheed, and Rockwell International together spent $16.8 m on their Washington offices in 1974 and 1975, or an average of $1.5 m each per year. Rockwell alone spent $7 m from 1973 to1975.

71.   See Adams, G. (see Note 63) (1982) chap. 8.
72.   Ibid, chap. 13.
73.   Ibid, chap. 13.
74.   Defense Budget Project (1985) (see note 2).

COMMENT

Christos Passadeos

The chapter is a corrective to the two dominant bodies of thought – that an arms build-up, from an economic point of view, is either all bad or all good. Thus those who regard it as 'all bad' have to try to explain why the US rearmament programme of recent years has coincided with apparent good general economic performance. However, how healthy is this upswing? What will be the future consequences of the rise in indebtedness to foreign countries, and what has happened to productivity?

Second, the chapter does not go along with the simple cliché that Japan's economic success can be explained by its low military expenditure. Obviously things are much more complicated than that.

Third, on spin-off: there are both spin-off and insularity in the military sector – and the whole subject deserves much more attention because with the strategic defence initiative and other new military programmes it will become even more important. There are many questions – who should look at the possibilities of spin-off, and how keen is the civil sector to pick up ideas originating in the military sector?

The chapter suggests that, despite intensive debate, until 1985 the Pentagon had obtained virtually all it requested. This suggested that the 'iron triangle' – with strong resistance to change, and in some ways isolated from the rest of the economy – has very considerable immunity to criticism.

There are some points which should be discussed more fully. The evidence surely does suggest that the military sector is becoming more capital-intensive: the rising share of procurement and of R & D in the budget suggest this. In considering the 'crowding-out' of other forms of expenditure as a consequence of rearmament, it is important to take into account the international aspect. Budget deficits are met by bonds bought by non-US residents. Financing the deficits creates great potential international instability.

Finally, there is the question of competitiveness. Will the effect of spin-off be such that it creates a technological gap in favour of the USA: alternatively, will the diversion of research to the military sector have the opposite effect?

14 Military-related Debt in Non-oil Developing Countries, 1972–82

Rita McWilliams Tullberg
STOCKHOLM INTERNATIONAL PEACE
RESEARCH INSTITUTE

Of the public foreign debt acquired each year from 1972 to 1982 by non-oil developing countries, about 20 per cent is estimated to have been directly or indirectly attributable to the purchase of foreign weapons. Domestic military spending, by contributing to overall budget deficits, has also led to increased foreign borrowing by developing countries. Budget deficits in developed countries have led to interest rates which increase the debt problems of developing countries.

I INTRODUCTION

More than on any previous occasion in world history, the 'debt crisis' of the current decade has highlighted the economic interdependence of the developed and the developing world. Recycling the flood of petro-dollars which followed increases in oil prices determined by the OPEC cartel during the 1970s, large amounts of money were lent by Western banking syndicates to Third World countries in anticipation of extrordinary returns. While, as a result of rapid inflation, real interest rates remained negative, loans were eagerly accepted by developing countries anxious to achieve economic 'take-off'.

Some of this money was used to finance development projects which it was hoped would generate sufficient income to repay the loans. Some was used for essential current consumption, some for conspicuous consumption, capital flight and the purchase of arms.

302

These latter uses were generally not income-generating and as such led, towards the end of the 1970s, to new net borrowing to pay interest on old debts.

If a country 'lives within its [foreign] income', it will not be a net [external] borrower. If it lives above its income, any item of foreign expenditure can be considered as contributing to the need to borrow. The purpose of this study is not to determine how specific loans were used, but to give a picture of total resource use by estimating how much smaller external debts might have been had specific purchases – in this case foreign arms – not been made.

After an introduction on the development of the debt problem since the beginning of the 1970s, an estimate will be made of the amount of debt of non-oil developing countries directly or indirectly attributable to their purchase of foreign arms. The contribution of budget deficits to the international debt problem is briefly examined, in particular the US Central Government deficit.

II EXTERNAL DEBT OF NON-OIL DEVELOPING COUNTRIES, 1972–82

Total debts of the non-oil developing nations have grown from $130 bn in 1973 to $730 bn in 1984 and account for 85 per cent of the external debts of all developing countries (see Table 14.1 and the Appendix to this Chapter). In real terms, the volume of external debt in these countries has more than doubled since 1973.[1] While this debt represented 114 per cent of export income in 1973, it had risen to 158 per cent in 1983. Table 14.2 shows the changing percentage of export earnings which has been devoted to debt servicing, that is, to the payment of interest and amortisation.

These figures *per se* do not give us any indication of the seriousness of the problem. Within integrated capital markets, it is normal for capital to flow from countries where it is in abundance and where returns are low to countries where it is in short supply and returns are high. Economic history offers few clues as to what is the 'right' amount of debt. However, in the normal course of this debtor–creditor relationship, something is felt to be wrong when a debtor is unable to keep up service payments and creditors are unwilling to extend new loans. Clear indications of a disturbance are the rash of reschedulings – from an annual average of four in the

Table 14.1   External debt of non-oil producing countries, 1972–85[a]

(*Figures are in current $bn*)

Duration	1972	1973	1977	1979	1981	1982	1983	1984	1985[b]
Long-term	97	112	238	340	464	523	580	627	676
Short-term	..	18	53	66	114	132	113	104	92
Total	..	130	291	406	578	655	694	731	768

Notes:
[a]Not including debt owed to the IMF
[b]Estimate

Sources: *World Economic Outlook*, 1981, Table 27; 1983, Table 32 and
1985, Table 47 (Washington, DC: International Monetary Fund,
1981, 1983 and 1985).

Table 14.2   Non-oil developing countries: debt service ratio[a] on short- and
long-term external debt

(*Figures are percentages*)

Region	1973	1977	1979	1981	1982	1983	1984	1985[b]
All non-oil developing countries	15.9	16.1	19.6	21.8	25.2	21.7	21.5	22.3
Africa[c]	..	11.9	15.0	16.7	20.9	22.7	28.3	30.0
Asia[d]	..	7.9	8.9	9.6	11.3	10.7	10.9	11.2
Western hemisphere[e]	..	28.7	38.9	41.5	51.6	41.1	39.4	40.5

Notes:
[a] Payments (interest, amortisation, or both) as percentages of exports of
goods and services.
[b] Projection
[c] Including Algeria and Nigeria
[d] Including Indonesia
[e] Including Venezuela

Source: *World Economic Outlook*, 1983, Table 35; 1985, Table 49
(Washington, DC: International Monetary Fund, 1983 and 1985).

years 1974–8 to thirty-two in 1983 – and the abrupt decline in the amount of new lending.[2]

From the point of view of both creditors and debtors, the precipitous rise in oil prices of 1973–4 and 1979–80 are central to the issues of the debt crisis. Higher oil prices contributed to the general rise in prices and to the slow-down in the economies of developed countries. Non-oil developing countries found themselves facing higher prices not only for oil but for all their imports and weaker markets for their exports. The oil bill of net oil-importers among the non-oil developing countries rose from $5 bn in 1973 to $67 bn in 1982, a total bill of $345 bn for those ten years. If oil prices had continued to rise over the decade at the same rate as the US wholesale price index, the total oil bill by 1982 would have amounted to only $85.5 bn at the same level of consumption. In other words, to the extent that oil prices increased more than the US wholesale price index, non-oil developing countries have had to increase their foreign currency income by $345 bn − $85 bn = $260 bn.[3]

The shock of the oil and general price increases gave fresh impetus to developing countries to exploit their own resources. It was therefore opportune to use OPEC funds, made readily available by Western banks, as the source of development finance. The model for the past decade has been loans from a group, often a large group, of banks to foreign governments or government-backed borrowers. Such loans entail payment of interest irrespective of whether or not a loan has generated any income and involves the whole of a nation in its repayment. The anonymity of the syndicate has the multiple effect of encouraging small banks to take bigger risks than otherwise, of complicating the relationship between debtor and creditor when problems arise and of allowing banks to by-pass domestic controls on certain types of investment.[4]

A second and closely associated problem for debtor countries has been the movements of the interest rates over the decade. In the 1960s, real interest rates were 4.1 per cent (deflating LIBOR with the US wholesale price index). Between 1971 and 1980, the average real interest rate was −0.8 per cent. Nominal rates rose sharply in 1979 and 1980 creating cash-flow problems for borrowers. Meanwhile tight monetary and fiscal policies in the developed countries had led to a significant decline in inflation, so that by 1981, the real interest rate was 7.5 per cent and by 1982 11 per cent.[5]

The market economies of the West were now in the grip of a severe slump. Growth rates which in industrial countries had averaged over

3 per cent in the 1970s fell to −0.5 per cent in 1982.[6] Developing countries found themselves facing falling commodity prices and an export recession at the same time as they needed to increase their dollar earnings to meet high real-interest rates. They were particularly badly hit by variations in interest rates, because of the increasing number of loans which had been taken at variable rates. Countries were finding it necessary to take expensive short-term loans to cover their new borrowing needs (from 14 per cent in 1973 to 20 per cent in 1982) as bankers became reluctant to lend more money at the same time as they required interest payments on their old loans. GDP growth in many of the big borrowing countries came to a standstill or declined since it was difficult with short-term credits to finance long-term projects.

Economic management under such conditions as these has not been easy in any country. High on the list of domestic policy errors committed in developing countries have been overvaluation of currency with subsequent poor export performance, high import levels and uncontrolled capital flight. Some of these policies have been maintained in an attempt to meet the growing expectations of the whole population. Others, such as the maintenance of fully convertible currencies, have favoured small sections of the community.[7] Similarly, the uses to which the flows of finance have been put vary from ambitious development projects aimed at raising general living standards to non-productive purchases for the benefit of the few. These latter include the purchase of foreign weaponry the purpose of which, in many cases, was to improve the status of the military and to suppress political rights.

III   ARMS PURCHASES AND DEBT

The value of arms transferred to non-oil developing countries more than doubled in real terms between 1972 and 1982 and their share of total world arms transfers has increased from 31 per cent to 41 per cent in the same period.[8] Arms purchases grew in importance during the 1970s, as the two major arms donors switched their policies from one of gifts to one of sales. As the arms industries of the industrial countries have grown, fuelled by and fuelling the tension between East and West, the expansion of arms sales to developing countries has filled both economic and political goals in producer-countries. Recipient-countries have used valuable resources to buy weaponry, and in doing so they have added to the debt burden of the whole population and mortgaged its future. Had they made no foreign arms purchases during the period, non-oil developing countries would have needed to borrow an estimated 20 per cent less each year and their accumulated long-term debts by the end of the period would have been roughly 16 per cent smaller (Tables 14.3 and 14.4). Prior to the oil-price shock of 1973–4, arms purchases formed a higher proportion of foreign expenditures by non-oil developing countries, which in the mid-1970s were forced to devote more resources to buying oil. The relative importance of arms purchases therefore declined and, as a consequence, so did arms-related borrowing. Nevertheless, at least one-fifth of new borrowing in the last ten years was not incurred for development purposes and has not generated income to cover its costs.[9]

IV MILITARY EXPENDITURES AND BUDGET DEFICITS

The relationship between military expenditure and debt is not restricted solely to the procurement of foreign weapons. Serious budget deficits have been run up by central governments in recent years, leading to large public debts. For developing countries, budget deficits entail the problems not only of debt in general but the particular problems of external debt.

A government which finds its spending plans are not covered by income can finance expenditures by non-bank borrowing or loans from commercial banks. The opportunities for such domestic borrowing by governments are limited in many developing countries. Often high inflation and political uncertainty discourage the purchase of government bonds, and personal savings may be put, by tradition and preference, into land, family business, gold or foreign balances.[10] Governments turn instead to money creation, that is (in modern times) by borrowing from central banks.

Unlike taxation, money creation requires no administrative machinery and its political consequences are not immediate. However, beyond a certain point, deficit-financing will lead to inflation, particularly in developing countries, since the increase in aggregate spending power cannot easily be matched by a sudden increase in the production or import of appropriate goods for consumption or investment. Unless governments are willing to adjust exchange rates to reflect the full rate of inflation, balance-of-payment

Table 14.3 Non-oil developing countries: alternative estimates of arms transfer credits as a percentage of net flows (disbursement − amortisations = net flows) 1972–82.

(Figures are in current US$)

	1972	1973	1974	1975	1976	1977	1978	1979	1980	1981	1982
1. Arms transfers (excluding China)	6005	7390	5165	5145	6120	7025	8565	11085	12690	12540	13895
2. US gifts	2400	3420	1520	1400	190	70	130	170	340	280	290
3. Soviet gifts	490	900	520	360	760	710	1040	2540	1580	1560	1720
4. Arms to be paid for	3115	3070	3125	3385	5170	6245	7395	8375	10770	10700	11886
5. Possibly paid for	165	590	615	80	15	255	870	465	500	1165	525
6. Estimated arms transfer credits (A)	2950	2480	2510	3305	5155	5990	6525	7910	10270	9535	11361
7. Net flows to non-oil developing countries (B)	8019	10262	16031	20177	24236	28641	34199	39525	41474	46151	43108
8. Net flows, alternative estimate (C)	8821	11288	17634	22195	26660	31505	37619	43478	45621	50766	47419
9. Estimated arms transfer credits as percentage of net flows											
A as percentage of B	37	24	16	16	21	21	19	20	25	21	26
A as percentage of C	33	22	14	15	19	19	17	18	23	19	24

Source: See Appendix to this Chapter.

Table 14.4   Accumulated military-related debt, 1972–82, for arms transfer credits taken 1972–82

(Figures are in current US$)

	1972	1973	1974	1975	1976	1977	1978	1979	1980	1981	1982	1972–82
Estimated arms transfer credits	2950	2480	2510	3303	5155	5990	6525	7910	10270	9535	11361	67991
Interest rates(%)	5.6	6.6	7.0	6.8	6.8	6.9	7.9	9.4	9.3	11.6	– –	– –
Interest payments on arms transfer credits and debt-service borrowing		165	340	527	764	1129	1567	2115	2907	3931	5148	18594
Total accumulated military-related debt, 1972–82												86585
Total accumulated military-related debt, 1972–82, as a percentage of total long-term debt 1982												16

Source: See Appendix to this Chapter.

problems will arise which must be met by borrowing. Inflation will further discourage domestic lending and force governments to look for loans abroad. Military spending by contributing to government deficits may well lead to inflation and thus indirectly to increasing external indebtedness.

Beyond a certain point, external indebtedness becomes a hindrance to development, diverting too many resources into exports and limiting essential imports in order to meet debt-service and requirements and to avoid further borrowing.[11] Its social costs can be very heavy as governments are forced to apply sudden and severe austerity measures to their indebted economies. Turning to the IMF for loans to tide them over the adjustment period, countries find that loan conditions invariably include substantial devaluation, the de-indexing of wages and the reduction of budget deficits by the elimination of food subsidies and price controls, cuts in services such as health and education and other deflationary measures. Though no other area of domestic policy seems sacred, the IMF, in public at least, seems reluctant to criticise levels of military spending which in many cases takes a major share of public spending. Ironically, public unrest resulting from a dose of IMF 'medicine' may be used as an excuse for further increases in military personnel and equipment.

Even in terms of the IMF's own data, which often underestimate military expenditure, spending on social welfare has not dominated budgets. At the beginning of the 1980s, the shares of Central Government Expenditure (CGE) in non-oil developing countries going to health was smaller in 68 per cent of cases and the share going to social security and welfare was smaller in 64 per cent of cases than the share devoted to the military sector.[12] In many non-oil developing countries, military expenditure in the past decade has grown faster than other government expenditures (Table 14.5). This is true of the four regions of the world which comprise mainly non-oil developing countries.

V BUDGET DEFICITS IN CREDITOR-COUNTRIES

In the opinion of the Managing Director of the IMF, the growth of public spending had been caused mainly by social expenditure.[13] He stressed that public services needed to be priced realistically and scrutinised hard to ensure efficiency and to contain public expecta-tions. The prescription has been carefully followed by the Reagan

Table 14.5   Annual average percentage growth rates, 1972–82

(*Figures are percentages*)

Region	Per capita income	Central government spending minus military spending	Military spending	Arms imports
South Asia	2.0	6.2	5.1	9.2
East Asia[a]	3.4	6.9	7.7	(−7.9)[b]
Latin America	1.6	6.0	12.4	13.2
Africa	0.3	6.5	7.8	18.5

Notes:
[a] Including Japan
[b] Reflecting US disengagement from Indochina. The figure for 1976–82 is 5.6 per cent.
Sources: Military expenditure figures from SIPRI sources. Remaining figures from *World Military Expenditures and Arms Transfers 1972–82*, (Washington, DC: US Arms Control and Disarmament Agency (ACDA), 1984) Table 1, pp. 12–14 and Table 2, pp. 53–6.

Administration in its attempts to reduce the US Government deficit which for fiscal year 1984–5 was over $200 bn. Health, education and housing budgets have been severely cut while military expenditure has been allowed to grow by 8.6 per cent in real terms since 1980, subject to only marginal efforts to ensure efficiency and contain the military sector's spending, which accounts for over 25 per cent of central government expenditure, the Reagan Administration has turned to borrowing to cover the budget deficit. The subsequent high interest rates and an appreciation of the dollar have had a pronounced effect on the international financial markets and led to a deterioration of conditions for debtor-countries. In 1982, 37 per cent of the debt of non-oil developing countries carried variable interest rates (interest rates that float with movement in a key market rate, such as the US prime rate). Only 7 per cent of such loans had been subject to variable rates in 1972.[14] To the extent that US military spending is a cause of the US budget deficit, it can also be said to be increasing the debt burden for the borrowing countries.

VI CONCLUSION

The symbiotic relationship between borrower and lender is clear. In order to repay their debts, developing countries must be able to sell their products to hard-currency countries. These countries are experiencing a recession with mass unemployment and are turning to protectionism to defend their markets from cheap Third World imports. Countries in debt difficulties are cutting their imports in an attempt to save on foreign earning, thus contributing to the reduction of exports and jobs in the industrial countries. A major factor affecting the ability of developing countries to repay their debts is the high US interest rate which is the result of heavy government deficits. Should some developing countries default on their debts, the subsequent reduction in capital to the rest of the financial system would heighten the recession in the industrial world. Default would further undermine the bankers' confidence in the Third World and lead to a drying-up of essential credit. Attempts by bankers to squeeze their money out of borrowing countries will create economic misery and political unrest.

Part of the developing world's demand for foreign loans has been in order to buy arms from developed countries who want to maintain the viability of their domestic arms industries. It is particularly ironic that some Third World governments feel obliged to expand arms exports from their nascent arms industries so that debts which were incurred to meet the requirements of the arms race may be repaid at the cost of adding to the availability of arms in the world.

APPENDIX DEFINITIONS, SOURCES AND METHODS

I Definitions

Non-oil developing: as defined by the IMF, and given, for example, in *World Economic Outlook* (WEO) September 1984, p. 25. It should be noted that countries that are not members of the IMF are automatically excluded from this group. Arms transfer figures are taken from *World Military Expenditure and Arms Transfers 1972–1982* (United States Arms Control and Disarmament Agency (ACDA) April 1984). In order to make these compatible with IMF data, the following adjustments were made. To the ACDA figures for its group 'developing countries' (ACDEA 1984, p. 103) are added Ecuador, Gabon and South Africa. From the same ACDA figures are subtracted those for OPEC, Albania, Angola, Bulgaria, Cuba, Mongolia, Mozambique, North Korea, Oman, Spain, Taiwan and the People's Republic of China.

Public/publicly guaranteed external debt: as defined by the World Bank and given, for example, in *World Debt Tables (WDT) 1982–83 Edition* (Washington, DC: World Bank, 1983) p. xvii. The extent to which military debt is included in the debt figures published by the World Bank is unclear. The sources of World Bank data are detailed (loan-by-loan) reports. The OECD in its *Survey of the External Debt of Developing Countries* 1983 (Paris: OECD, 1984) regards military debt as largely excluded from its data. The survey notes that the OECD external debt statistics do not cover:

> *Military* debt financed by *official* credits (military debt financed by private credits is indistinguishably included in private market debt). For a few creditors (for example, Iraq and Israel) unreported official military debt can be as high as total reported non-military debt. However, for non-OPEC LDCs as a whole, official military debt is estimated to represent in 1982 only some 10 per cent of total reported long-term debt and well under 10 per cent of total reported debt service (a large part of military imports of LDCs is paid in cash or provided on a grant basis). (OECD, *Survey of the External Debt of Developing Countries 1983* (Paris: OECD, 1984) Technical Note A.2, p. 78.)

The OECD estimate of unreported military debt is taken into account when estimating the proportion of total debt arising directly or indirectly from arms purchases (see Table 14.3 and below).

II Methods used in the Compilation of Table 14.3

1 Arms transfers

Arms transfers to the non-oil developing countries 1972–82 taken from ACDA, 1984.

2 US gifts

The value of arms given as gifts by the USA, 1972–82 are taken from *Foreign Military Sales, Foreign Military Construction Sales and Military Assistance Facts, September 1982*, Military Assistance Program Delivery/Expenditure (MAP), p. 47; and *Foreign Military Sales and Military Assistance Facts December 1978*, MAP, p. 19, both issued by Data Management Division, Comptroller, DSAA. USA MAP figures were converted from fiscal to current years on the assumption that deliveries were made evenly throughout the twelve months. For South Korea, Laos, Philippines and Vietnam, ACDA 1984 figures were used for the years 1972–5, since MAP figures include technical assistance.

3 Soviet gifts

The estimated value of arms given as gifts by the USSR 1972–82: the value of arms transferred to non-oil developing countries was estimated from cumulative Soviet transfers given in Table III of ACDA 1984 and ACDA 1979. Of total Soviet transfers to the world, the following percentages were estimated as having been delivered to non-oil developing countries: 1972–3: 34 per cent; 1974–7: 36 per cent; 1978–82: 45 per cent. The gift element of Soviet arms transfers was estimated from the figures given by Roger E. Kanet, 'Soviet and East European Arms Transfers to the Third World: Strategic, Political and Economic Factors', *External Relations of CMEA Countries: Their Significance and Impact in a Global Perspective*, NATO Colloquium 1983 (Brussels: NATO, 1983) using US Congressional and State Department sources. This gave the following percentages:

1972	50	1973	50	1974	35
1975	25	1976	40	1977	30
1978	30	1979	50	1980	35
1981	35	1982	35		

(In the absence of figures for 1982, the percentage for 1981 was repeated.)

4 Arms to be paid for

Row 1 *minus* rows 2 and 3, being an estimate of arms to be paid for.

5 Possibly paid for

Values of arms purchased by those countries and in those years for which new credits were not taken, directly or indirectly, to cover the purchase of foreign arms. Purchases of foreign goods and services: additions to reserves and debt-service payments must be covered by foreign income, changes in reserves plus new credits. If not credits are taken or if new credits are smaller than arms purchases, then it can be concluded that all or some of the arms have been purchased for cash. New credits are measured by disbursements as given in the *World Debt Tables*, December 1981, 1982–3 edn and First Supplement and 1983–4 edn. Arms figures are from ACDA 1984.

6 Estimated arms transfer credits (A)

Row 4 *minus* row 5 gives an estimate of credits taken as a direct or indirect result of arms purchases.

7 New flows to non-oil developing countries (B)

New debt of non-oil developing countries as measured by net flows (disbursements *minus* amortisation) from the *World Debt Tables*, cited in row 5. World Bank figures for developing countries have been made compatible with the IMF definition of non-oil developing countries by subtracting figures for Algeria, Asia, Others (including Taiwan), Indonesia, Nigeria, Oman, Spain and Venezuela. Figures for Afghanistan are added.

8 Net flows alternative estimate (C)

For this estimate, net flows to non-oil developing countries are increased for 10 per cent to cover the assumption made by the OECD (see above) that non-disclosed military debt is 10 per cent of total reported long-term debt.

9 *Estimated arms transfers credits as percentage of net flows*

Credits taken as a direct or indirect result of arms purchases as a percentage of new debt.

III Methods Used in the Compilation of Table 14.4

Table 14.4 gives an estimate of military-related debt accumulated by 1982. The assumption here is that debt-service payments are covered by new borrowing. In order to simplify the calculation, amortisation is disregarded – most debts have a grace period of several years before they begin to be amortised – and debt prior to 1972 is ignored. Only interest payments are considered as adding to the stock of debt. The interest rates used in this calculation are those given as the average rate on public debts from all creditors given in WDT 1982–3, p. 3, and WDT 1983–4, p. 3. It is assumed that both arms transfer credits and loans taken to pay interest on these credits are contracted at *fixed interest rates*.

In some few cases it would be possible for countries to meet their debt-servicing commitments without borrowing. For this reason, accumulated military-related debt has been rounded to $86 000 m when calculating it as a percentage of total accumulated debt in 1982.

The method used in constructing Tables 14.3 and 14.4 is derived from a technique developed by Michael Brzoska in 'Research Communiation: The Military Related External Debt of Third World Countries', *Journal of Peace Research*, vol. 20, no. 3, 1983.

Notes and References

1. *World Economic Outlook*, WEO Occasional Paper no. 27 (Washington, DC: International Monetary Fund, 1984) p. 60; calculated using an export deflator.
2. These figures include Cuba and Poland, see WEO April 1984 (note 1) p. 65. OECD figures for non-concessional net flows show a decline of 16 per cent in real terms between 1978 and 1982, see *External Debt of Developing Countries, 1983 Survey* (Paris: IECD, 1984) Table D, p. 28.
3. Cline, W. R., *International Debt and the Stability of the World Economy* (Washington, DC: Institute for International Economics, 1983) pp. 20–2.
4. 'The lender is not told precisely how this money will be spent (bankers making defence loans often admit they make a point of remaining ignorant) . . . there is the practical consideration that if corporate responsibility and full disclosure were pressed by bank shareholders, arms loans could spawn damaging criticism at home', Burgess, J., *Far Eastern Economic Review* vol. 109, no. 32, 1 August 1980, p. 89.
5. Cline (see note 3) p. 23, citing IMF data.

6. *World Development Report 1984* (New York: World Bank and Oxford University Press, 1984) Table 2.1, p. 11.

7. The Bank of International Settlements (BIS) estimates that $50 bn of capital left Latin America between 1978 and 1982. 'Substantial capital flight has aggravated, and is perhaps still aggravating, the external financial problems of some of the Latin American countries' (p. 170) . . . 'Clearly, the burden of interest charges would look much less frightening if it could be calculated in terms of net interest owed to the rest of the world, i.e. the interest to be paid on external debt minus the income received (but not necessarily repatriated) by the owners of the exported capital' (p. 171), Bank for International Settlements, *Fifty-Fourth Annual Report 1 April 1983–31 March 1984* (Basle, 1984). The BIS estimate is considered too low by some observers, see, for example, *Economist*, 23 June 1984; *El Pais*, 19 November 1984, p. 28.

8. *World Military Expenditure and Arms Transfers* (Washington, DC: US Arms Control and Disarmament Agency (ACDA), 1984) pp. 6–7.

9. For a study of military-related debt in Latin America including seven country studies, see Tullberg, R., *Military-related Debt in Latin America, Proceedings of the 7th RIAL Conference, Bogotá, November 1985* (forthcoming).

10. Goode, R., *Government Finance in Developing Countries* (Washington, DC: The Brookings Institute, 1984) p. 198 and Table 8.1.

11. Without entering into the argument as to whether development can successfully be export-led, it is clear that a massive diversion of resources into exports, particularly of primary products, in order to repay foreign debt will delay the development of alternative production.

12. *Government Finance Statistics*, vol. VII, 1983 (Washington, DC: International Monetary Fund, 1983) p. 27. Computed from data for seventy-six non-oil developing countries, 61 per cent of which claimed to spend more on education than on defence. IMF data on military spending tend to give low estimates. See Tullberg, R. and Millán, V., 'Military expenditure series: a comparison of five Latin American countries', in SIPRI, *World Armaments and Disarmament, SIPRI Yearbook 1983* (London: Taylor & Francis, 1983) Appendix 7C, p. 181.

13. J. de Larosière at the 40th Conference of the International Institute of Public Finance in Innsbruck, Austria, 27 August 1984, 'The Growth of Public Debt and the Need for Fiscal Discipline'; reprinted in *IMF Survey*, 3 September 1984, p. 266.

14. WEO, (note 1), p. 63.

COMMENT

Victor L. Urquidi
EL COLEGIO DE MEXICO

The accumulated figure of arms transfer credits for the period 1972–82, for non-oil developing countries, was $68 bn, not counting further debt to pay interest. It so happens that $68 bn was the total amount of Third World debt in 1970. This purchase of arms, by adding to debt, certainly complicated problems, not only in the late 1970s and early 1980s, but also – for example – in 1983, when they had to start meeting interest payments at a time when no new credits were available from any source. There is no doubt that these arms purchases have exacerbated the debt problem of Third World countries.

The US deficit has of course also contributed to the debt problem, because it has forced many Third World countries to borrow at very high interest rates. The capital flight from Latin America can also be partly considered as a consequence of the US rearmament programme.

The export of arms from developing countries is growing, and is being used to help to service the debt – not to repay it, because it is difficult to believe that any significant proportion of this debt will be actually repaid. This problem is how to meet interest payments – and in this way the debt problem is helping to spur the development of exporting military industries in Third World countries. Third World countries cannot in general now afford to purchase arms on a substantial scale. It is the non-market transfers – the military assistance to such countries as Honduras, El Salvador, or Nicaragua – which are rising.

Expenditure on arms has undoubtedly been excessive by any assessment, and damaging to the long-term development of those countries. Of course, arms transfers were not the only factor creating long-term difficulties. The over-valuation of the currencies in many Third World countries led to excessive imports and insufficient exports.

However, if the discussion is a more general one – about the relation between the development of military industry and economic growth, for example – then a certain agnosticism is appropriate. It is in some ways similar to the arguments about population – the economic consequences of rising, static or declining population. No clear generalisation can be drawn: the same is true of the economic consequences of starting a military industry.

The total debt of the less-developed countries increased some sixfold during the 1970s, and increased by a further 60 per cent between 1980 and 1984. This is one of the earth-shaking developments in the world economy. Just to meet interest payments the less-developed countries have to produce a real transfer of resources to the developed world – and this is unprecedented in history. It did not occur in the nineteenth century, partly because most of the loans were private loans, and many of them proved to be total losses for the lenders.

One additional relevant point; over the past decade the maturity of this debt increased, and the grace periods were reduced as well.

Part IV

Econometrics and Applied Microeconomics

15 Military Expenditure Dynamics and a World Model

A. R. Gigengack, H. de Haan, and C. J. Jepma
RIJKSUNIVERSITEIT, NETHERLANDS

This chapter reports the first results of a research project aiming to construct a world computer model which explicitly includes a conventional military production sector and 'arms race' dynamics to determine the size of military expenditures. Such a model is considered important because, as part of a 'model set', it can assist the high-level policy-maker, whether he is primarily responsible, for example, for economic policy, national security policy, foreign policy, etc., in recognising the full repercussions of his decisions on the world system. Based on an enhanced version of an existing world computer model called SARUM, and using an arms dynamics equation based on the 'Richardson Process' for which coefficients were estimated using ACDA data on military expenditures, a series of illustrative scenarios are compared. These simulations, which embody different assumptions about the way regions react to one another and determine the level of military expenditures, show that SARUM is a suitable candidate for the construction of such a world model, although more work is required before it can be used in actual decision processes.

I INTRODUCTION

The past decade has witnessed an increasing interest in the relationships between military expenditures and (inter)national economic performance. Partly this was the result of a heightened social awareness of the dangers which modern warfare entails. Another contributing factor was the widespread deterioration in economic performance while the costs of maintaining and developing (new) weapon systems rose sharply.[1] This served to highlight the vast amount of resources which are earmarked for the 'military–industrial complex (MIC)'. For instance, during the 1970s the rate of world economic growth fell from an average of around 4.5 per cent to less than 2 per cent, while global military expenditures rose from approximately $360 b to $450 b that is, one thousand million or (1978 prices).[2] In a world economy aggravated by the 'debt crisis', it also led many to wonder what role military expenditures play in the LDCs' development process. The economies of Third World countries were seen to stagnate, while their share of world military expenditures almost doubled.

In a world where poverty, famine, and human suffering are so glaringly apparent, many economic analyses understandably stress the 'wastefulness' and immorality of military expenditures. These studies then often go on to examine such questions as to how the resources tied up in the MIC can be efficiently reallocated to more peaceful and productive objectives. In contrast, some recent studies have suggested that the MIC plays an important beneficial role in the promotion and maintenance of economic growth. For example, some studies have concluded that the rate of return on private R & D is much higher than on capital investments, suggesting that, left alone, civilian industry underinvests in the former activity.[3] In addition, the emphasis on basic, long-term R & D by the MIC supposedly produces a rapid rate of technological progress and generates 'spin-off' to the rest of the economy. In the light of the prolonged economic recession of the 1970s, these studies bring new urgency to analyses of the interrelationship between the MIC and the civilian economy. Their conclusions suggest that if disarmament programmes are to be implemented the need may arise to design new institutions to (partially) replace the MIC, thus saving some of its beneficial characteristics, and avoiding a structural lessening in the rate of technological growth which disarmament would entail.

The growth in military expenditures has also attracted the attention of (inter)national economic policy-makers, whether they are responsible for the management of domestic economies, foreign affairs, or the distribution of (multilateral) aid flows. Since the amount of resources which are being devoted (some would say diverted) to military spending now represents around 6 per cent of world *GDP*, and since this category of government expenditures displays a rising trend, the feasibility or success of many (especially Third World) planning targets becomes increasingly dependent on exactly how this component of the government budget evolves. This is so for the targets of centrally-planned economies as well as for the less formal government 'projections' of the expected development of decentralised economies.

In order to help policy-makers to grasp the implications of (increased) military expenditures for the attainability and/or desirability of particular economic and social policy alternatives, as well as to heighten their awareness of the consequences of such policy alternatives for military spending (both at home and abroad), models should be developed which explicitly incorporate the links between the MIC and the civilian economy, both nationally and internationally. Since the questions which interest policy-makers are likely to range from detailed, short-term, country-specific matters to broad and long-term regional (even global) issues, no single model can hope to be adequate. Instead, a 'model set' should be available from which a policy-maker can choose, depending on the particular question at hand. One thing which the models should have in common, however, is an interdisciplinary approach. In particular, the models should contain insights from political science in order to portray the dynamics of national and regional military expenditure behaviour, in addition to economic theory.

The need for such an interdisciplinary approach in the case of the interaction between military expenditures and economic activity is especially vital because of existing institutional structures. Although military (or more generally 'national security') policies are recognised as having consequences for national economies, and economic policies are recognised as having consequences for the way countries perceive their security, in reality the decision-makers, because of the relatively compartmentalised bureaucracies of today's nation states, are responsible only for formulating and implementing policy within their own limited domain.[4] Since these two categories of government policy interact, however, it is essential for improved overall performance that these two categories of decisions are made with at least some minimum degree of mutual recognition. To help to achieve such coordination, a suitable quantitative framework, embodying interdisciplinary knowledge, can be used as a supplement to other modes of policy analysis for examining existing alternatives. This quantitative framework can consist of a set of computer models, for the reasons mentioned above. And since the effects of decisions concerning military expenditures are transmitted, from country to country, throughout the globe, a world model can be a helpful element in such a set.

This paper describes the results of an ongoing project to develop a world model for inclusion in such a 'model set'.[5] SARUM (which is an acronym for Systems Analysis Research Unit Model) an existing world model which we have previously modified to include a military production sector, has been further enhanced with a 'Richardson-Process'-inspired model of arms expenditure dynamics during a recent workshop held at the University of Groningen together with Professor R. W. Chadwick of the University of Hawaii and Dr F. Poldy of the Department of Arts, Heritage and Environment, Australia. This is described in section II. To examine the behaviour of the new version of SARUM, some illustrative scenarios have been performed which are described in section III. Section IV draws some conclusions, and outlines the work which still has to be done.

However, before continuing, a few brief remarks about why a world model is essential for the question at hand is in order. It is often said that because of the increased level of world trade and capital flows, no country can today afford to ignore the economic performance of its trading partners. This need to take into account the economic state of affairs of foreign countries goes even further, however, when immediate effects are no longer the only cause of concern. This is because countries with which no direct trade links exist can still exert an influence on a particular country's domestic economy by way of intermediate countries. In other words, in the medium term, links which are not immediately evident can still be the path through which major impulses influencing economic performance travel.

In a similar vein, the political links among nations extend further than the superficial alliances or divisions into hostile camps which characterise the modern world. More fundamentally, the fact that in today's world national security encompasses more than pure military might, including, for example, access to markets for consumer goods and supplies of raw materials, means that the aforementioned growth in world trade becomes an aggravating factor for world political stability. Ignoring these loops which travel through the rest of the world can be very dangerous when evaluating proposed foreign-policy alternatives. For this reason a world model, which offers the possibility of including these loops, should prove useful to policy-makers, especially when part of a set of models.

II THE MILITARY EXPENDITURE DYNAMICS IN SARUM

1 Some Brief Remarks on the World Model SARUM

SARUM divides the world into twelve regions (see Table 15.1) based mainly on geographic and economic development criteria. Each of the regions contains twelve sectors, or industries, which produce a single commodity (see Table 15.2), eight of which are traded. These trading links, together with aid transfers, form the interconnections between the regions. Decision on how much of each commodity to consume, produce, import, export, and so on,[6] are functions of prices, income, production capacity, and political–cultural patterns, and can be further influenced by population growth and income distribution. The form of the functions which related these variables are, for a large part, inspired by neoclassical economic theory. Since a thorough discussion of the economic reasoning underlying the SARUM model can be found in the SARUM Handbook,[7] no further attention will be devoted to this subject here.

The MILCOM (MILitary COMmodity) sector in SARUM corresponds roughly to the conventional armaments industry. The commodity which it produces (also called MILCOM) differs from the other SARUM commodities in that it is neither a final demand good that is a consumer good, aggregate purchases of which are dependent on regional population, *GDP* of a region, relative prices, and a series of Engel curves), nor is it an intermediate or capital good (required for the production of other commodities). It is produced for the sole benefit of governments, which are represented in the model through the government's budget. At present, attention is restricted solely to the conventional military expenditure component of the government budget. Part of these expenditures are spent on the military commodity MILCOM, while the rest is assumed to be allocated among final demand commodities in the same proportion as the region's overall consumption expenditures. The latter is not necessary in the model, but has been tentatively assumed for simplicity during the current developmental activities. The total expenditure on MILCOM includes imports from other regions, based on past patterns (as expressed by so-called 'trade biases') and relative prices. Concomitantly, a region's MILCOM sector produces partly for export.

Because of the assumptions described in the previous paragraph, the SARUM variable 'government budget' can be equated with

326

Table 15.1   SARUM regionalisation

EURCOM	Europe (Communist) Albania; Bulgaria; Czechoslovakia; German Democratic Republic; Hungary; Mongolia; Poland; Rumania; USSR
WANA	West Asia and Northern Africa Algeria; United Arab Emirates; Bahrain; Egypt; Iran; Iraq; Israel; Jordan; Kuwait; Lebanon; Libya; Morocco; Oman; Quatar; Saudi Arabia; Sudan; Syria; Tunisia; Yemen
NORAM	North America USA; Canada
AUS	Australia
NZ	New Zealand
CHINA	China
LACARB	Latin America and the Caribbean All of South and Central America
AFRICA	Africa Africa except for certain northern countries included in WANA
EUR	Europe (Western) Belgium; Denmark; France; Federal Republic of Germany; Ireland; Italy; Luxembourg; Netherlands; UK; Malta; Switzerland; Austria; Cyprus; Finland; Greece; Iceland; Norway; Portugal; Spain; Sweden; Turkey; Yugoslavia
JAPAN	Japan
ESEA	East and South East Asia Hong Kong; Indonesia; Kampuchea; North Korea; South Korea; Laos; Malaysia; Phillippines; Singapore; Taiwan; Thailand; Vietnam
SASIA	South Asia Afghanistan; Bangladesh; Bhutan; Brunei; India; Macao; Nepal; Maldive Islands; Pakistan; Sri Lanka

Table 15.2   SARUM commodity disaggregation (with attributes, if any)

MACHIN	Capital equipment; (traded) SITC section 7, excluding passenger cars
CONSTR	Construction
OMANUF	Other manufacturers; (traded; final demand good) SITC sections 5 through 9, excluding capital goods and chemicals for agriculture and subdivision 951
ENERGY	Primary energy; (traded; final demand good) SITC section 3, excluding refined petroleum products
MINRAL	Ore extraction; (traded) SITC divisions 27 and 28
OFLNP	Other flow limited natural products; (traded; final demand good) SITC sections 1 and through 4
SERVIS	Services; (final demand good)
FOOD	Agricultural food production; (traded; final demand good) SITC section 0
LAND	Development of arable land
IRRIG	Irrigation
FERTIL	Fertilisers and other chemicals for agriculture; (traded) SITC division 56
MILCOM	Conventional military commodities; (traded)

'military budget' in the present version of the model (the term 'military budget' will be used henceforth). This opens the door for incorporating the endogenous determination of the level of a region's military budget in SARUM. In order to identify suitable causal variables and specify the necessary relationships between them and the level of the military budget, an appeal is made to the research which political scientists have conducted in their studies of international conflict.

2   'Richardson Process' Models

In the political science literature, a widely used model for studying arms races is known as the 'Richardson Process'.[8] In its simplest and most common form, it consists of two linear differential equations describing the behaviour of the arms expenditures of two countries:

$$\dot{x} = k \cdot y - a \cdot x + g \tag{15.1}$$

$$\dot{y} = l \cdot x - b \cdot y + h \tag{15.2}$$

where x and y are, for instance, military budgets, with a dot above a variable used to indicate a derivative with respect to time.[9] the parameters a, b, k, l, g and h are all assumed to be positive.

It can be shown[10] that such a system of differential equations can be associated with a pair of linear reaction equations

$$x' = k \cdot y + g \tag{15.3}$$

$$y' = l \cdot x + h \tag{15.4}$$

and the following so-called dynamic assumption for each:

$$\dot{x} \overset{\Delta}{=} (x' - a \cdot x) \tag{15.5}$$

$$\dot{y} \overset{\Delta}{=} (y' - b \cdot y) \tag{15.6}$$

This dynamic assumption can be considered a special instance of (for the case of x):

$$\dot{x} = \rho \cdot \{x^* - \tau \cdot x\} \tag{15.7}$$

where

x^* is the target value
x is the actual value
ρ is the 'speed of response' parameter
τ is the 'current value weight' parameter

The dynamic assumptions (15.5) and (15.6) associated with equations (15.1) – (15.4) have $\rho = 1$ and $\tau = a$ and $\tau = b$, respectively.

Equations (15.1) and (15.2) are usually assumed to apply to two 'hostile' countries. This allows *a priori* restrictions to be placed on the signs of the coefficients, and leads to specific interpretations of the coefficients. In the literature the coefficient of the 'other' country's military expenditures (k, l) is usually called the 'fear coefficient', which appeals to the intuitive concept that, in a hostile climate, a country will increase its level of military spending as that of its opponent increases. Similarly, the coefficient of the 'own' level of military expenditure (a, b) is called the 'fatigue coefficient', which appeals to the intuitive concept that a country (in particular, its government) will experience more and more resistance in its attempt to increase military expenditures as the level of military expenditure rises. Finally, it is assumed that a country has an autonomous level of military expenditure, greater than zero, which reflects all the factors aside from the particular arms race being portrayed which influence military expenditures.

A number of variations on the above theme have been examined in the literature. For example, other variables, such as specific (classes of) weapon systems have been used instead of 'military expenditure'. The equations have also been extended to include more than one country, and theoretical 'special cases', such as the functioning of alliances, and the existence of inherently 'friendly' countries which imply negative values for the constant in equations (15.1) and (15.2), have been discussed.

In a world model such as SARUM, the restriction to pre-war (that is, war-oriented) or hostile (bilateral) arms races is too limited. In the first place, if interest is focused solely on two nations, then a smaller model is appropriate (unless the 'indirect' effects of such an arms race on the rest of the world are of interest). Second, the concept of a pre-war 'arms race' is too limited because the time horizon which SARUM covers is some twenty to fifty years in the future. It is unlikely that a true arms race in the 'pre-war' sense will continue over such a long period of time.

For these reasons it is of greater interest to focus on military expenditures in conditions of 'peace'. While arms races (these can now better be replaced by the more general concept of 'arms dynamics') can still occur, they are now caused, for example, by less-severe changes in political climate, or through changes in economic or technological conditions (of the region in question, or of its 'rival'). They could persist over long periods without leading to a 'hot' war, even indeed oscillating or disappearing.

Such behaviour, especially 'cold war'-type arms races can lay claim to vast resources, and so have significant effects on the level and distribution of economic activity. Of course, the possibility of (continuing) '(un)stable' and/or 'hostile' military expenditure dynamics – that is, pre-war arms races – is not excluded; it is not, however, explicitly assumed.

Given this broader framework, the category of causal variables which can appear on the right-hand side of the reaction equations is enlarged, and can include such factors as domestic and/or foreign *GDP*, technological growth, unemployment, trade flows, and so on. In addition, the signs of the coefficients can be either positive or negative, even if another region's military expenditures are involved. The latter reflects the possibility that regions 'share' the burden of military expenditure, either overtly in the form of alliances, or covertly (the so-called 'free-rider' phenomenon). It could also reflect that a 'friendly' nation's military expenditure is nevertheless perceived as requiring a *quid pro quo* (for instance, if an 'ally' is thought to be preparing for a major sale on the world's arms markets).

Furthermore, the more general analysis need no longer be restricted to a two-country situation. Indeed, the complexity of multi-country interrelationships, together with the additional causal variables as suggested above, offers a wide variety of linkages through which the dynamics of military expenditures can be expressed.

3   The Arms Dynamics Submodel in SARUM

A   General remarks

As a first step, the equation which has been incorporated in SARUM (one for each region) has military expenditures (domestic and foreign), trade in the military commodity (world-wide), and domestic GDP as causal variables in a linear specification for country 'i':

$$Z_{i,t+1} = \sum_{j=1}^{12} RCHDSN_{i,j} \cdot Z_{j,t} + \ldots$$

$$\ldots + \sum_{j=1}^{12} RIMARM_{i,j} \cdot MI_{j,\tau} + LFRGDP_i \cdot GDP_{i,\tau} + \ldots$$

$$\ldots + RCHCON_i \tag{15.8}$$

where *RCHDSN*, *RIMARM* and *LFRGDP* are coefficients, Z is the military variable (in our case, government military expenditures), *MI* is military imports, *GDP* is gross domestic product, and *RCHCON* is a constant. The indices 'i' and 'j' represent different countries, t

represents time, and τ can be either the present or past period index. Both the variable Z and the process underlying this equation can be interpreted in a number of different ways.

For example, Z could be seen as the level of actual military expenditures for a particular region. Statistical estimation techniques could be used to determine the coefficients, thus enabling Z to be calculated endogenously within SARUM for each simulation time step. In accordance with the way SARUM integrates many of its state variables, Z would be updated as:

$$\tilde{Z}_t = \tilde{Z}_{t-1} + \dot{\tilde{Z}}_t \tag{15.9}$$

where

$$\dot{\tilde{Z}}_t = (Z_t - \tilde{Z}_t)/T_Z \tag{15.10}$$

The tilde '$\tilde{\ }$' indicates a 'smoothed' Z, and T_Z the 'time constant' used for smoothing Z. The current value for Z is some function of a selected set of explanatory variables.

Alternatively, the interpretation can more closely follow the Richardson Process concepts. Equation (15.8) above could then be viewed as an expanded reaction equation. Since yearly data of government origin are used, it can be argued that the observations are points of equilibrium among governments in the same way that observed prices are assumed to be the intersection of supply and demand curves of firms and consumers in microeconomic theory. In this case, *a priori* assumptions about signs could be introduced. Subsequently a dynamic assumption of the following form could be postulated:

$$\dot{Z} = \ \cong \Delta Z = (z_t - \eta.Z_{t-1})/\rho^{-1} \tag{15.11}$$

where Z_{t-1} is the previous simulation step's value of Z. This is equivalent to the 'time constant' approach of SARUM if η equals 1. In this case ρ and η represent the general speed-of-response of the region, and the effect of the existing level of military expenditure on the change in military expenditure, respectively. If the above assumption about equilibrium observations is maintained, then $\eta = 1$ (note that the inverse of a 'time constant' is equivalent to a 'speed of response' parameter; that is why ρ^{-1} is used in (15.11).

While still other models and interpretations can be considered which give rise to similar specifications (for instance, distributed lag models), the rest of this chapter will concentrate on the way military expenditure dynamics have been implemented in SARUM.

B   *The introduction of arms expenditure dynamics in SARUM*

Although an expanded list of causal variables is planned for future use, the equation which has now been implemented is the following Richardson-Process-inspired reaction equation for region 'i':

$$Z^*_{i,t} = \sum_{j=1}^{12} RCHDSEN_{i,j} \cdot Z_{j,t-1} + RCHCON_i \qquad (15.12)$$

Here Z^*_i is viewed as the desired military budget of region 'i'. The dynamic assumption made now is:

$$Z_i = (Z^*_i - Z_i) \qquad (15.13)$$

where Z^*_i is the desired and Z_i is the actual level of region i's military expenditures. Substituting (15.12) into (15.13) and rearranging yields:

$$Z_i = \sum_{\substack{j=1 \\ j \neq i}}^{12} RCHDSEN_{i,j} \cdot Z_j + (RCHDSN_{i,i} - 1) \ldots (15.14)$$

$$\ldots \cdot Z_i + RCHCON_i$$

The interpretation which can be given to these coefficients is that the *RCHDSN* coefficients of foreign government's military expenditures reflect 'fear' and/or alliances, and the country's own ($RCHDSN - 1$) coefficient can represent the internal resistance to or pressure for (further) military spending. In order to estimate this equation, the first (forward) difference is taken instead of the derivative on the left-hand side to give:

$$\dot{Z}_i \cong \Delta Z_i \overset{\Delta}{=} Z_{i,\,t+1} - Z_{i,\,t} =$$

$$\sum_{\substack{j=1 \\ j \neq i}}^{12} RCHDSN_{i,j} . Z_{j,t} + (RCHDSN_{i,i} - 1) . Z_{i,t} + RCHCON_i$$

$$\qquad\qquad\qquad\qquad\qquad\qquad\qquad\qquad (15.15)$$

For the ith country this becomes:

$$Z_{i,\,t+1} = \sum_{j=1}^{12} RCHDSN_{i,j} . Z_{j,\,t} + RCHCON_i \qquad (15.16)$$

As a preliminary exercise, single equation stepwise OLS regression has been used on ACDA data of government military expenditures to estimate this equation for each of the regions distinguished by SARUM.[11] The estimates (see Table 15.3) were obtained during the workshop held in Groningen in June–August 1985. Since the purpose of the estimation was to obtain an illustrative set of coefficients, the step-wise algorithm was forced to include and maintain the 'own-country' military expenditures. The results, therefore, are not necessarily the statistically optimal set of coefficients, but correspond most closely with the original Richardson Process specification. For a further discussion of this and other estimation techniques, and an application to South-east Asian countries, see Chadwick (1986).[12]

In order to give an impression of the tracking performance of SARUM, the ACDA data for government military budgets and the series generated by SARUM are presented in Table 15.4. Table 15.5 gives series of regional *GDP* as presented in ACDA and as generated by SARUM. A thirty-year simulation using these equations constitutes the base run against which the alternative scenario simulations will be compared. It should be emphasised that the equations as presented above are of an experimental nature for illustrating and testing the military dynamics in SARUM.

III THE SCENARIOS

In order to examine how the arms dynamics equations behave within the SARUM model, a number of simple scenarios have been simulated. These simulations differ in their assumptions concerning the way the *RCHDSN* coefficients change through time. In addition,

Table 15.3 Matrix of estimated arms dynamics coefficients

	NORAM	JAPAN	AUS	NZ	EURCOM	EUR	LACARB	SASIA	ESEA	CHINA	WANA	AFRICA
NORAM	1.0263											
JAPAN		0.5960			0.1128							
AUS			0.0612						0.1205			
NZ				0.1582	0.0073							
EURCOM	0.1750				0.8931							
EUR	1.7744					0.6144						
LACARB	0.0669						0.9122					
SASIA	0.0684							-0.2632			0.0586	
ESEA	1.1355					0.1999			0.1409			
CHINA										0.0010		
WANA	0.1951										0.7699	
AFRICA	0.0481	-0.9075									0.1659	-0.1965

NB: The value for China has been set *ad hoc* in order to calculate the eigenvalues

Eigenvalues:
1.0263 0.7699 0.8931 0.9122 -0.2632 -0.1965 1.0527 0.0612 0.1409 0.1582 0.1576 0.0010

Constants:

NORAM	JAPAN	AUS	NZ	EUR-COM	EUR	LACARB	SASIA	ESEA	CHINA	WANA	AFRICA
-21177	-3862	836	-210	3531	13435	-4123	-2771	-8836	—	-7094	1424

Table 15.4   Regional military expenditures (billions (10^9) of 1981 US$)

Year	NORAM actual	NORAM SARUM	EURCOM actual	EURCOM SARUM	EUR actual	EUR SARUM
1972	155.4	155.4	213.9	213.9	92.4	92.4
1974	149.9	147.3	233.9	232.8	97.6	96.6
1976	138.3	146.4	251.3	246.6	101.0	100.6
1978	146.4	154.7	258.2	258.7	103.4	104.8
1980	162.5	174.2	269.1	272.8	109.9	109.5
1982	191.0	206.4	283.0	292.2	114.5	114.7

Notes
1. See Table 15.1 for a description of the regions.

Table 15.5   Regional expenditures (billions of 1981 US$)

Year	NORAM actual	NORAM SARUM	EURCOM actual	EURCOM SARUM	EUR actual	EUR SARUM
1972	2521	2075	1730	1754	2569	2803
1974	2667	2023	1941	1967	2782	3109
1976	2779	2279	2051	2205	2876	3235
1978	3050	2563	2182	2451	3039	3418
1980	3147	2836	2243	2661	3185	3677
1982	3158	3119	2297	2883	3180	3956

Notes
1. See Table 15.1 for a description of the regions.
2. - The SARUM results are based on an experimental revised
    INTERFUTURES data set.

some supplementary assumptions as to how investment propensities can change have been made. These supplementary assumptions reflect the *a priori* assumption that as governments decide to change their commitment to military expenditures, they can successfully undertake new initiatives, for example, in stimulating investment.

In the future, the WMP will undertake empirical studies to determine values for the effects of a reallocation of government revenues among other priorities. In these simulations, however, *ad hoc* values have been chosen for their illustrative effect. A description of the five scenarios follows below. Some selected results of these scenarios are presented in Table 15.6.

1 *'Peace'* The *RCHDSN* coefficients of NORAM *vs* NORAM, EURCOM *vs* EURCOM, and EUR *vs* EUR are reduced by 25 per cent between years 4(=1974) and 9(=1979). This scenario embodies the simple assumption that the 'internal' pressures influencing military expenditures, for instance the lobbying pressures of the MIC, or the perception of internal instability by the governing élites, falls. The *RCHDSN* coefficients fall from 1.026, 0.893, and 0.614 to 0.769, 0.6698, and 0.4607, respectively. As a result the growth rates of the government budgets alter radically, as can be seen in Table 15.5. The differences between the changes in growth rates for the three countries involved are in agreement with the relative magnitudes of the original *RCHDSN* coefficients, indicating that the model can discriminate fairly well between differences in specification. For all three regions, growth rates of aggregate expenditure rise. This shows that the size of the military budgets compared to other regional variables is sufficient to justify its separate treatment in the model.

2 *'War'* Here the same coefficients as in scenario 1 are increased by 10 per cent during the same period. The accompanying simple assumption is that internal pressures/fears increase. The *RCHDSN* coefficients rise from their original values (see scenario 1 above) to 1.128, 0.982, and 0.674, respectively. Because of the lack of feedback from the economy to the size of the military budget in the current version of the model, the explosive arms race to which this leads (note that the eigenvalues of the original system already indicated an unstable situation) causes budgets to increase astronomically. Indeed, before the simulation reaches 1992, the government's claim on regional resources has completely absorbed the civilian economy. This model behaviour is caused by the current lack of adequate feedback/feedforward loops from the economy and the rest of the political system back to military expenditures, (and points to the most urgent next step in model development). As can be expected, the growth rates of military budgets are more than twice as high as for the comparable period of the base run.

3 *'NATO peace with investment push'* Here *RCHDSN* of NORAM *vs* NORAM and EUR *vs* EUR drop by 25 per cent during the period 1974–9 (see scenario 1 above). This scenario examines a

Table 15.6 Scenario comparisons: average growth rates of selected variables

Variable	Base Run 72-82	Base Run 72-92	Scenario 1 72-82	Scenario 1 72-92	Scenario 2 72-82	Scenario 2 72-92	Scenario 3 72-82	Scenario 3 72-92	Scenario 4 72-82	Scenario 4 72-92	Scenario 5 72-82	Scenario 5 72-92
EXPEND												
NORAM	3.54	3.30	3.66	3.69	3.38	–	3.97	4.20	4.26	4.21	3.83	3.40
EURCOM	4.97	4.83	5.33	5.53	4.73	–	5.05	5.34	5.65	5.75	4.87	4.10
EUR	3.29	3.65	3.34	3.71	3.31	–	3.36	3.72	3.74	4.27	3.65	4.17
BUDGET												
NORAM	5.58	8.83	–19.40	–	12.20	–	–19.40	–	–	–	8.30	13.18
EURCOM	3.23	5.75	–9.10	–10.90	8.40	–	–0.02	0.00	–16.20	–13.40	5.91	9.90
EUR	2.22	2.56	–3.04	–3.37	4.50	–	–3.04	–3.23	–7.32	–4.50	3.86	4.74
JAPAN	na	na	–5.20	–	9.30	–	–5.20	–5.39	–	–	7.44	8.56
AFRICA	na	na	–7.67	–5.40	13.10	–	–7.67	–	–9.70	–5.00	8.99	13.55
ESEA	na	na	–7.39	–	11.20	–	–7.39	–	–	–	8.93	9.80
OUTPUT												
NORAM												
OMANUF	na	na	4.10	na	4.51	na	4.53	na	4.61	na	4.80	na
SERVIS	na	na	1.65	na	0.83	na	1.47	na	1.71	na	0.89	na
EURCOM												
OMANUF	na	na	3.91	na	4.39	na	4.08	na	4.02	na	4.29	na
SERVIS	na	na	4.53	na	3.15	na	3.92	na	4.83	na	3.47	na
EUR												
OMANUF	na	na	2.14	na	2.30	na	2.16	na	2.65	na	2.79	na
SERVIS	na	na	2.26	na	2.11	na	2.26	na	2.00	na	1.78	na

Notes:
1. See Table 15.1 for a description of the SARUM regions.
2. 'OUTPUT' is real production by the sectors. The commodity 'OMANUF' represents non-capital goods manufacturing; 'SERVIS' represents services.
3. The symbol 'na' refers to results which have not been examined; a '–' means that the growth rate calculation is inapplicable.

situation in which NATO unilaterally decides to decrease military spending. To supplement this strategy, an additional assumption is that NORAM succeeds in converting the associated freed resources (both the government component and privately managed resources) into productive investment. This could reflect the idea that 'economic' security replaces 'military' security in NORAM's defensive posture. The latter assumption is embodied by changing the 'cultural investment bias' or NORAM by 20 per cent (from 0.6 to 0.72) during the same period (see the *SARUM Handbook* for a description of this parameter). As could be expected, this leads to the same behaviour for the military budgets of NORAM and EUR as in scenario 1, while their overall growth rates are higher due to the 'investment push'. Of interest is the effect on EURCOM, which feels the influence of NORAM and EUR's policy through its arms dynamics equation: the growth rate of its military expenditure falls, becoming slightly negative in comparison with the base run. While its overall economic growth rate is lower than in scenario 1 in the period 1972–82, by 1992 it has managed to surpass the 'peace' scenario's value. This scenario has indicated that the model can successfully trace the effects on 'third parties' of changes in the (assumed) behaviour of selected regions.

4 *'World peace combined with economic expansion'*   In this scenario, all non-zero *RCHDSN* coefficients drop to 50 per cent of their original value at a rate of 20 per cent starting at year 4, while the cultural investment biases of EURCOM, EUR, JAPAN and NORAM rise to 20 per cent of their original value between years 4 and 9. While the levels of military expenditures fall sharply (even when compared with scenario 1) overall growth-rate increases do not display similar relative changes. An interesting result of this simulation is that the growth rate of the SERVIS sector, which can be seen as a proxy of the supply of consumer goods in the economy, is especially large (compared with scenario 3) for EURCOM and NORAM, while small for EUR. This could be the result of the relatively small share of *GDP* devoted to military expenditures in European countries.

5 *'War and government controlled investment'*   In this scenario, all the *RCHDSN* coefficients of NORAM, EURCOM and EUR rise by 5 per cent between 1974 and 1979, all *RCHCON* constants rise from 1974 at a rate of 10 per cent towards 120 per cent of their

original value, and the cultural investment biases of NORAM, EURCOM and EUR rise by 20 per cent between 1974 and 1979. In this scenario, a 'war drive' is assumed, which would reflect a situation of growing government management of the economy. As can be seen, this scenario (as well as the 'war' scenario 2) shows a markedly lower growth-rate in the SERVIS sector. Thus, while overall economic growth-rates rise (even when compared with a peaceful investment push), the implication is that this is not accompanied by increases in consumer welfare.

IV   CONCLUSIONS AND FUTURE PLANS

In its present stage of development the model is far from complete. There are still major linkages to be made, especially from the state of the economy back to the government's freedom to increase the military budget. Their inclusion should be relatively straightforward, for example by endogenising the values of the parameters in the military budget equations. In addition, further empirical work is required to discover plausible 'political reactions' (especially as concerns national security perceptions) to other nation's policies with respect to production, trade, aid, and so on. Finally, the significance of the government's military expenditures (in particular the R & D component) for the functioning of the 'civilian' economy needs further scrutiny.

The results of these exercises show that Richardson-Process-inspired military expenditure dynamics can be successfully introduced into SARUM. The behaviour over time of regional military expenditures can be modelled endogenously, and it is already possible to see some effect on overall economic performance. A number of examples, albeit simple ones, have also been given of the types of scenario which a world model incorporating military expenditure can be called upon to examine. While the examples have been mainly concerned with alternative policies in the sphere of 'national security policy', it is obvious that scenarios representing alternative economic policies could also have been simulated, allowing the consequences of such policy for 'arms races' to be examined. In this way an interdisciplinary tool designed to help bridge the gap between relatively isolated policy-makers can become a reality.

340   *Econometrics and Applied Microeconomics*

Notes and References

1. See, for example, Barnaby, F. (ed.) *Future War* (New York: Joseph, 1984).
2. For a thorough treatment of the interrelationships between armaments and Third World development see Ghosh, P. K. (ed.) *Disarmament and Development: A Global Perspective* (Westport, Connecticut: Greenwood Press, 1984).
3. See, for instance, Mansfield, E., *Technical Transfer, Productivity and Economic Policy* (New York: Norton, 1982).
4. A broader discussion of this and related issues is contained in Barney, G. O. (Study Director) *The Global 2000 Report to the President: Entering the 2st Century* (Harmondsworth: Penguin, 1984).
5. The current activities of the World Model Project (WMP), University of Groningen, The Netherlands, in the area of arms expenditure modelling is carried out in cooperation with Professor R. W. Chadwick, G–MAPP Project and University of Hawaii, and Dr D. MacRae and Dr F. Poldy of the Department of Arts, Heritage and Environment (formerly the Department of Home Affairs and Environment), Australia. Further information on the WMP can be found in Gigengack, A. R., Jepman, C. J., Lanjouw, G. L. and Schweigman, C. (eds) *The Use of a World Model for the Analysis of North–South Interdependence and Problems of Development and Security*, Special Issue, Working Group Development and Security (University of Groningen, Groningen, The Netherlands: 1985).
6. These and the following remarks pertain to the 'civilian' commodities of SARUM; a brief description of the military commodity is given in the next paragraph.
7. Systems Analysis Research Unit (SARU), Department of the Environment and Transport, *SARUM Handbook* (London: HMSO, 1978). A revised version of the *SARUM* Handbook, including corrections and a discussion of the military submodel in SARUM is currently being prepared. Interested parties can contact the authors of this paper, or contact Dr F. Poldy at the Australian Department of Arts, Heritage and Environment, Canberra, Australia.
8. See, for example, Zinnes, D. A. and Gillespie, J. V. (eds) *Mathematical Models in International Relations* (New York: Praeger, 1976) especially chap. 10 for a theoretical discussion. For a recent application, see for example, Chadwick, R. W., *Richardson Processes Applied to Selected Asia Pacific Nations, 1971–1980: A Preliminary Analysis* (Global Models and the Policy Process (G-MAPP) Project, University of Hawaii: 1985).
9. In the literature a number of other variables, such as missiles or other major weapons systems, have sometimes been used to model arms races using the Richardson Process Equations (see, for example, Intriligator, M. D. and Brito, D. L., 'Formal Models of Arms Races', *Journal of Peace Science*, vol. XXI, no. 1 (1976) pp. 77–88). This chapter presents a more qualitative discussion of the use of the Richardson Process equations and adheres to 'military budgets'

because it more closely reflects the notion of a general index of a rival's 'potential threat'. Nowhere in this chapter are terms such as 'threat', 'grievance', 'fatigue', and so on, given a precise meaning: the intuitive interpretation which these terms convey will suffice.;

10. See, for example, Boulding, K., *Conflict and Defense* (New York: Harper & Row, 1962).
11. United States Arms Control and Disarmament Agency (ACDA), *World Military Expenditures and Arms Transfers 1972–1982* (Washington, DC: ACDA, 1984).
12. Chadwick, R. W., 'Richardson Processes and Arms Transfers 1971–1980: A Preliminary Analysis', in *Journal of Peace Research*, 1986.

16 Time-series Estimates of the Macroeconomic Impact of Defence Spending in France and the UK*

Stephen Martin, Ron Smith
BIRKBECK COLLEGE, LONDON

and Jacques Fontanel
CEDSI, GRENOBLE

Measures of the effect of military expenditure on the economy had tended to rely on input–output or international cross-section models rather than time-series estimates. This chapter presents small simultaneous time-series models to estimate the effect of military expenditure on investment unemployment and growth in France and the UK. The impact and long-run multiples are calculated from the restricted and unrestricted reduced forms and the results compared. The relative advantages of time-series-based estimates as compared with other methods are then assessed. The main results suggest that military expenditure tends to reduce investment and increase unemployment. It has a positive immediate effect on growth, but when the system feedbacks are taken into account the net effect is negative.

I INTRODUCTION

Estimates of the effect of military expenditure on the economy have tended to rely on either input–output or international cross-sections. Aggregate time-series results for individual countries – the primary source of empirical information in most areas of economics – have played a comparatively minor role. The purpose of this paper is to investigate, within the context of a small simultaneous model, the light that aggregate time-series data shed on the impact of military expenditure in France and Britain on investment, unemployment and growth.

Time-series estimation has played a minor role in this area for a number of reasons:

1. Most theoretical models used as the basis for specification by the profession do not include an explicit role for military expenditure. Thus it is quite rare for economists concerned to explain macroeconomic phenomena to investigate the impact of military expenditure. There are of course exceptions such as Kormendi,[1] but relative neglect is the rule.

2. The main interest tends to be on the industrial and regional effects of changes in military expenditure and input–output models are better suited to revealing these. The classic study for the USA is by Leontief *et al.*;[2] similar exercises are reported for France in Aben,[3] and for Britain in Dunne and Smith.[4] Simulations of this sort also tend to suggest that changes in military expenditure, matched by other policy actions which leave the fiscal stance broadly unchanged, have relatively small macroeconomic effects. This might suggest that the macroeffect of military expenditure does not differ much from that of other government demand. However, it might merely be a product of the fact that these models constrain military expenditure to have effects similar to other government demands.

3. Peace-time military expenditures in OECD countries have shown relatively little variance around trend. This means that time-series estimates of its impact will tend to exhibit large standard errors. Wars have introduced more variance in military expenditure, but call into question the assumptions of structural stability on which time-series estimation is based. In these circumstances international cross-sections provide enough variability for more precise parameter estimation. In studies which do both time-series and cross-section estimation, such as Smith,[5] the large dispersion and standard errors of the time-series parameters contrast with the right cross-section estimates. However, the fact that the average time-series estimate matches the cross-section estimate provides some support for interpreting the former as picking up short-run impacts and the latter long-run ones.

4. Many of the important mechanisms by which military expenditure might influence macroeconomic performance resist quantification. These include technological spin-off; modernisation ethics and social discipline; effects of perceived security on discount rates; and the like. These effects, if present, are attributed to quantified variables in econometric estimation.

Despite these difficulties, it seems worthwhile to attempt a systematic investigation, using a small simultaneous macroeconomic system to estimate the defence expenditure multiplier on growth, unemployment and investment, for France and the UK.

Section II sets out the three-equation theoretical model used for each country; section III reports the estimation results and some diagnostic testing; and section IV summarises the quantitative conclusions and evaluates the strengths and limitations of the approach.

II THEORY

A principal aim of this analysis is to investigate the macroeconomic implications of military expenditure in France and the UK. Specifically, we will focus upon the consequences for investment, unemployment and growth. Previous single-equation studies have highlighted the direct impact of military expenditure, but these direct effects will feed through the macroeconomy interacting with one another. To identify these mechanisms a complete simultaneous equation model is required.

Since the purpose of this exercise is to produce comparative military expenditure multipliers for France and the UK, we have endeavoured to adopt similar model specifications. Comparison is also facilitated if the variables used are commensurable; therefore, where possible, the variables of interest should be unit free, for example as percentages, growth rates or shares. This approach has the added advantage that it is likely to reduce problems of heteroscedasticity (non-constant error variances). The three endogenous variables upon which we will focus are: the share of investment in GDP, the unemployment rate, and the growth rate of GDP. A variety of empirical work has suggested that the major impact of military expenditure is one investment, thus it deserves inclusion. Unemployment should also be examined because of the considerable political controversy surrounding the impact of military expenditure upon this important macroeconomic indicator. Lastly, since the growth rate of GDP is the most widely used measure of economic performance, the channels through which it is affected by military expenditure must be assessed. Clearly a more complete model of the macroeconomy would allow for monetary and trade linkages together with a variety of other feedbacks. However, a small model of the sort used here has the advantage that consistent systems estimators can be used, analytical results can be obtained, and the linkages can be easily identified.

1 Investment

The equation explaining the share of investment in GDP is,

$$i = a_0 + a_1g + a_2m + a_3u + a_4i_{-1} \qquad (16.1)$$

where

i = share of gross fixed capital formation in GDP
g = growth of constant price (1975) GDP
m = share of military expenditure in GDP
u = proportion unemployed

The detailed derivation of this equation is given in Smith,[6] where it is applied to fourteen countries, including France and the UK, for 1954–73. *A priori* expectations are that a_1 and a_4 will be positive, a_2 and a_3 negative.

2 Unemployment

The unemployment equation takes the form:

$$u = b_0 + b_1g + b_2m + b_3u_{-1} + b_4E + b_5t \qquad (16.2)$$

where

E = growth of exports
t = time trend

This equation is derived from a partial adjustment labour demand function of Okun's law form, which links unemployment to the growth rate of GDP, while allowing the demand factors of military expenditure and export growth to impart differential effects. Further, a time trend has been included to capture the impact of productivity improvements. We expect b_2, b_3 and b_5 to be positive, while b_1 and b_4 should be negative.

3   GDP Growth

To explain growth we assume that the full employment level of output is given by a Cobb–Douglas production function:

$$\bar{q} = \alpha_1 + \alpha_2 f + \alpha_3 k + p \qquad (16.3)$$

where the variables are logarithms of: full employment output, $\bar{q}$; labour force, f; capital stock, k; and total factor productivity/technology p. In general we use upper-case letters for the variables and lower-case letters for their logarithms.

The log of actual output, q, deviates from $\bar{q}$, by:

$$q - \bar{q} = \beta_1 (e - l) \qquad (16.4)$$

where e is the log of employment and l of measured labour force. Since the rate of unemployment is:

$$u = \frac{L - E}{L}$$

thus

$$e - 1 = \log(1 - u) \approx -u \qquad (16.5)$$

ignoring higher order terms in the approximation. Substituting (16.5) into (16.4) and then (16.4) into (16.3) gives

$$q = \alpha_1 + \alpha_2 f + \alpha_3 k + p - \beta_1 u \qquad (16.6)$$

Taking first differences yields an equation explaining the growth rate of GDP:

$$\Delta q = \alpha_2 \Delta f + \alpha_3 \Delta k + \Delta p - \beta_1 \Delta u \qquad (16.7a)$$

Since, Δk is roughly the proportionate growth rate in capital stock K; and $I = \Delta K + \delta K$, where I is gross investment and δ is rate of depreciation: then assuming a constant output–capital ratio, $v = Y/K$:

$$\Delta k = \Delta K/K = (I - \delta K)/K = vi - \delta \qquad (16.7b)$$

We shall also assume that over the longer run, $\Delta f = n$ a constant. Short-run variations in the size of the labour force will be allowed for by not imposing the first difference restriction on u.

Normally the growth rate of total factor productivity, Δp, is treated as a constant in econometric studies. However, we shall allow it to be determined by an error-correction term, catch-up effects and technological spin-off from military expenditure. The error-correction process removes deviations between GDP and a long-run trend and is modelled as

$$- \lambda_1 (q_{-1} - \beta_2 t)$$

where $\beta_2 t$ measures the long-run path. Second, 'catch-up', that is, international technological convergence to US levels is modelled as:

$$- \lambda_2 G_{t-1} \equiv - \lambda_2 [1nP_{t-1}/1n(P \overset{US}{\underset{t-1}{}} - P_{t-1})] \qquad (16.8a)$$

where P = manufacturing productivity.

The rationale for this variable rests upon intuitive notions of international convergence of technology; see Cornwall and Marris.[7,8] Specifically, it is assumed that the level of manufacturing productivity of a nation converges asymptotically to its target represented by the US productivity level. This US target is selected as it is likely to be a reliable indicator of international best practice. In the jargon of dynamic econometrics, this gap variable is a non-linear error-correction mechanism. Further, this term specifies the inherent long-run manufacturing-productivity equilibrium as productive homogeneity. However, such a state is only approached asymptotically over time. The long-run adjustment path is the familiar logistic function, where the target represents the ceiling towards which the adjustment converges (see Martin).[9]

Finally we shall endeavour to capture technological spin-off effects of military expenditure by including this variable directly as a determinant of technological change, $\lambda_3 m_t$. It should be noted that although military expenditure is included because of the spin-off argument, it may also have a Keynesian demand-expansion effect and we cannot distinguish these two mechanisms with this model.

Combining these elements:

$$\Delta p = -\lambda_1(q_{-1} - \beta_2 t) - \lambda_2 G_{t-1} + \lambda_3 m_t \tag{16.8b}$$

and our full model for GDP growth takes the form

$$\Delta q_t \equiv g_t = \alpha_2 \bar{n} + \alpha_3 (v i_t - \delta) - \lambda_1 q_{t-1} \ldots$$
$$\ldots + \lambda_1 \beta_2 t - \lambda_2 G_{t-1} - \beta_1 \Delta u_t + \lambda_3 m_t \tag{16.8c}$$

Removing the first difference restriction on unemployment, the estimating equation takes the form:

$$g = c_0 + c_1 i + c_2 u + c_3 u_{-1} + c_4 m_t + c_5 q_{-1} \ldots$$
$$\ldots + c_6 t + c_7 G_{-1} \tag{16.9}$$

The intercept c_0 ($= \alpha_2 n - \alpha_3 \delta$) represents a mixture of effects, thus we have no prior expectations concerning its sign. *A priori* c_1 ($= \alpha_3 v$), c_3 ($= \beta_1$) and c_6 ($= \lambda_1 \beta_2$) should be positive, as should c_4 ($= \lambda_3$) if military spin-off contributes to growth, while c_2 ($= -\beta_1$), c_5 ($= -\lambda_1$) and c_7 ($= \lambda_2$) should be negative. Note, if the specification of the model is correct, c_2 and c_3 should be of roughly equal magnitude and opposite in sign.

4   Simultaneous Equation Systems

The simultaneous system we propose to study is composed of the investment, unemployment and growth equations derived above (equations 16.1, 16.2 and 16.9 respectively). The complete system is thus:

$$i = a_0 + a_1 g + a_2 m + a_3 u + a_4 i_{-1} \tag{16.10a}$$

$$u = b_0 + b_1 g + b_2 m + b_3 u_{-1} + b_4 E + b_5 t \tag{16.10b}$$

$$g = c_0 + c_1 i + c_2 u + c_3 u_{-1} + c_4 m + c_5 q_{-1} \ldots$$
$$\ldots + c_6 t + c_7 G_{-1} \tag{16.10c}$$

The growth equation is just identified, the other two over-identified. The impact multipliers of military expenditure on the three endogenous variables are:

$$\frac{\partial g}{\partial m} = \pi_3 = \frac{c_1 a_2 + c_1 a_3 b_2 + b_2 c_2 + c_4}{1 - c_1 a_1 - c_1 a_3 b_1 - c_2 b_1} \qquad (16.11a)$$

$$\frac{\partial u}{\partial m} \equiv \pi_2 = b_1 \pi_3 + b_2 \qquad (16.11b)$$

$$\frac{\partial i}{\partial m} \equiv \pi_1 = (a_1 + a_3 b_1)\, \pi_3 + a_2 + a_3 b_2 \qquad (16.11c)$$

If the system is stable, that is, with roots which lie within the unit circle, the long-run multipliers from the final form give the effect of military expenditure when all the dynamic adjustment processes have worked through the system.

The long-run multipliers are:

$$\partial g/\partial m \equiv \phi_3 = \frac{a_2 c_1(1 - b_3) + b_2 a_3 c_1 + b_2(c_2 + c_3)\,(1 - a_4) + c_4(1 - a_4)\,(1 - b_3)}{(1 - a_4)\,(1 - b_3) - a_1 c_1\,(1 - b_3) - b_1 a_3 c_1 - b_1\,(c_2 + c_3)\,(1 - a_4)}$$

$$(16.12a)$$

$$\partial u/\partial m \equiv \phi_2 = \frac{1}{1 - b_3}\,\{b_1 \phi_3 + b_2\} \qquad (16.12b)$$

$$\partial i/\partial m \equiv \phi_1 = \frac{1}{(1 - a_4)\,(1 - b_3)}\,\{[a_1\,(1 - b_3) + a_3 b_1]\,\Phi_3 + b_2 a_3 + a_2(1 - b_3)\}$$

$$(16.12c)$$

It could be argued that the lagged effects which arise from the level of GDP, q_{-1}, should also be allowed for (when calculating these final-form multipliers); but, given our interpretation of this variable (in terms of an error-correction process), this does not seem appropriate.

III   ECONOMETRIC RESULTS

The system described in the previous section was estimated over the period 1954–82, for France and the UK by Three Stage Least Squares (3SLS). Definitions of the variables and results are given in the appendix to this chapter. A single system was estimated for the two countries together to allow for non-zero disturbance co-variances as a result of international influences to which both countries were subject.

Initially, some investigations of the specification was carried out using Ordinary Least Squares (OLS). This indicated that investment had a negative effect on growth in the French equation, and since this conflicts with standard economic theory, a zero coefficient was imposed. Inspection of the results also suggested that 1954 and 1955 were outliers and this was allowed for using a dummy variable for those two years denoted D55. This effect may be associated with the military activity at the time, post-Korea for the UK and Indo-China for France.

The regression results are shown in appendix Tables 16.1A–16.1C. The investment and unemployment equations fit well in both countries, the growth equation less well, but this is not unusual; there are severe difficulties in explaining growth. The system was subjected to a variety of diagnostic tests, which are described and reported in the appendix. Apart from some suggestion of higher-order effects in the unemployment equation there is no indication of serial correlation. Structural stability is accepted for France in all six tests. For the UK, there is an indication that the growth equation may have shifted in 1959 and the unemployment equation in 1973, but in both cases the null hypothesis of stability can be accepted at the 1 per cent level.

Except for the zero coefficient on investment in France, which was imposed, all the structural coefficients estimated have their expected signs. As the theory predicts, the coefficients of current and lagged unemployment in the growth equation have opposite signs. The hypothesis that the unemployment coefficients are equal with opposite signs can be accepted for the UK ($F = 0.072$) but is rejected for France ($F = 4.39$).

Overall, the differences between the estimates for the two countries are not large. Equality of the coefficients in the British and French investment equations can be accepted at the 5 per cent level ($F = 1.39$) and in the unemployment equations at the 1 per cent level ($F = 2.73$). Even in the growth equation where equality is rejected at the 1 per cent level, the test statistic ($F = 8.64$) is not that large given the extreme nature of the hypothesis tested.

The narrower hypothesis – that the coefficients of military expenditure are the same in both countries – can be accepted in all three equations at the 5 per cent level. Thus there is no evidence from these results that the effect of military expenditure differs between France and the UK. In both countries the structural coefficients indicate that military expenditure is associated with reduced investment, increased unemployment and higher growth in the first instance; though only the French investment and unemployment coefficient are significant.

The major problem with these results is that the UK estimates imply unstable dynamic behaviour. Whereas for France the roots of -0.59 and -0.91 indicate stability, those for the UK of -0.825 and -2.42 indicate explosive divergence. The UK instability seems to arise primarily from the coefficient of 1.01 on the lagged dependent variable in the unemployment equation. When the system is unstable, the long-run multipliers are undefined because the system does not return to an equilibrium after an exogenous shock.

The multipliers can be calculated either from the 'restricted reduced form', which is derived from the estimated structural equations, or the 'unrestricted reduced form', obtained by the regression of the endogenous variables on the whole set of predetermined variables. The estimates from the restricted reduced form will be more efficient if the over-identifying restrictions imposed on the structural equations are correct. There are five over-identifying restrictions on the UK system and six on the French. Since the failure of stability casts doubt on the specification, the unrestricted reduced form was also estimated and the results are given in the appendix, Tables 16.2A and 16.2B.

In comparing the two sets of estimates, it is noticeable that the estimated standard errors of regression (SER) are very similar between structural and reduced-form equations except in the case of UK unemployment, where the reduced form SER is considerably smaller. In general, the estimated coefficients of military expenditure are more precisely determined in the reduced-form estimates than in the structural estimates. The military expenditure coefficients are significantly different from zero at the 5 per cent level in all three UK equations, and all except the investment equation for France. This is exactly the reverse of the pattern in the structural coefficients. The differences between the reduced-form and structural estimates could be exploited through the use of a variety of statistical tests. For instance, conditional on the exogeneity assumptions, the over-identifying restrictions could be tested; or, conditional on the over-identifying restrictions, exogeneity could be tested. However, the small-sample properties of these tests are poor, and given the degree of prior belief in the specifications, it is not clear how revealing they would be.

The results are summarised in Table 16.1. This gives the various estimates of the coefficients of military expenditure. The structural coefficients measure the direct effect; the impact multipliers the effect in the current year, once allowance has been made for the simultaneous feedbacks through the endogenous variables. The long-run multipliers allow for the total effect once the dynamic responses through lagged endogenous variables have been allowed for. Long-run multipliers are not given for the UK because the

Table 16.1   The impact of military expenditure

		i	u	g
Structural coefficients				
UK		−0.290	0.560	0.070
France		−0.500	0.360	0.650
Impact multipliers				
UK	A	−1.580	2.090	− 6.950
	B	−0.650	1.180	− 3.940
France	A	−1.050	0.710	− 2.930
	B	−0.660	0.820	− 5.310
Long-run multipliers				
UK	A	−	−	−
	B	−0.686	1.025	− 2.400
France	A	−9.700	6.700	−14.500
	B	−2.350	1.380	− 3.190

Notes: A   From restricted reduced form
         B   From unrestricted reduced form
         i share of gross fixed capital formation in GDP
         u proportion of labour force unemployed
         g The change in the logarithm of constant price GDP

structural system is unstable. The unrestricted reduced form is stable for both countries, with convergent cyclical solution for France.

Cross-section results (for example, Smith)[10] suggest that military expenditure has a strong negative effect on investment; a small direct positive effect on growth, but a negative total effect on growth when allowance is made for the linkage through investment; and no clear relation with unemployment. The results in Table 16.1 are broadly consistent with this pattern as far as growth and investment are concerned; but the negative effects of military expenditure seem implausibly large by comparison with cross-section estimates. The result – that higher military expenditure tends to be associated with higher unemployment – is not in accord with the cross-section results.

It should be remembered that all government policy multipliers are sensitive to the Lucas critique. Large changes in military expenditure are likely to change the patterns of private sector behaviour and thus the coefficients on which the estimates are based. This is the reason that wartime observations are usually regarded as being the product of a different regime. It is unlikely, however, that this would be a serious problem for inferences about the effect of changes of the same order of magnitude as those observed over the sample period.

IV   CONCLUSION

Econometric results always have to be treated with some caution, but the quantitative conclusion suggested by these estimates is that military expenditure tends to be associated with reduced investment and increased unemployment, and that these damaging effects are magnified when the system feedbacks are taken into account. With respect to growth: the direct effect of military expenditure, whether through technological spin-off or demand expansion, is positive, but this is more than offset by the negative indirect effects through investment and unemployment. Thus the net effect is for higher military expenditure to be associated with lower growth. These conclusions are broadly in line with previous empirical results. Interestingly there was no significant difference between the direct effects of military expenditure in Britain and France.

These results can be regarded as a useful contribution to a general strategy of investigating the effects of military expenditure from as many different perspectives as possible. This is the strategy of methodological pluralism advocated in Fontanel and Smith.[11] The results in this paper can be regarded as complementary to those in Aben and Smith.[12] The two studies try to bracket the question by doing both aggregate time-series analysis and disaggregated input–output analysis. However, the questions about the relative advantages of aggregate time-series analysis against other methods of investigation remain.

Although the results are useful, they have obvious limitations. They are dependent on the particular theoretical model used as a framework for estimation, and other models might produce different results. In particular the effect of variables excluded from the model will be attributed to military expenditure, to the extent that they are correlated with it. Clearly, there is no shortage of potential excluded variables; but testing for their inclusion raises the familiar difficulties of specification searching, multicollinearity and interpretative complexity. The use of a single aggregate variable, the share of military expenditure in output, is very limited. The presence of conscription, the balance between personnel and equipment, the use of domestic or imported weapons, and all the other details of defence posture will have a differential effect. The aggregate time-series results can only capture simple empirical regularities. Finally, the degree of aggregation means that relatively little is revealed about the detailed transmission mechanisms involved. Nonetheless, despite these limitations, the results provide a little more information on the impact of military expenditure.

APPENDIX

Variables

Unless otherwise specified the data are taken from OECD National Accounts Statistics, or national sources.

i :   Gross fixed capital formation as a proportion of GDP
u :   the proportion of the labour force unemployed
g :   the change in the logarithm of constant price GDP
m :   military expenditure as a share of GDP (SIPRI)
E :   growth rate of exports (OECD)
G :   logarithm of manufacturing productivity differential between the USA and UK/France
$D55$:   dummy variable for 1954 and 1955
t :   time trend
q :   logarithm of real GDP
Estimation period: 1954–1982

Statistics

$\bar{R}^2$ is the coefficient of determination corrected for degrees of freedom. With 3SLS estimates the interpretation of this statistic is not straightforward.

SER is the Standard Error of Regression.

DW is the Durbin Watson Statistic which tests for First Order Serial Correlation.

LMF( ) are small sample versions of a Lagrange Multiplier test for higher order serial correlation. They are obtained by regressing the equation residuals on 4 and 2 lagged residuals plus equation regressors. The *F* statistic given (with degrees of freedom in parentheses) tests that the coefficients of the lagged residuals are zero.

SSF( ) are tests for structural stability. The sample is split at the year given and an *F* statistic calculated for the hypothesis that the coefficients are the same in the two subperiods. The 1959 break is suggested by the return to convertibility by European countries, the formation of the EEC, and in the case of France the change from old to new SNA. The oil price increase and the demise of the Bretton-Woods system suggest the 1973 break.

For the *3SLS* results, *F* statistics are given to test the hypotheses:
1. The coefficients of military expenditure are the same in each country;
2. All the coefficients in the equation are the same.

356

Table 16.1A   Three Stage Least Squares results: investment

	UK		France	
Const	0.056	(1.47)	0.12	(2.72)
g_t	0.147	(3.47)	0.133	(1.77)
u_t	−0.13	(−2.51)	−0.23	(−2.08)
i_{-1}	0.79	(6.25)	0.59	(4.62)
$D55$	0.0003	(0.06)	−0.005	(−1.16)
m_t	−0.29	(−1.18)	−0.50	(−2.4)
$\bar{R}^2$	0.9040		0.9350	
$SER \times 100$	0.427		0.390	
DW	2.199		1.60	
$LMF(4)$	1.16	(4.19)	1.06	(4.19)
$LMF(2)$	1.88	(2.21)	0.65	(2.21)
SSF (1959)	0.226	(6.18)	1.69	(6.18)
SSF (1973)	2.28	(9.15)	2.64	(9.15)

Cross-country Parameter Equality Tests

1. $M(UK) = M(FC)$ $F_0(1,131) = 0.630$
2. $a_i(UK) = a_i(FC)$ $F_0(6,131) = 1.39$

Note: t statistics for coefficients and degrees of freedom for tests are given in parentheses.

Table 16.1B   Three Stage Least Square results: unemployment

	UK		France	
Const	−1.93	(−1.23)	−2.34	(−2.57)
g_t	−0.22	(−2.71)	−0.12	(−3.76)
t	0.00097	(1.24)	0.0012	(2.59)
E_t	−0.021	(−1.12)	−0.0063	(−1.44)
u_{-1}	1.01	(6.34)	0.73	(7.55)
D55	−0.008	(−1.02)	0.0054	(2.09)
m_t	0.56	(1.27)	0.36	(1.96)
$\bar{R}^2$	0.9234		0.9915	
$SER \times 100$	0.649		0.159	
DW	2.02		2.41	
LMF(4)	7.91 (4,18)**		3.45 (4,18)*	
LMF(2)	4.04 (2,20)*		6.09 (2,20)**	
SSF (1959)	0.127 (6,17)		0.170 (6,17)	
SSF (1973)	3.28		1.65 (9,14)	

Cross-country Parameter Equality Tests

1. $M(UK) = M(FC)$ $F_0(1,131) = 0.189$
2. $b_i(UK) = b_i(FC)$ $F_0(7,131) = 2.73*$
            *reject at 5%   **reject at 1%

Table 16.1C   Three Stage Least Square: GDP growth

	UK		France	
Const	−34.76	(−3.52)	−29.62	(−2.22)
i_t	1.89	(4.26)	–	–
u_t	−1.93	(−5.25)	−5.03	(−4.20)
u_{t-1}	1.80	(5.67)	3.07	(4.31)
q_{t-1}	−0.96	(−4.89)	−0.24	(−2.35)
G_{t-1}	−0.077	(−2.16)	−0.029	(−1.64)
t	0.023	(3.78)	0.017	(2.27)
D55	0.019	(1.61)	0.015	(0.74)
m_t	0.07	(0.09)	0.65	(0.52)
$\bar{R}^2$	0.6792		0.6908	
$SER \times 100$	0.10		0.90	
DW	2.13		2.13	
LMF(4)	0.68 (4,16)		0.35 (4,17)	
LMF(2)	0.15 (2,18)		0.25 (2,19)	
SSF (1959)	4.29 (6,15)*		2.28 (6,15)	
SSF (1973)	1.6 (9,12)		0.314 (9,13)	

Cross-country Parameter Equality Tests

1. $M(\text{UK}) = M(\text{FC})$ $F_0(1,131) = 0.198$
2. $C_i(\text{UK}) = C_i(\text{FC})$ $F_0(9,131) = 8.644^{**}$
   *reject at 5%   **reject at 1%

Table 16.2A   Unrestricted reduced form

	UK		
	i	*u*	*g*
m	−0.646	1.184	−3.935
	(−2.3)	(3.7)	(−4.8)
E	0.040	−0.062	0.218
	(2.4)	(−3.2)	(4.4)
t	−0.007	0.013	−0.008
	(4.0)	(6.8)	(−1.5)
*D*55	−0.001	−0.005	0.035
	(−0.3)	(−1.0)	(2.5)
q_{-1}	0.235	−0.401	0.007
	(4.0)	(−5.9)	(0.04)
G_{-1}	−0.024	0.040	−0.225
	(−1.32)	(1.9)	(−4.1)
u_{-1}	0.099	0.32	0.631
	(0.54)	(1.5)	(1.2)
i_{-1}	0.200	0.71	−1.300
	(0.925)	(2.8)	(−2.0)
Const	10.73	−21.51	15.35
	(4.0)	(−6.94)	(1.91)
$\bar{R}^2$	0.9099	0.9599	0.7115
DW	2.16	1.75	2.34
SER × 100	0.396	0.457	1.182

Table 16.2B   Unrestricted reduced form

	France		
	i	u	g
m	−0.655	0.818	−5.305
	(−1.4)	(3.7)	(−4.4)
E	0.018	−0.008	−0.011
	(1.1)	(−1.1)	(−0.3)
t	−0.001	0.003	0.007
	(−0.2)	(1.8)	(0.7)
$D55$	−0.008	0.015	−0.080
	(−1.1)	(4.25)	(−4.2)
q_{-1}	0.003	−0.021	0.260
	(0.1)	(−0.7)	(−1.7)
G_{-1}	0.001	0.010	0.106
	(0.1)	(1.8)	(−3.6)
u_{-1}	−0.211	0.577	−0.248
	(−0.5)	(3.0)	(−0.2)
I_{-1}	0.595	0.099	−1.047
	(3.3)	(1.2)	(−2.3)
Const	1.6	−5.7	−9.1
	(0.3)	(−2.0)	(−0.6)
$\bar{R}^2$	0.9472	0.9885	0.6273
DW	1.56	2.16	1.80
$SER \times 100$	0.381	0.179	0.975

Notes and References

* We are grateful for financial support from the Centre Nationale de la Recherche Scientifique and the Economic and Social Research Council for a collaborative study on the defence efforts in France and the UK.

1. Kormendi, R. C. 'Government Debt, Government Spending and Private Sector Behaviour', *American Economic Review*, vol. 73, no. 5 (December, 1983) pp. 994–1000.
2. Leontief, W. *et al.* 'The Economic Impact – Industrial and Regional – of an Arms Cut', *Review of Economics and Statistics*, vol. 47, (August 1965) pp. 217–41.
3. Aben, J. 'Désarmement, Activité et Emploi' *Défense Nationale*, (mai 1981) pp. 105–23.
4. Dunne, J. P. and Smith, R. 'The Economic Consequences of Reduced Military Expenditure', *Cambridge Journal of Economics* (September 1984).
5. Smith, R. P. 'Military Expenditure and Investment in OECD Countries 1954–1973', *Journal of Comparative Economics*, vol. 4, 1980, pp. 19–32.
6. Smith (see note 5).
7. Cornwall, J. 'Diffusion, Convergence and Kaldor's Laws', *Economic Journal*, 86 (June 1976) pp. 307–14.
8. Marris, R. 'How Much of the Slow Down was Catch-up?' in RCO Matthews (ed.), *Slower Growth in the Western World* (London: National Institute of Economic and Social Research, 1982).
9. Martin, S. 'Convergence as an Empirical Determinant of Long-run Productivity Growth', Birkbeck Discussion Paper no. 158 (1984).
10. Smith, R. P. 'Military Expenditure and Capitalism: A Reply', *Cambridge Journal of Economics*, Vol. 2 (Sep 1978) 299–304.
11. Fontanel, J. and Smith, R. 'Analyse économique des dépenses militaire', *Stratégique*, no. 3, 1985, pp. 73–116 and Fontanel, J., 'Formalised Studies and Econometric Analysis of the Relationship between Military Expenditure and Economic Development', *United Nations*, 1980.
12. Aben, J. and Smith, R. P. 'Defence and Employment in the UK and France' (this volume).

COMMENT

H. de Haan
FACULTEIT DER ECONOMISCHE WETENSCHAPPEN,
RIJKSUNIVERSITEIT

In such a model as that of *Martin, Smith and Fontanel*, there is a case for disaggregating military expenditure, at least into such components as research and development, investment, consumption, etc. Different parts of military expenditure will have very different impacts on growth and employment.

Further, in the analysis of the effects of military expenditure, it is important to compare the situation with an alternative in which civil expenditure of one kind or another takes the place of military expenditure. This can, of course, be considered particularly for R & D – where, for example, there are very big variations between countries in the share of total R & D taken by the military. So it is important to think of alternatives.

In all these models, it will of course, make a difference whether the general model is neoclassical or Keynesian – particularly in such questions as long-term employment effects from changes in Government expenditure. The point was made that time-series econometrics is unlikely to pick up the effects of research and development, whether military or other – simply because of the very long and variable time-lags: any specific research project is likely to have effects on the macroeconomy with time-lags which can vary between five and thirty years, or indeed more.

17 NATO Burden-sharing: Rules or Reality?*

Todd Sandler
IOWA STATE UNIVERSITY

In 1978 and again in 1985, the NATO ministers pledged to increase their real military expenditures by 3 per cent per year. The purpose of this paper is to demonstrate that fixed-percentage pledges of this kind are unworkable policies since they do not account for an ally's income cycles, its incentive to rely (or to free ride) on other allies' military expenditures, or an ally's contingencies or future threats. A secondary, but related, purpose here is to re-examine what the true determinants of defence burdens are. To accomplish this task, we formulate a reduced-form demand equation for an ally's defence expenditures, and then present ordinary-least-squares estimates of this equation for nine NATO allies. The estimated coefficients of these equations are used to forecast real growth in defence expenditures. These predicted growth rates are in significant contrast with the fixed 3-per-cent pledges. Except for the USA, no ally is predicted to come near to their agreed-upon pledges.

I INTRODUCTION

In the face of an ever-increasing perceived Soviet military threat, the North Atlantic Treaty Organisation (NATO) allies pledged in 1978 to increase their *real* military expenditures by 3 per cent annually. This pledge was given in a NATO ministerial meeting where a long-term defence programme was discussed. The purpose of this paper is to demonstrate that fixed percentage pledges of the kind solicited in 1978 and reiterated in May 1985 are unworkable policies since they do not account for an ally's income cycles, its incentives to rely (or to 'free ride') on other allies' military expenditures, or an ally's contingencies or future threats (for example, the Falklands War fought

363

by the UK). Hence, this paper argues that fixed pledges are naive policies that ignore the underlying determinants of defence expenditures and, consequently, are doomed to failure. With the exception of the USA and the UK, none of the NATO allies came near to fulfilling their 3 per cent pledge. This chapter explains why.

A secondary, but related, purpose here is to re-examine what are the true determinants of defence burdens. In so doing, we formulate and test a reduced-form demand equation for defence expenditures of a nation belonging to an alliance. We then present ordinary least squares (OLS) estimates of this equation for nine NATO allies for the period 1955–1981. Burden-sharing behaviour is also examined using non-parametric statistical tests on cross-sectional data. These latter tests, when taken in conjunction with our time-series regressions, provide a fuller picture of burden-sharing behaviour.

II TWO MODELS OF DEFENCE EXPENDITURES FOR ALLIES

1 Two Models

When analysing alliance behaviour, economists have called attention to the free-rider problem where smaller allies rely on the larger allies for defence protection.[1] That is, large allies take on a disproportionately large defence burden. This hypothesis is based on the notion of a pure public good.

A pure public good exhibits two crucial characteristics. First, the benefits of the good are *non-rival in consumption*. This means that more than one nation (or individual) can simultaneously consume the *same unit* of the good without detracting from the benefits available to others. Consider the case of deterrence, which is typically characterised as purely public. The threat of punishment embodied in NATO's strategic triad can protect any number of allies. Taking additional allies under the deterrent umbrella does not *necessarily* diminish the protection of the original allies, provided that the retaliatory threat is credible.

The second characteristic of a pure public good is that it is prohibitively expensive to exclude nations (allies) from using the good once it is provided. This characteristic of *non-excludability* leads to the free-rider problem, since both contributors and non-contributors receive the good's full benefits. Obviously, in the absence of exclusion, it is in many nations' self-interest to undercontribute to the public good, knowing that the contributions of others will provide enough of the good for their needs. Such selfish behaviour allows the free riders to spend their scarce resources on other things, which they cannot get without contributing. Again consider deterrence. Once a strategic triad is deployed and the associated threat is credible, it is not always possible to deny an ally protection. Because of fallout, misses, and wind direction, a nuclear attack on Canada would kill millions in the USA. Clearly, the USA could not deny Canada deterrent protection. Judging from Canadian defence burdens,[2] the Canadians are aware of this and are free riders, relying on the USA for their protection. In general, however, the second characteristic of pure publicness is less certain to apply to deterrence. It applies whenever an attack on a nation's allies inflict unacceptable damage, in terms of fallout or the loss of foreign investment interests and/or military personnel, on the nation(s) providing the deterrence.

Researchers have found strong evidence of free riding in NATO throughout the 1950s and during the first half of the 1960s.[3] In particular, the wealthy allies shouldered the defence burdens of the smaller, poorer allies who rode free. Throughout the 1950s and 1960s over 90 per cent of the NATO defence burden, when calculated as a proportion of total NATO defence expenditures, fell on the four largest allies – that is, the USA, the UK, France and the Federal Republic of Germany. These results follow because, during the 1950s and 1960s, NATO relied on its strategic arsenal to deter the USSR's use of conventional forces in Western Europe, since NATO's conventional forces were no match against Soviet tanks and ground troops.

In the 1970s and 1980s, there has been a closing of the 'share gap'. To explain this closing, researchers have put forth a *joint product* model, which generalises the pure public good model by allowing an ally's arsenal to produce more than one output.[4] In particular, an arsenal provides deterrence, damage-limiting protection (needed when deterrence fails and conflict begins), and private or country-specific benefits. Each of these three types of benefit possesses varying degrees of publicness. For example, most country-specific benefits must be paid for by the nation itself if it is ever to receive the benefits. Conventional forces are not purely public, since they are subject to *thinning* as the same-sized arsenal is spread along a longer perimeter. In other words, the degree of protection provided by a conventional arsenal, unlike deterrent missiles, depends on how much land or border is being defended. The addition of an ally with large areas needing defending (for example, Spain in 1980) would diminish the damage-limiting capabilities of an alliance arsenal, unless sufficient armaments are added. Moreover, conventional forces and their damage-limiting benefits can be withheld at will. This degree of excludability also cuts down on intra-alliance free riding for conventional forces.

The joint product model predicts that the extent of free riding is inversely related to the proportion of excludable defence outputs produced by the arsenal.[5] Alliances whose sole purpose is deterrence would be characterised by many free riders; an alliance whose primary purpose is country-specific or damage-limiting protection would have fewer. If the proportion of excludable defence outputs grew in the late 1970s and in the 1980s, then the closing of the share gap can be explained. Any viable alliance will always produce a certain amount of deterrence. Even in the presence of purely public outputs, free riding is still reduced, whenever the deterrence-producing weapons need to work in conjunction with the conventional weaponry. Benefits or goods that are best consumed together are termed complements (for example, missiles and missile launchers). If deterrent weapons are now complementary to conventional weaponry, then an increase in spillins (for example, increased deterrence provided by one's allies) may stimulate the ally's demand for its own conventional forces. Thus, we view the joint product model as more volatile than the pure-public-good model since changes in strategy and/or technology, by altering the mix of joint products, can create significant differences in an ally's demand for military expenditure.

During the period 1970–4, the NATO alliance changed is emphasis from a strategy of mutual assured destruction (MAD) to one of flexible response. The flexible response doctrine is not new, but a great deal of new interest has been and is being shown in it since 1970.[6] This doctrine allows NATO to respond in different ways to a Warsaw Pact challenge; conventional forces or strategic forces may be used and, in the latter case, a missile exchange may be limited or complete. With this doctrine, the European allies must be prepared to defend themselves against conventional aggression in the European theatre, since the initial stages of warfare are expected to involve conventional and tactical nuclear weapon exchanges. No longer can these allies rely solely on nuclear weapons' deterrence for their external security. An ally which does not increase its military activity in response to other allies' increased military activities could invite aggression, since an opposing alliance might have a better chance to gain an advantage in a conventional war fought on that ally's soil. By tying warfare to a sequence of measured responses involving the deployment of all three kinds of weaponry, flexible response enhances the importance of the conventional, non-nuclear arsenals relative to strategic deterrence. The nuclear and non-nuclear arsenals contribute to one another's value; they become Hicksian complements and must therefore be used together.

This increased complementarity affects an ally's defence expenditure response as the rest of the alliance increase their expenditures; in particular, increases in one's allies' expenditures (or spillins) could increase an ally's own defence expenditures.[7] This positive spillin effect holds when the complementarity influence is strong and outweighs the diminishing marginal rate of substitution (MRS) influence to substitute out of defence expenditures in response to spillins. For normal goods, the income effect, associated with spillins, will reinforce any complementarity influence, thus pushing the spillin effect in the positive direction. A positive spillin prediction would hold for most non-nuclear allies, but would not apply to the same extent to the nuclear allies. The nuclear allies provide all three classes of weapon and, unlike the non-nuclear allies, can substitute their military expenditure for those of any of the other allies. The doctrine of flexible response may actually enhance the ability of nuclear allies to ride free if, as appears to be the case, strategic weapon budgets are increased as a proportion of these allies' total defence expenditures. This follows because relatively more non-excludable benefits are then produced.

A non-nuclear ally who can still ride free even under the doctrine of flexible response is the crucial flanking nation of the Federal Republic of Germany, whose strategic position requires NATO troops to be stationed on its soil. In 1984, 330 000 troops from other NATO allies were stationed on German soil.[8] To a smaller extent, Italy also receives NATO troops because of its flanking nation position; in 1984, 3800 non-Italian NATO troops were on Italian soil. These allied forces relieve pressures somewhat for these flanking allies to provide their own forces.

2   The Demand for Military Expenditures Equation

We now utilise the joint product model to derive a demand for military expenditure equation for an ally. Consider an n-country alliance like that of NATO. For a representative ally, let x stand for the private defence output, z for the public defence output (that is, deterrence), and q for the military activity. The joint product relationships are:

$$x = f(q) \tag{17.1}$$

and

$$z = g(q) \tag{17.2}$$

where $dx/dq = f' > 0$ and $dz/dq = g' > 0$, where both $f(q)$ and $g(q)$ are strictly concave, twice continuously differentiable functions.[9]

An ally is assumed to take the amount of deterrence ($\tilde{Z}$) provided by the other allies as given when choosing its own level of military activity. Thus, Nash–Cournot behaviour is hypothesised to characterise participants.[10] Deterrence spillins are the difference between alliance-wide deterrence (Z) and the deterrence provided by the representative ally, so that:

$$Z = \tilde{Z} + z \tag{17.3}$$

The level of $\tilde{Z}$ that spills in is a function of the *aggregate* military activity (Q) of the *other* allies. Hence:

$$\tilde{Z} = h(Q) \tag{17.4}$$

in which $h' > 0$ and $h'' < 0$.

The preferences of a representative, though not necessarily identical, ally are depicted by a well-behaved, strictly concave, non-satiable utility function:

$$U = U(y, x, Z; E) = U(y, x, \tilde{Z} + z; E), \tag{17.5}$$

where y is a private numeraire activity and E is a shift parameter, denoting environmental changes. In particular, E includes changes in either strategic doctrine or external threat. Using (17.1), (17.2) and (17.4), the utility function can be expressed in terms of activity space:

$$V = V(y, q, Q; E). \tag{17.6}$$

To derive an ally's demand equation for military activities, (17.6) must be maximised subject to the budget constraint:

$$I = y + pq, \tag{17.7}$$

where I is the nation's income, p is the relative costliness of the military activity, and the price of good y is one. Finding the first-order conditions and invoking the implicit function theorem yield an ally's demand for military activity.

$$q = q(I, p, Q; E). \tag{17.8}$$

An alternative specification of the budget constraint permits us to account for the influence of one of the primary inputs – that is, oil – on military activity. This specification is:

$$R(O) + I = y + C(O)q, \tag{17.9}$$

where O represents the price of oil, $C(O)$ is the unit cost of military activity (assuming constant returns to scale), and $R(O)$ is a nation's net oil revenue (positive for exporters and zero for importers). Maximising (17.6) subject to (17.9) yields the alternative demand specification,

$$q = q(I, R(O), C(O), Q; E) = q(I, O, Q; E). \tag{17.10}$$

Changes in the price of oil give a host of effects which depends on the elasticity of substitution, income effects, and substitution effects. The specification in (17.9) and (17.10) assume that oil prices impinge on the military sector differently from the way they impinge on the non-military sector, thus yielding relative price changes. Input substitution possibilities exist for both sectors when the price of oil rises, but are assumed to be more limited in the military sector.

Equation (17.11) denotes the basic form for the demand for military expenditure equation, estimated in section III.

$$ME = F(PRICE, INCOME, SPILLIN, OIL, E) \qquad (17.11)$$

There are five primary influences or variables that determine an ally's military expenditure (ME). As for all demand relationships, military expenditure depends on the relative price (P) of military goods as compared with all other goods. Because countries do not maintain indices of the price of military activity, data on price are not available.[11] $INCOME$, as measured by an ally's GDP, is a crucial determinant of military expenditure. As GDP rises, an ally has both more resources to protect and greater means to provide protection. Thus, we hypothesise that ME and $INCOME$ are positively related, thereby implying that defence is a 'normal' good.

Another influence on an ally's military expenditure is the defence expenditures of the other allies as measured by $SPILL$. For free riders, military expenditure and spillins are negatively related; an increase in spillins causes a decrease in defence expenditure. If this relationship has a coefficient of -1, then a dollar increase in the military expenditure of the other allies serves to replace a dollar of one's own defence spending. This -1 value corresponds to a high degree of free riding. When complementarity exists between allies' arsenals, we would predict a positive relationship or a very small negative relationship between ME and $SPILL$.

In (17.11), we have included oil prices (OIL). Since oil is a major input into an ally's military activity, we would expect that changes in its price would have a 'derived demand' effect. The effect of a change in oil prices depends on whether other fuel sources, whose prices have not risen by as much, are easily substituted for oil. If oil is not easily replaced, then the *quantity* of oil purchased will remain unchanged in spite of the price rise; thus, the higher price will increase the ally's military expenditure on oil. In the short- and medium-run, most allies cannot substitute other fuels for oil, since military equipment (especially conventional forces) runs on oil-based fuels. Hence, we would expect a positive relationship between OIL and ME. It would be expected that this positive relationship would become especially important in the analysis of the period after 1973.

Equation (17.11) also includes environmental factors (E), such as a change in strategic doctrine. Other environmental factors include population and threat, as measured by Warsaw Pact defence expenditure. Increases in either population or threat is hypothesised to increase ME.

III BURDEN-SHARING REALITY: TWO VIEWS

1 Cross-sectional Analysis

This section gives a cross-sectional analysis of (17.11). In particular, we intend to determine which of the hypothesised influences are highly correlated with military expenditures. The use of cross-sectional data requires that we somehow scale the data, so that relative comparisons between countries can be facilitated.[12] Since the primary focus here is on burden-sharing and defence spending, we have chosen to scale the data by the relevant totals of the NATO alliance. This means that each variable measures the 'slice' of the total NATO pie attributed to each ally.

The measures used and their definitions are presented in Table 17.1. *DEFBURDEN* measures an ally's contributions to the total military spending of the alliance. As this measure grows for a particular ally, that ally is shouldering more of the defence burden for the alliance. The remaining variables of Table 17.1 represent some of the hypothesised determinants for defence burdens. The variable *GDPBENEFIT* measures the size of each ally's gross domestic product (*GDP*) is relation to the total income generated by the NATO members. We expect *GDPBENEFIT* and *DEFBURDEN* to be positively and significantly correlated to one another. *POPBENE-FIT*, *EXPOSED*, and *AREA* are also hypothesised to have positive influences on *DEFBURDEN*. Each of these measures represents a benefit to an ally from being in the alliance. *POPBENEFIT* proxies the benefits of saving citizens as a result of forestalling war with an enemy. *EXPOSED* measures the percentage of NATO's total exposed borders attributable to each ally. Luxembourg, for example, is completely surrounded by friendly nations; therefore, it has zero miles of exposed borders. Turkey, however, has many miles exposed to direct attack.

EXPOSED provides for a unique test of our hypothesis concerning the doctrine of flexible response. In the 1950s and 1960s, the miles of exposed borders were relatively unimportant to the NATO allies because deterrence relied primarily on MAD. With the adoption of a flexible response, exposed borders need to be defended. Those allies with more miles to defend are therefore induced to spend more on defence to counter the thinning of their forces. If our hypothesis is correct, then *EXPOSED* and *DEFBURDEN* should be positively

Table 17.1   Description of the variables used in the cross-sectional analysis of military spending

Variable	Description
DEFBURDEN	Defence burden. Calculated as the military spending of the ally divided by the total military spending in NATO (in percentage terms).
GDPBENEFIT	An ally's share of GDP. Calculated as the GDP of the ally divided by the total GDP of NATO (in percentage terms).
POPBENEFIT	An ally's share of population. Calculated as the population of the ally divided by the total population of NATO (in percentage terms).
EXPOSED	An ally's share of NATO's total miles of exposed border (in percentage terms).
AREA	An ally's share of NATO's total land mass (in percentage terms).

Note: All expenditure values were initially expressed in 1980 prices using each country's GDP price deflator and were converted to US dollars using 1980 exchange rates.

Sources: Stockholm International Peace Research Institute, *World Armaments and Disarmament: SIPRI Yearbook* (New York: Crane, Kussak, 1983) and International Monetary Fund, *International Financial Statistics Yearbook* (Washington, DC: IMF, 1983).

correlated during the years under the doctrine of flexible response. In fact, the strength of the relationship should grow as the allies become more adapted to the new doctrine. Many of the same arguments apply to *AREA*, which measures an ally's share of NATO's total land area.

The data for *DEFBURDEN*, *GDPBENEFIT*, *POPBENEFIT*, *EXPOSED*, and *AREA* are presented in Table 17.2 for each ally for the years 1978, 1980, and 1982, respectively. Because the miles of exposed borders and the square miles of land area remain constant over time, these measures are only presented once.

The hypothesis concerning *DEFBURDEN* and *GDPBENEFIT* cannot be rejected on the basis of the estimated correlation coeffi-

Table 17.2 Relative defence burdens and benefits in NATO: 1978, 1980, 1982
(as percentage of total)

Country	DEFBURDEN			GDPBENEFIT			POPBENEFIT			EXPOSED[1]	AREA[1]
	1978	1980	1982	1978	1980	1982	1978	1980	1982		
USA	54.9	56.2	56.7	45.4	44.8	45.0	39.2	39.4	39.7	27.4	42.3
Canada	2.1	1.8	2.1	4.4	4.4	4.3	4.1	4.1	4.2	20.0	45.1
Belgium	1.6	1.5	1.4	2.0	2.1	2.0	1.7	1.7	1.7	0.1	0.1
Denmark	0.6	0.6	0.5	1.2	1.2	1.2	0.9	0.9	0.9	2.2	0.2
France	10.5	10.3	11.4	11.2	11.3	11.5	9.4	9.3	9.3	4.4	2.5
FRG	10.9	10.4	9.1	13.8	14.1	13.9	10.8	10.7	10.5	2.7	1.1
Greece	1.1	0.9	1.3	0.7	0.7	0.7	1.6	1.7	1.7	5.8	0.6
Italy	3.7	3.7	3.4	6.5	6.9	6.8	10.0	9.9	9.6	9.1	1.4
Luxembourg	0.0	0.0	0.0	0.1	0.1	0.1	0.1	0.1	0.1	0.0	0.0
Netherlands	2.1	2.1	1.8	2.9	2.9	2.8	2.5	2.4	2.4	0.9	0.2
Norway	0.7	0.7	0.7	0.9	1.0	1.0	0.7	0.7	0.7	5.7	1.5
Portugal	0.3	0.3	0.4	0.4	0.4	0.5	1.7	1.7	1.7	1.5	0.4
Turkey	1.2	1.0	2.0	1.0	1.0	1.1	7.5	7.7	7.9	10.7	3.5
UK	10.3	10.4	9.1	9.5	9.1	9.0	9.8	9.7	9.5	9.3	1.1

Notes: Columns may not sum to 100 because of rounding errors.
[1]These measures remain constant over time. Kendall's coefficient of concordance is 0.8
for all three years. The Kendall coefficient of concordance measures the degree of
correlation between the variables. The rather high concordance value of 0.8 indicates
that, taken together, all the variables appear to be correlated with one another.

cients (Kendall's tau) between these measures.[13] The correlation coefficient was 0.89 in 1978, 0.85 in 1980, and 0.82 in 1982. In each year the measure is positive and statistically significant at the 0.01 level. The correlation coefficients between *DEFBURDEN* and *POP-BENEFIT* was 0.74 in 1978 and 1980, while increasing somewhat to 0.76 in 1982. These measures are not inconsistent with the hypothesis that population has a significant influence on defence expenditures.

Positive and significant correlations are also evidenced between *DEFBURDEN* and *EXPOSED*. The correlation estimates are 0.38, 0.42 and 0.49 for 1978, 1980 and 1982, respectively. In 1965, the same correlation was only 0.36. The increase in this measure over time is consistent with the hypothesis concerning the doctrine of flexible response. Similar findings are evidenced by the correlation coefficients with respect to *DEFBURDEN* and *AREA*. In 1965, the measure stood at 0.41; by 1978, it was 0.49; and in 1982 it was 0.63. The steady increase in these correlation coefficients agrees with our prediction concerning flexible response. In the time-series analysis, both *EXPOSED* and *AREA* must be dropped since each has remained constant over time.

2 Time-series Analysis

In this section statistical estimates of the military expenditure equations are presented for nine NATO allies. Estimating an equation for each ally requires data for a time period sufficiently long to ensure credibility. The nine allies considered here satisfy this requirement, whereas the other allies do not. The allies in the sample include the USA, the three major Northern European allies (that is, France, UK, and FRG), Belgium, the Netherlands, Denmark, Norway, and Italy. According to Table 17.2, these nine allies accounted for approximately 94 per cent of NATO's total expenditure in 1982; hence, the allies left out of the sample are indeed a minor consideration. Our estimates cover the period of 1955–81.

The variables and their definitions are presented in Table 17.3. All expenditure data are expressed in billions of constant US$, making direct comparisons of the estimates across countries possible. By holding prices and exchange rates constant, the variations in the data are isolated to *real* changes, not changes in currency valuations. *OIL* is the Saudi crude price per barrel. For each ally, the Saudi price has been divided by the country's *GDP* price deflator before being converted to US dollars. Therefore, *OIL* measures the *relative price*

Table 17.3   Definitions of the variables used in the time-series analyses of military spending

Variable	Definition
ME	Military expenditures in 1980 prices. Converted to US dollars using 1980 exchange rates (billions of US dollars).
GDP	Gross domestic product in 1980 prices. Converted to US dollars using 1980 exchange rates (billions of US dollars).
SPILL	Spillins from NATO allies lagged one year. Calculated as total NATO defence spending minus the military expenditures of the country under consideration. Expressed in 1980 prices, converted to US dollars using 1980 exchange rates (billions of US dollars).
THREAT	Military expenditure of the Soviet Union lagged one year. Expressed in 1980 prices using SIPRI's conversion to US\$ (billions of US\$).
POP	Population in millions.
OIL	Saudi crude oil price per barrel. For each country the Saudi price was divided by its GDP price deflator before converted to US\$ using 1980 exchange rates.
D	Dummy variable, equal to zero for the years 1955–73 and equal to one for the years 1974–81.
D·SPILL	*D* times *SPILL*.
D·OIL	*D* times *OIL*.

Sources: Stockholm International Peace Research Institute, *World Armaments and Disarmament: SIPRI Yearbook* (New York: Crane, Kussak, 1983) and International Monetary Fund, *International Financial Statistics Yearbook* (Washington, DC: IMF, 1983).

of oil when compared to all other goods in the country. If the oil prices and other prices change in the same manner year after year, then there will not be any change in *OIL*.

Since the hypothesised relationship of *ME* with *GDP*, *OIL*, and *SPILL* have already been discussed, we focus our remarks on the relationship between *ME* and *D·SPILL*. In section II, we argued that an alliance's strategic doctrine and the mix between conventional and strategic forces determine an ally's response to *SPILL*. In particular, we hypothesised free-riding behaviour for all allies up until NATO's new emphasis on flexible response in the early 1970s. Before this new emphasis, the alliance's reliance on strategic deterrence (MAD) meant the sharing of a purely public benefit, which, in turn, would lead to free riding. This free riding will show up as a significant *negative* coefficient on the spillin term in the ally's demand for *ME*. After this new emphasis, three classes of allies must be distinguished: nuclear allies, non-nuclear flanking allies (FRG and Italy), and all others. For nuclear allies, the doctrine of flexible response allows for greater substitution possibilities, since, for example, the build-up in one ally's strategic stockpile relieves the pressures for another to build up its own stockpile. The flanking allies could also ride free to a greater extent after this new emphasis on flexible response, since they would automatically receive conventional troops from other allies. Under the doctrine, the other non-nuclear allies would find that their conventional forces were complementary to the nuclear nations' strategic and tactical nuclear forces. This complementarity would induce the small non-nuclear allies to ride free *to a smaller extent*; hence, the coefficient of their spillin terms should be positive or less negative after the early 1970s.

Equation (17.11) was estimated in linear form using various possible formulations, in which some influences such as population, threat, and oil prices have been added or dropped. Our remarks focus on the best-case result, reported in Table 17.4. Equation (17.2) denotes the military expenditure equation that we estimated for each of the nine allies:

$$ME = \beta_0 + \beta_1 GDP + \beta_2 SPILL + \beta_2 D{\cdot}SPILL \ldots$$
$$\ldots + \beta_4 OIL + \beta_5 D{\cdot}OIL + \epsilon \qquad (17.12)$$

The term $D{\cdot}SPILL$ is in (17.12) to test for a structural change in an ally's response to spillins occurring after 1973.[14] If such a change occurred, and if the change is in the direction that we predicted, then this would provide evidence not inconsistent with our predicted impact of the doctrine of flexible response. Similarly the term $D{\cdot}OIL$ tests for a structural shift in an ally's response to oil prices after 1973.

Table 17.4 gives the estimated value of the coefficients for each of the independent variables. Out of the fifty-four coefficients estimated, thirty-three are significant at the 0.10 level. Moreover, with the exception of the US equation, the *R*-squares are high, and the

Table 17.4 Estimated coefficients for the military expenditure equations by country: 1955–1981

Independent variable	USA	France	FRG	UK	Belgium	Netherlands	Denmark	Norway	Italy
GDP	0.018	0.016*	0.009	0.015*	0.022*	0.022*	0.006*	0.029*	0.022*
SPILL	0.058	−0.037*	−0.043	−0.010	0.002	0.003	0.002*	0.003*	−0.010*
D·SPILL	−0.927*	−0.038*	−0.049*	−0.005	0.001	0.002	−0.0005	0.001*	−0.008*
OIL	−9.187*	−0.805*	−1.656*	0.380*	0.030	0.055*	−0.028*	0.012	−0.049
D·OIL	11.025*	1.061*	1.820*	−0.219	−0.013	−0.056	0.035*	−0.027*	0.083
Intercept	137.081*	23.985*	34.263*	15.986	0.027	0.578	0.604*	−0.479*	3.822*
R-Square	0.61	0.92	0.77	0.97	0.95	0.95	0.98	0.97	
Durbin-Watson	0.72	1.37	1.13	1.07	1.24	1.34	1.14	1.19	
	0.94								
	1.43								

*Statistically significant alpha level equals 0.10.
Notes: The dependent variable is ME.
Ordinary Least Squares estimates.
OIL included as an independent variable.

Durbin-Watson statistics are in the uncertain range. The addition of the oil measures improves the estimates significantly over previous estimates.[15]

As expected, most of the coefficients on *GDP* are positive and significant. Interestingly, there is a wide variation between allies with respect to their marginal responses to *GDP*. For France, a dollar increase in *GDP* induces a 1.6-cent increase in *real* military expenditure. In FRG, a one-dollar increase in *GDP* induces only a 0.9-cent increase in military spending. Similar to France, the UK's marginal response is 1.5 cents. The USA's reponse to *GDP* is also quite close to that of the other two nuclear allies. Four of the smaller non-nuclear allies had significant marginal responses of 2.2 to 2.9 cents; these included Belgium, Denmark, Italy, and Norway.

The estimated coefficients for *SPILL* and *D·SPILL* are given in the second and third rows of Table 17.4, respectively. The post-1973 responses are calculated *as the sum* of the two coefficients presented. Therefore, for France, the marginal response in the late 1970s and early 1980s is estimated to be −0.075. In FRG this response is −0.092, and in the UK it is −0.015. Of special interest is the USA's post-1973 spillin response of −0.869. This measure indicates that if the US allies increase (decrease) their total military expenditures by one dollar, the USA will respond (holding *GDP* and *OIL* constant) by cutting (raising) its defence spending by 87 cents.

Our hypothesis concerning the doctrine of flexible response cannot be rejected on the basis of our estimated coefficients for *D·SPILL*. For the UK, France, and the USA, the negative sign provides evidence that is not inconsistent with the hypothesis that the new doctrine has enhanced the substitution possibilities of the nuclear allies, causing their free-riding behaviour to worsen. Furthermore, as flanking nations, FRG and Italy were predicted to exhibit free riding. The evidence supports this contention. The positive signs of *D·SPILL* for Belgium, the Netherlands, and Norway suggest increased complementarity between the public and private defence outputs, and reduced free riding in the post-1973 period. Denmark's equation yields the only inexplicable sign with respect to *D·SPILL*.

The results of Table 17.4 also show that a $1 increase in spillins results in a 7.5-cent reduction in military expenditures for France, a 9.2-cent reduction in FRG and a 1.5-cent reduction in the UK.[16] In total, *an increase in one dollar of US expenditures means a reduction of about 18 cents in the Northern European military expenditures.*

Finally, we consider the estimated coefficients on *OIL* and *D·OIL* as presented in the fourth and fifth rows of Table 17.4. To measure the response of the allies to *OIL* in the post-1973 period, it is necessary to sum the coefficients for *OIL* and *D·OIL* in each equation. For France, the response is $(-0.805 + 1.061 =)\ 0.164$ and in the UK it is $(0.380 - 0.219 =)\ 0.161$. The positive response indicates that, as an important input into defence, oil has relatively few substitutes in these countries. Hence, since 1973, increases in oil prices have led to increases in military expenditures for the oil importers as predicted. The *D·OIL* term is positive and significant for the USA, France, FRG, and Denmark. For the other oil importers, the coefficient has the wrong sign, but is insignificant.

The estimated equations reported in Table 17.4 clearly demonstrate that burden-sharing is significantly related to *GDP*, *SPILL*, *OIL*, and changes in environmental factors. True burdens are shared in an interactive fashion, in which allies are keenly aware and responsive to their allies' expenditures and to changes in their environment. Hence, income cycles, strategic policy changes, and oil-price shocks have an influence on an allies' demand for military expenditures.

IV AN ASSESSMENT OF BURDEN-SHARING RULES

In Table 17.5, we report projected *percentage* changes in the three medium-sized allies' military expenditures under different income growth and spillin-growth scenarios. Our forecasts are based on the estimated income and spillin elasticities for 1981 that are computed from Table 17.4. The income elasticities for France, FRG, and the UK are 0.38, 0.27, and 0.31, respectively; the spillin elasticities for France, FRG and the UK are: -0.60, -0.74, and -0.13, respectively. Each of these measures has shown almost no variability since 1975;[17] hence, this stability gives greater credence to our projection procedure. In Table 17.5, four different growth projections are given for the three allies. The range of growth projections has been chosen after intensive review of growth forecasts provided by Chase Manhattan, Data Resources, Inc., OECD, IMF, and others.[18] The current economic climate and the reduced pressures on oil prices have led us to conclude that oil prices will not change appreciably in the near future. We have, therefore, held oil prices constant when computing our forecasts.

Table 17.5 Forecasts of percentage changes in military expenditures for France, FRG, and the UK, based on different scenarios for *GDP* and *SPILL*

% GDP / % SPILL	FRANCE				FRG				UK			
	−1	0	+1	+2	+1	+2	+3	+4	0	+1	+2	+3
−3	1.42	1.80	2.18	2.56	2.49	2.62	2.89	3.30	0.39	0.70	1.01	1.32
−2	0.82	1.20	1.58	1.96	1.75	2.02	2.29	2.56	0.26	0.57	0.88	1.19
−1	0.22	0.60	0.98	1.36	1.01	1.28	1.55	1.82	0.13	0.44	0.75	1.06
0	−0.38	0.00	0.38	0.76	0.27	0.54	0.81	1.08	0.00	0.31	0.62	0.93
+1	−0.98	−0.60	−0.22	0.16	−0.47	−0.20	0.07	0.34	−0.13	0.18	0.49	0.80
+2	−1.58	−1.20	−0.82	−0.44	−1.21	−0.94	−0.67	−0.40	−0.26	0.05	0.36	0.67
+3	−2.18	−1.80	−1.42	−1.04	−1.98	−1.72	−1.45	−1.14	−0.39	−0.08	0.23	0.54

Note: Assuming no change in the price of oil and using the estimated and spillin elasticities for 1981.

The defence-growth forecasts in Table 17.5 are computed by multiplying the projected income growth by the income elasticity and *adding* the resulting product to the product of the spillin elasticity and the spillin growth projection. Seven different spillin scenarios are indicated in the left-most columns varying between −3 and +3 per cent change in spillins. Since all three allies respond negatively to spillins and positively to income, defence projections increase either by moving up each column in Table 17.5 (as spillins fall) or by moving rightwards along each row (as income increases). Insofar as the USA is the major contributor in NATO, the most important determinant of spillins for France, FRG, and the UK is US spending. Currently, US defence-spending increases, coupled with other allies' responses, makes the bottom row of Table 17.5 the most-likely scenario of those displayed. US increased defence-spending is predicted to *keep* the medium-sized allies from achieving their pledges owing to free riding. Table 17.5 indicates that both France and FRG *will cut* their defence expenditures by 1 to 2 per cent under this scenario. The UK will increase its expenditures by less than one-half of 1 per cent. Other entries in Table 17.5 show that under no reasonable scenario will these three allies meet their pledges, provided that their past behaviour can be used to forecast their future actions.

The lesson learned from Table 17.5 is that a spending policy that instructs each ally to pledge a real increase in defence, while ignoring future economic realities and interactive spending behaviour is unworkable and naive. Interactive spending behaviour arises from the publicness of some defence joint products. This publicness leads the major allies to reduce their defence expenditures in response to increases in the defence expenditures of their allies. For fixed pledges to work, spillin elasticities must be zero and income must grow to support the required defence increase.

V CONCLUSIONS

Based on the analysis contained in this paper, we have reached the following conclusions:

1. Under current growth scenarios, no medium-sized ally is expected to come close to their pledged 3 per cent real increase in defence expenditures.

2. A policy that asks allies to meet a targeted real growth in defence expenditures would be a near-impossible task. Sensible policy must account for economic and free-riding behaviour.

3. Every time NATO allies spend $1 less on defence, the USA spends 87 cents more. Moreover, every time the USA spends $1 more, the medium-sized allies (that is, France, FRG, and the UK) in total spend about 18 cents less.

4. The doctrine of flexible response appears to have had a significant effect on NATO's spending behaviour in the 1970s. Conventional weaponry has taken on an increased importance in Western Europe. This is evidenced by the increased influence of the thinning variable as shown by our statistical analysis.

5. Oil-price increases after 1973 were a crucial determinant of defence spending among the NATO allies. For most allies, increases in oil prices raise military spending because of an inability to find suitable substitutes for the higher-priced fuels.

Notes and References

* The author gratefully acknowledges the help of James C. Murdoch who jointly developed the statistical analysis presented in this paper.

1. On public goods and free riding, see the following: Olson, M. and Zeckhauser, R., 'An Economic Theory of Alliances', *Review of Economics and Statistics*, vol. 48, (August 1966) pp. 266–79; Olson, M., *The Logic of Collective Action* (Cambridge, Massachusetts: Harvard University, 1965); Sandler, T., 'Impurity of Defense: An Application to the Economic Theory of Alliances', *Kyklos*, vol. 30 (Fasc. 3, 1977) pp. 443–60; Sandler, T. and Cauley, J., 'On the Economic Theory of Alliances', *Journal of Conflict Resolution*, vol. 19 (June 1975) pp. 330–48; Sandler, T. and Forbes, J. F., 'Burden Sharing, Strategy, and the Design of NATO', *Economic Inquiry*, vol. 18, (July 1980) pp. 425–44; Sandler, T. and Murdoch, J. C., 'Defense Burdens and Prospects for the Northern European Allies', in Denoon, D. (ed.) *Constraints on Strategy: The Economics of Western Security* (New York: Pergamon, 1986); Murdoch, J. C. and Sandler, T., 'A Theoretical and Empirical Analysis of NATO', *Journal of Conflict Resolution*, vol. 26, (June 1982) pp. 199–235; and Murdoch, J. C. and Sandler, T., 'Complementarity, Free Riding, and the Military Expenditures of NATO Allies', *Journal of Public Economics*, vol. 25 (November 1984) pp. 83–101.

2. See Sandler and Forbes (see note 1).

3. Researchers include Olson and Zeckhauser (see note 1) and Sandler and Forbes (see note 1).

4. See Sandler (see note 1), Murdoch and Sandler (1984, see note 1), Sandler and Murdoch (see note 1), and Sandler and Forbes (see note 1).

5. See Sandler and Forbes (see note 1) and Sandler, T. and Culyer, A. J., 'Joint Products and Multijurisdictional Spillovers', *Quarterly Journal of Economics*, vol. 97, (November 1982) pp. 707–16.

6. See the discussion of this doctrine in Murdoch and Sandler (1984, see note 1), pp. 90–1; Sandler and Murdoch (see note 1), footnote 10; and Ball, D., *Déja Vu: The Return to Counterforce in the Nixon Administration* (Los Angeles: California Seminar on Arms Control and Foreign Policy, 1975).

7. See Murdoch and Sandler (1984, see note 1).

8. International Institute for Strategic Studies, *The Military Balance: 1984–1985* (Oxford: Alden Press, 1984).

9. Other joint products, such as damage-limiting protection, can be added to the model. On this issue, see Murdoch and Sandler (1982, see note 1). To avoid undue complications, we stick to just two joint products.

10. McGuire, M. C. and Groth, C. H., 'A Method for Identifying the Public Good Allocation Proceeds Within a Group', *Quarterly Journal of Economics*, vol. 100 (1985).

11. Price can be dropped from the equation without biasing our results, provided that the price of military activities has inflated at the same general rate as that of non-defence activities. Evidence to this effect is provided by Stockholm International Peace Research Institute, *World Armaments and Disarmament: SIPRI Yearbook* (New York: Crane, Kussak, 1983) chap. 8.

12. For this reason, we could not examine the effects of oil prices and spillins until we switched to time-series analysis.

13. Kendall's tau is used, rather than Spearman's rho, because the distribution of the Kendall measure approaches the standard normal distribution for sample sizes greater than 10.

14. In examining the data for structural change, we noted evidence of structural change throughout the period 1969–75, with the peak of the change concentrated in 1974. Hence, we settled on 1974 as the shift year.

15. See Murdoch and Sandler (1984, see note 1) and Sandler and Murdoch (see note 1).

16. We ignore the other allies since in total their spillin influence nets out to a fraction of a one-cent change.

17. Sandler and Murdoch (see note 1) Table 17.22 and 17.23.

18. Sandler and Murdoch (see note 1).

18 Defence and Employment in the UK and France: A Comparative Study of the Existing Results*

Jacques Aben
UNIVERSITY OF MONTPELLIER

and Ron Smith
UNIVERSITY OF LONDON

This chapter reviews the available, input–output based studies of the relation between military expenditure and employment in Britain and France. It has a substantive objective: to contrast the employment impacts in the two countries within a comparable framework; and a methodological objective: to investigate the limits to comparison posed by differences in measurement procedures, definitions and military structure in the two countries. Although the UK spent a higher proportion of GDP on defence than France, the proportion of the labour force devoted to military activities is similar in the two countries. However, within these similar totals the structure of employment is quite different because of the high productivity of the French defence industries and the substitutions induced by the availability of conscripts. The distribution of employment by industry differs between the countries, but interpretation of the difference is complicated by diversity in industrial classification. As for the regional distribution, the UK shows more concentration, perhaps because of the absence of a policy of decentralisation for military and political reasons.

I   INTRODUCTION

The study of the relationship between military expenditure and employment, while not quite a mainstream topic, has been the subject of numerous studies, mainly based on input–output models.[1] These studies differ in a variety of ways, such as the nature of the change in military expenditure examined; the accompanying policy stance and economic scenario assumed; the second-round effects and feedbacks allowed for; the degree of detail on industrial and regional disaggregation provided; and the character of the model employed. Some are primarily concerned with the general economic consequences of military expenditure, others focus on the employment aspects.

Given the size of military expenditures and their economic influence, the desire to measure the employment impact is understandable. However, the numbers have political dimensions, thus their interpretation needs to be considered. In particular, it is important to avoid the common tendency to judge the desirability of public spending not in terms of its direct consequences (the security, health or education that it provides) but in terms of the indirect macroeconomic consequences for such variables as employment, the balance of payments, inflation, etc. Such indirect effects may play a part in the calculation of the opportunity cost of the programmes, but exclusive concern with them can obscure the real priorities and distort budgetary allocations: the in direct consequences creating a pressure for the public-spending programmes to persist after the direct need has disappeared or changed. Economic arguments alone can neither substitute for an analysis of the direct strategic utility of military expenditure nor be used to dismiss the possibility of disarmament.

Technological spin-off is a typical indirect consequence used to justify military spending, though there is little evidence for its economic importance in recent years. For example the director for international affairs of the Délégation Général pour l'Armement (DGA), a French ministerial body, asked, in a recent interview, whether the great French technological innovations since the war (Concorde and Ariane) would have taken place in the absence of military R & D spurred on by the arms race. British observers might be sceptical about whether Concorde was either wholly French or a wholly successful technological innovation. In addition the DGA official also undermined his case by appearing to suggest that military engineers were incapable of directly developing effective systems for civil uses. Nonetheless, Ministries do tend to emphasise the high-technology, high-productivity nature of the defence industry to justify support.

With respect to employment, the Ministry of Defence (MoD) in each country tends to present the figures in such a way as to show the additional benefits of military spending. This attitude transcends the political divide. M. Hernu, when French Socialist Minister, never missed an opportunity to underline the importance of his budget and arms exports for employment. Mr Heseltine, British Conservative Secretary of State, used exactly the same type of argument against his Labour opponents' proposals for reduced military expenditure. But, for a given expenditure, maximising estimates of the employment generated by the defence budget implies reducing estimates of the productivity associated with its provision. This poses a problem for publicists who wish to emphasise both the employment generation and the high-technology, high-productivity, nature of the industry. In addition, the employment required by military expenditure is both a benefit (since unemployment is a major policy problem) and a cost (since those human resources could have been used to produce alternative civilian products). Academic studies have tended to suggest that in the final analysis military expenditure has no especially beneficial economic effects, and that various combinations of civil expenditures could more than compensate for the employment and technology effects.

This chapter is not concerned with alternative policies or interpretation of the political significance of the numbers; instead the objective is merely to bring together existing French and UK studies[2] to see if any comparison of the employment effects of military expenditure in the two countries is possible.

II   ISSUES IN COMPARISON

In any international comparison, the first problem is exchange rates, since market rates do not necessarily correspond to purchasing power parities. The sterling–franc rate is influenced by the fact that France, unlike the UK, belongs to the exchange-rate mechanism of the European Monetary System; while sterling, as a petro-currency, reacts to fluctuations in the oil market. Removal of exchange controls in the UK in 1979 and reinforcement of them in France in 1981 may also have influenced the rate. There is no completely satisfactory way of dealing with this problem,[3] and in this chapter the average market-exchange rate has been used. The results will also be sensitive to the date at which the comparison is made. Most of our comparisons relate to 1981, with a rate of 11 F/£. This is very close to the estimated purchasing power parity rate for the year.

Even, when one considers the direct military employment – that is, those serving in the armed forces – problems arise because the military institutions in the two countries have somewhat different functions. In France the *gendarmerie* are included in the defence budget, whereas in Britain such policing functions performed by the *gendarmerie* are regarded as civil expenditures. It would seem logical to remove the expenses for the *gendarmerie* from the defence budget, and the French MoD does this, in certain publications, when it compares its budget with foreign countries. However, the *gendarmerie* do fill certain military functions, and have been increasingly taking over certain significant tasks which were previously the function of the army. Also the British army does have certain policing functions, particularly in Northern Ireland. Comparisons both with and without the *gendarmerie* will be given.

The other major problem in comparing the armed forces arises from the differences in the modes of recruitment, arising for political and historical as well as economic reasons. Britain has tended to use professional volunteer forces, regarding being a soldier as a job like any other. In France, there has been a tendency for politicians to distrust the military, regarding it as a potentially subversive force, which conscription helps to keep under control. In addition, French defence doctrine, at least implicitly, regards the conscripts – the citizens in uniform – as representing the nation in defending its vital interests. Conscription also acts as a tax in kind, adding to the real defence budget to the extent that conscript wages are below market rates.

While logic seems to require some correction for conscription, it is not obvious how the adjustment should be made. In France conscripts represent more than a third of the active military forces. In 1981 the annual costs of a conscript and a volunteer were assessed as 21 849 F and 43 200 F.[4] These figures can be used to give two extreme bounds. On the other hand it can be assumed that without conscription, the size of the armed forces would have been exactly the same, and the defence budget would have increased to make up this difference. This gives the constant forces correction. Alternatively, it can be assumed that the defence budget would have remained the same and the size of the forces reduced accordingly. This gives the constant budget correction. Corrections on both bases will be used.[5]

The final issue in comparison concerns the method used to estimate the industrial employment generated by military expenditure. The simplest method involves surveying defence contractors and asking them how many workers they employ on defence contracts. Such enquiries were conducted in the UK until 1973, but were abandoned because of their alleged unreliability. In France similar enquiries were conducted through the *Service de Surveillance de l'Armement*, but these are not published. Despite their simplicity, direct enquiries have disadvantages, since it may be difficult to distinguish those working on defence contracts from those working on civilian contracts in the same enterprise, particularly when certain tasks or overheads are shared; and they do not allow for the indirect employment required to produce intermediate inputs used in production.

Given the difficulties with direct enquiries, most estimates of defence industrial employment are derived from input–output based models, from which estimates of the direct and indirect labour inputs required can be derived. In the British and French estimates discussed below, two different types of model are used. One type uses standard input–output tables supplemented by average labour coefficients; these will be referred to as static models. The other type augments the input–output table (which may have trending coefficients) with econometric equations to determine final demands and factor demands; these will be referred to as dynamic models.

The two types of input–output model will give different estimates of the employment effect of military expenditure, partly because the dynamic models allow for feedbacks and partly because the static models use average labour requirement and the dynamic models use marginal labour requirement. The average and the marginal effects will differ for a variety of reasons, and the econometric estimates of the marginal employment–output elasticity will be influenced by the extent to which the defence contractors treated their work-force (design teams, skilled labour, etc.) as a fixed asset to be maintained in the face of fluctuating demand, over the estimation period. It might be expected that high average labour requirements, associated with holdings of under-utilised labour would be associated with a low marginal requirement.

III COMPARISONS OF EMPLOYMENT

The comparison begins with the direct personnel employed in the armed services and the MoD. In 1981 the UK spent around £434 m on personnel costs, equivalent to 48 609 m francs (mF): 61.4 per cent for military employees and 38.6 per cent for civil employees. In that year, France spent only 37 946 mF or 30 772 mF excluding *gendarmerie* (exG), of which the military received 84 per cent or 80 per cent (exG). On these numbers the UK devoted either 28 per cent or 58 per cent (exG) more than France on personnel costs.[6]

Under the assumptions given in the last section about the relative wage of conscripts and volunteers, the total professionalisation of the French forces in place in 1981 would have cost 5600 mF making total payments for personnel 45 546 mF or 36 372 mF (exG). Thus with the existing force structure the corrected personnel costs are still substantially higher (11 to 33 per cent) in the UK than in France.

The UK expenditures enabled it to field 331 000 service personnel, while France fielded 573 000 or 495 000 (exG). The British military cost on average £8200 each, about 90 200 F, while the corresponding French military cost between 49 600 and 55 300 F, about 60 per cent of the British figure. The constant budget conscription correction reduces the effective French forces to 443 000 (366 000 exG) and raises the average cost to between 67 000 F and 71 600 F. Thus conscription does not explain all the difference in average salary costs. One possibility is that British military pay is more responsive to market pressures in order to maintain recruitment, and this results in a bonus of 8–10 per cent. In addition the British forces, being mainly long-service professionals are, on average, older and of higher rank with higher rates of pay, increasing total costs.

The comparison of numbers of civilian defence-ministry employees does not pose the same problems, since they include neither conscripts nor *gendarmerie*. However, the boundaries between provision of a function by military personnel, civil servants, or the employees of industrial enterprises outside the ministry is very flexible and differs between countries. The UK records 203 000 civil servants (UK-based, excluding the Royal Ordnance Factories), while France has about 80 000. Each UK employee costs £8400 (about 92 400), while the French counterpart costs about 77 800 F. These differences are explained partly by the fact that in the UK much of the central administration and non-combat functions have been civilianised, while in France they are done by the military, notably qualified conscripts (*scientifiques du contingent*), and partly by the fact that in the UK more industrial workers are included in the MoD, even after the Royal Ordnance Factories are subtracted. In the UK there has been pressure to privatise not only state-owned industrial facilities, like the Royal Ordnance Factories, but also functions carried out by members of the armed forces (like repair and maintenance) and by civil servants. The UK civil service numbers have been reduced by about 30 000 since 1981.

The figures so far refer to those employed directly by the defence budget; to these must be added those employed, upstream, to make the equipment and other inputs used in defence. The UK information for 1981 comes from Ministry of Defence calculations, using input–output tables supplemented by some information on the direct employment of defence contractors. Subsequent estimates are based on estimates from the Cambridge Growth Project dynamic input–output system.[7] Both sets of French figures are produced by the Ministry of Defence, those for 1981 (and also for 1982 and 1983) are from an input–output model called *Analyse Variantielle* (AVA-TAR) of INSEE. In 1984 it used a more complex INSEE dynamic model called PROPAGE.[8]

In 1981 UK military demand for goods and services was around £6180 m (67 980 mF) generating employment of around 600 000; while in France expenditures of around 66 550 mF only generated 341 000 jobs. This puts the cost of induced employment per person at 0.113 mF in the UK, against 0.195 mF in France. The British MoD employs 1.7 times the number of workers in industry as the French ministry, for a given expenditure. This could be accounted for by differences in productivity. There are major difficulties involved in international comparisons of productivity, and differences in industrial classification between the two countries. But on the basis of rough estimates, in 1980 UK productivity (value added per employee) in the aerospace and shipbuilding industries was £9070 per worker (89 000 F per head) as compared with 130 000 in France. In electrical machinery it is £7877 (78 000 F) against 127 000 F; and for total industrial production it is £9054 (89 000 F) as compared with 144 000 F. Thus in these three examples, workers' productivity in France is respectively 46, 63 and 62 per cent higher than in the UK – roughly in accord with the figures concerning defence employment. In general French manufacturing productivity is higher than that in Britain, but the difference in the productivity of the defence industries is larger than national averages would lead one to expect. Size of firms and scale of plants seem to be similar in the two countries, as does the degree of domestic competition. The greater export orientation of the French industry may lead to improved efficiency however, particularly in the development of low-cost designs. But these explanations are speculative at the moment.

The estimates above give the total employment generated by military expenditure, using the average coefficients of the static models. The dynamic input–output models enable some estimate of the effect of marginal changes to be obtained. The UK and French studies used differ in some respects. The UK study considered a reduction of 35 per cent in the total defence budget, giving a reduction of 191 600 in employment over five years, with 149 000 in the first year. The model runs gave a reduction in public employment including the armed forces, of only 65 400 which is very small given the size of the cuts. The low elasticity of the ratio, military employment:expenditure, has appeared in other econometric studies,[9] but this is implausible for a large change, and the study gives an adjusted number of a reduction of 150 000 in public employment. The French study considered a 0.75 per cent increase in the defence spending on purchases of goods and services of 1 000 mF which gave an employment figure of 1985 in the first year rising to 5271 after five years.

Although the size of the stimulus differs between the two studies, the UK model concerned appears to be close to linear and symmetric so the results can be rescaled for comparison to the effect of a 1000 mF change. The British model estimates are then 2346 and 3051 after one and five years respectively or 3396 and 4364 using the adjusted public sector figures, as compared with the French estimates of 1985 and 5271. The impact effect in France is smaller, but the long-run effect is much larger. One can convert the French figure, which is based on a stimulus to military goods and services, to the British basis of a stimulus to the total defence budget, by splitting the 1000 mF into 364 mF renumeration (which has a multiplier of 3.982 jobs/mF for a professional army) and 636 mF goods and services. Given these estimates a 1000 mF increase in the total defence budget gives employment in France of 5244 at the end of one year and 7334 at the end of five. Thus this increases the difference.

The final element in the employment consequences of military expenditure is arms exports, production to meet the demand generated by military expenditures abroad. Arms exports are closely linked to domestic defence production decisions.[10] In 1981, on official figures, British military exports were £1746 m, about 19 200 mF, as compared with a French total of 28 500 mF, 48 per cent more than the UK. The definition of what constitutes military equipment is not very precise, and the figures may not be completely comparable. A third source reinforces this suspicion, since SIPRI estimates that in 1981 France exported 115 per cent more than did the UK.

The British MoD estimated that arms exports generated employment of 140 000 in 1981, whereas the calculations for France indicated between 100 000 and 110 000 – 20 to 30 per cent less than the UK. Each French employee produces about 271 000 F of exports, as compared with 137 000 for a British employee. Export productivity is 49 per cent less in the UK, similar to the 44 per cent less for the production of domestic defence equipment, which is not surprising given the similarity in the methods of calculation.

Pulling the results together for the year 1981, Table 18.1 indicates that military expenditure occupied 1.275 million persons in the UK, or 5.4 per cent of the work-force. On the same basis military

Table 18.1 Military-related employment in the UK and France in 1981

	UK		France	
	10^3	%	10^3	%
Services	331	26.0	495	45.0
Gendarmes			79	7.0
Ministry	203	16.0	80	7.0
Industry, domestic demand	600	47.0	341	31.0
Industry, exports	140	11.0	110	10.0
Total	1274	100.0	1105	100.0
Employment generated by defence budget	1134		995	
Percentage of work-force		4.8	915	4.6
Deduction of *gendarmerie*				
Percentage of work-force		4.8		4.2
Deduction for 50 per cent of conscripts			787	
Percentage of work-force		4.8		3.7
Share of defence expenditure in GDP		4.8		3.9

expenditure occupied 1.105 million people in France, including *gendarmerie* and conscripts, and 896 000 correcting for *gendarmerie* and conscripts, or 5.1 per cent of the work-force. Removing exports, the domestic defence budget in the UK occupied 4.8 per cent of the work-force, the same percentage as the share of military expenditure in GDP. In France, the share of the defence budget in GDP was 3.9 per cent, occupying 4.6 per cent of the work-force in total, or 3.7 per cent after correction for conscripts and *gendarmerie*.

IV   THE STRUCTURE OF EMPLOYMENT

One can analyse structure in a multitude of ways, since the criteria of classification such as sex, age, qualifications, area of activity, and region, are numerous. In the absence of sufficiently detailed information, we cannot retain all these criteria, thus we shall focus upon industry and region. However, it is worth mentioning the role of women in each country's forces. This question is topical in view of the wish of the French Minister of Defence to feminise the army. In fact the French forces have more women in their ranks today than have the British: 18 500 compared with 13 400; although proportionately women make up 3.3 per cent of the French forces as compared with 5.8 per cent of the British forces.

The estimates for industrial structure come from the dynamic input–output models already discussed. The major difficulty is the difference in classification of industry by Britain and France, and we have aggregated the information into eight broad categories to try to establish some comparability, although the match between the sectors in the two countries is very rough. The figures in Table 18.2 have been rescaled as proportions of the total change.

The pattern of the British effects is heavily influenced by the estimated output–employment elasticities by sector, which lead to what are almost certainly underestimates for the effect on electrical engineering and overestimates of the effect on building and civil engineering.

The regional breakdown of the employment impact of military expenditure is given in Table 18.3 and on Map 18.1. The primacy of the capital in both countries is clearly evident, because of the role of central administration. The south-east of England is a larger region than the Isle de France. In addition the contract data on which the UK estimates are based tend to overestimate the importance of

Table 18.2   Effects by sector of a change in military expenditure
(percentages of total change)

	France	UK
Agriculture, energy and mining	2.8	1.8
Electrical engineering	3.5	0.9
Aerospace, shipbuilding and mechanical engineering	22.6	22.7
Building and civil engineering	4.8	21.5
Commerce	10.0	10.5
Transport and communications	10.9	2.4
Services	5.2	3.7
Other	40.0	36.5

London.[11] The other feature is the importance of coastal regions. In France there is a policy of distancing the production of arms from the northern and eastern frontiers which were traditional invasion routes. The coefficient of variation for the UK data is roughly twice that for France, indicating the greater decentralisation of the employment induced by military expenditure in France. There has been a tradition in France of using the location of military facilities and contracts as an instrument of political management.

V   CONCLUSION

Quantitative comparison inevitably raises difficulties. The problems caused by exchange rates, differences in classification methods, institutional functions and estimation procedures inevitably produce large, though unknown, standard errors which must be attached to the numbers. Disregarding this uncertainty the review above suggests that while the UK devoted a higher proportion of GDP to defence than France (4.8 per cent against 3.9 per cent), the proportions of the labour forces occupied by defence were very similar (4.8 per cent and 4.6 per cent). Using the term productivity loosely as expenditure per employee, in the UK productivity in the defence sector in total was thus almost exactly the same as productivity in the economy as a whole. The French figures show lower productivity in the defence sector than for the economy as a whole, but when the employment figures are corrected for the *gendarmerie* and conscripts, the defence share of the work-force drops to 3.7 per cent, matching the GDP share.

Within the defence industry, productivity, on an 11 F/£ exchange rate, is between a third and a half higher in France than in the UK. The combination of conscription, differential industrial productivity and, perhaps, differences in the distribution of bureaucratic influence means that the total defence labour force is distributed in quite different ways in the two countries. The UK total of 1.134 million people is split 29 per cent in the armed services, 18 per cent in the Ministry of Defence, and 53 per cent in industry. The French total of 0.915 million people (excluding *gendarmerie*) is split 54 per cent services, 9 per cent ministry, 37 per cent industry. With respect to arms exports 110 000 French workers produce 50 per cent more foreign military sales than 140 000 British workers.

The regional distribution of military employment is rather more dispersed in France than in the UK, perhaps as a result of policy decisions which promote decentralisation. The low UK employment expenditure elasticities clouded conclusions about the marginal effects of changes in military expenditure on different industries. These low elasticities might be interpreted in terms of traditional accounts of UK economic inflexibility, but together with the difficulties of matching industrial classifications they make comparison of effects on different industries even more uncertain than the rest of the conclusions.

Table 18.3   Regional distribution of military-related employment

Regions of France	1	2	3	4
Ile de France	57.5	151.3	20.7	4.1
Languedoc–Roussillon				
Provence–Cote d'Azur	45.6	93.7	12.8	5.5
Bretagne–Pays de la Loire	35.7	85.6	11.7	4.6
Aquitaine–Midi-Pyrénées	34.8	79.3	10.9	5.0
Rhône–Alpes–Auvergne	20.7	62.9	8.6	2.9
Centre–Bourgogne	27.1	57.2	7.8	4.4
Alsace–Lorraine	29.1	54.6	7.5	4.2
Nord–Pas de Calais–Picardie	18.4	49.4	6.8	3.7
Haute Normandie et Basse Normandie	10.0	33.8	4.6	3.3
Champagne–Ardennes Franche-Comté	16.2	32.3	4.4	3.8
Poitou-Charentes-Limousin	14.0	30.1	4.1	4.0

Regions of UK	1	2	3	4
South-east	97.9	423.0	41.0	6.0
South-west	53.2	183.9	17.8	12.9
Scotland	18.9	79.4	7.7	4.5
East Midlands	14.4	65.0	6.3	4.2
North-west	2.2	62.6	6.1	2.8
West Midlands	9.7	58.6	5.7	3.1
North	1.2	42.0	4.1	3.8
East Anglia	15.6	40.5	3.9	6.6
York and Humberside	13.6	35.0	3.4	2.4
Wales	66.3	20.8	2.8	2.6
Northern Ireland	11.6	20.1	1.9	6.3

Notes: 1   number in armed services ($\times$ 1000).
         2   total military-related employment ($\times$ 1000).
         3   share of employment generated by region.
         4   share of military-related employment in work-force.

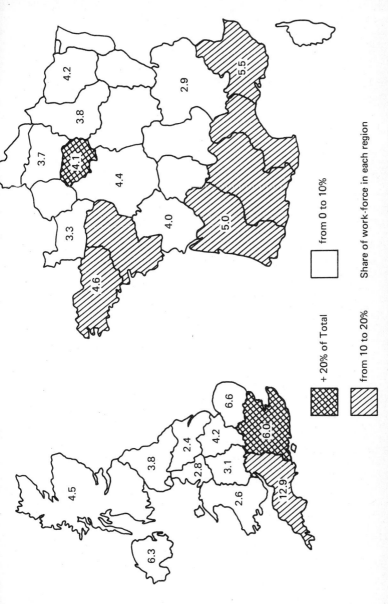

Map 18.1   Regional structure of employment generated by defence

from 0 to 10%

Share of work-force in each region

+ 20% of Total

from 10 to 20%

Notes and References

* We are grateful for the financial support provided by the CNRS and ESRC for a study on the defence efforts in Britain and France. We are also grateful for comments from Tony Humm of Birkbeck College, Jacques Fontanel, Grenoble University, and participants at the Stockholm Conference.

1.　The classic studies are: Leontief, W. *et al.* 'The Economic Impact – Industrial and Regional – of an Arms Cut', *Review of Economics and Statistics*, vol. 47, no. 3, 1965, for the US; and Leontief, W. and Duchin, F., *Military Spending* (Oxford: Oxford University Press 1983) for the world.

2.　The UK studies include: Economist Intelligence Unit, *The Economic Effects of Disarmament* (London: EIU 1963); Pite, C., 'Employment and Defence', *Statistical News*, no. 51 (November 1980); Dunne, J. P. and Smith, R. P., 'The Economic Consequences of Reduced Military Expenditure', *Cambridge Journal of Economics*, vol. 8 (September 1984); Bellany, I. *British Defence Expenditure and Its Impact on Jobs and Energy Use* (Bailrigg Papers on International Security No 8, University of Lancaster, 1985).

　　　The French studies include: Aben, J., 'Désarmement, activité et emploi', *Défense Nationale* (mai 1981); Aben, J., *Défense et aménagement du territoire* (Montpellier: Cahiers du Séminaire Ch. Gide, Vol. XV, 1981); Aben, J. et Daures, N. *Défense Nationale et emploi en France* (Montpellier: CSG 1981) vol. XV; Ministère de la Défense, *Analyse économique des dépenses militaires* (Paris: 1982 et 1984).

3.　Fontanel, J., 'La comparison des dépenses militaires' *Défense Nationale* (novembre 1982).

4.　*Le Monde*, 13 décembre 1981.

5.　The corrections correspond to assumptions of zero and unit elasticities of substituting between labour and capital in the production of armed services, see Fontanel, J., Humm, A. and Smith, R. P., 'La Substitution Capital Travail dans les Dépenses Militaires', *Arès: Défense et Sécurité*, Special issue 1985–6, Grenoble.

6.　The sources for the figure are: for the UK, *Statement on the Defence Estimates* (London: HMSO, annually); and for France, *La défense en chiffres* (Paris: SIRPA annually).

7.　The UK static results come from Pite (see note 2) the dynamic results from Dunne and Smith, (see note 2).

8.　The French results come from *Analyse Economique* (see note 2).

9.　Hartley, K. and Lynk, E., 'Budget Costs and Public Sector Employment: the Case of Defence', *Applied Economics*, vol. 15, 1983.

10.　Fontanel, J., Humm, A. and Smith, R. P., 'The Economics of Exporting Arms', *Journal of Peace Research* (September 1985); Aben, J., 'Commerce de Guerre ou commerce de paix, un dilemme pour les relations entre la France et la Tiers Monde', *Défense Nationale* (février 1985).

11.　Short, J., 'Defence Spending in the UK Regions', *Regional Studies* (no. 2, 1981).

19 Reducing Defence Expenditure: A Public Choice Analysis and a Case Study of the UK

Keith Hartley
UNIVERSITY OF YORK

Public choice theory is used to explain the behaviour of agents in the defence sector. Public choice embraces the economics of politics, bureaucracies and interest groups. Consideration is given to a government wishing to reduce the level of defence spending or to change its composition (for example, 'mix' of nuclear and conventional forces). How are the armed forces, the Ministry of Defence and weapon firms likely to respond to defence cuts? Identification of the groups likely to lose from disarmament and of the arguments they will use to protect themselves are essential for explaining behaviour in the military–industrial complex. The predictions of public choice theory are outlined and the framework is applied to the UK. Defence reviews are taken as examples of spending cuts and it is shown how agents in the political market have reacted and adjusted. The results of some limited empirical tests are presented. These include estimates of the effects of defence reviews on employment; whether defence spending is different from other forms of government and private expenditure; and the impact of the governing party on military budgets. It is recognised that the analytical and empirical work is still in its infancy.

I INTRODUCTION[1]

Economists delight in suggesting Pareto-type policies. Yet actual policy changes often involve substantial departures from Paretian ideals. Why do governments frequently fail to exploit obvious opportunities for increasing social welfare? One possible explanation (there are others) arises in the political market place where policy choices are made and implemented and which economists have traditionally regarded as 'black box'. Government decisions are likely to be the result of actions by various interest groups in the political market place, each seeking to influence policy in its favour. This paper outlines the possible role of these interest groups in formulating defence policy. The relative infancy of public-choice theory means that the approach will be exploratory, seeking to determine whether the paradigm can be usefully applied, and mapping out a possible research agenda. In this chapter we consider how the various agents in the political market-place will seek to influence the level and composition of defence expenditure, with UK experience providing case-study material. What, for example, is the likely response (and success) of the Armed Forces and the domestic weapons industry to government proposals to reduce the level of defence spending and to change the 'mix' from nuclear to conventional forces? Debates about the desirability or otherwise of UK membership of NATO, US bases in the UK, cruise missiles, Trident, and so on, cannot ignore the behaviour and influence of agents in the political market on the formulation of defence policy. In particular, some of these agents represent barriers to proposed reductions in the level of military spending and to changes in its composition. Inevitably, questions arise as to who is likely to gain and who is likely to lose from such a policy and what arrangements, if any, will be made to compensate the potential losers? Clearly, those likely to lose will oppose any policy change, particularly if there are no arrangements for adequate compensation.

II THE STYLISED FACTS OF UK DEFENCE SPENDING

The level and composition of UK defence spending is summarised in Table 19.1. Total expenditure is some £18 bn (1985 prices) which employs an all-volunteer force of over 330 000 military service personnel, with some 46 per cent of the budget allocated to equipment. It total, the UK defence sector accounts for 1.25 million jobs which obviously represents a major barrier to sudden, large-scale defence cuts. Some of the main trends in military spending and other components of aggregate expenditure are shown in Table 19.2. Defence shares have followed a general downward trend via a series

Table 19.1　The UK defence sector, 1985

Expenditure[a]	£m
Nuclear strategic forces	509
Navy combat forces	2 505
European ground forces	2 764
Other army forces	205
Air force	3 702
Reserves	360
R & D	2 304
Training	1 294
Repair facilities	917
Stocks	535
Other support functions	2 998
Total[c]	18 059
Expenditure on　(i)　personnel	6 271
(ii)　equipment	8 355

Employment[b]	000's
Numbers of armed service personnel	334.2
Civilians employed by Ministry of Defence	208.6
Employment in UK defence industries (direct, indirect and export sales)	710.0
Total	1 252.8

Notes:
[a] Expenditure data for 1985–6
[b] Industrial employment data for 1983–4. Employment figures exclude multiplier effects – for example, effects of expenditure by military service personnel in local communities. Also, there are 284 000 reservists. [c] Total expenditure includes miscellaneous expenditures and receipts of minus £34 m.

Source:　Cmnd 9430, *Statement on the Defence Estimates* (London: HMSO 1985).

of steps, with the rising share after 1978 reflecting the UK's commitment to NATO to raise military spending by 3 per cent annually in real terms.

Table 19.2   Trends in shares

Year	D/Y (%)	NHS/Y (%)	E/Y (%)	I/Y (%)
1960	6.4	3.4	3.6	16.4
1961	6.3	3.4	3.7	17.3
1962	6.4	3.4	4.1	17.0
1963	6.2	3.4	4.2	16.8
1964	5.9	3.4	4.2	18.3
1965	5.9	3.6	4.4	18.4
1966	5.8	3.7	4.6	18.4
1967	5.9	3.8	4.9	19.0
1968	5.6	3.8	4.9	19.4
1969	4.9	3.8	4.9	18.8
1970	4.8	3.9	5.1	18.9
1971	4.8	3.9	5.2	18.8
1972	4.8	4.1	5.6	18.7
1973	4.7	3.9	5.4	20.0
1974	4.9	4.6	5.5	20.6
1975	4.9	4.9	6.2	20.1
1976	4.9	4.9	5.8	19.5
1977	4.7	4.6	5.4	18.5
1978	4.5	4.6	5.2	18.5
1979	4.6	4.6	4.9	18.8
1980	4.9	5.1	5.3	18.1
1981	4.9	5.3	5.4	16.4
1982	5.2	5.1	5.3	16.6

D   defence expenditure
NHS   National Health Service expenditure
E   education expenditure
I   gross domestic fixed capital information
Y   GDP at market prices

Source: CSO, *UK National Accounts* (London: HMSO, 1960–82).

III   A PUBLIC CHOICE APPROACH TO UK DEFENCE POLICY

Critics and supporters of military expenditure disagree about the appropriate level and composition of a nation's defence spending. In the UK, opponents point to lower defence spending by other

European members of NATO, particularly France and the FRG, while supporters will argue for increased spending to match the military capabilities of the Warsaw Pact. To neoclassical economists, a rational decision-maker would determine the optimal level of defence expenditure on the basis of equating benefits and costs at the margin. Efficiency criteria and output measures would be central to such a marginal evaluation. The public goods characteristics of defence usually involve government in interpreting society's preferences on the level and composition of military expenditure.

Ideally, individual preferences are recorded through the ballot box at elections. But voting mechanisms, certainly in the UK, have major limitations as a device for registering society's preferences. Elections do not occur continuously but at irregular intervals thereby imposing constraints on the opportunities for re-contracting. Votes are cast for a general package of measures (an election manifesto) in which defence policy is only one among a heterogeneous set embracing economic, social, technological and other policies and between which voters cannot accurately indicate the intensity of their preferences. Nor are voters provided with much meaningful information allowing an evaluation of defence policy. The Official Secrets Act means that voters are given little indication about what alternative defence budgets might buy in the form of such final outputs as protection and the probability of survival in different conflict situations. Finally, the paradox of voting creates further difficulties in compiling society's preferences in a majority voting system.[2] For example, in the 1983 UK election, was a vote for the Conservative Party a vote for the continuation of the NATO commitment to raise defence spending by 3 per cent, continued membership of NATO, US military bases in the UK, cruise missiles, Trident and generally 'strong defences'; or, was it a vote for tax cuts, increased individual incentives, lower public expenditure, privatisation, owner-occupation, 'free' collective bargaining and continued membership of the EEC? Of course, defence is not unique since similar problems of interpreting voter preferences apply to other components of government expenditure (for example, education, health, transport). Moreover, as with other exchange relationships where there are possible gains from trading, political markets can generate alternative non-voting mechanisms which allow individuals and groups to express their preferences and thus overcome any deficiencies in society's voting rules. The possibilities for individual and group action include log-rolling (voting agreements) between elected politicians, increased participation in political parties either existing ones or creating new ones, interest groups and lobbying, private provision, mobility and revolution. In the case of defence policy, examples include lobbying by British arms firms for new contracts, lobbying by CND over nuclear weapons policy, individuals or groups voluntarily providing their own nuclear fall-out shelters or moving from industrial areas and major military targets.[3] The opportunities for such behaviour raise the interesting question of the meaning of market failure in political as well as commercial markets in a dynamic and uncertain world. If private agents pursuing their self-interest on an individual or group basis seek to exploit the available opportunities for beneficial exchange subject to the costs of transactions, then it is possible that at any moment of time (with given resource endowments, technology and factor prices), all worth-while opportunities will have been exploited. It follows that the constitutional and voting arrangements, together with the scope, size and organisation of the public sector must be deemed to be Pareto-efficient: otherwise utility-maximising individuals and groups would seek to exploit worthwhile opportunities for change.[4] One alternative view is that interest groups in political markets are inefficient (for example, price controls, subsidies, protection), inequitable and adversely affect growth.[5] In these circumstances, there is a role for government tackling a standard collective action problem in which all might gain if everyone is willing to make a small sacrifice of their special privileges on the basis of other groups also sacrificing their special rights. Similar problems arise with multilaterial disarmament where all nations would gain from a balanced reduction in armaments but no one country is willing to risk unilaterial disarmament.

The limitations of the voting system as a means of accurately registering society's views on the level and composition of defence expenditure allows opportunities for governments, bureaucracies and other interest groups to interpret the 'national interest' and influence defence policy. UK defence as a political market involves all agents with preferences for alternative defence policies.[6] These agents consist of:

(A)   *Large numbers of utility-maximising voters, with only limited infcrmation on such specialised topics as the 'threat', NATO, defence strategy, nuclear weapons, the role of a surface navy, the effectiveness of manned aircraft and the contribution of British troops based in Germany.*   Since the collection of information is not costless (nor is voting), there are opportunities for producers and other interest groups with specialist knowledge to influence voters and political parties.[7]

(B) *Small numbers of vote-conscious political parties, comprising existing parties and new entrants.* Advocates of reduced defence spending and opponents of nuclear weapons have to decide whether to influence policy by seeking to change the policies of an established political party (compare a take-over) or by creating a new party. Neither solution is costless. For a new party in the UK there are entry barriers in such forms as legal restrictions on access to TV advertising. Nor must it be forgotten that any political party seeking office cannot ignore voter-preferences. However persuasive a particular defence (or other) policy might be to its advocates, it will not be implemented if the party fails to attract votes.

(C) *State bureaucracies concerned with utility-maximisation, including a desire for larger budgets.* UK examples include each of the Armed Forces, the Ministry of Defence and the Home Office (civil defence), although other Ministries will be concerned with the jobs, technology and balance-of-payments implications of defence policy and weapons procurement choices (for example, the foreign-exchange costs of British troops in Germany; US *v* UK weapons). Bureaucracies are usually monopoly suppliers of defence information and defence services, with each of the armed forces seeking to protect their traditional property rights in the air, land and sea domains. The absence of rivalry and of clearly defined measurable end outputs (protection, survival), together with employment contracts which lack efficiency incentives, provides defence bureaucracies with opportunities for discretionary behaviour.[8] Nevertheless, some aspects of bureaucratic behaviour are constrained by the investigations of Parliamentary Committees (for example, House of Commons Defence Committee and Public Accounts Committee) as well as by the activities of pressure groups.

(D) *Interest groups of producers and consumers, each seeking to influence government policy in its favour through such mechanisms as lobbying, sponsorship of politicians, advertising, large-scale demonstrations and civil disobedience.* Producer groups will consist of weapon contractors seeking domestic orders and protection from foreign competition, especially from the USA, as well as favourable rules for regulating profits on defence contracts. Trade unions and professional associations with members in the defence industries will similarly support domestic weapon producers with the aim of protecting the jobs and favourable income prospects of their members. In contrast, other pressure groups represent specific consumer interests such as those opposed to nuclear weapons (for example, CND, SANA); those in favour of disarmament such as the Society of Friends; and those in favour of strong defences (for example, Peace through NATO; Academic Council for Peace and Freedom). Finally, a number of groups exist specialising in the independent analysis and evaluation of UK defence policy, thereby providing voters and political parties with an alternative source of information outside the state bureaucracy (for example, Jane's, IISS, university research centres).

(E) *The international community of foreign nations and international agencies with an interest in influencing UK defence policy* Examples include NATO and the United Nations; foreign governments such as the USA and the FRG which will oppose reductions in UK defence spending as well as foreign arms firms seeking UK contracts.

IV   THE PREDICTIONS OF PUBLIC CHOICE THEORY

Economic models of politics, regulation and bureaucracies suggest a number of predictions which are relevant to explaining defence policy:

1   Consensus Politics

In a two-party democracy, both political parties agree on any issues favoured by a majority of voters. Both parties will offer similar and vague policies. For example, neither party seeking office is likely to *continue* offering a defence policy which appeals to only a few voters at the extreme of the political spectrum and involves the potential loss of large numbers of moderate voters. The emergence of a third party in the UK raises the possibility that either voter preferences are no longer single-peaked or that the new grouping is seeking the middle ground with the two traditional parties likely to respond by moving towards the centre.

2   The Policies of Democratic Governments Tend to Favour Producers More than Consumers

Examples include supporting a domestic defence industry through subsidies and preferential treatment in allocating government contracts. In addition, economic models of regulation suggest that regulation benefits the industry (that is, the regulated or producers) rather than society.[9]

3   Political Business Cycles

Once elected, the governing party can use its policies to influence voter preferences to increase it chances of re-election. To increase its popularity, it can adopt an expansionary aggregate demand policy prior to an election. As part of such a policy, new weapon contracts might be allocated to major firms in areas of high unemployment or in marginal constituencies; or a military establishment which is 'vital' to a local community might be expanded or saved from closure.

4   Bureaucracies are Likely to be X-efficient and 'Too Large'

As a result, services supplied by state bureaucracies are likely to cost more than similar services supplied by competitive firms in the private sector; industries supported by a monopoly Ministry of Defence will be 'too large' and bureaucrats will rationalise their activities by overestimating the demand for their preferred policies and underestimating the costs of projects. Examples of such behaviour include MoD and NATO emphasis on the apparent numerical superiority of Warsaw Pact Forces (more aircraft, ships, soldiers and tanks) and evidence of cost escalation, delays and 'gold plating' on weapons. Interestingly, the existence of inefficiency suggests that proposed reductions in military spending (disarmament) might produce a 'shock effect' leading to the elimination of organisational slack and improved efficiency in defence activities.

V   SOME APPLICATIONS TO THE UK

The UK has experienced a series of Defence Reviews affecting both the level and composition of military expenditure. There were major Reviews in 1957, 1964–8, 1974–5 and 1981. In contrast, between 1979 and 1986, the UK supported the NATO commitment to raise defence spending by 3 per cent annually in real terms, with this commitment ending in 1985. In other words, the UK Defence Reviews and the end of the 3 per cent commitment provide case-study material on the actual experience of efforts to cut military spending. Such a case study can identify the barriers to defence cuts, with implications for disarmament policies. Questions arise as to:

- whether policy was implemented – that is, plans versus outcomes: what policy-makers aimed to achieve, what actually happened and why the difference?
- the effects of policy changes on the British armed forces, NATO and the British economy;
- whether a public choice approach explains the facts.

Once again, the exploratory and illustrative nature of the exercise needs to be stressed. Ideally, a public choice approach needs to be compared with alternative explanations of defence spending and there is clearly scope for more satisfactory empirical testing with less emphasis on casual empiricism.[10] Nevertheless, a public choice approach identifies some of the agents most likely to oppose policies designed to reduce defence spending and to change its composition. In particular, it shows how the armed forces respond to cuts, the types of argument that bureaucracies are likely to use to protect their budgets and how domestic defence industries are likely to react to cancellations. As a result some of the myths of defence and procurement can be exposed to critical scrutiny and empirical evidence.

A brief outline of the major Defence Reviews is required. Reviews provide an indication of society's preferences and views about the maximum acceptable levels of defence spending and its appropriate composition. In 1957, the Conservative Government's Review aimed to reduce defence spending from its previous share of almost 10 per cent of *GNP* which was regarded as 'too high'. The Review announced the substitution of nuclear weapons, rockets and missiles for large-scale conventional forces and manned aircraft, with implications for the future size and form of the RAF. Conscription was to be abolished and replaced by a relatively small all-volunteer force. The economics of politics would explain the abolition of conscription as a potential vote-winner, with the two major parties having an inducement to adopt similar policies favouring volunteer forces.

The Labour Government's Defence Reviews of 1965–8 aimed to reduce defence spending further to 5 per cent of GNP by 1972–3. The

UK's overseas defence commitments were reduced with the planned withdrawal from east of Suez; land-based RAF aircraft were to replace naval carrier-borne aircraft; and US aircraft with work-sharing arrangements replaced British projects. Next, was the Labour Administration's Defence Review of 1975 which sought to reduce spending from $5^1/2$ per cent to a lower target of $4^1/2$ per cent of *GNP* by 1984. This involved further withdrawal from the UK's remaining non-NATO commitments (for example, Mediterranean) and associated reduction in the Navy's amphibious forces and surface warships and in the RAF's transport fleet and maritime-patrol aircraft. However, as a result of the 1977 NATO agreement, the Labour Government accepted a commitment to raise defence spending by 3 per cent annually in real terms for 1979–81: an example of the influence of NATO on the level of UK defence spending. Finally, the Conservative Government's 1981 Review reflected resource constraints and technical change, particularly the vulnerability of major platforms such as aircraft and surface ships. Significantly, it proposed solutions which are 'less glamorous than maximising the number of large and costly platforms in our armoury, but it is far the better way of spending money for real security value'.[11] As a result of the Review, substantial reductions were announced in the size of the Navy's surface fleet and in the scale and sophistication of new ship-building, the stress being on 'total capability rather than Service shares'.[12] References to 'less glamorous' weapons and 'Service shares' suggests that the armed forces represent major interest groups seeking to protect their military service with a preference for 'prestige and glamorous' weapon projects (that is, those which satisfy the preferences of the military users rather than of the society seeking protection). This outline of Defence Reviews raises questions about the meaning of cuts, the response of the military–industrial complex and whether there were any benefits to the British economy.

1 The Definition of Cuts; Plans Versus Outcomes and the Adjustment Period

The definition of a cut in military spending is not without its problems. Evidence from Defence Reviews suggests that cuts are publicly announced reductions in actual or planned expenditure. However, since the armed forces usually bid for more funds than they are allocated, defence budgets (and other Ministry budgets) are cut annually as part of the public expenditure review. Doubts also arise about the meaning of savings based on future reductions in long-term spending plans. For instance, the 1975 Labour Government's Review announced *annual* savings of some £500 m by 1983–4 and a *total saving* of some £4.7 bn (1974 prices) on the estimated cost of its predecessor's plans;[13] but this assumes that its predecessor's plans would have been implemented. Defence choices are made under uncertainty and plans can be affected by unexpected changes in, say, technical progress, international tensions, wars (for example, the Falklands conflict), budget constraints, NATO commitments and the attitudes of Ministers. In relation to new equipment programmes some ten years ahead, one Defence Secretary has stated that, 'There is no need to make decisions until you have *got* to make decisions':[14] a view which suggests flexibility rather than rigidity in long-term forward plans. Nonetheless, by aggregating modest annual savings over a ten-year time-horizon, the armed forces and Ministry of Defence can present an impressive picture of cuts and a vote-conscious government can show its supporters and the electorate that it is taking 'decisive action' to reduce military spending. Of course, by offering substantial future cuts, the armed forces and the Ministry of Defence can always hope for a change in the financial climate or a change in government, or a transfer of the problem to their successors! Significantly, even *annual* plans often fail to be achieved! Table 19.3 shows the level and percentage growth of real defence expenditure on an annual basis for 1974 to 1984. Note the general tendency for annual plans to exceed out-turns and the UK's performance against its 3 per cent NATO commitment after 1979.

A government's defence preferences will also be constrained by contractual and treaty commitments, thus affecting the extent and speed with which it can reduce expenditure. There are long-term commitments to military service manpower and new weapon projects. For example, in the year immediately ahead, over 90 per cent of major equipment expenditure is effectively committed by past decisions and the proportion remains at some 50 per cent for three years ahead. In other words, there are major constraints on achieving large-scale cuts in defence spending in the short run. An adjustment period of more than five years seems to be required: hence a UK government aiming at substantial reductions in military spending will have to be re-elected (*ceteris paribus*). Table 19.1 provides evidence on defence shares that show the extent to which the spending targets of the various Defence Reviews were actually achieved.

Table 19.3   Defence expenditure 1974–84

Year	Defence expenditure (£m, 1975–6 prices)		Percentage real growth (% p.a.)	
	Plans	Out-turns	Plans	Out-turns
1974–5	5349	5185		
1975–6	5478	5419	2.4	4.5
1976–7	5500	5321	0.4	−1.8
1977–8	5324	5202	−3.2	−2.2
1978–9	5293	5171	−0.6	−0.6
1979–80	5449	5322	3.0	2.9
1980–1	5503	5467	1.0	2.7
1981–2	5582	5548	1.4	1.5
1982–3	5747	5881	3.0	6.0
1983–4	6154	6010	7.1	2.2

Source: Defence Committee, *Defence Commitments and Resources and the Defence Estimates*, vol. II, (1985) pp. 4–5.
   (a)   Data are in constant 1975–6 prices, using defence-specific price deflators.
   (b)   Figures are based on UK definitions of defence expenditure. NATO definitions give higher figures.
   (c)   Falklands Islands costs are included from 1982–3 onwards.

2   The Response of the Armed Forces and the Ministry of Defence

Faced with Defence Reviews and cuts, the armed forces are likely to respond by protecting their established property rights and their high-technology 'prestige' weapon systems. The 1957 Review announced the end of manned combat aircraft for the RAF; the 1965–8 Review signalled the end of the navy's aircraft carriers and carrier-borne aircraft; and the 1981 Review was designed to reduce further the Navy's surface fleet. All these decisions were subsequently modified, often under the same government! This suggests two hypotheses: first, the behaviour is consistent with utility-maximising armed forces, supported by domestic weapon producers, successfully protecting their traditional property rights and their 'glamorous' weapons; or second, they could be the rational economic response to changes in strategy, technology and in relative factor prices. It is difficult to distinguish these as alternative hypotheses capable of being tested by independent economists. Similarly, faced with cuts, the armed forces are likely to respond by cutting civilian manpower, especially overseas civilian personnel and cutting back on training, exercises, support functions and stocks (for example, of ammunition), rather than sacrificing their major new equipment programmes. Preferences for inputs are likely to differ between the military services, with the capital-intensive air force willing to sacrifice personnel rather than combat aircraft and the labour-intensive army aiming to protect manpower as its most valuable asset. Such hypotheses need more careful specification, although actual behaviour in response to cuts could reveal the inputs and forces that each of the military services regard as marginal and hence are willing to sacrifice. Also, it is interesting to note that the budgetary shares of the army, navy and air force show a remarkable degree of stability (for example, 1975–6 to 1985–6). This relative stability has occurred despite Defence Reviews and technical progress which might have been expected to produce changing comparative advantages for each of the armed forces. One explanation of the stability in shares has been the UK's desire to maintain 'balanced forces'; alternatively, it could be that the data on annual expenditure flows are poor indicators of trends in the stock of productive assets for each of the military services; or, it could reflect pressures from established military-service interest groups, each protecting their property rights and, over the long-run, agreeing on 'equal misery' in any cuts.[15]

The Ministry of Defence is also likely to oppose efforts to cut defence spending. It will stress the 'dire consequences' of cuts, pointing to the growing threat from the Warsaw Pact, the employment effects of cancelling weapon projects and the employment and social consequences of closing military bases in remote rural areas which lack alternative job opportunities. References will also be made to the loss of high technology (the UK will become a nation of 'metal-bashers'), the loss of national independence and the loss of prestige (such as cancellation of Trident). Other ministries such as the Department of Trade and Industry, the Manpower Services Commission and the Foreign Office are likely to support the arguments about jobs, technology and the international prestige of a world military power. Vote-conscious governments might be influenced by some of these arguments if the cuts are likely to lead to electoral harm, particularly if they are concentrated in marginal constituencies. Also, in an effort to protect themselves, the military services and the Minstry of Defence will promise future efficiency improvements through reorganisation, rationalisation, civilisation, contracting-out, more competition and international collaboration. This suggests that Defence Reviews might have a 'shock effect' resulting in efficiency improvements, so that is is possible to maintain defence output or protection with a reduced budget. It should also be noted that civilisation policies can increase the problems of defining a weapon for disarmament purposes (for example, oil tankers can be converted to aircraft carriers within a few days!).

Some limited empirical tests were undertaken to estimate the manpower effects of Defence Reviews. Governments often claim that Reviews result in the release of military and civilian manpower employed by the armed services and the Ministry of Defence. On this basis, Reviews were expected to have two effects on manpower. First, a shock effect on labour inputs resulting in a 'once-and-for-all' release of manpower. In the case of civilians, it was predicted that civil servants in the Ministry of Defence would tend to shift downward adjustments in manpower to other groups of staff. Second, a positive relationship between employment and expenditure would mean that if the Reviews reduced military spending below its actual or planned level, there would be a corresponding release of labour. The hypotheses were tested using a standard employment function incorporating a dummy variable for the Defence Reviews and examples of the results are shown in Table 19.4.[16] It can be seen that with the possible exception of the air force, Defence Reviews have not resulted in any separate 'shock effect' on military service and civilian employment (see coefficients for dummy variables DV). However, changes in defence spending have the predicted effect on armed service manpower (positive coefficients for D), but surprisingly, no influence on any category of civilian employment. Interestingly, there was evidence of a significant *negative* trend in the employment of civilian industrial staff and tentative support for a *positive* trend in the employment of civil servants.[17] Such results are useful tests of Government claims about Reviews releasing manpower. However, they are only a starting-point for public choice analysts who need to model the bargaining process associated with Reviews and where such complexities cannot be represented by a simple dummy variable.

Table 19.4 Employment effects of defence reviews

Dependent variables: employment (L)	Constant	log D	log Q, t	DV1	DV2	log of lagged dependent variable (L_{t-1})	$\bar{R}$
1. log RN	0.53 (0.73)	0.18* (0.09)		-0.008* (0.003)	0.004 (0.008)	0.59** (0.11)	0.96
2. log RA	-2.37 (1.35)	0.41* (0.16)		-0.005 (0.004)	-0.012 (0.014)	0.86** (0.09)	0.92
3. log RAF	-0.31 (1.01)	0.23 (0.13)		-0.011* (0.005)	-0.029* (0.012)	0.73** (0.09)	0.98
4. log T	-2.79** (0.57)	0.45** (0.08)		-0.004* (0.002)	-0.016 (0.009)	0.88** (0.04)	0.99
5. log NOI	5.55* (2.63)	0.14 (0.21)		0.007 (0.003)	-0.014 (0.019)	0.42 (0.22)	0.83
6. log IN	5.28 (2.85)	0.09 (0.21)		-0.013* (0.006)	-0.016 (0.021)	0.51* (0.19)	0.95
7. log Aerospace	0.94 (1.67)		0.20* (0.09)	-0.005 (0.007)	0.025 (0.014)	0.66* (0.24)	0.96
8. log Shipbuilding	-0.14 (0.84)		0.29 (0.14)	-0.001 (0.002)	0.019 (0.012)	0.78** (0.11)	0.95

Coefficients

Notes

(a) RN, RA, RAF and T = military personnel in the Navy, Army, Air Force and the total in all three Services, respectively

(b) NOI and IN = employment of non-industrial staff (NOI = civil servants) and of civilian industrial staff (IN) employed in the UK by the Ministry of Defence, respectively

(c) Aerospace and shipbuilding = employment in each of these industries

(d) D = UK defence expenditure in constant prices

(e) Q_t = industry output measured by the value of sales in constant prices

(f) t = a time-trend for 1952–78 in equations 1–4; for 1955–78 in equations 5–6 and for 1959–76 in equations 7–8

(g) $DV1$ = dummy variable for Defence Reviews with 1 = 1957, 1965–8, 1974–5 and 0 elsewhere; $DV2$ = alternative dummy for Reviews allowing for a one-year lag. In equation 8, the dummy is 1 = 1963, 1964, 1967, 1973–5

(h) All equations are log-linear with 1–3 estimated using Cochrane–Orcutt iteration and 4–8 with OLS; there was evidence of auto-correlation at the 5 per cent level in equation 4

(i) $\bar{R}^2$ is adjusted for degrees of freedom

(j) Standard errors are shown in brackets

* Significant at the 5 per cent level

**Significant at the 1 per cent level using a two-tail test

3   The Concept of a Powerful Producer Group

Producer groups have a major role in public choice models but few efforts have been made to operationalise the concept. What are the characteristics of a 'powerful' producer group in the sense of a group which is favoured by government? Critics of defence spending claim that the military–industrial complex represents a powerful and influential pressure group. In which case, an analysis of the major UK weapon producers and their market environments suggests that powerful producer groups have some of the following characteristics:

(A)   Market structure

Firms are large both in absolute and relative size. For example in 1983–4 ten UK firms in the aerospace, shipbuilding, electronics and ordnance sectors each received Ministry of Defence contracts exceeding £100 m. Usually, these firms were domestic monopolies or oligopolies (some state-owned) operating in protected markets.

(B)   Dependence on defence business

UK defence contracts form a substantial proportion of their business, so that the firm's fortunes are closely linked with government decisions. 'Substantial' needs operationalising but the Ministry of Defence believes that it is a dominant customer for the aerospace, shipbuilding and electronics industries, accounting for 45, 30 and 20 per cent of their output, respectively, in 1984.

(C)   Location

Vote-conscious governments are likely to be influenced by firms located in marginal constituencies or in high-unemployment areas.

(D)   Types of contract

Firms which receive non-competitive cost-plus, incentive and fixed-price contracts will have close and continuous links with the Ministry of Defence procurement agents. The government's profit rules on such contracts are designed to provide defence firms with a 'fair' return on capital, defined as a return equal to the average return earned by British industry. A specialist regulatory agency monitors the government's profit rules and can renegotiate any 'excessive' profits. In this context, it is possible that the type of contract and the regulatory arrangements are the result of successful lobbying by producer groups, with both contracts and profit rules favouring contractors.

(E)   Lobbying activities

Once again, this is a black box which economists have neglected but which is obviously a potentially important mechanism in the set of linkages in the political market. Examination of actual behaviour identifies at least two features: first, the existence of an active specialist trade association, for example, the Parliamentary Defence Committee's investigation of procurement received evidence from trade associations representing aerospace, electronics, engineering, naval equipment and defence manufacturers suggesting that these are important groups worth further study;[18] second, business appointments by staff leaving the Ministry of Defence and armed forces. Clearly, senior military and civil staff have contacts and expertise which is especially valuable to defence contractors seeking more business.

Faced with cuts in the level of defence spending and the cancellation of major weapon projects, producer groups will respond in two ways: first, they will use all available arguments and threats to oppose the cuts and to stress their 'invaluable' contribution to the British economy. The science and technology lobby will point to the dangers of cutting defence R & D spending and to the prospect of the UK losing out on advanced technology and the next industrial revolution. Firms will threaten to cut jobs and close plants; and trade unions and professional associations will also lobby on behalf of their members in defence industries.[19] Second, firms will adjust to the expected changes by seeking new defence contracts and new markets. They can press for work-sharing on imported weapons (for example, UK purchase of US Phantom aircraft); they can stress the advantages of international collaboration (one of which might be that it is more difficult to cancel a project!); seek government funding for new civil ventures; increase exports and withdraw work from subcontractors.

Defence Reviews are supposed to release scarce manpower, particularly scientists, technologists, and skilled labour from weapon industries, thus making these resources available for more 'socially desirable' civil industries, especially engineering. This hypothesis was tested using a standard employment function incorporating a dummy variable for Reviews. The empirical tests showed no evidence that

Reviews produced a 'shock effect' in securing a 'once-and-for-all' release of manpower from the defence-intensive aerospace, electronics and shipbuilding industries. However, the estimating equations for these industries showed a significant and positive coefficient for output, suggesting some release of manpower following a reduction in an industry's actual or future planned military sales. Examples of the results are shown in Table 19.4.[20,21]

4   The Economic Benefit of Cuts

Critics of military spending claim that it adversely affects investment, economic growth, the balance of payments, taxation, and government civil expenditure, especially on health, welfare and education: hence the argument that Defence Reviews will release resources for expanding these 'socially desirable' activities. Supporters of military spending point to the jobs, exports, import-saving and technological spin-off benefits from defence.[22,23] Some of these arguments can be tested empirically; others, particularly the spin-off argument are more difficult to test, although it has to be recognised that the difficulties of testing might reflect the fact that there is nothing to be measured!

Satisfactory empirical tests of these opposing claims require a fully specified economic model identifying the underlying causal factors linking different levels and components of military spending with the major macroeconomic variables in the UK.[24] The model needs specifying and estimating in a general equilibrium framework, and, ideally, similar evaluation and estimation are required to identify the true economic effects of other components of government expenditure and aggregate demand. Is defence spending 'different' or do other components of government and private expenditure also have adverse economic effects? As an *exploratory exercise*, some simple tests were undertaken to estimate the effects of defence and other components of government and private expenditure on economic growth and unemployment. Critics of military spending claim that it will adversely affect both these variables. These hypotheses were tested using OLS techniques and examples of the results are shown in Table 19.5.[25] In addition, some limited tests were undertaken to identify the determinants of defence expenditure in the form of the government in power, Defence Reviews and the NATO commitment to raise spending by 3 per cent annually. Positive coefficients were predicted for Conservative Governments and the 3 per cent commitment and a negative coefficient for Defence Reviews.

A number of equations were affected by serial correlation, especially those for unemployment. Accepting the *ad hoc* nature of the estimating equations, it can be seen that defence is not the only component of government expenditure which adversely affects economic growth; similar adverse effects appear for various health service expenditures. Education gave a significant and positive coefficient but, in the same equation, the investment share showed an unexpected negative impact on growth. There was no evidence of defence shares being affected by Defence Reviews, nor by the political composition of the government. Although the coefficient for the Conservative Government had the predicted sign, it was not quite significant at the 5 per cent level using a one-tail test. However, the 3 per cent NATO commitment had the predicted positive effect on military spending.

VI CONCLUSION

Public choice models are useful in identifying how agents in the political market are likely to respond to defence cuts. Identification of the groups likely to lose from disarmament and of the arguments they will use to protect themselves are essential for explaining behaviour in the military–industrial complex. The myths of defence and procurement policy need to be exposed through critical scrutiny and empirical testing. This paper has shown that defence cuts do not necessarily mean disarmament (less defence): the system might be 'shocked' into improved efficiency and there might be a willingness to sacrifice other objectives (for example, support for the British defence industry). While the paper has identified the agents, their behaviour and potential linkages in the defence market, it is recognised that there is a further need to model and quantify the effectiveness of the various agents: do they influence policy, how and by how much?

Table 19.5 Economic effects of defence spending

Dependent variable	Constant	D/Y	NHS/Y	HHSPS/Y	E/Y	I/Y	t	g_1	DVR	DVG	DVE	$\bar{R}^2$
					Coefficients of							
1. g_1	89.59** (5.35)	-372.98** (84.91)					1.43** (0.008)					0.085
2. g_1	73.68** (7.50)		-616.03** (168.08)			63.68* (26.46)	2.26** (0.16)					0.986
3. g_2	17.79** (4.96)			579.08** (120.90)		-209.27** (41.86)	-0.48** (0.16)					0.574
4. g_1	69.51** (1.41)			-107.52* (39.69)			1.87** (0.09)					0.979
5. U	-20.46** (3.86)	324.51** (61.25)					0.60** (0.07)					0.862
6. U	8.58** (2.94)				-217.34** (71.59)		0.52** (0.06)					0.773
7. U	21.44** (2.41)					-120.09** (13.28)	0.39** (0.02)					0.935
8. D/Y	0.15** (0.02)						0.002* (0.0005)	-0.001** (0.0003)	-0.0001 (0.001)			0.816
9. D/Y	0.15** (0.02)						0.002** (0.0005)	-0.001** (0.0003)		0.002 (0.001)		0.839
10. D/Y	0.13** (0.02)						0.0007 (0.0005)	-0.0009** (0.0003)			0.005** (0.002)	0.878

Notes

(a) g_1 = growth rate measured by output per person employed in UK.

(b) g_2 = growth measured by annual percentage rate of change of *GDP* at constant factor cost.

(c) U = UK employment rate (%)

(d) D/Y = share of defence expenditure in *GDP* at market prices; NHS/Y = share of National Health Service expenditure in *GDP*; $NHSPS/Y$ = share of National Health Service and Personal Social Services expenditure in *GDP*; E/Y = share of education expenditure in *GDP*; I/Y = share of gross domestic fixed capital formation.

(e) t = linear line trend, 1960–82.

(f) DVR = dummy variable (0,1) for Defence Reviews; DVG = dummy for Conservative Governments (= 1) with 0 for Labour Governments; DVE = dummy for 3 per cent NATO commitment = 1 for 1979–82 and 0 elsewhere.

(g) Equations 1, 2, 5, 6, 8 and 9 were affected by serial correlation.

(h) $\bar{R}^2$ is adjusted for degrees of freedom.

(i) Standard errors are shown in brackets.

* significant at the 5 per cent level.

**significant at the 1 per cent level, using a two-tail test.

422   *Econometrics and Applied Microeconomics*

Notes and References

1. Statistical assistance was provided by Geoff Hardman, IRISS, University of York, UK. Thanks are also due to the discussant, Dr S. Deger, Economics Department, Birkbeck College, London.
2. Arrow, K. J., *Social Choice and Individual Values* (New York: Wiley, 1951).
3. Geographical mobility is subject to uncertainty – for example, during the 1970s, the Falkland Islands seemed to be a relatively safe haven!
4. Culyer, A., 'The Quest for Efficiency in the Public Sector', in *Public Finance and the Quest for Efficiency*, Proceedings of the 38th Congress of International Institute of Public Finance (Detroit, Michigan: Wayne State University Press, 1984).
5. Olson, M., *The Rise and Decline of Nations* (New Haven, Connecticut: Yale University Press, 1982).
6. Mueller, D., *Public Choice* (Cambridge: Cambridge University Press, 1979).
7. Downs, A., *An Economic Theory of Democracy* (New York: Harper & Row, 1957).
8. Niskanen, W., *Bureaucracy and Representative Government* (Chicago: Aldine Atherton, 1971).
9. Stigler, G., 'The Theory of Economic Regulation', *Bell Journal of Economics and Management Science* (Spring 1971).
10. Smith, R., The Demand for Military Expenditure, *Economic Journal* , vol. 90, (1980) pp. 811–20.
11. Cmnd. 8288, *The UK Defence Programme: The Way Forward* (London: HMSO, 1981) p. 4.
12. See Cmnd. 8288 (note 11) p. 4.
13. Ministry of Defence, *Our Contribution to the Price of Peace* (London: HMSO, 1975). p. 4.
14. Defence Committe, *Defence Commitments and Resources and the Defence Estimates*, 1985–6, HCP 37-III (May 1985) p. 57.
15. Hartley, K., 'UK Defence Policy: A Case Study of Spending Cuts' in Hood, C. and Wright, M. (eds) *Big Government in Hard Times* (Oxford: Martin Robertson, 1981).
16. The model is $L=f(Q, t, DV, L_{t-1})$, where L = employment, Q = output, t = a time-trend for Defence Reviews (0,1) and L_{t-1} is a lagged dependent variable. Alternative specifications were estimated with similar results. The use of a dummy for Reviews reflected the lack of published data on future defence-spending plans before and after Reviews.
17. Hartley, K. and Lynk, E., 'Budget Cuts and Public Sector Employment', *Applied Economics*, vol. 15 (1983) pp. 531–40.
18. Defence Committee, *Ministry of Defence Organisation and Procurement*, vol. II, HC 22-II (London: HMSO, 1982).
19. Dunne, J. and Smith, R. P., 'The Economic Consequences of Reduced UK Military Expenditure', *Cambridge Journal of Economics*, vol. 8 (1984) pp. 297–310.

20. Hartley, K. and Lynk, E., 'Labour Demand and Allocation in the UK Engineering Industry: Disaggregation, Structural Change and Defence Reviews', *Scottish Journal of Political Economy*, vol. 30 (1983) pp. 42–53.
21. Lynk, E. and Hartley, K., 'Input Demands and Elasticities in UK Defence Industries', *International Journal of Industrial Organisation*, vol. 3 (1985) pp. 71–83.
22. Chalmers, M., *Paying for Defence* (London: Puto, 1985).
23. Smith, D. and Smith, R., *The Economics of Militarism* (London: Puto, 1983).
24. Martin, S. *et al.*, 'Time-Series Estimates of the Macroeconomic Impact of Defence Spending in France and Britain' (Chapter 16, this volume).
25. The estimating equations were:

$$g = f(X/Y,\ I/Y,\ t) \tag{a}$$

where g = growth, X/Y = share of defence or other government expenditure in GDP, I/Y = share of investment, t = a linear time-trend.

$$U = f(X/y,\ I/Y,\ t) \tag{b}$$

where U = UK unemployment rate.

$$D/Y = f(g,\ t,\ DV) \tag{c}$$

where DV is a dummy variable for Defence Reviews, Conservative Governments and for the 3 per cent NATO commitment.

The equations were estimated in linear form with and without a time-trend; the trend was designed to capture any trend influences in the time-series data (for example, productivity).

20 The Conversion of Military Activities: A Strategic Management of the Firm Perspective

Pierre Dussauge
CENTRE D'ENSEIGNEMENT SUPERIEUR DES AFFAIRES

Studies on the conversion of military industrial activities up to now have largely ignored one of the main actors of the conversion process: the firm. Adopting a strategic management of the firm perspective, the purpose of this chapter is to give some insight on the way the conversion process will affect firms that have military activities. The first stage in the analysis is aimed at clearly identifying the main characteristics of defence-oriented activities, pointing out the specific part they play in a firm's business portfolio, and understanding how they affect the formulation and implementation of a firm's global strategy. Military industrial activities appear to have three main strategic impacts on firm's business portfolio: (i) a technological impact; (ii) an impact in terms of financial resources and profitability; and (iii) an impact on the firm's global risk level. Taking these points into account, one can suggest that the main impulse to proceed with a conversion process must necessarily be given by the State and that firms involved will generally oppose the process. A general framework for evaluating the effect on the firms of the conversion of their military activities is presented as a conclusion. It seems to imply that different firms face different problems and that they therefore require differentiated government measures; the central consideration for designing the government measures is the strategic impact of military activities on the business portfolio of the various firms.

The firm is one of the main actors of economic activity; it therefore appears to be not only legitimate but necessary to take the firm's viewpoint into account when trying to analyse, on an economic basis, the possibility of converting military industrial activities into civilian activities.

A firm's defence-oriented activities cannot generally be considered globally, as a whole; they are often disseminated among what business strategists call the firm's 'Strategic Business Units' (SBUs), that is to say the elementary activities or 'businesses' that make up its business portfolio. Converting its military activities into civilian activities means that a firm will progressively eliminate the military SBUs in its business portfolio and eventually replace them by civilian SBUs. As defining the composition of the firm's business portfolio – that is deciding what activities or 'businesses' it should be in – is one of the main tasks of top management, we will centre our analysis on a strategic management perspective.

Being primarily defence-oriented is obviously a very important characteristic of any given strategic business unit. Understanding what the main constants of most military activities are, underlining what part they play in a firm's business portfolio and how they affect its overall strategy is a preliminary but essential phase of any action aimed at converting – or suppressing – military industrial activities.

I   THE STRATEGIC IMPACT OF MILITARY ACTIVITIES IN A FIRM'S BUSINESS PORTFOLIO

For a firm, having military activities in its business portfolio seems to have, at a strategic level, three main implications: (i) in terms of technological capacity; (ii) on its overall financial results and profitability; and (iii) on the global risk for the firm.

1   Military Activities and Technological Development

The first and most publicised impact of military activities for a firm is technological; military programmes which are very demanding in terms of technical performance play an important part in developing a firm's technological know-how. They enable a firm to build up, develop and maintain its technological capacities and subsequently apply its know-how to other non-military activities that it may have.[1] Corporations such as TRW in the USA or Matra in France, are well known for having exploited technologies developed for military programmes in civilian activities.[2]

In military programmes, the main emphasis is put on technical performance, and cost or price considerations only come in eventually under the form of constraints or secondary objectives.[3] In most civilian activities the cost constraints are much stronger; technical performance is very seldom the sole objective and the prevailing perspective is generally that of a performance/cost ratio. All this explains why military activities play such an important part in technological development for the firm. That President Reagan's Strategic Defense Initiative (SDI) should be termed as a 'technology pump' for US industry illustrates the fact.[4] Government funding of almost all military research and development is obviously one of the vital features of defence-oriented activities.

The technological know-how acquired from defence-oriented activities, however, is directly aimed towards military applications. According to the exact nature of these applications the possibilities of exploiting a determined technology in civilian areas can vary immensely. In some cases a military-oriented technology may have direct civilian applications, whereas in other cases, the civilian applications may be practically nil. Radar equipment, air control systems, airborne electronics or helicopter manufacturing are good examples of activities for which the synergies between military and civilian applications are very strong. Nuclear weapons and nuclear-power plants, contrary to what is often thought, have very few connections at an industrial level even if they both rely on a common base of fundamental scientific research; in the same way, the technologies linked to the manufacturing of armoured vehicles have relatively few civilian applications.

The point here is that the more dependent on military-generated technology the civilian activities of a firm are, the more difficult it will be trying to convert its military activities. On the other hand, if the military technology is specific to military activities, the conversion process will not affect non-military activities and can be analysed within the framework of pure business-portfolio-management techniques. If the technologies acquired through its military activities are vital for the whole of the firm's activities, their conversion – in other words their disappearance – could endanger the firm's survival. Aerospatiale's civilian helicopter business would not have existed in the first place without its military counterpart and would not survive very long if this one were to disappear.

The only alternative to technologically vital military programmes would be equivalent civilian 'technology pumps', that is to say, high-technology, government-funded, civilian development programmes. The 'Apollo-man on the moon' project in the USA or civilian space programmes in general fit into that scheme. The European 'Hermes' space shuttle project or 'Ariane' launcher, and up to a point the 'Eureka' programme, can be analysed as such civilian 'technology pumps'. In a conversion perspective, such programmes would have to be launched as substitutes to existing military programmes and be addressed basically to the same group of firms.

Cost constraints, however, will always weigh more heavily on civilian commercial programmes than on military programmes because of their very nature: a space shuttle may at some point have to compete in the market place and be profitable when launching satellites, whereas these requirements will never be placed on a fighter aircraft or a nuclear submarine, they will only have to be as technologically advanced and effective as possible and eventually fit into the defence budget. In pure technological terms, defence programmes are therefore likely to be more efficient than civilian programmes.

The emphasis put on technical performance in military programmes and the lack of cost constraints have been said to have peculiar side-effects on the way in which defence industry firms function, making them unable to be cost-effective and compete successfully on civilian markets where price considerations, as much or more than technical performance criteria, are the key factors of success. That obviously would make conversion to civilian activities even more difficult.

The last point, in a technological perspective, is that the main impulse for converting military activities must come from the government. From a business-policy point of view, the first steps to maintain and develop their technological know-how and potential, will not be taken spontaneously by firms which are dependent on the military contracts they can obtain.

2   The Financial and Economic Aspects of the Conversion of Military Activities

The second strategic impact of military activities is their generally regular and high profitability, which can be analysed as a result of the pricing systems set up by the military administrations within their weapon-acquisition process, to compensate for the absence of a real market.[5] Export markets, which are said to have extremely high profit margins, much higher in most cases than those of the domestic markets, also add to the overall profitability of defence activities.[6] Boeing Aircraft Corporation's military activities, for instance, generated over 80 per cent of the firm's profits in 1984, while they only accounted for about 40 per cent of its total sales.[7]

Military activities are also very strong cash-generating activities for the firms. The fact that they generate a strong and positive cash flow practically right from the beginning is due to the government financing of a large part of all the investments incurred. That implies that firms do not have to invest a major part of their financial resources into their military activities to keep on developing them, but that, on the contrary, the cash flow they generate can be invested into other activities, most other activities while they are in the early stages of their life cycles and as long as they keep on growing at a rapid pace, however profitable they may be, absorb more cash than they generate, and therefore require a firm to concentrate part of its global financial resources on them. Military activities, on the contrary, tend to generate continuously more cash than they absorb. It is therefore no surprise that military activities have often been said to be 'cash cow' activities.[8] As a result, military activities are an excellent base for diversification and have made it possible for most defence firms to diversify much more widely and rapidly than their dominantly civilian counterparts. Matra, one of the French leading missile and aerospace equipment manufacturers was able to diversify into activities such as automobile manufacturing, public transport systems, telecommunications, satellites, electronic components, multi-media communications, and so on, thanks to the financial resources generated by its defence activities while maintaining its dominant position in those activities. J. L. Lagardère, Matra's chief executive, acknowledged the fact publicly on various occasions.[9]

These financial characteristics of military activities enable them to balance the financial impact of other long-cycle activities a firm may have in its business portfolio. Very heavy high-technology activities, such as aircraft construction or electronic equipment, may require long-term investments, especially in R & D, and such long-term investments could not be carried out by the firms if they did not also have strong cash-generating activities to compensate. It is actually not surprising that most civilian aircraft manufacturers also make military aircraft or have other military activities; the complementarity and the synergy between both activities is based at least as much on financial considerations as it is on technological considerations; most civilian aircraft manufacturers could not survive without the financial resources generated by their military activities.

The conversion of military activities would imply, for firms involved in military production, the disappearance of some of their main cash-generating activities. This could, as we have mentioned, jeopardise the development of other business areas the firms may have. If it did not produce military helicopters, Aerospatiale could not produce civilian helicopters both for technological and financial reasons; if it did not have important, stable military activities, the firm would not be able, on purely financial grounds to support the Airbus programme, even though the technical links it has with military activities are really quite limited.

From the firm's point of view, giving up its military activities would considerably limit the financial resources available for growth and diversification, making future development more difficult. It would therefore be totally unrealistic to hope that the firms themselves might willingly give up their military activities on their own. As we stressed previously while pointing out the technological impact of military activities for the firms, any tentative conversion would require the government to make the first moves and keep the process going both by putting pressure on the industry and by setting up easing measures to accompany the conversion process; we will examine this point in more detail in section II.

3   Military Activities and the Firm's Global Risk

The third strategic impact of military activities for the firm is related to its global risk level. Empirical studies seem to show that military activities do not follow the same economic cycles as civilian activities.[10] Firms which have both military and civilian activities can therefore partially rely on their military activities when their civilian activities are depressed. That has recently been the case for most aerospace companies; both the passenger-aircraft market and the civilian-helicopter market have gone through a very difficult phase in the early 1980s and a corporation like Aerospatiale in France – but the same would apply to Bell Helicopters or Boeing Aircraft in the USA, British Aerospace or Westland in the UK or Messerschmidt–Bolkow–Blohm in the FRG – has been more and more dependent on its military markets; Aerospatiale Helicopter Corporation (Aerospa-

tiale's helicopter subsidiary in the USA) which sells almost exclusively civilian helicopters has been in a much more difficult situation
than the French mother-company whose helicopter sales are about 60
per cent military and 40 per cent civilian. As long as firms are not
excessively dependent on exports, military activities seem to have a
relatively low risk level. There are two major causes of this.

First of all, the defence administration's acquisition programmes in
most countries are planned so as to be as regular as possible.
Obviously there may be variations during a long-term equipment
programme because of budgetary causes for instance, but those
variations are generally a lot milder than in most civilian markets; in
1982 and 1983 Airbus Industries did not sell a single plane after
having thirty-one in 1981, while it sold thirty-two again in 1984; such
strong unforeseen variations in such a short period of time are
practically impossible in military domestic markets. Had Aerospatiale not been able to rely on its other activities and mainly on its
military activities (Airbus represents about 20 per cent of Aerospatiale's sales, military activities 60 per cent) the situation of the Airbus
programme would have been desperate.

The second reason for the low risk level of military activities is that
state intervention in most countries, including the USA, is constant in
defence-oriented industries and aimed at protecting the national
defence potential. The acquisition process takes into account the
situation of the various potential supplier firms, and one of the
criteria – more or less explicit according to the prevailing official
procurement doctrine in each country – for awarding markets is how
badly each firm needs the job to stay in the business. In France, one
of the more extreme examples on this subject – the defence procurement system – is in fact at the same time a real government-oriented
industrial policy.[11] The same could be said in most developing
countries which are trying to build up a local defence industry. Even
in the USA, it can be argued that the Department of Defence would
not let free competition drive one of its important suppliers out of the
market.[12]

Clearly identifying the main characteristics of defence-oriented
activities, pointing out the specific part they play in a firm's business
portfolio, and understanding what their impact on its global strategy
can be, will now help us to determine the main obstacles that any plan
to convert military industrial activities would encounter; it should
also provide some insight into the conditions under which the
conversion process might affect the defence firms in the least harmful

way and into those accompanying measures that could help the process to be as successful as possible.

II PERSPECTIVES FOR A SUCCESSFUL CONVERSION OF EXISTING MILITARY ACTIVITIES

The conversion of its military activities means for a firm the progressive, but certain, loss of part of its business and, eventually, the possibility, but not the assurance, of developing new activities; it implies losing part of both its global activity and its sales and subsequently trying to create new products, and new markets for them. Creating new activities, or more precisely new 'strategic business units', and developing them to compensate for the disappearance of military activities is probably a more serious problem than the purely technical conversion, which implies adapting – or even completely changing – the production units and giving the work-force new qualifications. The technical aspects of the conversion of military activities – which we will not examine closely in this paper – can be solved relatively more easily because of the generally highly skilled work-force in the defence industry and because of the large amount of subcontracting. Rather than 'how', finding 'what' to convert to seems to be the main difficulty.

1 The Government's Central Role in the Conversion Process

The above analysis of the strategic impact of military activities for the firms clearly suggests that corporations involved in the defence industry will not willingly accept giving up a profitable, cash-generating, technology-creating, low-risk part of their business. For the firms, the conversion of their military activities is, *a priori*, a very risky operation in which they have little to gain and a lot to lose, and which will in any case drastically alter the composition of their business portfolio, probably reduce its global profitability, affect its financial balance, and limit its growth potential.

Firms in the defence industry will not, in most cases, spontaneously decide to convert their military activities. This implies that the main impulse must come from exterior forces. For a process of conversion of military industrial activities actually to get on its way, it is absolutely vital that the government be firmly decided about carrying it out. Because of the central part they play in the activity of the defence industry, the government as a whole, and state bodies such as the military authorities, the administration in charge of defence procurements and even the state's industrial policy-makers, must be the main actors in the conversion process.

As the only domestic client for the defence industry, by the control it has over exports, and because of the importance of state funding of military R & D, and more generally of most investments in the sector, the government has considerable bargaining power over the firms. Simultaneously it can take industrial policy decisions or adopt more specific measures to make the conversion process less damaging for the firms.

The crucial question at this point is how determined the government really is in wanting to convert the country's defence industry. We will not examine here the reasons or circumstances that can incite any specific government to start converting its defence industry, as that analysis probably has more to do with political science or international relations than it has with economic analysis or business policy. The government's political determination to carry out the conversion process is however one of the key elements; the French experience in 1981–2, after the socialists came to power, is quite revealing. Though the socialists had pledged in their government programme that they would drastically reduce French arms exports and convert any military industrial capacity that was not strictly necessary for the equipment of France's own armies, they never put that into practice because of lobbying by the military–industrial complex and because of very serious economic constraints such as foreign-exchange earnings, unemployment and rising costs of military equipment.

The French experience is also interesting on another account; it has shown that when addressing the question of converting military activities, it is extremely difficult to separate the production of weapons for domestic needs on the one hand and the production of weapons for exports on the other, at least in smaller countries where the domestic demand is not large enough to keep the costs at an acceptable level. Furthermore, exports are usually the most profitable portion of the firms' military activities and reducing exports would therefore affect them directly.

2   A Framework for Analysis

The difficulties that conversion of the firms' military activities can create should not be underestimated, as the first section of this chapter tried to show. However, though military activities tend to have similar characteristics, their strategic impact can vary quite a lot from one firm to another according to two main factors:

1. The relative importance of military activities in the firm's global activity: this can be measured quite simply by the proportion of the firms net sales which come from military activities; it can also be argued that it should be measured by the relative contribution of military activities to the firm's global profit; in any case what is to be assessed at this point is the economic importance of military activities for the firm. Table 20.1 shows the relative importance of military activities in the total sales of the ten major weapon suppliers in the USA and in France for 1983.

Table 20.1   Relative importance of military activities of weapons firms, 1983

Companies		Total sales 1983	Defence contracts 1983	(%)
USA		(in million dollars)		
1.	General Dynamics	7 146	6 818	95
2.	McDonnell Douglas	8 111	6 143	75
3.	Rockwell International	8 098	4 545	55
4.	General Electric	26 797	4 518	15
5.	Boeing	11 129	4 423	40
6.	Lockheed	6 490	4 006	60
7.	United Technologies	14 669	3 867	25
8.	Tenneco	14 363	3 762	25
9.	Hughes	4 938	3 240	65
10.	Raytheen	5 937	2 720	45
France		(in million francs)		(%)
1.	Thomson group	50 000	15 000	30
2.	Aerospatiale	24 000	14 500	60
3.	Dassault Bréguet	13 500	12 270	90
4.	CEA	13 000	6 400	50
5.	Snecma	6 700	5 000	75
6.	Matra	6 000	4 200	70
7.	Snpe	2 300	1 600	70
8.	ESD	2 100	1 500	70
9.	Sagem	3 000	1 400	45
10.	Turbomeca	2 000	1 200	60

2. The importance of the technological know-how generated by the
    firm's defence activities for its other non-military activities: what
    is to be measured here are the technological synergies existing
    between the firm's military activities on the one hand and its
    civilian activities on the other.

By simply rating the two above factors 'high' or 'low' for each firm
examined, it is possible to evaluate the strategic impact of the
conversion process for each firm considered and to determine what
kind of response, in terms of industrial policy or of specific government aids, is more adequate. A simple two-by-two matrix (Figure
20.1) will help in visualising this approach:

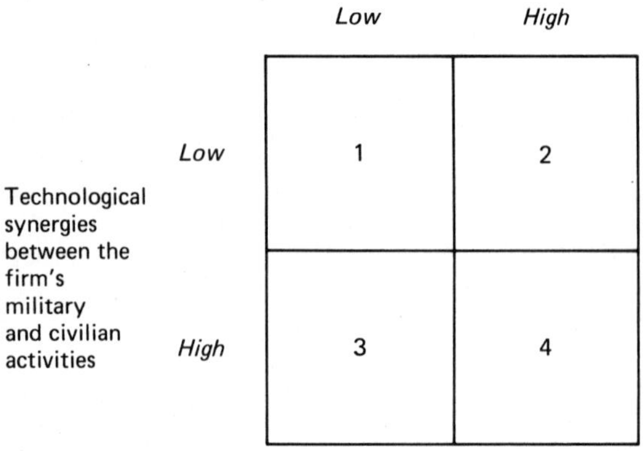

Figure 20.1   Revaluation of the strategic impact of a firm's military

In a more operational perspective than the one we have adopted in
this paper, it would obviously be important to define and quantify the
threshold points between the 'low' and 'high' ratings on each factor: it
could even be necessary to adopt a more detailed and progressive – perhaps even quantified – scale for determining the position of
the firms according to both dimensions. Just to illustrate our
approach in this paper, however, we will keep the matrix in its more
simple form.

Firms situated in the 'number 1' zone of the chart are those for
which the conversion process will be easiest and have less long-term
strategic consequences. Their military activities only account for a

relatively small part of their global activity and are not technologically related to their civilian activities. In this case a progressively conducted conversion process should not require any specific form of state intervention; it can be managed by the firm as a normal evolution of the composition of its business portfolio. In 1983, CIT–ALCATEL, one of the French leading firms in the telecommunications sector gave up all its military activities, which accounted for only a small part of its total sales and were technologically fairly independent from the rest of its activities, selling them to Thomson, another French electronics group, at the government's request. That operation did not affect CIT–ALCATEL's corporate strategy or create any problems for the firm; the conversion of the military activities of firms positioned in zone number 1 of the chart could be compared to the above example.

For firms situated in zone number 2, their military activities account for a significant portion of their global activity (roughly 20 to 25 per cent or more) though they are not technologically related to other non-military activities. Examples of firms in this case would be the Thomson group or Luchaire in France, Enasa of Spain, General Electric in the USA. The conversion of their military activities would affect the overall level of activity of these firms; it is therefore vital that they develop into new activities to make up for the lost business. The government would probably have to offer some kind of help in the more serious cases, by giving the firms in a difficult situation priority for the awarding of government contracts, on new developing civilian programmes. Firms in this case could also try to expand their existing non-military activities, which are not affected technologically by the conversion process, at an international level for example; multinationalisation can be a satisfactory alternative to diversification for providing new business.

The situation of firms positioned in the third zone of the matrix is in general more difficult. The conversion process, though it does not imply a short-term loss of a large part of the firm's activity will affect its non-military activities in the long run by drying up their main source of technology. The Matra group in France, TRW or Rockwell in the USA could be mentioned as examples of firms in this category, though their military activities still account for a relatively important part of their total sales. Firms in this case would require some kind of state intervention to replace their military government-subsidised source of technology. The most appropriate form of intervention appears to be the launching of civilian so-called 'technology pump'

programmes such as NASA's space-shuttle or orbital-station programmes in the USA, 'Ariane' satellite-launcher or 'Hermes' space-
shuttle projects in Europe or again the European 'Esprit' or 'Eureka'
programmes – though the latter has not been clearly defined as either
military or civilian. Space programmes in general seem to have many
common characteristics with defence programmes and are organised
in much the same way; indeed, many defence-industry firms also
have space activities. Therefore these appear as a natural substitute
for military activities. However, they are obviously not the only
possible 'technology pump' activities that can progressively replace
military activities in the course of a conversion process.

Firms in the fourth zone of the chart are obviously in the most
difficult situation and represent the most dramatic cases. The conversion process directly hits a significant position of their overall
activity – and most probably the more profitable part of it – and will
also affect their non-military activities in the long run by cutting off
the main flow of technology on which they depend. Most firms in the
aerospace industry are good examples of firms in this case; the
helicopter division of Aerospatiale is quite typical in this respect:
military sales account for 60 per cent of its total sales and most
civilian helicopter models are directly derived from military projects
or at least incorporate a considerable amount of technological
know-how acquired from military programmes; the civilian part of
Aerospatiale's helicopter activity would not survive the disappearance of its military counterpart for very long, as we mentioned
previously.

In the course of a conversion process, some of the firms in this case
would probably have to disappear; that would be the case in
particular for firms like Panhard in France or General Dynamics in
the USA whose activities are predominantly or even exclusively
military. Other firms in a less extreme situation would probably have
to undergo a restructuring process, selling their non-military activities
to other groups with technologically complementary activities or
associating with firms where it is possible to create synergies.

Most of the research work on the conversion of military industrial
activities centres on technical, industrial, political or macroeconomic
questions; it very rarely focuses on some of the parties most affected
by the conversion process: the defence-industry firms. The approach
we have tried to develop in this paper, however simplistic it may
seem, should provide a framework within which it is possible to
understand and analyse the firms' perspective of the questions and

problems raised by the conversion process. Centring on the strategic impact of the military activities in a firm's business portfolio – as opposed to a global sectorial analysis of the defence industry as a whole, which neglects the case of each individual firm – makes it possible to work out a typology of the various situations faced by the different firms and eventually offer a more adapted response to the specific nature of the problems that the conversion process would create for each of them.

Notes and References

1. See, for instance, Gazier, P. and Gloaguen, J., 'L'Armée vecteur de la Technologie', *Le Nouvel Economiste*, 18 juillet 1983.
2. See Dessarts, R., 'La Stratégie Mondiale de TRW: Inventer avec les Crédits Militaires et Développer dans le Secteur Civil', *Le Nouvel Economiste*, 2 décembre 1983.
3. See Schmidt, C., 'L'Appréhension Economique du Service de Défense Nationale. Le Système des Armements', *Défense Nationale*, décembre 1981. Also see Anastassopoulos, J. P. and Dussauge, P., 'Transformer les Avances Technologiques Nationales en Avancées Stratégiques Mondiales', *Revue Française de Gestion*, no. 42, septembre–octobre 1983.
4. See Bellon, B., 'La Politique Industrielle de l'Etat Fédéral aux Etats-Unis' (working paper), Commissariat Général du Plan, juin 1985.
5. See Gansler, J. S., *The Defense Industry* (Cambridge, Massachusetts: MIT Press, 1980); also see Dussauge, P., 'Formation des Prix, Evolution des Coûts et Performances Economiques de l'Industrie d'Armement', *Défense Nationale*, mai 1985.
6. See Jannic, H., 'Les Dividendes du Réarmement', *L'Expansion*, 18 avril 1980.
7. See 'The Military Build-up at Boeing', *Business Week*, 11 March 1985.
8. See Dussauge, P., *L'Industrie Française de l'Armement* (Paris: Economica, 1985) chap. IX.
9. See the firm's annual report for 1981 or 'Matra: Le Civil Marque le Pas', *Le Nouvel Economiste*, 1 février 1985.
10. See Dussauge (note 8), forward by Schmidt, C.; also see Bellon (note 4).
11. See Ponssard, J. P., and de Pouvourville, G., *Marchés Publics et Politique Industrielle* (Paris: Economica, 1982), or Anastassopoulos, J. and Dussauge, P., 'L'Armement, une Spécialité Industrielle à la Française', *Revue Française de Gestion*, no. 31, mai–juin–juillet–août 1981.
12. See Gansler (note 5).

Index

Notes: references to authors' contributions to this volume and the pages of their contribution are in **bold** type; t denotes table; f denotes figure; n denotes note.

Index